PCI Compliance

The Definitive Guide

PCI Compliance

The Definitive Guide

Abhay Bhargav

CRC Press
Taylor & Francis Group
Boca Raton   London   New York

CRC Press is an imprint of the
Taylor & Francis Group, an **informa** business
AN AUERBACH BOOK

CRC Press
Taylor & Francis Group
6000 Broken Sound Parkway NW, Suite 300
Boca Raton, FL 33487-2742

© 2014 by Taylor & Francis Group, LLC
CRC Press is an imprint of Taylor & Francis Group, an Informa business

No claim to original U.S. Government works

Printed on acid-free paper
Version Date: 20130919

International Standard Book Number-13: 978-1-4398-8740-0 (Hardback)

Library of Congress Cataloging-in-Publication Data

Bhargav, Abhay.
   PCI compliance : the definitive guide / author, Abhay Bhargav.
      pages cm
   Includes bibliographical references and index.
   ISBN 978-1-4398-8740-0 (hardcover : alk. paper)
   1. Credit cards--Security measures--Handbooks, manuals, etc. 2. Data
protection--Standards--Handbooks, manuals, etc. I. Title. II. Title: Payment-card industry
compliance.

HG3755.7.B43 2014
332.1'780681--dc23   2013036711

Visit the Taylor & Francis Web site at
http://www.taylorandfrancis.com

and the CRC Press Web site at
http://www.crcpress.com

Contents

Preface

The payment-card industry (PCI) security standards have become the most important security-compliance standards in recent times. Any entity storing, processing, or transmitting cardholder information is required to comply with payment-card industry standards. However, most entities find it challenging to comply with and meet the requirements of this prescriptive and technically rigorous standard.

This book explains the PCI standards from an implementation standpoint and clarifies the intent of the standards on key issues and challenges that entities must overcome in their quest to meet the compliance requirements. Beyond detailing the requirements of the PCI standards, this treatise also delves into multiple implementation strategies to achieve PCI compliance.

The book presents various case studies and examples from different industry verticals undergoing compliance, such as banking, retail, outsourcing, software development, and processors to articulate specific compliance issues and challenges and to explain solutions from real-world PCI implementations.

The Payment Application Data Security Standard (PA-DSS) has been created for commercial applications that are to be deployed in a PCI environment, and the book examines the PA-DSS in terms of application development and implementation strategies for PA-DSS validation. This book additionally focuses on audit and assessment strategies for assessors to effectively assess PCI environments.

Individuals or companies who seek PCI compliance are often hindered by their inability to visualize and conceptualize the compliance requirements and apply these to their organizations or to the organizations they are assessing. This book addresses that very issue by (a) presenting various case studies and examples from different industry verticals undergoing compliance and (b) examining specific compliance issues, challenges, and solutions from real-world PCI implementations.

The target readers for this book include

- Individuals in companies undergoing PCI compliance
- IT managers, CTOs, CISOs, and quality-management personnel in charge of compliance for the following types of organizations: retail, payment processing, banks, software companies, outsourcing companies, merchants
- Information-security professionals who need to grasp the concepts of PCI compliance for assessments
- Software developers and architects who are developing customized or commercial off-the-shelf applications that are deployed in a payment-card environment. (These readers would benefit from the discussion of PA-DSS requirements included in this book.)

The book is structured in a way that is easy for the reader to understand and grasp. It begins with a basic introduction of PCI compliance, including its history and evolution. The book then thoroughly and methodically examines the specific requirements of PCI compliance. The PCI requirements are presented along with assessor notes and assessment techniques for auditors and assessors.

About the Author

Abhay Bhargav is the founder and chief technical officer of the we45 Group, a Bangalore-focused information security solutions company. He has extensive experience with information security and compliance, having performed security assessments for many enterprises in various domains, such as banking, software development, retail, telecom, and legal. He is a qualified security assessor (QSA) for the payment-card industry and has led several security assessments for payment-card industry compliance. He is also the coauthor of *Secure Java for Web Application Development*, published by CRC Press.

Abhay is a specialist in Web-application security with broad experience in vulnerability assessment and penetration testing, and he has served as a consultant for a wide array of enterprises and governmental/quasi-governmental entities. He was recently awarded the prestigious SANS Certified GIAC Web Application Penetration Tester certification. He has been interviewed by leading media outlets for his expertise on information security, particularly application security.

Abhay is a regular speaker at industry events. He was a featured speaker at the JavaOne Conference in September 2010 at the Moscone Center in San Francisco. He also regularly speaks at OWASP (Open Web Application Security Project) conferences around the world, notably in New York at the world's largest application security conference, the OWASP AppSec Conference, in September 2008. He has also spoken at various other conferences and seminars, such as the PCI summit in Mumbai in December 2008. He is a regular speaker at industry events such as the Business Technology Summit and events organized by the Confederation of Indian Industry (CII). He has also delivered several talks to government entities and their stakeholders on information security and application security. He is also a trainer in information security and has led several public workshops on PCI, PA-DSS, and risk assessment.

Abhay is well versed in risk assessment and risk management, with rich consulting experience in the OCTAVE* Risk Assessment and NIST SP 800-30 methodologies. His expertise also extends to providing solutions on information security based on the ISO-27001, HIPAA, SOX, GLBA, and other security-compliance standards.

Previously, Abhay was the leader of application security and PCI compliance at SISA Information Security Pvt Ltd. Prior to that, he was involved in implementing enterprise IT solutions for various verticals, including manufacturing and retail. He has developed various business applications in Java and proprietary object-oriented program languages such as TDL. He has also written various articles on application security and security compliance.

Apart from his professional interests, Abhay is also a trained Carnatic classical flutist and has delivered several concerts. He is also a theater enthusiast and playwright with an English comedy play to his writing credits. He blogs actively and maintains a security blog and a personal blog. He also writes a weekly article on computer education in a leading Kannada daily newspaper for rural youth.

1

Payment-Card Industry: An Evolution

Payment has become the lifeblood of today's economy. They are used by millions of people all over the world to buy goods and services in stores, online, through the mail, or over the phone. People often have multiple credit cards for their personal and business purchases. The use of these cards has resulted in an incredible growth for the payment-card industry. This chapter tracks the evolution of the payment-card industry and identifies key highlights in its incredible growth path.

1.1 THE DEVELOPMENT OF A SYSTEM: THE COMING OF THE CREDIT CARD

1.1.1 The Need for Credit: A Historical Perspective

The concept of *credit* is essential to the understanding of business. Indeed, it is perhaps the most integral aspect of doing business. The earliest motivation for credit or virtual money was that real money—gold, silver, or otherwise—could be stolen. This paved the way for a system of credit and "virtual money" that has existed for over 5,000 years and continues to dominate the present environment for business and personal finances.

1.1.1.1 Credit in the Mesopotamian Civilization

Some of the earliest instances of credit and debt can be traced back to the Mesopotamian civilization. At that time, the largest institutions in the system were temples and palaces, where the administrators established a system of debit and lines of credit. Debts were measured in silver, but payments were made in produce—barley or any other item that was acceptable to both parties. Debts were recorded in cuneiform tablets and kept as evidence of the transaction for both parties involved. Innkeepers also developed a system of credit, where they served drinks and rented out rooms to customers who would run up a tab and pay the innkeepers during the subsequent harvest. The innkeepers developed a list of trustworthy clients and only provided credit to these clients, thus creating a system of credit.

Interest is an important facet of debt and credit. It is calculated as the additional payment (usually calculated on a particular rate over a particular period of time) that is made for providing the debt/credit over a particular period of time. The earliest traces of interest can be found in Egypt, where interest rates of 20 percent were fixed over a period of 2,000 years. However, this had adverse social effects as well. In the years when there were bad harvests, the farmers were constantly in debt and sank deeper in debt, giving up the land and then the family, becoming bonded laborers to a class of rich people in the kingdom. Slavery has been the leading cause of most uprisings, and on several occasions these bonded workers went up in arms against the establishments, either in agitation or by becoming bandits and thieves.

1.1.1.2 Credit in the Era of Coins and Metal Bullion (800 BC to AD 600)

The era of coins came at a time when the East was experiencing a significant rise in importance in world affairs. The coming of coins was also appropriate for an age where metals were in vogue as weapons of warfare. Precious metals like gold and silver were used for trading. It is surprising to note that the merchants and trading community did not adopt coins until very late. Coins were first created to pay soldiers. One of the prominent trading nations, Carthage, adopted coins very late, and did so only to pay their foreign soldiers.

Rulers encouraged the development of markets and the capture of slaves for the kingdom. Slaves were one of the important forms of debt. Coins used to be mined by slaves, and markets were created from the consumption of soldiers who would be paid in coins and currency.

1.1.1.3 The Rise of Virtual Money Transactions (AD 600 to AD 1500)

Religion played a major role in the economies of most countries in this period. International trade was established on the basis of relationships between merchants of different nations, but it was monitored and regulated by the religious authorities. Even though coins had been introduced in the world, they were not universally adopted. Tally sticks were used to record small debts during this period, where notched pieces of wood were broken in two, with one given to the creditor and one to the debtor as the indication of the debt and relationship between them. This age also saw the emergence of bills of exchange to record larger debts. A typical example of a bill of exchange would be that one has sold goods to another and the bill (for the sale) is given to a regulating authority (like a bank) in exchange for the amount of the bill (minus some exchange fee levied by the authority). When it is time for the customer to pay the bill (upon completion of a credit period), the customer pays the bank. One can observe that there are several similarities between this system of bills of exchange and the modern day credit card payment system.

International trade also facilitated the commercial practices and conventions of different countries to be known all over the world. For instance, the Arab word *sakk* is the original word for cheque/check, which was only used in England starting in 1220.

The East also had its conventions and practices. For instance, pawn shops were introduced in Buddhist places of worship to aid poor farmers. This was done against the Chinese state, which had appointed local lenders to provide credit to merchants and farmers. The Buddhist temples acted to save the farmers from the clutches of these local lenders. However, the state ultimately exercised its authority and established interest rates, and it moved away from bullion by establishing paper money.

1.1.1.4 The Reemergence of Coins and Precious Metal Currency (1500–1971)

This period without doubt can be termed as the *Rise of Europe*. Empires across Europe rose in conquest against the rest of the world. There was a great deal of annexation, invasion, and conquest of Eastern civilizations. One of the main factors for this was the move back to precious metals (or bullion). The Chinese Ming Dynasty dethroned the paper currency regime and decided to move back to silver as a form of exchange. This prompted an incredible demand for silver, and the silver that had been plundered by the Spanish conquistadors from Mexico ended up in China.

Credit was in vogue, even among the states, as they had to finance their expensive wars. Deficit financing (the practice where the government spends more money than it receives as revenue, the difference being met either by borrowing or by minting new funds) was the order of the day, as most of these countries were fighting expensive wars and campaigns, and funding them required extensive deficit financing.

1.1.1.5 The Rise of Debt (1971 Onwards)

Many believe that the current age of debt began when Richard Nixon suspended the convertibility of the US dollar into gold and created the current state of floating currency. Several countries, including in the United Kingdom and the European Union, have floating currency regimes. A system of virtual money has been established where the consumers in developed countries don't even use paper currency for the bulk of their transactions. In many cases, consumer debt and consumption rather than savings drives national economies.

One of the major harbingers of this modern system of consumer spending and debt has been the credit. In the subsequent sections of this chapter, I will detail the evolution of the credit card, debit card, and the payment-card industry in general.

1.1.1.6 The Need for Credit

As you have read in the previous sections, the concepts of *debt* and *credit* are not new to the world. They have existed since the days of the ancient Mesopotamians. However, like everything else in the modern world, access to credit and debt have become easier, thereby fueling a debt culture in most countries (as highlighted in Section 1.1.1.5). Debt and credit have always had a close relationship with businesses. Businesses work on credit and debt all the time, because they need to be able to find working capital (capital required for day-to-day activities) as well as long-term capital. Their suppliers provide them credit for the goods and services supplied, so that they can complete their sales cycle and pay them back at a later date. These businesses might provide the same credit facilities to their customers as well.

Credit and debt have made their way into personal finances in a big way. People use credit and debt extensively for their personal needs. Acquisition of assets is a common requirement, where people buy assets like cars, homes, etc., on debt and pay them back in easy installments. People also use debt for shorter-term benefits like a holiday or for large purchases such as appliances, electronics, etc. This is made possible because of a singular and extremely significant creation known as a credit card.

1.1.2 The Credit Card: A Means to Address the Need for Credit

1.1.2.1 The History of the Credit Card

The creation of the credit card arrives as a natural progression in the history of debt. They entered the scene in a very small way in the early 1900s and then completely dominated the latter part of the century and on into the current century. There are two critical concepts that had to evolve before the arrival of credit cards. One, of course, is that of *debt*, where one party provides the debt (supplier/bank/regulatory authority) and the other party is a debtor (the consumer of the debt). The other is that of *installments*, as that is the foundation of the modern credit card system. It is said that in 1730, Christopher Thompson, a furniture merchant, offered furniture that could be paid off weekly. Furniture was naturally a high-cost item, and this idea gave buyers access to expensive furniture without having to pay for it all at once. They could make regular payments until they eventually paid off the cost of the furniture.

The idea was used by garment traders right from the eighteenth century to the twentieth century. These traders were called "tallymen." They sold clothes that buyers could pay for with small weekly installments. They used a notched wooden stick to keep a tally of the debt and payments of each person who bought clothes on credit.

1.1.2.2 The First Credit Cards

In the early 1900s, several companies recognized the need to provide some of their customers with credit and build loyalty for their products and services. In 1914, Western Union gave some of their important clients a metal card. This card was used by the clients to defer payments to Western Union, interest free.

The concept was then adopted in 1924 by General Petroleum Corporation, when they offered a metal card for the purchase of gasoline and automotive services. Gradually, other corporations began to follow suit. AT&T created a "Bell System Credit Card" in the 1930s. The furious pace of loyalty cards (the first credit cards) only slowed momentarily because of World War II. The post-world-war scenario was very different, in that spending went up immensely and the US economy was booming.

"Charg-It" was a card created by John Biggins of the Flatbush National Bank in Brooklyn. The concept was simple: The customer could make a purchase using the Charg-It card, and the merchant would forward the bill to Biggins' bank. Periodically, the bank would reimburse the merchant and charge the customer. However, the purchase could only be made locally, and the Charg-It cardholders had to possess accounts in the Flatbush National Bank. Later, New York's Franklin

FIGURE 1.1
Specimen of a Diners Club Card in the 1950s.

National Bank also came up with a credit card that could be used only by their bank's account holders.

The Diners Club Card was a significant development in the creation of the modern credit card industry. The card was born from a business meal in which the founder, Frank McNamara, had forgotten his wallet and didn't have the cash to pay for a restaurant bill that he had run up at a New York restaurant. This gave birth to Diners Club. McNamara created Diners Club, mostly for travel and entertainment purposes. Customers could use it at establishments that accepted the Diners Club Card and had 60 days to make payment for the bills they had run up with the card. By 1951, Diners Club had more than 42,000 members, and the card was being accepted in all major cities in the United States (see Figure 1.1).

1.1.2.3 The Development of a Credit Card Industry

Soon after Diners Club became one of the early entrants into payment cards, American Express entered the fray in 1958 with their plastic cards for travel. One of the big developments to occur in 1958 was the creation of the "floating payment" regime in credit cards, which meant that customers could pay a fraction of their complete bill and elect to pay the balance over time. However, this did run the risk of incurring finance charges and defaults, but it provided customers more flexibility in making their payments.

1.2 DEBIT CARDS AND AUTOMATED TELLER MACHINES

1.2.1 The Coming of the Debit Card

Debit cards were introduced initially by Seattle's First National Bank for business executives. They were substitutes for checks. The card would be presented, the transaction would be recorded, and the bank would guarantee payment for the goods purchased by the cardholder. The bank had required a large savings account to be maintained by the cardholder to cover the funds. The cards were only issued to people who the bank could trust, i.e., people with a long association with the bank with sizable bank balances.

In 1984, Landmark created a national debit system where users of the debit card could use it for purchases all over the country. This gradually expanded to Canada.

Funds were directly debited from the customer's account, thus differentiating them from credit cards. Over time, debit cards became more and more popular. From bank-specific debit cards, banks tied up with payment brands to deliver a common brand experience for the debit cards. Debit cards were also combined with ATM cards to create debit-ATM cards that can be used for purchase transactions as well as for withdrawing money from a bank's ATM.

1.2.2 The Automated Teller Machine

In 1960, the predecessor for the modern ATM, a machine called a Bankograph, was installed by New York's First National Bank (now Citicorp) in several branches. This machine was meant for users to be able to pay their utility bills without a teller.

The first cash-dispensing machine was installed by Barclays Bank in London in 1967. Over the course of 1967 and 1968, the cash-dispensing machines utilized a system of plastic cards, where the customer could buy plastic cards from the teller and perform a transaction on the cash-dispensing machine. However, this proved to be inconvenient, as the customer would have to get a new card for every new transaction.

With the coming of the mag-stripe cards, a company called Docutel installed an ATM in New York's Chemical Bank. Docutel was the first to get a patent for this machine and has been listed as the inventor of the ATM. Chemical Bank made this innovation famous by advertising, "On September 2nd our bank will open at 9:00 and never close again." Figure 1.2 is a picture of a modern ATM.

1.2.3 E-Commerce and Online Payments

The e-commerce revolution began largely in 1995 with the coming of Amazon and the AuctionNow website that was rechristened eBay. With the coming of e-commerce, businesses needed ways to facilitate payments online. One of the first companies to facilitate payments on the Web was PayPal, which is now part of eBay. Based on the success of e-commerce, several payment gateways, payment aggregators, and so on, have sprung up to support the burgeoning demand for the online payments space.

1.3 THE FUTURE OF PAYMENTS

1.3.1 Trends for the Future of Payments

The future of the payment industry is an exciting one and is being made as we speak. Mobile payments, contactless payments, near-field communication, and so on, are changing the face of payments as we knew it. Some of the key trends that I see in the world of payments are as follows:

- Mobile payments
- Contactless payments
- Chip and PIN cards

1.3.1.1 Mobile Payments

Mobile payment is an exciting and fascinating concept. The pitch is simple: "Your mobile phone becomes your wallet." Everyone carries a mobile phone today. Many companies are finding ways to develop applications interfacing customers'

FIGURE 1.2
A modern ATM.

credit card accounts on the mobile phone for payments. Some companies are developing technology to embed payment-card information into the SIM card of the mobile phone. When the user swipes the phone in front of a contactless card reader, the payment information from the SIM card is read and the payment process ensues. Companies and governments all over the world are working on developing and regulating mobile-based payments. Payment brands like Visa, MasterCard, Amex, and so on, are getting involved in making mobile payments a reality.

There is another dimension to mobile payments. While customers can benefit from the convenience of paying for goods and services with their mobile phones, merchants can also easily accept payments over mobile devices that are hardware and software based. For instance, Square provides a small hardware device that can be plugged into a mobile device to accept payments for a merchant (see Figure 1.3). Nonconventional merchants like babysitters and home tutors can now start using these simple devices to receive payments for their services.

FIGURE 1.3
Square payment card reader for mobile phone.

1.3.1.2 Contactless Payments

Contactless payments are another innovation worth watching. This method uses radio-frequency identification (RFI) to perform secure payments. The embedded chip and antenna recognize the wave of a card in front of the contactless machine and read the payment information in the chip and PIN card (see Figure 1.4). Contactless payments are also utilizing mobile-phone-based payments (as mentioned previously) to achieve contactless payments.

1.3.1.3 Chip and PIN Cards

Chip and PIN cards are great for cardholder-data security. As opposed to the regular magnetic stripe cards, chip and PIN cards have an embedded smart card. The smart card holds the payment-card information as well as encryption, key exchange information, and so on. This makes it more secure for communication with card readers and other machines. As the information cannot be read in plaintext like in a magnetic stripe card, chip and PIN cards are also more resistant to card skimming.

1.4 SUMMARY

This chapter explored the history and the future of the payment-card industry. We began with a historical analysis of money and credit. We learned that the need for the payment-card industry arose from the need for debt that fueled economies after the 1970s. The first credit cards were provided by merchants like the General Petroleum Company for their loyal customers. Banks started entering the fray by providing cards to their trustworthy customers for shopping, and so on. This paved the way for the larger acceptability and recognition of the payment card as an instrument of payment. This gradually led to the development of interbank networks that paved the way for the advent of payment cards as an acceptable and

FIGURE 1.4
Google Wallet contactless payment reader.

pervasive medium of payment all over the
world.

2

Card Anatomy: The Essentials

Before we delve into the Payment Card Industry Data Security Standards (PCI-DSS), it is very important to understand the structure and workings of a payment card. A payment card has many instances of data embedded in the card, and a lot of this data constitutes sensitive information, which needs to be secure. In this chapter, I will provide a detailed view into the anatomy of a credit card, some of the key terminologies used in the payment-card industry, and some of the data sets that are considered sensitive and need to be protected.

2.1 PAYMENT CARDS: TYPES OF CARDS

2.1.1 Payment Card with Magnetic Stripe

In the previous chapter, we discussed that the payment-card industry has evolved over time. The evolution has gone from the days when the face of the card was the only place where information could be held to the present, when the entire credit card process can be replicated on a mobile phone.

2.1.1.1 Magnetic Stripe Cards: A Brief History

The magnetic-stripe (or the "magstripe," as it is popularly called) card was first created by IBM in 1960. It was created by Forrest Parry, an IBM engineer. He had the idea of embedding a magnetic stripe to the card base as a means of storing information. He tried several adhesives and methods to secure the magnetic stripe to the base of the card, with unsuccessful results. One day, he came back from the office frustrated at constant failure, while his wife was ironing their clothes. Looking at him frustrated, she told him to give her the card and that she would iron the magnetic stripe on the card base. Surprisingly, the technique worked, and the magnetic stripe was fused together with the card. Ever since then, the magnetic-stripe card has been used all over the world, not only for credit, debit, and ATM cards, but for other purposes like hotel rooms, drivers' licenses, and so on.

The magnetic-stripe cards follow multiple ISO standards that define the physical characteristics and payment-card transaction standards, like ISO/IEC 7810, 7811, 7812, 7813, and 8583.*

2.1.1.2 Magnetic-Stripe Coercivity

The magnetic-stripe card has multiple types of coercivity based on the utility of the card. Payment cards or financial cards are used on a regular basis over an extended period of time by their users. Therefore, these cards need to be of a higher coercivity, as high-coercivity cards are harder to erase. Low-coercivity cards are typically used for hotel rooms and the like, as they are generated using cheap machines, and they are not highly critical. High-coercivity cards have a black magnetic stripe, (see Figure 2.1), while the low-coercivity cards usually have a brown magnetic stripe.

2.1.1.3 Magnetic Stripe: A Primer on Data Sets

The data is the most important aspect of the mag-stripe. The magstripe contains data that is used to process and approve/decline the transaction, as the case may be. The data on the mag-stripe traverses

multiple networks once it is swiped. The magstripe typically contains three tracks of data that are called, quite simply, Track 1, Track 2, and Track 3 (see Figure 2.2). These three tracks contain the information relating to the card, the cardholder, and some other supplementary details. Once the card is swiped on the point-of-sale (POS) machine or the electronic-data-capturing (EDC) machine, in the case of a retail sales transaction, or an ATM kiosk, in the case of an ATM banking transaction, then the information held in the magstripe is transmitted for the processing of the transaction. We will discuss in detail the constitution of the data sets on Tracks 1, 2, and 3 in later sections of this chapter.

2.1.2 Chip and PIN Cards

Chip and PIN cards are a recent development for the payment-card industry. Over time, the industry has seen the need to reduce fraudulent card transactions to ensure that the system remains safe and profitable for all of its constituents. The chip and PIN cards—promulgated by the Europay MasterCard and Visa specifications (commonly known as the EMV Specifications) for payment systems—are a step in that direction. The EMV specifications, first published in 1996, are used for debit and credit card payments as well as ATM transactions, and it is estimated that around 16 million chip and PIN cards are in circulation today.

The difference between a chip/PIN card and a magstripe card is that the consumer payment information in the former is contained within a chip that is embedded onto the payment card. This card is commonly referred to as a *smart card*. The chip in the card provides three critical functionalities

---

* ISO-7810 defines the physical attributes of a card. ISO-7811 defines the recording techniques on an identification card. ISO-7812 defines the numbering system for the issue of identification cards to users. ISO-7813 specifically defines the physical characteristics of financial cards like credit cards, ATM cards, debit cards, etc. ISO-8583 defines the processing of a financial transaction made using a payment card. The standard defines interchange messages, data elements, and codes that are used in the processing of payment transactions. Any application that is used in the processing of payment card transactions has to comply with ISO-8583.

FIGURE 2.1
A typical magnetic-stripe payment card.

FIGURE 2.2
Chip and PIN card.

that differentiate itself quite starkly from a magnetic-stripe card. First, it can store payment-card information. Second, it is an active participant in the processing of transactions, and lastly, it is also secure, as it is capable of performing cryptographic operations, thereby protecting stored payment information as well the confidentiality and integrity of information in transit (during the payment cycle).

The greatest difference between a chip/PIN card and the magnetic-stripe card is the fact that, in the case of the mag-stripe card, the magnetic stripe is merely a storage medium for the payment information.

However, a smart card can perform certain processing operations, in that it actually determines some of the rules of payment of a particular transaction. For instance, the chip might determine a rule of payment set by the issuer* of a particular card that the user has to authorize a transaction using a PIN that is to be entered by the user at the time of payment processing. In such a case, the terminal reads and enforces this rule, set by the chip.

---

* Issuer typically refers to the bank that has issued the payment card. We will delve into the role of the issuer in Section 2.4, which discusses payment card terminology.

We will delve into chip and PIN cards in greater depth in this chapter and discuss the payment process and the data sets used by the chip and PIN cards. Figure 2.2 is an image of a chip and PIN card.

2.2 PAYMENT CARDS: AN ANATOMY

2.2.1 Payment Card: External Visage (Front)

The entire payment card (either debit or credit) contains information that is used in the processing of a transaction. It is simple to understand how a transaction is performed when the cardholder is present in a merchant establishment and the card is swiped on the EDC machine, which subsequently processes the transaction. In an increasing number of scenarios, the cardholder is not present in front of the EDC machine and, instead, is usually transacting for goods and services online with the use of his/her payment card. In such a case, it is essential for certain data to be present on the face of the card. The front of a credit or debit card looks like the image given in

Figure 2.3. We will now explore these data sets in greater detail.

In some cases, there are variances based on the issuing bank. For instances, some issuing banks have the photo of the cardholder on the face of the card. But the data sets that we are discussing are mandatorily present on the face of the card. Here you have the following details, namely:

- The card issuer's logo
- The payment brand logo and hologram
- The card number
- The expiration date
- The cardholder's name (first and last name)

2.2.1.1 The Card Issuer's Logo

The issuing bank is the bank that issues the card to the cardholder. For instance, if Citibank issues a credit card to a cardholder, then the card-issuing bank's logo is printed on the top right corner of the card. In the case of closed-loop systems like American Express, Discover, and JCB, the issuer is, respectively, American Express, Discover, or JCB, and their names and logos are therefore printed on top of the card. In some cases, however, the payment brand has cobranded

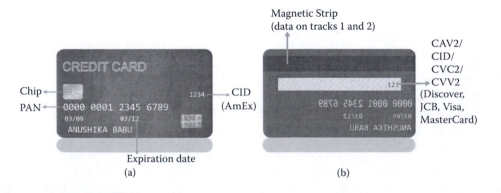

FIGURE 2.3
Front and back of a typical payment card.

the card, and the cobranded logo appears in the top right corner of the card.

2.2.1.2 The Payment Brand Logo and Hologram

A *payment brand* refers to the brand of a specific payment-card organization. For instance, Visa, MasterCard, JCB, American Express, and Discover are payment brands. These brands set transaction terms for the merchants and provide an interlink network for transactions to traverse multiple countries and continents. The payment brands also provide dispute-settlement services and operating rules and guidelines for the entire network to ensure that the payment process is unencumbered.

The payment brands have their logo and hologram placed in the right corner of the card. This applies to debit, credit, and ATM cards as well. Some of the popular brands are Visa, MasterCard, JCB, Discover, American Express, and Diners Club. For debit and ATM cards, the popular brands are Maestro, Cirrus, Visa Debit, Visa Electron, and so on.

Apart from these payment brands, there are several payment networks that work in a specific geography, such as within a country. For instance, China's UnionPay is a large payment network that operates in China, where 14 banks in the mainland, Macau, and Hong Kong are connected to this network, providing ATM and debit card functionality. China UnionPay is also affiliated with Visa, MasterCard, and American Express; therefore, these cards can be used in over 104 countries due to their affiliation with these international payment brands. Similarly, there is the Malaysia Electronic Payment System (MEPS) in Malaysia as well as other geographically restricted payment networks that act within a particular geography.

2.2.1.3 The Card Number (PAN)

The card number is perhaps the most important piece of data that is present on the card. It is the primary identifier of a particular card and its cardholder, and is mandatorily used (as the primary identifier) in every single transaction that has been made with the card. The card number is also known as the primary account number (PAN).

The PAN typically ranges from 12 to 19 digits, based on the payment brand. For instance, Visa cards usually have 16 digits, while American Express cards have PANs that are only 15 digits. In fact, the magnetic stripe has a field to hold the PAN that limits the data to 19 characters. The numbering system for payment cards follows the ISO-7812 standard of numbering.

There is a great deal of significance as to how the PAN of any payment card is derived. Let us explore this concept in greater depth:

The first digit of any PAN refers to something known as the *major industry identifier*. This single digit represents the category of the organization that issues the payment card to the user. There are different single digits for different industry verticals. They are as follows:

0 ISO/TC68 and other industries (This number refers to the technical committee of the International Organization for Standardization.)
1 Airlines
2 Airlines and other industry segments
3 Travel and entertainment
4 Banking and financial
5 Banking and financial

6 Merchandizing and banking/financial

7 Petroleum

8 Health care, telecommunications, and other future industry segments

9 National assignment

Based on this, one can glean that American Express, Diners Club, and JCB are grouped under the category of "Travel and Entertainment," whereas Visa, MasterCard, and Discover are grouped under the category of "Banking and Financial."

Another important aspect of the PAN is the issuer identification number (IIN), previously known as the the bank identification number (BIN). Different payment brands have different IIN ranges. They are as follows:

Visa card numbers always begin with the number 4.

MasterCard card numbers always begin with the numbers 51 through 55.

American Express card numbers begin with numbers 34 or 37.

Diners Club card numbers always begin with 36 or 38.

Discover card numbers begin with 6011 or 65.

JCB card numbers begin with 35.

Of course, the IIN consists of more than just the initial digits of a card number. The first six digits of a card number constitute the IIN. The IIN, simply put, is a number that can be issued to identify the name of the bank that has issued the card and the payment brand used to issue the card. For instance, 421323 is the IIN of ICICI Bank Gold Visa Debit Card in India; 414716 is the IIN of the Bank of America–Alaska Airlines Signature Visa Credit Card.

The subsequent digits of the card (after the IIN's first six digits) constitute the account number of the card, with the exception of the last digit. Based on probability, each issuer has a million possible account numbers that can be issued.

The last digit of the card number is known as the *check digit*. It is used to check the validity and accuracy of the credit card number.

All cards issued by the major payment brands under the card schemes have one thing in common: the Luhn algorithm (also known as *Modulo 10*). This algorithm is used to validate identification numbers like payment-card numbers. The name derives from IBM scientist Hans Peter Luhn, who created the algorithm. The algorithm has been adopted by ISO-7812 and is used primarily for error checking to ensure accuracy and validity of the identification number (like PAN). Let us explore the workings of the Luhn algorithm.

The rationale behind the Luhn algorithm is that after applying a series of calculations on the PAN, the product should be perfectly divisible by 10. If so, the PAN satisfies the requirements of the Luhn algorithm and is most likely a valid PAN. There are other checks and balances done during a transaction when it is being processed, but the Luhn check is an initial, base-level check to ensure validity.

The calculation begins from the rightmost end of the number. Let's take the example of a dummy PAN, e.g., 4111 1111 1111 1111:

- Every number beginning from the penultimate number (the number next to the check digit) should be multiplied by 2; other numbers should be multiplied by 1.

TABLE 2.1

Demonstration of the Luhn Algorithm on a Dummy Credit Card PAN

4	1	1	1	1	1	1	1	1	1	1	1	1	1	1	1
×2	×1	×2	×1	×2	×1	×2	×1	×2	×1	×2	×1	×2	×1	×2	×1
8	1	2	1	2	1	2	1	2	1	2	1	2	1	2	1

Note: Total = 30; modulo 10 = 0 and, therefore, the PAN is valid based on the Luhn algorithm.

- The products of the multiplied numbers, if in double digits, need to be added together. For instance, if the product of a number is 12, 1 + 2 must be added to derive 3.
- Finally, all the products from multiplying by 1 and 2 need to be added to derive a total value.
- If this value modulo 10 = 0, then the number is valid as per the Luhn algorithm.

Table 2.1 demonstrates the use of the Luhn algorithm for the dummy PAN 4111 1111 1111 1111.

2.2.1.4 The Expiration Date

The expiration date is in the format of MM/YY. The expiration date is the end of the month and year when the payment card expires, and transactions with the same card cannot be processed after the date. For instance, if a payment card has an expiration date 05/13, then the card expires on the 31st of May 2013. Issuer banks usually send a new card to the cardholder a short while before expiration of the current card to ensure that the cardholder is not inconvenienced and can carry out transactions without being interrupted.

2.2.1.5 The Cardholder's Name

The cardholder's name is embossed near the bottom of the card. The name is embossed in first-name and last-name format. The cardholder's name is transmitted along with other information in a typical transaction, where the cardholder is physically present with the card and the card is swiped on an EDC machine. In the case of Internet payment transactions or a transaction where the cardholder is not present, then the transaction oftentimes mandates that the cardholder's name be exactly as mentioned on the face of the payment card.

2.2.2 Payment Card: External Visage (Back)

There is a great deal of information contained in the back of the card as well. The back of the card (in the case of a mag-stripe card) is in fact the most useful when the payment card is used to perform transactions, where the cardholder is physically present with the card. The information contained on the back of the card is described in the following subsections.

2.2.2.1 The Magnetic Stripe

The magnetic stripe consists of iron-based magnetic particles placed on a band of magnetic material. When contacted with a magnetic-stripe reader, the data contained in the magnetic stripe is read, and the transaction is subsequently processed. In the case of most magnetic stripes on a payment card, the mag-stripe is located about 0.223 inches from the edge of the card and is 0.375 inches wide.

The magnetic stripe contains up to three tracks of data, namely Track 1, Track 2, and Track 3. We will explore track data in greater detail in Section 2.3. As mentioned previously, the magnetic stripe is of a different color based on its coercivity. High-coercivity cards are nearly black, whereas lower-coercivity cards are brown or a light brown color.

2.2.2.2 Signature Strip

The signature strip is located right below the mag-stripe. The signature strip is used for merchant authentication and to indicate the validity of a payment card. The card is considered to be valid only if the cardholder signs the signature strip. The signature strip is also provided as a method of protection and authentication for the merchant. When the transaction is carried out at a physical merchant establishment, the merchant swipes the card and, after the payment has been successfully processed, the merchant generates a charge slip that is evidence that the transaction has been successfully processed for a particular amount. The cardholder has to sign on the merchant's copy of the charge slip and give it back to the merchant. A prudent merchant can verify the signature on the charge slip by comparing it with the one on the signature strip on the payment card. If both match, it provides a level of assurance that the individual using the payment card is probably authentic and not an impostor or a fraudster.

2.2.2.3 The CVV

The card verification value (CVV) code is also known as CVV2 for Visa and CVC2 for MasterCard. The CVV2 is a three-digit number printed as a separate entity, adjacent to the signature strip. It is known as the CVV2, because the CVV1 is present in the card's magnetic stripe in the track data. This CVV2 is printed on the card for authorization purposes during a card-not-present transaction, like an Internet transaction or telephone-based payment transaction using the payment card. In case of an Internet transaction, when the card is not present physically, there is a greater need for authorization. This is used as an additional authorization measure to prevent card fraud. In many countries, providing the CVV2 is mandatory. For instance, in India, all online merchants are mandatorily required to accept CVV2 information in addition to a password authentication just before a transaction is processed.

2.2.2.4 Service Disclaimer

The service disclaimer is printed right below the signature strip of the payment card. The service disclaimer states that by the use of the payment card, the cardholder has received and acknowledged the cardholder's agreement. The cardholder agreement is an agreement between the payment-card issuer and the cardholder. This agreement usually contains information on the following:

- Charges incurred on the card: the responsibility of the cardholder's use of the card
- Indicates whether the card can be used for cash advances at ATMs
- Indicates whether there are any insurance benefits on the card
- Billing and settlement details: cycle Information, service charges, unpaid charges, etc.
- Information in the event of loss of payment card

- Termination of the cardholder's agreement
- Claims, liabilities, and miscellaneous information
- Governing laws and information about arbitration in the case of a dispute
- Information about rewards programs linked to the card

2.2.2.5 Bank Address and Contact Details

The issuing bank prints the bank address and emergency contact information to report a lost or stolen card. Customers are advised to call this number immediately after their card is misplaced/stolen to prevent any further transactions from occurring on the card. The address is also provided to inform a potential finder of the card to mail to the given address.

2.2.2.6 Customer Service Information

Customer service information is provided below the address of the issuing bank. This information is provided for the cardholder to contact the customer service department for any inquiries relating to the card, including:

- Billing and settlement issues
- Reporting loss of stolen card
- Miscellaneous inquiries

2.3 DATA SETS: PAYMENT CARD

2.3.1 Track 1 Data

The most important aspect of a magnetic-stripe card is the track data that is contained in the magnetic stripe. This data is stored and used for processing during a payment-card transaction. When the card is swiped on a reader, the magnetic card reader head reads the track information on the payment card and transmits this information to the processors.

Every magnetic-stripe card has up to three tracks of data. These tracks have to be loaded in 0.223 inches of width (width of the magnetic stripe). Card readers only read Track 1 and Track 2 data, or sometimes both when one of them is unreadable. Track 3 is not usually read.

Track 1 was developed by the International Air Transport Association (IATA). It was the first track that was standardized for usage in the payment-card industry. The track contains 79 alphanumeric characters, and its recording density is 210 bpi (bits per inch). Track 1 data is organized as given in Figure 2.4.

Start sentinel (%): The start sentinel is the first character in the Track 1 data. It begins with the character "%".

Format code (B): The format code is a one-byte alpha character. The standard specified by financial institutions is the alpha character "B".

Primary account number (PAN): The PAN is a 16–19-digit number that is stored in the Track 1 data. Track 1 can store up to 19 characters of the PAN.

Field separator (^): The field separator is a logical character that is used to demarcate between the different fields in Track 1 data. The field separator is usually the character "^".

Name: The cardholder's full name (up to 26 characters) is stored in the Track 1 data strip.

Additional data: Additional data includes the expiration date (in YYMM)

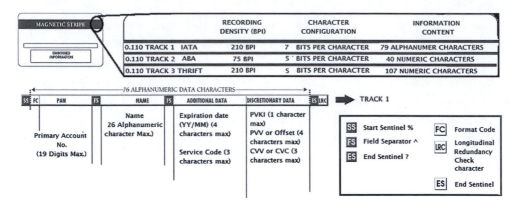

FIGURE 2.4

Organization of Track 1 data on payment card (with legend).

format—four characters—and the service code in three characters.

Discretionary data: Discretionary data includes the PIN value key indicator (PVKI), the PIN verification value (PVV), and the card verification value (CVV)/card verification code (CVC) in the case of a credit card. The value of the CVV/CVC in the track information is the CVV1/CVC1, which is different from the one next to the signature panel. Let's spend some time discussing the PIN, the PVKI, and the PVV.

The personal identification number (PIN) is used as a means of authorization during the payment cycle to provide assurance that the transaction is legitimate and not fraudulent. The PIN is mostly used in the case of debit cards and ATM cards. The PIN is generated and stored in the track data. The PIN is generated by encrypting a combination of the 11 rightmost digits of the customer's PAN, a constant of 6, a PIN value key indicator (PVKI) of 1 digit, and a 3-digit validation field. These digits are concatenated, encrypted, and decimalized

to yield a PIN value that consists of 4 digits. This value is called the natural PIN. The natural PIN is stored in the Track 1 information. There is something known as a PIN offset, which is the difference between the PIN value provided by the institution and the PIN value chosen by the customer. This offset value is stored in Track 3 of a magnetic-stripe card.

End sentinel (?): This is encoded at the end of the data, indicating that the data ends at this section.

Longitudinal redundancy checker: This is a redundancy check digit that is present for error checking.

2.3.2 Track 2 Data

Track 2 data was developed by the American Banking Association (ABA). It consists of 37 characters that are encoded in the track of the card. They are as follows:

Start sentinel (;): This indicates the start of the Track 2 data. It denotes hexadecimal B or the ";" character.

Primary account number (PAN): The PAN is a 16–19-digit number that is stored in the Track 2 data. Track 2 can store up to 19 characters of the PAN.

Field separator (=): The field separator indicates a logical separation of data elements. In the case of Track 2 data, the field separator is the "=" character or hexadecimal D.

Expiration date: The last day of the month and year on which the card expires.

Service code: The service code indicates some rules of the payment cycle to the merchant's terminal that are to be followed with a specific payment card.

Discretionary data: The discretionary data includes the PIN value key indicator (PVKI), the PIN verification value (PVV), and the card verification value (CVV)/card verification code (CVC) in the case of a credit card.

End sentinel (?): This is encoded at the end of the data, indicating that the data ends at this section.

Longitudinal redundancy checker: This is a redundancy check digit that is present for error checking.

Figure 2.5 is a representation of Track 2 data on a magnetic-stripe card.

2.3.3 Track 3 Data

Track 3 data has been created by the thrift. Track 3 data is a relatively new track in the payment-card scheme. It is governed by ISO-4909:2006. This track, however, is virtually unused by most card payment brands, and in some cases it is not even present on the face of the card because of the narrow magnetic-stripe requirements. This track is mainly used to permit interchange based on the use of the magnetic-stripe card. Track 3 consists of 104 characters and contains the following information:

Start sentinel (;): This indicates the start of the Track 3 data. It denotes hexadecimal B or the ";" character.

Primary account number (PAN): The PAN is a 16–19-digit number that is stored in the Track 3 data. Track 2 can store up to 19 characters, nothing more.

Field separator (=): The field separator indicates a logical separation of data elements. In the case of Track 3 data, the field separator is the "=" character or hexadecimal D.

Use and security data: This consists of a large number of data sets, including:

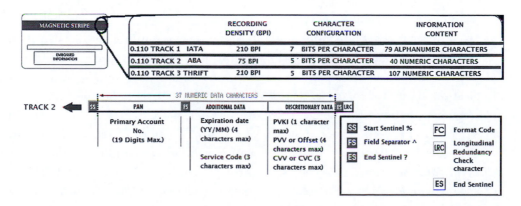

FIGURE 2.5
Track 2 data with legend.

Country code (3 digits to indicate the country to which the transaction should be routed)

Currency (3 digits to calculate the update in the home currency)

Currency exponent (1 digit to indicate the base value of the amount authorized and the amount remaining)

Amount authorized per cycle period (4 digits)

Amount remaining in this cycle (4 digits)

Cycle beginning (4 digits in the form of YDDD to indicate the date on which the card becomes valid)

Cycle length (2 digits to denote the period during which the accumulated total of all the charges to the card shall not exceed the authorized amount)

Retry count (1 digit to denote the number of times of attempted false PIN entry before the card is locked out)

PINPARM (6 digits to indicate the algorithm code and PIN verification value)

Interchange control (1 digit to indicate whether interchange is permitted on the card)

Type of account and service restriction (2 digits to define the type of account recorded in the individual field and the interchange restriction control of debits and credits)

Expiration date (4 digits), and card sequence number (1 digit to distinguish between cards issued with the same PAN)

Additional data: Additional data consists of several data sets. They are as follows:

First and second subsidiary accounts (refers to subsidiary card accounts [add-ons]) linked to the main cardholder's account

Relay marker (1 digit to provide a facility to check to verify whether the length of Track 3 that passed during the transaction may be reduced to exclude the additional data)

Crypto check digit (6 digits to provide a cryptographic check on the integrity of all the data elements on Track 3)

Discretionary data (same as provided in Tracks 1 and 2)

End sentinel (?): This is encoded at the end of the data, indicating that the data ends at this section.

Longitudinal redundancy checker: This is a redundancy check digit that is present for error checking.

Figure 2.6 is a representation of Track 3 data.

2.4 PAYMENT CARD: TERMINOLOGY

2.4.1 The Payment Card Processing Cycle

The payment processing cycle for a card transaction has multiple aspects to it (see Figure 2.7). All of us use payment cards with utmost ease. We simply go to a store; buy some products; hand the card over to the cashier, who swipes it on a machine; and within a matter of seconds, the transaction is authorized and the payment goes through. Online, it's even easier: We enter our card details, and the payment is authorized from the card account. However, there are several parties to a payment-card

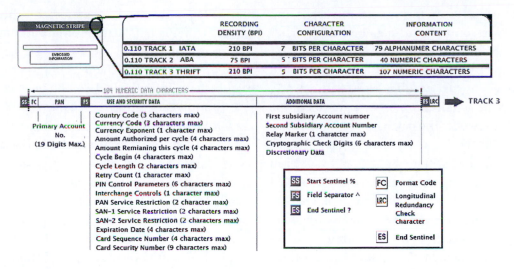

MAGNETIC STRIPE		RECORDING DENSITY (BPI)	CHARACTER CONFIGURATION	INFORMATION CONTENT
0.110 TRACK 1	IATA	210 BPI	7 BITS PER CHARACTER	79 ALPHANUMER CHARACTERS
0.110 TRACK 2	ABA	75 BPI	5 BITS PER CHARACTER	40 NUMERIC CHARACTERS
0.110 TRACK 3	THRIFT	210 BPI	5 BITS PER CHARACTER	107 NUMERIC CHARACTERS

FIGURE 2.6
Track 3 data with legend.

transaction. These parties make the processing cycle possible.

When a cardholder swipes his/her card on the merchant's card terminal, the transaction is routed first to the acquirer. The acquirer is the one who has provided the terminal to the merchant and has agreed with the merchant to process all or some of the merchant's transactions. The acquirer is the organization that typically "acquires" the transactions from the merchant and processes them on the merchant's behalf.

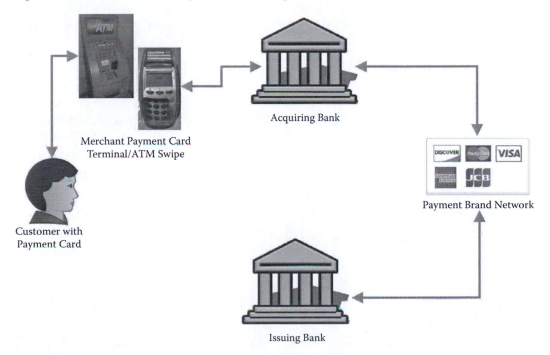

FIGURE 2.7
Typical payment-processing process.

The acquirer performs certain checks and balances on the card data and then routes the transaction to the payment brand's payment network. For instance, if the card swiped by the cardholder is a Visa card, then the acquirer routes the payment to the Visa network. The payment brand performs certain checks and balances on the card information sent to be processed. It then identifies the issuer—the organization that has issued the card to the cardholder—and routes the card details to the issuer along with the amount, etc., for authorization of the card payment. The issuer has the cardholder's file and performs checks and balances on the transaction, identifies if there are any anomalies with the information sent or the authorized amount, and posts the amount that is authorized. The transaction is routed all the way back to the merchant, where the cardholder signs on a charge slip to complete the transaction.

This cycle applies in a very similar way for ATM transactions. However, in the case of an ATM transaction, the card is swiped at an acquirer's ATM terminal instead of a merchant's card terminal.

2.4.2 Merchants

Merchants are one of the most important players in a payment process. They are generally the point of origin of most payment-card transactions. Merchants can be of multiple types: online retailers, point-of-sale merchants, and so on. The need for payment cards is validated by merchants and their need to accept payment cards as a form of payment for goods and services rendered. The merchant ties up with one or more acquirers. The acquirers are usually banks that provide the merchant with the capability to accept payment-card transactions by supplying the merchant with credit card terminals, APIs (application programming interfaces), or links to their payment network through the merchant POS (point of sale) system. Initially, PCI compliance was largely aimed at getting merchants compliant with the PCI requirements, because the possibility of a card breach was highest at a merchant location, as they processed a great deal of customer card information on a daily basis. The PCI standard categorizes merchants in different levels for PCI compliance. We will discuss that in Chapter 3, where we examine the issue of PCI compliance in greater detail.

2.4.3 Acquirers

Acquirers or acquiring banks are a critical component of a payment processing cycle. Acquirers are organizations that associate with merchants to provide them with payment-processing services. As a part of their duties as acquirers, they provide credit card terminals for merchants to physically process payment cards at their stores. Some acquirers also provide payment gateway services to online merchants for them to process their online transactions using the acquirer's payment gateway. For larger merchants, where they have their own credit card processing terminals, acquirers provide the merchant's point-of-sale (POS) system with access to their payment-processing network, and the merchant can directly process card transactions in their own POS terminals. In some cases, acquirers also expose their payment gateway API to the merchant's Web application, which allows the application to directly process payment-card transactions from the merchant's website, rather than routing the same to the acquirer's payment gateway.

2.4.4 Payment Networks

Payment networks refer to the networks that have been created by payment brands like Visa, MasterCard, Amex, JCB, and Discover. These payment networks are used to facilitate authorization, clearing, and settlement functions for the payment network. These payment brands firstly provide the brands for which cards are issued by banks and accepted by merchants.

Authorization is one of the most important functions of the payment process. The payment brand network is required by the acquirer bank to contact the issuer bank to authorize the payment made from the card. The payment brand network receives the information from the acquirer, identifies the issuing bank, and contacts the issuing bank with details. If the transaction is approved, an authorization code is sent by the payment brand network to the acquirer.

The clearing function is another key role of the payment brand network with reference to the payment processing cycle. The merchant bank or the acquirer sends the card transaction information to the payment brand network. The payment brand network sends the relevant information to the relevant issuing bank for reconciliation. The payment brand network in this case provides reconciliation services to the acquiring bank, thus acting as a clearing agency.

Settlement is the process where the merchant bank pays the merchant after settling its dues with the issuing bank, with the payment brand network is the via intermediary. Additionally, it is also a process where the issuing bank bills the cardholder for the purchase.

Another important function of the payment brand is to provide dispute resolution and charge-back services. In certain situations, there are issues where the cardholder might dispute a transaction for reasons ranging from fraudulent occurrence of the transaction to the cardholder forgetting the existence of the transaction itself. In such cases, the cardholder raises a dispute request with the issuing bank, and the issuing bank in turn raises a dispute request through the payment network with the acquirer and its merchant for information regarding the transaction, such as the sales receipt, charge slip, or any other form of evidence to prove that the transaction is legitimate. If the transaction is legitimate, then the cardholder's dispute is repudiated by the card-issuing bank. If the cardholder's dispute is legitimate, then the cardholder is not liable for the transaction, and there is a chargeback to the card, in which case the merchant is forced to forfeit the amount from the transaction. A dispute situation proves to be very costly for the merchant, as it means that the amount arising from the transaction is lost, and in some cases, the merchant also incurs an additional processing fee for a chargeback.

2.4.5 Issuers

Issuers are commonly known as *issuing banks*. Issuing banks are those banks that issue payment cards branded with one of the payment brands to their customers, who become the cardholders. In many cases, acquiring and issuing banks may be the same entity with reference to a particular transaction. Issuing banks store the card files of the cards they have issued to their customers. These card files contain the details relating to the payment card and the cardholder, such as the PAN, name, address, expiration date, and so on. Based on the system, sometimes even the CVV/

CVV2/PVV/PIN may be stored by the issuing bank's card-management system.

2.4.6 Processors

Apart from certain conventional entities in a payment-card process, there are also several service providers in the payment-card cycle or related to the payment processing cycle. There could be service providers providing various types of services, for instance a back-office company providing settlement services for payment-card transactions or providing evaluation of credit card applications. There could also be service providers providing fraud-management services to issuers, acquirers, and merchants.

One of the most important types of service providers in this category are the "payment processors." These are the entities that provide payment processing infrastructure to issuing and acquiring banks. They are like the outsourced payment-processing departments of banks. For instance, let us say Bank X wants to issue and acquire payment cards and payment-card transactions, but they don't have the infrastructure or the qualifications to do so. Instead, they engage the services of a payment-processing company. This company has the infrastructure to perform the issuing function of the bank, from accepting the application for payment cards from the customers, to embossing the card with the cardholder's details, to mailing PIN details to the cardholder, to mailing the monthly statement to the cardholder, and so on. They also would perform acquiring functions, such as equipping merchants of the bank with card-processing terminals and machines, and providing APIs to online merchants for online transactions, etc. Payment-processing organizations can perform processing for multiple issuing and acquiring banks. In some cases, some processors might choose to only perform the acquiring function; in other cases, they may choose to do both.

2.4.7 Other Service Providers

There may be various types of service providers in the payment processing or settlement cycle. Service providers are entities that are part of the payment processing, clearing, or settlement cycle, or with whom cardholder information is shared by entities in the payment processing, settlement, or clearing cycle. For instance, a BPO (business process outsourcing organization), which performs collections for a merchant's customers where customers share their credit card information to make payment for the merchant's goods or services, is considered a service provider, because the merchant has authorized the BPO to collect their customers' payment-card information to initiate payment for their goods and services. Other service providers include payment aggregators, who handle multiple merchant accounts and have transactions processed through an acquirer for these merchants. This is usually seen with small online merchants that have a payment aggregator or gateway service.

2.4.8 Independent Sales Organizations

Independent sales organizations (ISOs) are also referred to as merchant service providers (MSPs). These organizations are third-party organizations that sign on merchant accounts for payment processing. They are tied up with acquiring banks, and they are responsible for signing on merchant organizations, in exchange for a fee, as a percentage of the merchant's sale. Acquirers prefer being very selective when it comes to choosing merchant accounts, because certain merchants, such as online auctions and adult entertainment, are riskier than other merchants with reference to payment-card fraud. Therefore, ISOs can, despite an elevated risk, take on such merchant accounts for payment processing as well.

2.5 PAYMENT CARD TRANSACTIONS

2.5.1 Card-Present Transaction

A card-present (CP) transaction is the oldest type of card transaction. This is the type of transaction where the card (and the cardholder) are physically present during the transaction. Typically, this would be when a cardholder steps into a merchant establishment and uses his/her card for the transaction. The merchant usually swipes the card on the credit card terminal and the transaction is processed. This type of transaction is considered less risky for the payment entities (merchant, acquirer, issuer, payment brand) because the card is physically present for verification and, consequently, the transaction carries a lower fee as compared to online or telephone transactions.

2.5.2 Card-Not-Present Transaction

A card-not-present (CNP) transaction is the opposite of a card-present transaction. This is a transaction where the cardholder's card is not present for verification or examination in a physical sense. This occurs usually in the case of online transactions, mail-order/telephone-order (MOTO)

transactions, interactive voice response (IVR) transactions, and so on.

Online transactions are typical e-commerce transactions, where the cardholder shops at an e-commerce merchant and pays for goods and services with a payment card. The cardholder enters the requisite details on the merchant's website or a payment gateway, and the payment is processed online. MOTO transactions are those CNP transactions where the cardholder typically provides the card information along with certain information over the telephone or over a filled-out application form, and the merchant processes the transaction without the cardholder's card being physically present. This usually happens for magazine subscriptions of telephone sales, where the cardholder fills out a physical form with card information and personal information and the merchant charges the card with the amount due. IVR transactions are telephone-based CNP transactions, where the cardholder keys in the card information at a telephonic prompt using his/her normal telephone/mobile phone. The keys punched in by the cardholder is the card information, and this is processed for payment.

2.5.3 Open-Loop Payment Systems

An open-loop payment system is also commonly known as a *four-party payment system*. The open-loop payment system typically involves two banks and a payment brand, apart from the merchant. A typical open-loop payment transaction is as follows:

- A cardholder uses the payment card at a merchant establishment.
- The merchant sends the card details (CP or CNP transaction) to an

acquiring bank (that the merchant has signed up with).

- The acquiring bank requests authorization through a payment brand to an issuing bank.
- The payment brand sends the information to an issuing bank (the bank that has issued the cardholder's payment card).
- The issuing bank (based on the information provided) authorizes or denies the transaction, thereby completing the transaction cycle.

The open-loop payment system is used by Visa and MasterCard. These payment brands do not issue the cards, and they do not set interest fees that are to be paid by cardholders. These are rules that are to be set by the issuing banks. Additionally, these payment brands do not sign on merchants or establish merchant transaction fees for the transactions or discounts, etc. This is a function of an acquiring bank. The payment brands that operate in an open loop are responsible for branding, payment flow, settlement, and clearing. Figure 2.8 represents an open-loop payment system

2.5.4 Closed-Loop Payment Systems

Closed-loop payment systems are typically known as a *three-party payment system* involving the cardholder, the merchant, and the payment network (brand). In this system, the payment brand is responsible for the acquisition and issuance of payment cards in the network. The payment process typically works as follows:

- A cardholder uses the payment card at a merchant establishment.
- The merchant sends the card details (CP or CNP transaction) to a payment network (brand) acting as the acquiring bank.
- The payment network (brand) authorizes or declines the transaction, and the payment cycle is complete.

Payment brands that operate a closed-loop payment system are typically American Express and Discover. They do not provide acquiring and issuing functions to financial institutions. However, in recent times, they have begun to open their network to financial institutions in the issuing functions, thus behaving

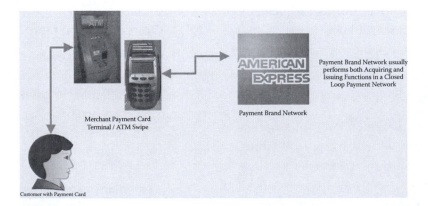

FIGURE 2.8
Open-loop payment system.

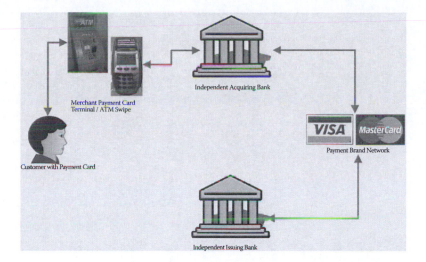

FIGURE 2.9
Closed-loop payment system.

like open-loop networks in some aspects. Figure 2.9 represents a closed-loop payment system.

2.6 SUMMARY

We began this chapter with a view of the history of a magnetic-stripe card. We described its origins and the evolution of the payment card to the chip and PIN card that is being adopted the world over today. We then described the physical attributes of the card in great detail, explaining the appearance of the card in the front and back. We delved into the various data elements on the card, including the primary account number (PAN), expiration date, and so on. Further, we described the data present in the magnetic stripe of payment card. We delved into the intricacies of the three tracks of data on the magnetic-stripe payment card. Subsequently, we explored the payment processing cycle and described the various entities that are involved in this cycle. Finally, we explored the different types of payment-card transactions and the differences between an open-loop and a closed-loop payment system.

3

Security and the Payment-Card Industry

The increasing adoption of payment cards as a medium of business transactions has resulted in an exodus of people from using traditional media like cash, checks, and notes to the mass usage of payment cards for their daily personal and business transactions. The payment-card industry has systemically ensured that businesses and consumers constantly embrace the payment-card industry for ease of use and sheer convenience. However, this has also attracted a more nefarious brand of individuals and organizations. The ubiquity of payment cards has also ensured that attackers are constantly looking to extract this information from banks, merchants, and any other entities handling card information. This chapter details a brief history of credit card fraud and some of the key security incidents in the payment-card industry that prompted the requirement for security to become a key aspect of this industry and its ecosystem.

3.1 A BRIEF HISTORY OF CREDIT CARD FRAUD

Before the advent of e-commerce, credit card fraud was largely a physical act. The compromise of payment-card information largely revolved around compromising an individual's card (physically) and then using the card to perform transactions (impersonating the legal holder of the card). Card fraud usually centered around activities such as skimming and physical theft.

Card skimming is an act of duplicating the data that is present on a magnetic stripe of a payment card to create other fake cards that may be used by fraudsters to perpetrate card fraud. For instance, a waiter at a restaurant might have a skimming machine near the card terminal machine where he/she swipes the card to process a payment. This skimming machine captures the magnetic-stripe data on the customer's card, which can then be used to regenerate fake cards and perform transactions as the cardholder. This kind of fraud relies on physical access to the customer's cardholder data. The attacker typically uses a specific card-reading machine (popularly known as a skimming machine) to read the track data on the magnetic stripe. Another popular skimming attack is an ATM skimming fraud that is perpetrated by attackers who steal confidential ATM and debit-card information from customers visiting bank ATMs for cash withdrawals, balance verifications, etc. The attacker could rig an ATM by adding a card-reading device to it to capture the magnetic stripe and a small camera to capture the customer's PIN as he/she is entering it. The device logs several cards that are used by the bank's customers at an ATM location, and the attacker is able to capture all their card details, including the PIN, thereby completely compromising the cardholder's data.

Figure 3.1 shows images of an ATM skimming fraud, where the ATM machine has been fitted with a special card reader that has been inserted by the fraudster. Apart from that, there is a small camera just above the PIN entry device panel, where the fraudster visually captures the cardholder PIN.

Another form of card fraud that was popular earlier is known as *carding*. Fraudsters use this practice to verify the validity of a stolen card. The fraudster may run the card on some popular website or e-commerce portal to see if the card works. If it works, the fraudster knows that the card is still valid and can be used to carry out more transactions.

Another dimension of carding was to use a card generator to generate millions of credit card numbers and data. The fraudster would then use this data to test the valid card numbers that were generated. Earlier, fraudsters would even use the fake cards in locations where credit card processing was not done online, like conventions, conferences, and shows, and use the fake card to perform transactions. However, both these practices are largely obsolete now because of various fraud-management systems that banks, merchants, and payment portals have online. Additionally, card terminals require additional details such as an address or a PIN or last four digits to validate a card.

These attacks largely address the compromise of individual cardholder information, on a model that does not scale to tens of thousands of card numbers being stolen, unless the institutions fail to detect them. However, modern-day card fraud is more a game of numbers. Attackers who are looking to compromise cardholder information are looking for large numbers to be compromised. Additionally, they are looking to compromise identity data along with card information to be able to perform a more comprehensive and monetarily rewarding attack against a particular institution. We will explore some of the most significant incidents in cardholder-data theft in the subsequent section.

3.2 A BRIEF HISTORY OF SIGNIFICANT CARD DATA BREACHES

3.2.1 The CardSystems Breach

CardSystems is a large payment processing company. It processes payments on behalf of merchants and banks on both the issuing and acquiring fronts. It suffered a massive breach in 2005, when almost 40 million cards were exposed by attackers who had been able to attack and compromise its IT environment. While the company issued a statement that only about 200,000 cards had been stolen by attackers, about 40 million cards were exposed due to the breach.

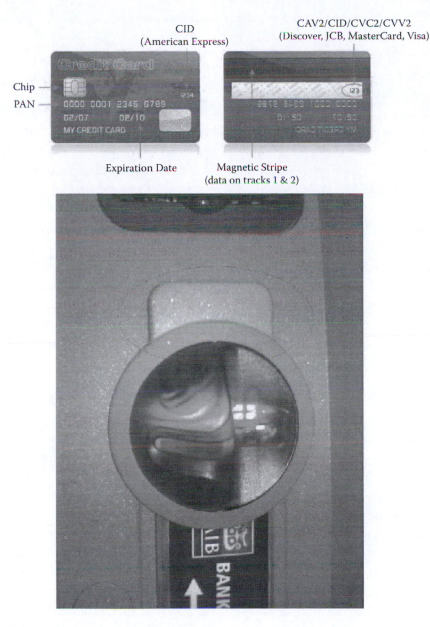

FIGURE 3.1
ATM skimming fraud.

CardSystems had been breached because of an SQL-injection attack. The attack, which had been perpetrated by external attackers, relied on compromising a back-end database that was being used by a Web application that was used by the customers of CardSystems. SQL injection is an attack that allows an attacker to enter crafted SQL queries into the application's form fields and parameters and get access to the back-end database. The attackers in the CardSystems breach were able to run crafted database queries through the vulnerable Web application. These database queries were run every four days, and the data was zipped into a smaller file and sent to the attackers over FTP. The 200,000 card numbers that were stolen were stolen using this method.

It was seen that CardSystems had been negligent with the protection of its IT environment, its applications, and its data. It was found that CardSystems was storing information in an unencrypted manner, thereby resulting in an easy extraction for the attackers, once they were able to find the vulnerabilities in the Web application. In fact, in a complaint filed by the Federal Trade Commission (FTC), it was seen that CardSystems had not taken basic measures like strong passwords to protect its systems against the breach.

The CardSystems breach was actually discovered because of a high volume of fraudulent transactions happening through counterfeit cards. These counterfeits contained the magnetic-stripe and track data that matched those that were being processed and stored by CardSystems as part of its issuing operations.

CardSystems was found to be non-compliant with Visa CISP (Cardholder Information Security Program), which had been adopted by the other payment brands, as well as MasterCard's security program.

Unhappy with the remediation efforts taken by CardSystems, Visa issued a statement precluding CardSystems from the ability to process Visa card payments. This was soon followed up with a similar statement from American Express.

MasterCard, however, gave CardSystems until August 31, 2005, to comply with the standard. CardSystems was acquired by Pay-by-Touch later in 2005.

At that time, the CardSystems breach had been the largest breach in history and was the first time that card payment brands had intervened to issue sanctions against CardSystems and its ability to process card payments.

3.2.2 The T.J. Maxx Card Breach

The T.J. Maxx card breach was a watershed event in the history of data breaches, especially payment-card-industry security breaches. The breach was one of the largest breaches of a mainstream merchant organization, and it revolved around credit card details as well as personal information of customers at T.J. Maxx and its partner organizations.

The breach was one of massive proportions. There were about 95 million cards that were said to be exposed. Several banks around the world reported fraudulent transactions that had been carried out by cards that seemed to have a common point of origin in T.J. Maxx. In early 2007, T.J. Maxx released a statement that its network had been compromised by attackers and that these attackers were able to access credit card information in its network.

The attack had been carried out by attackers who were able to compromise an insufficiently protected wireless network at one of the T.J. Maxx stores. After compromising the store IT system, the attackers were able to elevate their access from a single store to T.J. Maxx's central systems and databases. For the greater part of 2006 and 2007, and possibly 2005, attackers were able to constantly gain access to T.J. Maxx's central database, where they egressed sensitive information like card data, user personal data, etc. T.J. Maxx had not encrypted card information or its users' personal data, thereby easing the attackers' access to data. This resulted in one of the most expensive and historically significant data breaches in world history.

T.J. Maxx suffered heavy financial losses due to the breach. In September 2007, T.J. Maxx was the target of a class action lawsuit, where it had to furnish $30 vouchers to all the customers who had been affected by the breach. Later in 2007, Visa imposed a heavy fine on T.J. Maxx to the extent of $880,000. T.J. Maxx also paid Visa the reissue cost for reissuing all the cards that had been stolen or feared stolen in the breach. This amounted to a substantial $40.9 million. MasterCard imposed reissuance charges of $24 million on T.J. Maxx, along with other fines and penalties to the tune of almost $15 million.

3.2.3 The Heartland Payment Systems Breach

In early 2009, Heartland Payment Systems, the sixth largest payment processor in the United States, declared that it had been breached in 2008. Heartland has been in the merchant-acquiring processing business for several years now. They acquire transactions on behalf of acquiring banks for merchants, and they process card payments from debit cards, credit cards, and other payment cards. Over 160 banks were affected by the Heartland Payment Systems breach, as Heartland processed somewhere along the lines of 100 million card transactions per day.

The Heartland Payment Systems breach was due to a Web application vulnerability. Attackers were able to attack Heartland's databases with an SQL-injection attack through one of Heartland's Web applications. Once the attackers were able to gain access to the internal network zone at Heartland, they ran sniffing programs that were able to sniff the traffic on the servers and gain access to network traffic

containing unencrypted card information. Heartland suffered heavy penalties and reissuance costs from payment brands.

It is interesting to note that the hacker group that was behind the T.J. Maxx breach was the one behind the Heartland breach. The group perpetrated many other incidents in other companies, including 7-Eleven.

3.2.4 The Sony Playstation Network Breach

The Sony Playstation Network is one of the most successful gaming networks in the world. Millions of users access the network to play online games and to buy products and services relating to their Playstation gaming consoles from the site. In April 2011, Sony disclosed that their Playstation network had been compromised. The company disclosed that over 70 million customer records including names, addresses, and credit card information, along with user IDs and passwords, were compromised.

Sony issued a statement later that, while other information like names and addresses were unencrypted, credit card information was encrypted. However, there was no proof that those details were not accessed by the attackers.

This would be the first of several times in the same month that Sony ands its partner organizations would be affected by major data breaches that caused them a great deal of embarrassment and loss of reputation. At the time of writing this book, details are yet to be disclosed as to the exact means of attack and the details. The matter is being investigated by law enforcement agencies. However, this is one of the largest data breaches in history, with over 77 million records compromised and the company attacked several times over in the short span of a few months.

3.3 CARDHOLDER SECURITY PROGRAMS

3.3.1 Card Brand Cardholder Security Programs

One of the critical roles of the payment brand is to ensure that a safe umbrella is provided to all parties of a card transaction, from consumer to merchant. Payment cards are a ubiquitous medium for making payments. However, there may easily come a time when consumers are afraid to use their credit and debit cards for their daily transactions. This is a perception that is very prevalent in Eastern economies like India, where people within the age group of 35–60 are very afraid of using their credit cards for shopping online because they fear that their card details and sensitive information will be stolen. Such perceptions cost the card schemes and the payment-card industry in general a lot of money. Therefore, to improve the overall security of entities handling cardholder information—and consequently to improve the perceptions of stakeholders and customers—the card payment brands have created their compliance programs for cardholder-data security.

Visa has a cardholder-data security program called the Visa Cardholder Information Security Program (Visa CISP). The CISP is a set of requirements that merchants and service providers who store, process, or transmit Visa cardholder data have to be compliant with. The program has been mandated by Visa since June 2001. However, now the compliance requirement has changed from Visa's CISP to the PCI-DSS (Payment-Card Industry Data Security Standard) by the PCI-SSC (Payment-Card Industry Security Standards Council), as discussed in Section 3.3.2.

MasterCard has a program called the MasterCard Site Data Protection Program, which applies to entities such as merchants and service providers. American Express has a Data Security Operating Policy (DSOP) that is a set of compliance requirements that American Express has laid out for merchants and service providers that are storing, processing, or transmitting American Express cardholder information.

3.3.2 The Formation of the PCI-DSS and PCI-SSC

In 2006, the payment brands came together in a move that would unify security standards across the payment-card industry. They created an independent entity known as the Payment-Card Industry Security Standards Council (PCI-SSC). The PCI-SSC is responsible for the creation, development, and promulgation of the PCI standards. It also appoints assessing organizations for the payment-card industry.

3.3.3 Structure of the PCI Standards

Any industry is constantly evolving. The payment-card industry is no different. There are always changes in technology, operating environments, and IT (information technology) deployments. IT deployments probably change at the most furious pace because of the developments that have been taking place in the IT environment. For instance, the cloud is and has been one of the most discussed aspects of IT in recent times. Organizations have seriously started considering the cloud to host their applications and leverage common infrastructure, platform, or applications from a common service provider or organization. Because of its cost benefits and value proposition, the cloud is being adopted by organizations all over the world. In fact, there is an organization promoting and promulgating security information about the cloud, known as the Cloud Security Alliance.

The constant change in the industry requires that a prescriptive and rigorous standard like PCI has to be updated with the latest trends in IT. This means that the standard requires review over time. Both the PCI-DSS and PA-DSS (Payment Application DSS) go through a life cycle that is decided by the PCI-SSC as part of their standards life cycle, and it works as follows:

Stage 1: Standards are published. Stage 1 of the PCI and PA development life cycle is undertaken in October of the year. This is timed to coincide with the SSC's community meetings that are held for stakeholders of the standards. Stakeholders may choose to adopt the standard, but they are not required to do so until they become effective on a particular date.

Stage 2: Standards become effective. The published standards become effective in January of the following year. Stakeholders should implement the new version of the standard on that date, but the older standards are allowed for the next 14 months, after which they are invalidated.

Stage 3: Implementation. The market begins to implement the new standards as of this point. During the implementation, there are aspects of assessment of the standards that have to addressed, relative to a stakeholder's environment. Changes are assessed, and their applicability to a stakeholder's environment is determined.

Stage 4: Feedback. Every new standard released by the SSC will have several points of response from the market. Stakeholders continually express their views on specific points of the standards and provide feedback to improve them in any way. There are several special-interest groups that add their thoughts to aspects of the applicability of their specific special-interest group, such as cloud, virtualization, and so on. This happens from November to March of the year. This would be the second year, as the standard would have been published in October of the previous year.

Stage 5: Retirement of the old standard. In December of the second year, the old standard that has been grandfathered by the SSC for 14 months will be retired by the SSC. The old standards are officially invalidated, and the new standards alone shall be used for purposes of compliance.

Stage 6: Feedback and review. This is the stage where the SSC gathers feedback and comments from several participating organizations. This stage of the life cycle happens sometime in August of the second year. The feedback consists of the following:

- *Clarifications*: Participating organizations and stakeholders might find the language and verbiage of certain requirements of the standards to be confusing. Clarification feedback helps the SSC understand the origin of clarification ambiguity and ensures that words are used precisely to convey the intent of the requirement.

- *Additional guidance*: On several occasions, a large body of stakeholders has requested additional guidance from the SSC on matters of specific requirements. For instance, if the community requires information on the concept of "one primary function per server," which is a requirement in the PCI-DSS (which we will cover later), they might want additional guidance from the SSC with reference to the meaning of the requirement or the specific implementation requirement for the guidance. The SSC will review such cases where additional guidance has to be given with reference to the requirements.

- *New/evolving requirements*: Some requests for new or evolving existing requirements also come in from the community. These requests are considered by the SSC during this stage.

Stage 7: Drafts. Based on the data received as feedback, special-interest groups, research, and so on, the SSC will draft new standards and circulate them within the SSC. There will be several iterations of these drafts, based on the inputs received by them. This stage occurs from November of the second year to April of the third year.

Stage 8: Final reviews. The final drafts of the new standards and supporting documents are maintained for review. The standards are first circulated in-house. Comments from the board of advisors are also invited. Subsequently, the SSC releases a document called the "Summary of Changes" that briefly delves into the changes that will be incorporated, comparing the proposed requirements to the previous standard to provide a roving view to the community on what to expect. The standards and supporting documents are prepared and finalized over May to June of the third year to ensure that they are ready for the community meetings in September–October.

3.3.4 The PCI Assessment Environment

3.3.4.1 PCI-QSAs and PCI-QSACs

The PCI standards are technically rigorous standards that require very detailed assessment and review requirements. The SSC needed to create an ecosystem where they would be able to empanel certain entities to assess and certify downstream entities for PCI-DSS. These entities are called QSACs (qualified security assessor companies). The QSACs are empaneled by the PCI-SSC to assess, report, and certify qualifying organizations for the PCI-DSS. Although it is not necessary that all organizations undertaking PCI compliance need to be assessed and certified by a QSAC, assessment and validation by a QSA (qualified security assessor) are mandatory for organizations that store, process, or transmit cardholder information beyond a particular threshold. We will discuss this in detail in the next chapter. The PCI-QSAC has to consist of one or more PCI-QSAs. The QSA is an employee of a QSAC that has been certified by the SSC to validate, assess, and certify an organization's adherence to PCI-DSS.

In addition to their basic role, PCI-QSAs are not precluded by the PCI-SSC from providing consulting services, remediation services, or even products that will help their clients meet the requirements of the PCI-DSS. However, they cannot mandate that the organization undertaking PCI compliance must use such products or services to obtain compliance. This has been a cause of some debate in the community about the conflict of interest that a QSA and a QSAC have in relation to the organization undergoing compliance, as they may both act as brokers for an organization to achieve compliance.

3.3.4.2 The PCI ASV (Approved Scanning Vendor)

Another important player in a PCI-compliance process is the approved scanning vendor (ASV). One of the requirements of the PCI-DSS is that an organization must undergo quarterly scans by an ASV of the PCI-SSC and obtain passing results upon said scans of their external-facing devices that are within the scope for the PCI-compliance effort.

An ASV is an organization qualified by the PCI-SSC to undertake the external vulnerability scanning requirement for the organization undertaking PCI compliance. In fact, the ASV scan is mandated for any organization undergoing PCI compliance.

3.3.4.3 The PCI Internal Security Assessor

Large merchant organizations and third-party processors must adhere to a significant PCI-DSS compliance program. In such cases, it may be more feasible for the company to nominate a suitable candidate (or set of candidates) as internal security assessors (ISAs). The PCI-SSC has introduced this qualification for companies that would like to build their internal payment-card security assessment process, apart from other benefits like enhanced understanding of the payment-card industry requirements.

Following an application process and acceptance process, the ISA must undergo training that is provided by the SSC. Upon successful completion of the training, the ISA designation is provided to a specific individual employed by the company, and the company can now perform its own security audits based on PCI-DSS requirements.

3.3.4.4 The PCI Special-Interest Groups

Constant change in the business and technology landscapes has necessitated the creation of PCI special-interest groups. These groups are formed from participating organizations of the PCI-SSC that contribute to the evolution of the standards and their applicability to various entities that would undergo PCI compliance.

The special-interest groups (SIGs) have been formed to address specific industry or technological changes faced by the industry at large. They address these dimensions by constant analysis of these trends in business and technology based on a specific subject, and they provide guidance or clarification to the PCI-DSS as necessary. The various SIGs are related to wireless technology, virtualization technology, cloud, point-to-point encryption, and so on. The SIGs cannot bring change to the standard, but they can provide guidance and clarifications while suggesting enhancements in the standards based on the topics that they represent.

3.3.5 Payment Application Compliance

3.3.5.1 PCI's PA-DSS

Earlier, one of the key challenges that most enterprises faced in their efforts at PCI compliance was relating to applications. Enterprises would deploy a bevy of applications that would store, process, or transmit cardholder data and be part of the payment processing cycle. However, some of these applications did not provide any capability to be secured based on the requirements of the standards. As a result of this divide, applications would essentially negate an entity's capability to achieve PCI compliance. The applications in question were commercial applications that were available "off the shelf" for an organization to use, such as POS applications, payment middleware, etc.

Over time, the PCI-SSC has created a standard that applies to commercial applications within the payment-processing cycle that store, process, or transmit cardholder information. These requirements are derived from the PCI-DSS and specifically address commercial applications that are part of the payment-processing cycle. These applications have to meet with 13 requirements that must specifically be met for an application to be validated as a PA-DSS–validated application. This application would be conducive for deployment within a PCI environment of an organization undergoing PCI or one that has achieved PCI compliance.

We discuss PA-DSS compliance and its requirements extensively in Chapter 5.

3.3.5.2 PA-QSA and PA-QSAC

Just as the SSC has developed an ecosystem for certified and approved organizations to assess and certify organizations for PCI compliance, the SSC has created a similar ecosystem for PA-DSS, with the PA-QSAC (PA qualified security assessor company) and the PA-QSA (PA qualified security assessor). The PA-QSAC is an entity that is certified by the PCI-SSC, through its employees, to carry out assessments and validation process for PA-DSS. The PA-QSAC must have one or more qualified PA-QSAs that perform the assessment of the payment application, validate the application's adherence to the PA-DSS requirements, review documentation, and generate the report on validation (ROV).

3.4 SUMMARY

We began this chapter with a brief history of payment-card fraud. We explored instances of fraud involving theft of individual payment cards and card records. We then examined the fraudulent practice of skimming and carding that is still popular with ATMs and kiosks. Subsequently, we delved into a brief exploration of some of the largest card breaches in history: from the CardSystems breach to the T.J. Maxx breach to the Sony Playstation breach. After that, we explored the concept of cardholder security programs and their origins to the card payment brands. Subsequently, we studied the evolution of the PCI standards and their adoption by the payment brands as a unifying standard. PCI-SSC (PSI security standards council) is the entity that is responsible for developing, promulgating, and enhancing the standards. We discussed the life cycle of the requirements and the process adopted by the SSC for development and review of the PCI standards. We also discussed some of the entities that form part of the PCI ecosystem.

4

Payment Card Industry Data Security Standard (PCI-DSS)

The Payment Card Industry Data Security Standard (PCI-DSS) is perhaps the most well-known standard in the family of standards developed and maintained by the Payment Card Industry Security Standards Council (PCI-SSC). The standard applies to environments that store, process, or transmit payment-card information. In this chapter, we will explain some of the peripheral aspects of the PCI-DSS with reference to compliance for enterprises the world over. We will also explain some of the validation levels and requirements for various entities that are to be assessed and certified for PCI compliance. We will also briefly delve into some business models of companies that typically undergo PCI compliance. Finally, we will discuss different compliance options and possibilities for entities that are undergoing PCI compliance.

4.1 BRIEF HISTORY OF THE PCI-DSS

The PCI-DSS is one of the most significant compliance requirements in the world today. It has been enforced and adopted across the world by payment brands, acquirers, and issuers on their respective payment ecosystems, thereby resulting in several compliant and certified companies.

The reason for the creation of the PCI-DSS relied on the fundamental concepts of singularity and threat. Around 1999, Visa's Cardholder Information Security Program (CISP) had taken shape. It was a standard created by Visa for companies that were storing, processing, or transmitting Visa-branded cards. This included merchants, service providers, etc. In 2001, the CISP became a standard for Visa's ecosystem of acquirers, issuers, merchants, and service providers. At around the same time, MasterCard released its Site Data Protection (SDP) program, which was very similar to Visa's standard. This program was a set of security compliance requirements that entities who stored, processed, or transmitted MasterCard cardholder information had to adhere to. At around 2003, American Express created its own security compliance program for its ecosystem. At the time, merchants, service providers, and other entities under the scope of compliance would have to go through multiple validations by assessors from different payment brands. This situation had the potential to create a great deal of inconvenience owing to the fact that multiple payment brands would have to assess and validate an entity, even though the protection requirements for the various payment brands were similar, for the most part.

There was a clear need for a unifying standard that would provide a singular route to compliance for entities under the purview of PCI compliance. This prompted the creation of the unifying standard known popularly as the PCI-DSS. The PCI-SSC (Security Standards Council) was created in 2004. All the payment brands— Visa, MasterCard, JCB, American Express, and Discover—came together to form an independent entity that would govern the standards relating to the payment card industry as well as manage and promulgate the standard.

After the formation of the PCI-SSC, the massive CardSystems breach occurred in 2005. During the year, the PCI-SSC stated that approximately 235 million card records had been breached thus far, demonstrating the need for a regulatory entity to govern and manage security for the payment card industry.

In September 2006, the PCI-DSS version 1.1 was released by the PCI-SSC. The standard consisted of 12 requirements, ranging from security requirements on networks to physical security, documentation, and risk management.

The year 2007 was the proverbial *annus horribilis* for information security and the payment card industry because of the high-profile breaches of T.J. Maxx, Hannaford, Shell, and other companies. Millions of cardholder information records were stolen by attackers as part of these attacks. This increased the need for PCI compliance and also increased the pressure on the payment ecosystem by the payment brands and, in some cases, regulatory laws and requirements to impose security standards on the payment card industry.

In October 2008, the PCI-SSC released the PCI-DSS v 1.2. This version of the standard had certain changes and clarifications based on the previous versions of PCI-DSS. There were also several aspects relating to wireless implementations, virtualization, and encryption that were illuminated in the PCI-DSS v 1.2. The next version of the standard was v 1.2.1, released in August 2009. There were very minor changes in the standard at this time, with the PCI-SSC terming the changes as "administrative." There were some clarifications, supporting documents, etc., in this version of the standard.

Business models and technology undergo constant change, and it is essential that a security standard keep pace with this change. The PCI-DSS also undergoes change based on the change cycle defined by the PCI-SSC. (See Chapter 3 for further discussion about the PCI change cycle.) At the time of this writing, the latest standard from the PCI-SSC relating to the PCI-DSS is the PCI-DSS v 2.0. This version of the standard has 130 amendments to the previous version. There have been several new issues that have been clarified and supported, relating to virtualization, Web application security, cloud computing, encryption, and so on. We will delve into the requirements of the PCI-DSS v 2.0 in Chapters 8–20 of this book.

4.2 PCI COMPLIANCE LEVELS: PAYMENT BRANDS

4.2.1 Payment Brand Compliance Programs and PCI-DSS

The creation of the PCI-DSS has brought a great deal of structure to the payment card industry compliance process. Organizations have to comply with a single, unifying standard (i.e., the PCI-DSS), and they have to be assessed and validated against the 12 requirements of the PCI-DSS. Their adherence to the requirements allows them to be either certified or otherwise against the PCI-DSS.

We have already explored cardholder information security requirements from payment brands in Chapter 3 and in this chapter as well. It would be prudent to learn the interplay between these compliance requirements and the PCI-DSS.

The compliance programs for each of the payment brands like Visa, MasterCard, American Express, and so on, are still applicable. If an organization complies with the PCI-DSS, the organization does not automatically comply with these individual compliance programs. The organization has to obtain a certification and present a report on compliance to each of the payment brands. Upon examination of the documentation and a (possible) certification of PCI-DSS by a qualified security assessor (QSA), the organization complies with individual cardholder security programs of the different payment brands. While the compliance processes for these cardholder information security programs are not automatically fulfilled because of the PCI-DSS compliance and certification, it is the most essential requirement for compliance with individual cardholder security programs from payment brands.

4.2.2 Compliance Levels and Compliance Requirements

Any entity that stores, processes, or transmits cardholder information must comply with the PCI-DSS. However, based on the number of cardholder information records stored, processed, or transmitted by the entity, the level of compliance with the individual cardholder security program changes. For instance, if entity ABC is processing around 50,000 Visa cards per year, then the entity would have to comply with the PCI-DSS. However, they may be able to fill out a self-assessment questionnaire and perform the external vulnerability assessment by an approved scanning vendor (ASV) to comply with the PCI-DSS. However, if merchant XYZ was processing more than 6 million Visa cards, then the merchant would have to have the scoped environment assessed by a PCI-QSA and have an external vulnerability assessment by an ASV to comply and certify, based on the PCI-DSS requirements.

Each payment brand has multiple compliance levels that are specified for different types of entities like merchants and service providers. Let's tabulate these levels.

TABLE 4.1

Visa Merchant Compliance Validation Levels

Level	Criteria	Validation Requirements
Level 1	Merchants processing over 6 million Visa transactions annually or global merchants identified as Level 1 by any Visa region	• Annual report on compliance (RoC) by qualified security assessor or internal auditor if signed by officer of the company • Quarterly network scan by ASV • Attestation of compliance form
Level 2	Merchants processing 1 million to 6 million Visa transactions annually	• Annual self-assessment questionnaire (SAQ) • Quarterly network scan by ASV • Attestation of compliance form
Level 3	Merchants processing 20,000 to 1 million Visa transactions annually	• Annual self-assessment questionnaire (SAQ) • Quarterly network scan by ASV • Attestation of compliance form
Level 4	Merchants processing less than 20,000 Visa e-commerce transactions annually and all other merchants processing up to 1 million Visa transactions annually	• Annual self-assessment questionnaire (SAQ) • Quarterly network scan by ASV • Compliance validation requirements set by acquirer

TABLE 4.2

Visa Service Provider Compliance Validation Levels

Level	Criteria	Validation Requirements
Level 1	VisaNet processors or any service provider that stores, processes, or transmits over 300,000 Visa transactions annually	• Annual on-site assessment by qualified security assessor • Quarterly network scan by ASV • Attestation of compliance form
Level 2	Any service provider that stores, processes, or transmits less than 300,000 Visa transactions annually	• Annual self-assessment questionnaire (SAQ) • Quarterly network scan by ASV • Attestation of compliance form

4.2.2.1 Visa Merchant and Service Provider Validation Levels

Table 4.1 contains the merchant levels for Visa's compliance. The validation for each merchant level is dictated by the transaction volume. Similarly, service providers storing, processing, or transmitting cardholder information also have multiple validation levels for their compliance with Visa. They are listed in Table 4.2.

4.2.2.2 MasterCard Merchant and Service Provider Validation Levels

The MasterCard merchant and service provider compliance validation levels are listed in Tables 4.3 and 4.4, respectively.

MasterCard considers third-party processors in the payment card industry as Level 1 service providers. They are also referred to as TPPs. The other class of service providers

TABLE 4.3

MasterCard Merchant Compliance Validation Levels

Level	Criteria	Validation Requirements
Level 1	• Any merchant that has suffered a hack or an attack that resulted in an account data compromise • Any merchant having more than 6 million total combined MasterCard and Maestro transactions annually • Any merchant meeting the Level 1 criteria of Visa • Any merchant that MasterCard, in its sole discretion, determines should meet the Level 1 merchant requirements to minimize risk to the system	• Annual on-site assessment by qualified security assessor[a] • Quarterly network scan by ASV
Level 2	• Any merchant with more than 1 million but less than or equal to 6 million total combined MasterCard and Maestro transactions annually • Any merchant meeting the Level 2 criteria of Visa	• Annual self-assessment[b] • On-site assessment at merchant discretion • Quarterly network scan conducted by an ASV
Level 3	• Any merchant with more than 20,000 combined MasterCard and Maestro e-commerce transactions annually but less than or equal to 1 million total combined MasterCard and Maestro e-commerce transactions annually • Any merchant meeting the Level 3 criteria of Visa	• Annual self-assessment • Quarterly network scan conducted by an ASV
Level 4	• All other merchants	• Annual self-assessment[c] • Quarterly network scan conducted by an ASV

[a] Level 1 merchants for MasterCard may choose to be audited/assessed by an internal auditor. However, that internal auditor must have taken the PCI-DSS ISA (internal security auditor) training and be certified as an ISA.

[b] Level 2 merchants, when opting to complete a self-assessment questionnaire, must have a PCI-DSS ISA (internal security auditor) perform the audit and complete the self-assessment questionnaire. The organization may also choose to engage with a PCI-QSA for an external assessment.

[c] Level 4 merchants must consult with their acquirers as to whether compliance validation is required or not.

TABLE 4.4

MasterCard Service Provider Compliance Validation Levels

Level	Criteria	Validation Requirements
Level 1	• All third-party processors • All DSEs with a combined total of more than 300,000 MasterCard and Maestro transactions annually	• Annual on-site assessment by QSA • Quarterly external vulnerability assessment by ASV
Level 2	• All DSEs with 300,000 or less MasterCard and Maestro transactions annually	• Annual self-assessment • Quarterly external vulnerability assessment by ASV

as defined by MasterCard is called a data-storage entity (DSE). The compliance validation levels for these entities are defined by the transaction volume of MasterCard card records that are stored, processed, or transmitted.

4.2.2.3 *American Express Merchant and Service Provider Compliance Validation Levels*

The American Express merchant and service provider compliance validation levels are listed in Tables 4.5 and 4.6, respectively.

4.2.2.4 *Compliance Validation Levels: Identification and Implementation*

The compliance validation levels for each of the payment brands also change based on the region in which they are operating. For instance, there may be some minor changes to the compliance validation between Visa Asia Pacific and Visa CEMEA (Central Europe Middle East and Africa).

The transaction volumes that have been provided in the tables are determined by the acquirer that the merchant or the service provider reports to. In the case of a franchise model, the transaction volume is determined by the model of "Doing Business As" (DBA) or a chain of stores. This does not mean that it applies to the corporation owning several chains. For instance, if a corporate entity has several franchise locations that are not owned by the corporation, then for the purposes of identifying transaction volumes, the following will have to be considered:

- The number of payment cards processed by the entity in corporation-owned locations.
- The number of transactions handled by the corporation on behalf of the franchise owners, if any.
- If the payment-card processing is routed through the corporation's infrastructure, then the number of cards processed is determined to establish the compliance validation level of said corporation.

TABLE 4.5

American Express Merchant Compliance Validation Levels

Level	Criteria	Validation Requirements
Level 1	2.5 million American Express Card transactions or more per year, or any merchant that American Express otherwise deems a Level 1 merchant	• Annual on-site assessment by QSA (mandatory) • Quarterly network scan by ASV (mandatory)
Level 2	50,000 to 2.5 million American Express Card transactions per year	• Annual self-assessment questionnaire (mandatory) • Quarterly network scan by ASV (mandatory)
Level 3	Less than 50,000 American Express Card transactions per year	• Annual self-assessment questionnaire (highly recommended) • Quarterly network scan by ASV (recommended)

TABLE 4.6

American Express Service Provider Compliance Validation Levels

Level	Criteria	Validation Requirements
Level 1	Service providers storing, processing, or transmitting 2.5 million American Express Card transactions or more per year, or any merchant that American Express otherwise deems a Level 1 merchant	• Annual on-site assessment by QSA (mandatory) • Quarterly network scan by ASV (mandatory)
Level 2	Service providers storing, processing, or transmitting 50,000 to 2.5 million American Express Card transactions per year	• Annual self-assessment questionnaire (mandatory) • Quarterly network scan by ASV (mandatory)
Level 3	Service providers storing, processing, or transmitting less than 50,000 American Express Card transactions per year	• Annual self-assessment questionnaire (highly recommended) • Quarterly network scan by ASV (recommended)

4.3 PCI-DSS: APPLICABILITY

4.3.1 Applicability of PCI Compliance and Interplay with Compliance Validation Requirements

After learning about the various levels of PCI compliance, one might be inclined to ask the following question: "Does that mean that merchants/service providers below Level 1 that are required to only go through self-assessment or that have to consult with their acquirer have to comply with only some parts of PCI-DSS?" The answer to that question is a simple "No."

Merchants and service providers have to get compliant with PCI-DSS. This means that they have to adhere to all the PCI-DSS requirements that apply to them. Failure to adhere to even one of the applicable requirements without a suitable compensatory control will result in them being noncompliant with PCI-DSS. The PCI-DSS is not a self-directed standard like the ISO-27001, where an organization can choose the controls it wants to adopt.

However, it also does not mean that organizations have to mandatorily comply with every single one of the 12 broad requirements of the PCI-DSS. Organizations must simply adhere to requirements that apply to them. For instance, if a service provider is not storing cardholder data at all, and merely transmitting the information over an encrypted channel, then the requirements relating to "Protection of Stored Cardholder Information" will not apply to that service provider.

Another example would be in the case of an application (app) development organization that was developing an e-commerce application for its client that is undergoing PCI compliance. In this case, the app development organization would have to attain PCI compliance because its principal organization is obtaining compliance, and a key aspect of its card-management operations (in the form of the customized e-commerce application) will be deployed in the principal's environment. However, let us assume, that the app development organization only does the development of the application, does not come in contact with live card numbers, and only uses test card numbers to test the card-processing aspect of its e-commerce application. In this case, several requirements relating to protection of stored cardholder information and to protection of cardholder information in transit will not apply to the application development organization.

The next question relates to compliance validation. Compliance validation does not mean that merchants and service providers below Level 1 have to comply with a diluted version of the PCI-DSS. It just means that they can choose to fill out a self-assessment questionnaire (SAQ), which is very similar to the report on compliance (RoC) that is filled out by the PCI-qualified security assessor (QSA). The only difference would be that this form is filled out by the representatives of the organization, who have internally assessed the organization for compliance and have found the organization to be compliant with the applicable requirements of the PCI-DSS.

4.3.2 Merchant Organizations

Merchants are an important target group of the PCI-DSS. Merchants traditionally have the highest instance of the storing, processing, or transmitting of cardholder information the world over. Merchants may be both traditional brick-and-mortar merchants with card-management operations in physical establishments, or they may be online merchants where they accept payment cards in exchange for goods and services. In many cases, merchants have both physical "card present" operations and online "card not present" operations.

However, there are some merchant organizations where some requirements of PCI will not necessarily apply because their access to cardholder information is either limited or nonexistent. For instance, let us take a physical merchant establishment that accepts payment cards in its store. The merchant uses a bank (service provider)-provided card-processing machine. The cards are swiped on these machines, and the card number or any additional detail relating to the card is not stored anywhere in the environment. In fact, the card number is also masked in the customer's charge slip that is provided to the merchant. In such cases, this merchant may not even be required to become PCI-compliant because there is no storage, processing, or transmission. The merchant is not storing any cardholder information. The merchant is not processing it either; the machine provided by the merchant's service provider is processing the transaction and is out of the merchant's scope. The merchant is transmitting the card information only via the machine provided by the service provider, which is, again, out of scope. Therefore, the merchant may effectively be removed from PCI compliance.

In a similar instance for an online commerce merchant, the merchant redirects the user to a payment gateway, where all the card details are entered and the transaction is processed subsequently, with only an authorization code appearing in the database of the online commerce site. The site does not store, process, or transmit cardholder data, thereby technically negating the need for PCI compliance.

PCI compliance for merchants is mostly driven by the acquiring banks. Acquirers are required by the payment brands to get their ecosystem compliant and certified with the PCI requirements to prevent card fraud and other card breaches. Merchants below a certain level, for instance, Level 4 merchants, may be required to first consult with their acquiring bank about whether they need to achieve PCI compliance in the first place.

4.3.3 Service Providers: Processors

Payment processors have to be compliant with PCI-DSS. Processors have higher instances of storage, processing, and transmission of cardholder information than most other entities. Payment processors may be acquiring processors or issuing processors or both. In the case of acquiring processors, they acquire the transactions from the merchants (and on behalf of the banks). Subsequently, they route the transactions to the right payment brand and finalize the transaction on the return from the payment brand with either an approval or decline of the transaction. In such cases, cardholder information is only processed and transmitted by the processor. However, if the processer issues cards as well, then the processor is responsible for the generation of cards for several banks. Generation includes handling the form, embossing the card, PIN mailers, etc. In such cases, processors store a great deal of information relating to the card and cardholder.

4.3.4 Service Providers: Everybody Else

The other class of service providers in the eyes of the PCI-DSS are those service providers that provide support functions to merchants, banks, and processor service providers. These may include companies that develop customized payment applications, call centers, and business process outsourcing centers (BPOs), among others. PCI-DSS for these companies is largely driven by their clients and principals that happen to be merchants, banks, or other service providers undergoing PCI compliance. For instance, if a bank has outsourced the collection for its credit cards to a BPO in India, then the bank will have to ensure that its service provider, which is handling the bank's card data, is compliant with the requirements of the PCI-DSS. In fact, Requirement 12.8.4 of the PCI-DSS requires that organizations track and monitor the status of their service providers' PCI compliance at least annually.

4.3.5 Cloud Service Providers

At the time of this writing, PCI-SSC released a new information supplement for cloud computing through its Special Interest Group on Cloud Computing. Cloud computing is a form of distributed computing that has gained in acceptance and popularity. Organizations deploy their services on the cloud to realize cost, efficiency, and management gains. However, there are various aspects of security that have to be thought out in depth, especially from a security standpoint. Security over cloud services is usually shared between the cloud service provider and its clients. There are different types of cloud deployments, they are:

Private cloud: As the name suggests, private cloud refers to cloud infrastructure that is provided for a single client. This cloud infrastructure is managed either by the organization or the cloud service provider. The infrastructure may be either on the premises of the client or in the service provider's location. For instance, a major telecom company has a private cloud that has been set up by a leading IT services company. The private cloud is dedicated only to the telecom company and has been hosted by the IT services company in their data center.

Community cloud: Community cloud refers to infrastructure shared by several organizations that share requirements or business-model considerations. It is managed by a cloud service provider and may be on or off the premises.

Public cloud: This refers to cloud infrastructure that is available to the general public or to a specific industry. It is owned and managed by a cloud service provider.

Hybrid cloud: Hybrid cloud is an amalgamation or two or more cloud services (private, public, or community). Hybrid clouds are utilized for load balancing and capacity requirements. For instance, a public cloud of a major ticket-booking service provider might utilize the resources of its private cloud when there is a great demand for capacity on its public cloud.

There are three major cloud service models. They are as follows:

Software as a service (SaaS): This model is where the cloud service provider provides the software on the cloud for its customers to use. The customer has very little control over the application, infrastructure, and resources. The customer may be able to change some application configuration settings on the application.

Platform as a service (PaaS): This model is where the cloud service provider provides an application platform for its clients to develop and deploy applications. The client is responsible for developing and deploying the application on a platform. However, the client has no visibility into the hardware infrastructure, the operating systems, or the platform infrastructure resources that have gone into developing/deploying the platform for the client to use.

Infrastructure as a service (IaaS): Some cloud service providers provide infrastructure for the client to control and manage. For instance, the client is provided with servers or server infrastructure on which the client can deploy any operating system of choice, applications, and so on. Often clients also have the ability to define their firewall rules, security configurations, and so on.

The responsibility of PCI compliance differs on the cloud service model adopted by the client. In a SaaS scenario, the cloud service provider has the responsibility to achieve PCI compliance, as the client has little or no control over the application or the infrastructure. However, the client must achieve PCI compliance for other operations handling cardholder data like physical point-of-sale (POS) billing, and so on. I recently was consulting with a company that provided end-to-end merchant payment solutions. This company set up and managed e-commerce portals for small merchants and provided payment-gateway integration. In this case, the end-client (the merchant) has no control over the application or the cardholder data. This was similar to the SaaS model of cloud computing and, therefore, the onus was on the cloud service provider to achieve PCI compliance and certification.

Similarly, in a PaaS scenario, the responsibility and applicability is shared between the client and the cloud services provider (CSP). The CSP must achieve compliance with applicable requirements for the infrastructure, network, and operating-system security. However, the client must achieve compliance for the application security requirements, cardholder-data security requirements (Requirement 3 and 4), and so on.

4.4 PCI: ATTESTATION, ASSESSMENT, AND CERTIFICATION

4.4.1 The Role of a PCI-QSA

The PCI qualified security assessor is an assessor who is approved by the PCI Security Standards Council (PCI-SSC). The QSA is authorized to perform audits against the PCI-DSS requirements and certify an organization based on the PCI-DSS Requirements. The PCI-QSA is required to be a security professional who is a qualified certified information systems auditor (CISA) or a certified information systems security professional (CISSP) or who possesses relevant experience of 5 years or more.

Annual on-site evaluation by a QSA is a mandatory requirement for Level 1 merchants and service providers. However, merchants and service providers below the mandatory Level 1 status may decide to use the services of a QSA for an on-site PCI assessment and certification.

The PCI-QSA completes the PCI-DSS assessment and identifies whether the entity has met all of the requirements for PCI-DSS

certification. Subsequently, the PCI-QSA prepares the report on compliance (RoC) based on the documentation requirements of the PCI-DSS and submits the same to the company along with the PCI certification. The QSA also needs to complete the attestation of compliance (AoC) and affix his/her signature on the document, along with the requisite details required to complete the document.

4.4.2 The PCI-DSS Requirements

Although we will deal with the PCI-DSS requirements extensively in the chapters to come, let us have a brief view of the 12 requirements of the PCI-DSS and support them with basic explanations. They are:

Requirement 1: Install and maintain firewall configuration to protect cardholder data. This requirement delves into specific details through multiple requirements into the network security requirements that have to be met by an entity undergoing or maintaining PCI compliance. The requirement details several specific sections relating to firewalls, network segmentation, intrusion prevention systems, and other network security controls that have to be adopted by the entity.

Requirement 2: Do not use vendor-supplied defaults for system passwords and other parameters. This requirement specifically prohibits the use of vendor-supplied default password credentials in the PCI environment. This requirement provides specific guidance on change default settings for network devices, wireless access points, and other system components that are in scope for the compliance.

Requirement 3: Protect stored cardholder data. This is a key requirement that exclusively discusses the protection of cardholder data at rest. There are some requirements relating to data classification and need for storage. Additionally, the requirement details multiple options for protecting stored cardholder information at rest. The requirement also explores in detail the key management requirements for entities that encrypt stored cardholder data.

Requirement 4: Encrypt transmission of cardholder data across open, public networks. While Requirement 3 details the protection of cardholder data at rest, Requirement 4 delves into encryption of cardholder data across open public networks. The requirement details the use of encryption for securing Wi-Fi deployments in PCI environments.

Requirement 5: Use and regularly update antivirus software or programs. This requirement exclusively deals with antivirus management for the PCI environment of an organization.

Requirement 6: Develop and maintain secure systems and applications. This requirement encompasses secure systems from the point of view of patching and patch management and development of secure software that is used in the PCI environment. The requirement details development security practices, including systems development life cycle (SDLC), segregation of testing environment, etc. This requirement also delves into application security practices.

Requirement 7: Restrict cardholder information by business need to know. This requirement deals mostly with access controls. The requirement describes best practices for access control, including authentication and authorization best practices that are to be implemented in a PCI environment.

Requirement 8: Assign a unique ID to each person with computer access. This requirement completes the access control requirements of authentication, authorization, and accountability with specific requirements relating to accountability, password controls, and two-factor authentication requirements under certain conditions.

Requirement 9: Restrict physical access to cardholder data. This requirement deals almost exclusively with physical security controls and media-management controls. The requirement explores physical security practices, including physical access control, video monitoring of the cardholder-data environment, and visitor management. Additionally, the requirement also details security practices for media management of tapes, data storage, data destruction, and so on.

Requirement 10: Track and monitor all access to network resources and cardholder data. This requirement deals with logging, log management, and monitoring controls deployed across the cardholder environment. The requirement discusses the need for audit trails of access to cardholder information. The requirement also details security practices relating to monitoring for administrative access and other user access to cardholder information. The requirement goes on to specify the details that are to be captured as part of the audit trail.

Requirement 11: Regularly test security systems and processes. This requirement calls for security testing to be performed in the PCI environment. The requirement details the need for the wireless access point testing to discover rogue access points within the environment. The requirement also details the need to have an external vulnerability assessment every quarter by an approved scanning vendor (ASV). Additionally, the requirement dictates the performance of internal vulnerability assessment and penetration testing as well as the use of intrusion prevention systems and file integrity monitoring solutions for sensitive system files.

Requirement 12: Maintain a policy that addresses information security for all personnel. This requirement deals with documentation and risk-management controls. The requirement deals with the need to maintain a risk-management framework in the organization for its PCI environment. Additionally, the requirement discusses some policies, procedures, and practices that are to be implemented by the organization to meet with PCI compliance.

4.4.3 Compensatory Controls

The PCI-DSS is a technically rigorous and prescriptive standard. On occasion, organizations find it difficult to implement certain controls of the standard because of a technical constraint or a business constraint.

In such cases, organizations may choose to adopt a different set of controls than the ones prescribed by the standard. While these controls are not exactly the controls required by the standard, they are able to sufficiently mitigate the risk in the form of compensatory controls.

Compensating controls must mandatorily meet the following criteria:

- Meet the intent and rigor of the original PCI requirement
- Provide a similar level of security as the original PCI requirement
- Be above and beyond the existing PCI requirement

Existing PCI-DSS requirements cannot be considered as compensating controls. For instance, if the organization is not able to "render the PAN [primary account number] unreadable" (Requirement 3.4) with encryption, one-way hashing, or tokenization, then the organization cannot cite "access control" with username and password as a compensating control, as the control is already required by the PCI-DSS.

4.4.4 Documentation: The Report on Compliance

The report on compliance (popularly known as the RoC, pronounced "rock") is the most important document in a PCI-compliance process. The RoC is a document containing all 12 requirements of the PCI-DSS along with an executive summary containing the organization's key information relating to business areas, network topology, etc. The RoC is the document validating the PCI-compliance effort of an organization. It is documented by the PCI-QSA when he/she validates the organization against each control in the PCI-DSS that is applicable to the organization. If the organization is found to be noncompliant with even one of the requirements, without a valid compensating control, then the organization is not PCI-DSS-compliant. The PCI-QSA documents the observations, interviews, and tests conducted to validate a requirement in the RoC, and then stipulates whether the requirement has been met based on the intent and rigor required by the PCI-DSS requirement.

4.4.5 Documentation: The Attestation of Compliance

The attestation of compliance (AoC) is a document that has to be filled out by the QSA upon completion of the PCI-DSS assessment for the purposes of certification. The AoC is meant as a declaration of compliance of a merchant or service provider entity against the requirements of the PCI-DSS. The AoC form captures some details about the company and its industry of operation. The AoC form also contains details requiring the organization to declare that it is compliant with all the requirements of the PCI-DSS.

4.5 SUMMARY

In this chapter, our prime focus was on PCI-DSS. We began with a brief history of the PCI-DSS. We then focused our attention on understanding compliance validation levels. We identified that the compliance validation levels for merchants and service providers were dictated based on the transaction volume of a particular entity. We then specified transaction volumes and compliance validation levels for different payment brands. Subsequently, we learned about PCI-DSS applicability and how multiple entities like merchants, service providers, and so on, come under the purview of the PCI-DSS requirements. We ended the chapter with a brief description of some of the documentation requirements of the PCI-DSS, including the report on compliance (RoC), the attestation of compliance (AoC), and the role of the PCI-QSA in the compliance process.

5

The Payment Application Data Security Standard (PA-DSS)

Applications form the backbone of the payment-processing cycle. Applications are essential for entities that store, process, or transmit cardholder information because they facilitate the routing, encryption, storage, and transmission channels and also functionally allow an entity to manage card operations. There are several readily available off-the-shelf applications that are procured by entities and that are an integral section of the entity's payment-processing life cycle. It is critical for such applications to facilitate and support the entity's PCI (payment-card industry) compliance process. In this chapter, we will delve into a standard popularly known as the PA-DSS (Payment Application Data Security Standard). This is a subset of the PCI-DSS (Payment-Card Industry Data Security Standard) and applies specifically to commercially available off-the-shelf applications that are part of the payment-processing life cycle.

5.1 HISTORY AND OVERVIEW OF THE PA-DSS

5.1.1 The Need for Payment Application Validation for PCI

The payment-card industry relies heavily on applications in the payment-processing cycle. There are a multitude of relevant applications, including point-of-sale (POS), e-commerce, card-fraud-management, payment-switching, card-processing middleware, etc., to name a few. These applications are deployed by entities that traditionally store, process, or transmit cardholder information. Several of these applications are commercial in nature, i.e., they are readily available off-the-shelf applications that may be procured by an entity with little or no customization and deployed in the environment to manage the payment life cycle. An organization's PCI compliance hinges heavily on these applications because they are closest to cardholder information, and attackers specifically target these applications or related infrastructure to compromise and breach cardholder information. In fact, quoting a research report from Verizon's 2009 Business Data Breach Report, 85 percent of data that was breached is cardholder information, and 32 percent of breaches were targeted against POS systems, 30 percent against databases, and 30 percent against application servers. The trend is clear. Attackers look to compromise cardholder data through applications that are used to store, process, or transmit said information.

In light of this fact, it is essential that commercial or customized (either internally developed or outsourced) applications need to be under the scope of an entity's PCI-compliance program. For instance, if a merchant establishment is undergoing PCI compliance, then the POS application and related infrastructure would most definitely be in scope for compliance. If that application did not support PCI compliance, for instance, or if the application did not support the PCI requirement for strong encryption to be used to protect cardholder information or did not provide functionality to enforce the quality of certain passwords, then the application would not allow the entity to achieve PCI compliance. Earlier, in fact, a massive roadblock to PCI compliance was the applications that had not implemented security features per the requirements of PCI, thereby preventing the entity from achieving PCI compliance.

This divide between the payment applications and the PCI standards was the reason for the creation of the PA-DSS. The PA-DSS was adopted from Visa's Payment Application Best Practices (PABP), which was Visa's validation program for commercially available off-the-shelf applications

that were part of the payment-processing cycle. The PA-DSS is a subset of the PCI-DSS with 13 requirements that payment applications must comply with and then have them validated by a payment application qualified security assessor (PA-QSA).

The PA-DSS does not apply to the following types of applications:

- Applications that are developed in house (by the entity) or outsourced to an application developer (considered as in-house developed as it is customized), as these applications would be covered under the organization's PCI-compliance process.
- Applications that are available as a service online for customers, without being sold or licensed to customers. Typically, these are e-commerce or SaaS (software as a service) applications. These would be covered under the application developer's PCI-compliance program, merchant's PCI-compliance program, etc.
- Applications that are not actively part of the payment-processing cycle, such as operating systems, databases, or back-office systems that purely store/report cardholder information and are not part of the payment cycle.

The PA-DSS does apply to the following types of applications:

- Commercially available off-the-shelf applications with little customization that are part of the payment-processing life cycle.
- Applications that are developed as modules, where the module of the application is part of the payment-processing life cycle.

The PCI-SSC (Payment-Card Industry Security Standards Council) manages and maintains the PA-DSS. The PCI-SSC also publishes a list of validated payment applications that have been assessed, validated, and found to be in compliance with the requirements of the PA-DSS. These applications include POS applications, payment middleware, e-commerce applications (commercial), payment gateway applications (commercial), fraud-monitoring and -management applications (commercial), and payment switches.

5.1.2 A Brief History of the PA-DSS

Visa was the first payment brand to take cognizance of the growing divide between the PCI and payment applications. Therefore, in 2005, Visa developed the Payment Application Best Practices (PABP). The PABP was a set of 14 requirements that focused on the application-security best practices that need to be implemented, documented, and validated by developers of payment applications to ensure that their applications could be used in a PCI environment and as part of the payment-processing cycle. Visa would have qualified security assessors (QSAs) validate these applications and submit a report on validation to Visa, and Visa would subsequently list the validation applications on its website.

In 2008, the PABP was adopted by the PCI-SSC. The PCI-SSC adopted the standard and provided the name PA-DSS for the standard's version 1.1. It accepted the PABP until 15 October 2008, after which all new payment application validations would be under the PA-DSS requirements. The PCI-SSC also instituted a program where it selected and appointed payment application qualified security assessors (QSAs) to validate applications against the PA-DSS requirements and document its assessment in the form of a report on validation (RoV). Upon scrutiny of the RoV and its acceptance by the PCI-SSC, the application is validated under the PA-DSS and is listed in the "List of Validated Payment Applications" on the PCI-SSC's website, pcisecuritystandards. org. The current version of the PA-DSS is version 2.0.

5.1.3 Primer on the PA-DSS Standard

We have already explored the PA-DSS requirements briefly. The PA-DSS is well known as a subset of the PCI-DSS. As it is meant to help companies become PCI-compliant, none of the requirements in the PA-DSS are in conflict with the PCI-DSS, and all are natural extensions of the PCI-DSS specifically relating to applications that are part of the payment-processing cycle. The PA-DSS requirements also link to specific PCI-DSS requirements to reiterate the parent-child relationship that the PCI-DSS has with the PA-DSS.

The PA-DSS consists of 13 requirements. These requirements specifically apply to commercially available off-the-shelf applications that are part of the payment-processing life cycle. The PA-DSS requirements only apply to the validation of the application and not of the company developing it. Therefore, if a company develops a PA-DSS–validated application, it does not mean that the company is PCI-DSS-compliant. It simply means that an application/application component that it has developed has been tested and validated against the requirements of the PA-DSS.

Similarly, if an entity deploys a PA-DSS–validated application in its PCI environment, it does not mean that the entity has automatically achieved PCI compliance. While the entity might have met some of the requirements of PCI relating to applications and protection of cardholder information, several other requirements of the PCI-DSS that are applicable to the entity have to be met with the same intent and rigor that is demanded by the standard.

5.1.3.1 The PA-DSS Requirements

The PA-DSS has 13 requirements that have to be met by the payment applications undergoing validation for PA-DSS. Unlike the PCI-DSS, there is no concept of compensating controls for the PA-DSS. All applicable controls have to be met with the intent and rigor that has been required by the standard. The 13 requirements are as follows:

1. Do not retain full magnetic stripe, card verification code or value (CAV2, CID, CVC2, CVV2), or PIN block data
2. Protect stored cardholder data
3. Provide secure authentication features
4. Log payment application activity
5. Develop secure payment applications
6. Protect wireless transmissions
7. Test payment applications to address vulnerabilities
8. Facilitate secure network implementation
9. Never store cardholder data on a server connected to the Internet
10. Facilitate secure remote access to payment application
11. Encrypt sensitive traffic over public networks
12. Encrypt all nonconsole administrative access
13. Maintain instructional documentation and training programs for customers, resellers, and integrators

We will be exploring each of these requirements in great depth in Chapters 8–20 of this book.

5.2 PA-DSS VALIDATION

5.2.1 The PA-DSS Validation Process

The PA-DSS validation is a distinct and unique process. Firstly, the application development company must identify a PA-QSA to validate the application against the PA-DSS requirements. The PA-QSA first assesses the application against the requirements of the PA-DSS. There is also a requirement for the PA-QSA to test the application in a laboratory environment belonging to the QSA or to the application development company or other. The testing lab environment details also have to be documented for the purposes of the report on validation (RoV).

Subsequently, the application development company must develop an implementation guide for the application as required by the PA-DSS. The PA-DSS implementation guide is a comprehensive guide to the application's security functionality and features, and it derives its documentation requirements from the PA-DSS standard.

Once the PA-QSA has completed the validation of the application and has found the application to have met all the applicable requirements of the PA-DSS, the QSA prepares a report on validation (RoV). The RoV has to meet the documentation requirements and criteria laid down by the PCI-SSC. After the QSA submits the RoV to the PCI-SSC, it is scrutinized in conjunction with the implementation guide prepared by the application development company in great detail. When the SSC is satisfied with the report and with the evidence presented as part of the assessment, the RoV is accepted, and the application is subsequently included in the list of validated payment applications on the PCI-SSC's website.

5.2.2 The Differences in PCI-DSS and PA-DSS Validation

There are some differences between the PCI-DSS compliance and certification and PA-DSS validation. The first difference is the use of the word *validation* instead of the word *certification*. The PCI-DSS compliance and certification is given to a particular entity that has achieved PCI-DSS compliance for a specific scoped environment. However, an application is *validated* against the PA-DSS requirements and listed as a validated application. To many people, the view of validation in this context probably encompasses certification, but the terminology of the PCI-SSC is that of *validation*.

There is no concept of "compensating controls" in the case of PA-DSS validation. Unlike PCI-DSS, where compensating controls can be applied for certain requirements, PA-DSS requires the application to meet all the applicable requirements to avoid diluting the PCI-compliance process of a user organization (of the validated application) in the future.

5.2.3 Technical Testing and Validation for the PA-DSS

The PA-DSS requires a laboratory environment for testing the payment application. The testing lab is an essential aspect of the PA-DSS requirements, as the requirements have several specific requirements relating to testing the application in a lab environment.

The lab environment may be at the location of the PA-QSA or at the location of the software vendor (application developer). The requirement states that the application has to be tested in a real-world simulated environment. In the event that the PA-QSA is reviewing the application in the lab environment of the software vendor, the PA-QSA has to ensure that a clean install of the application is performed and, subsequently, that a real-world simulation of the application's use is provided for the test by the PA-QSA. This is to prevent tampering of the environment by the software vendor and creating a more biased environment toward validation.

In addition, the PA-QSA has to ensure that all of the requirements of the PA-DSS with reference to secure application deployment are met by the testing laboratory set up by the software vendor. The PA-QSA has to perform a security test of the application using industry-standard penetration-testing methodologies like the OWASP, SANS CWE, CERT Secure Coding, etc. Additionally, the PA-QSA might have to use forensic tools and techniques to identify potentially sensitive authentication data from the card data (like track data, CVV [card verification value]) that may be stored by the application. The testing process for PA-DSS also has to be exhaustive. The PA-QSA must ensure that all versions being covered as part of the PA-DSS validation scope are be reviewed. Additionally, the PA-QSA must ensure that all of the platforms listed in the PA-DSS application scope for validation are included in the testing process. This ensures that the application's security functionality, implementation, and deployment do not revert to a nonsecure state for some platforms.

5.2.4 The Role of a PA-QSA

The role of the PA-QSA is very similar to that of the PCI-QSA. The PA-QSA is an individual who is employed by a PA-QSAC (payment application qualified security assessor company). The company has its selected employees trained to become PA-QSAs, who need to undergo PA-QSA training provided by the PCI-SSC and pass the examination that has been set forth by the SSC.

The PA-QSA is authorized by the SSC to validate, assess, and prepare the RoV for an application that needs to be validated against the requirements of the PA-DSS. The PA-QSA's primary responsibility is to assess and validate the application against the 13 requirements of the PA-DSS. The PA-QSA must also go over the implementation guide prepared by the application vendor organization to ensure that all relevant points and details required by the PA-DSS are covered.

The application provided by the application vendor needs to be signed off with a vendor release agreement. The PA-QSA and her team must also test the application in a lab environment. This lab (as discussed previously) may either be at the PA-QSA's location or at the application vendor's location. The QSA must also ensure that all of the requirements governing the integrity of the lab environment are maintained as prescribed by the standard.

Finally, the PA-QSA must complete the RoV after validating the application successfully against all of the PA-DSS requirements and verifying that there are no requirements that the application has not fulfilled. The PA-QSA's internal QA (qualified assessor) team must first review the RoV to determine whether it meets the quality standards prescribed by the PCI-SSC.

The PA-QSA must then hand over the RoV, along with applicable documentation, to the PCI-SSC, which then conducts a stringent review. The SSC might subject the QSA to some inquiries about the application and its compliance with the requirements of the PA-DSS. If the SSC finds that the application meets the requirements of the standard through an acceptable documentation review process, the SSC initiates the process for the application to be added to the list of validated payment applications. The SSC first countersigns on the attestation of validation (AoV) and returns a copy to the application vendor organization. The vendor organization would also have to pay a fee to the SSC to have its application accepted. Subsequently, the list of validated payment applications is updated and the review process is complete.

5.3 PA-DSS DOCUMENTATION

5.3.1 The PA-DSS Report on Validation

The PA-DSS RoV is the most important report in the context of a PA-DSS validation. The RoV is prepared by a PA-QSA upon completion of the review of the application that is within the scope for the PA-DSS validation. The RoV is a document that first describes the payment application as well as details relating to the company that has developed it, the target market, previous versions, hardware details, etc. Subsequently, the RoV contains all 13 requirements of the PA-DSS, and the PA-QSA has to mark whether or not the application is compliant against each requirement. The QSA also has to document specific testing procedures, points of review, or observations that were used to validate the application against the requirement. This validation has to be aligned with the documentation requirements of the PA-DSS as prescribed by the PCI-SSC. This ensures consistency and quality for the report presented to the SSC.

The report captures key details of the application, including:

- Payment application name, version: e.g., Ajax POS version 6.3
- Payment application type: e.g., POS suite
- Target market, e.g.: retail, gas/oil, e-commerce, etc.

The RoV requires an executive summary that captures the following details (not limited to):

- Brief description of the payment application
- Resellers of the payment application
- Operating systems and hardware that the application can be used with
- Databases that the application utilizes
- Flow of payment-card-related information into and out of the application
- All software and hardware dependencies

In addition to the above, the QSA must also describe in detail the audit approach that she used to test and validate the application against the PA-DSS requirements.

5.3.2 The PA-DSS Implementation Guide

The PA-DSS implementation guide is one of the many documents that have to be created by the application vendor organization when the application is being validated

against the PA-DSS requirement. The implementation guide serves as a reference to customers, resellers, integrators, and implementers of the application to educate them about the security functionality of the application and the security functionality that has to be maintained over the application's infrastructure. For instance, the implementation guide must document the need for two-factor authentication if a vendor can log in remotely to the application. The PA-DSS implementation guide must also detail specific implementation techniques to set up and configure the application to be secure "out of the box" when it is being deployed in the PCI environment or any environment that handles payment-card data. In addition to the implementation guide, the application vendor organization must prepare adequate documentation for customers, partners, resellers, integrators, and implementers of the application.

The implementation guide must be prepared and submitted to the QSA during the time of validation, along with the other documents. The PA-QSA will also submit the RoV and the implementation guide (with other documents if necessary) to the PCI-SSC to review the adequacy of the implementation guide and review the application's validation against the PA-DSS.

5.3.3 The PA-DSS Attestation of Validation

The attestation of validation (AoV) is very similar to the attestation of compliance (AoC) in the case of PCI-DSS. In this case, the PA-QSA fills out the AoV as a declaration that the target application has been successfully validated against the requirements of the PA-DSS standard. The PA-QSA has to fill out several details relating to the application, target market, description, and compliance with the PA-DSS, among other details. This application has to be signed by the PA-QSA and submitted to the PCI-SSC. Once the SSC has satisfactorily reviewed the RoV and other documents relating to the application provided by the QSA, the SSC signs off on the AoV and sends a copy to the application vendor.

5.3.4 The PA-DSS Vendor Release Agreement

The PA-DSS vendor release agreement is signed by the application vendor and the PA-QSA. This is done before commencement of the PA-DSS review process by the PA-QSA. The vendor release agreement is accompanied by a nondisclosure agreement signed by the PCI-SSC and the application vendor organization. The agreement discusses the need for maintaining confidentiality for the materials that are provided by the vendors to the QSA. The agreement also details the requirements of the application and related materials needed by the PA-QSA for testing and validation.

The agreement also explores the aspect of vulnerability/breach disclosure. This addresses the possibility of a vulnerability being discovered in the application or a breach occurring against the vendor payment application, as it may have a bearing on the validation state of the application, especially in the case of breach of data.

The agreement also details the need for a QSA to maintain confidentiality of vendor-provided information, even in communications with the PCI-SSC. The agreement stresses the need for reasonable encryption practices when the PA-QSA is transmitting data to the PCI-SSC for review, validation, etc.

5.4 PA-DSS APPLICATION REVALIDATION

5.4.1 Annual Revalidation

Payment applications that have been validated against the PA-DSS and are in the list of validated payment applications need to be revalidated annually. The application vendor must submit an AoV to perform the revalidation process annually.

The annual submission of the AoV is just a declaration by the application vendor to affirm that there have been no significant updates to the validated payment application. In addition, the process also prompts a new validation process in the event of a significant change. PCI-SSC defines the nature of changes based on their impact and severity. Depending on the nature of the changes, the application may or may not need to be revalidated.

5.4.2 Changes to Payment Applications

Payment applications naturally undergo change over time. The application vendor might make some changes to the application in terms of user interface or through the addition or removal of components and modules. However, not all changes impact the validation of the application against the requirements of the PA-DSS. The PCI-SSC measures changes to the applications in the following ways:

- No-impact change
- Low-impact change
- High-impact change

5.4.2.1 No-Impact Change

No-impact changes are minor changes that have no impact on the PA-DSS requirements. They may be administrative- or software-related changes. These include minor updates like changes to design or to modules that have no bearing on the payment-processing function of the application.

5.4.2.2 Low-Impact Change

A low-impact change constitutes a minor change to the application that has a limited (low) impact on the application's payment-processing capability. The application's vendor organization submits a new version of the application with detailed documentation of changes. This is subject to a partial review.

5.4.2.3 High-Impact Change

As the term would suggest, a high-impact change is one where the application undergoes a major change that significantly impacts the PA-DSS requirements. For instance, changes to the payment-processing function of the application or changes to the way the application renders the PAN (primary account number) unreadable during storage would fit the definition of a high-impact change. The application vendor must submit details of such changes. The PA-QSA might require a partial reassessment or might go in for a full reassessment based on the PA-QSA's discretion.

5.4.3 Change-Impact Documentation

In the event of a change in an already-validated payment application, the application vendor must submit a change document to the PA-QSA that contains some details

relating to the change. Some of those details are:

- Name of the payment application
- Version of the payment application
- Description of changes
- Indication of the severity of the change: high, low, or no impact
- Reason the change was made
- Impact on cardholder information
- Impact on effect of the PA-DSS validation requirements
- Practices/implementation strategies used to ensure that negative impact on PA-DSS requirements did not occur

5.4.3.1 No-Impact Change-Impact Documentation

We have already defined the meaning of a no-impact change. It is a minor change that does not affect the PA-DSS requirements in any way. The application vendor must document the change in the vendor-change document and furnish the details to the PA-QSA. The application changes may be of an administrative nature[*] or of a software nature.[†]

All of the requisite details relating to the change needs to captured in the vendor-change form. The vendor fills out the AoV along with the vendor-change form and then sends it across to the PA-QSA, who reviews the document and transmits the information to the PCI-SSC. Upon acceptance of the changes, the PCI-SSC issues

[*] Changes of an administrative nature occur when the application's ownership, management, or branding have undergone a change and the changes have to be taken into cognizance for the application's validation with PA-DSS. This occurs in the event of change of name, branding, etc.
[†] Software changes of a no-impact nature refer to changes in the application or its module with no bearing on the payment-processing aspect of the application.

an invoice for the change to the application vendor and makes the appropriate changes to the list of validated payment applications.

5.4.3.2 Low-Impact Change-Impact Documentation

A low-impact change is defined as one that has a minor bearing on the payment-processing function of the payment application. Examples of such changes are:

- Updates to some modules like reporting and administration
- Addition or deletion of supported payment processors
- Recompilation of code base with a different compiler

However, any change that impacts the following data sets is considered to be a high-impact change by the PCI-SSC. They are:

- Sensitive authentication data
- Remote access
- Default passwords
- Protection of cardholder data at rest and in transit
- Logging
- Wireless

The application vendor fills out the attestation of compliance (AoC) along with the vendor-change form with all the change details and then sends these to the PA-QSA. Once the PA-QSA agrees with the vendor-change form, the PA-QSA must notify the application vendor. The PA-QSA must perform an assessment of the changes based on the vendor-change form and document them as changes in the original RoV. The

new version of the RoV is sent along with the AoV as well as the vendor-change form to the PCI-SSC, where it is reviewed and, upon approval, is included in the list of validated payment applications with the changes. The PCI-SSC then invoices the application vendor for changes.

5.4.3.3 High-Impact Change-Impact Documentation

If a PA-QSA determines that the changes to an application are not low-impact changes, the PA-QSA must carry out a full PA-DSS assessment of the application. While the application vendor may first submit changes to the PA-QSA, the QSA decides the nature of the changes and performs the assessment as seen fit.

5.5 SUMMARY

This chapter was entirely focused on the PA-DSS. We began with a brief history of the PA-DSS. We explored how the PA-DSS was born from a need by entities undergoing PCI compliance to have their applications support the compliance process. The PA-DSS standard is meant for commercially available off-the-shelf applications that are part of the payment-processing cycle. We identified the 13 requirements of the PA-DSS. We also discussed the validation process of the PA-DSS and its differences from PCI-DSS. We closed the chapter with a description of the PA-DSS documentation requirements and the content and substance of these documents that are critical to the PA-DSS validation process.

6

Enterprise Approach to PCI Compliance

PCI (payment-card industry) compliance is a reality that organizations in the payment-card industry have to contend with. Enterprises have to adopt the compliance requirements, as they usually are essential for the enterprise to even operate in a certain business environment that involves storing, processing, or transmitting cardholder data. PCI compliance is a gigantic challenge for the unprepared. In this chapter we focus on how enterprises should handle PCI compliance. We will not focus on the technical aspects of the compliance, as that will be covered in subsequent chapters, but we will detail some good practices that enterprises can adopt to smoothen the compliance process and make it more efficient.

6.1 INDUSTRY VERTICALS AND PCI COMPLIANCE

6.1.1 PCI Approaches for Different Industry Verticals

We have learned that PCI compliance applies to entities that store, process, or transmit cardholder information. We have also detailed the types of entities that would be typically under the purview of the PCI compliance. While the PCI standard does not change in its requirements for different industry verticals, the approaches to PCI compliance for different industry verticals are markedly different. For instance, the PCI-compliance approach adopted by a merchant would be quite different from the approach adopted by a third-party processor or a bank. This is due to some of the factors described in the following subsections.

6.1.1.1 Basic Business Function

Business functions play an important role in the approach to enterprise PCI compliance. A merchant's key business function is to sell (and buy) goods and services to customers. While selling these goods and services, merchants need to accept cardholder information, as it is a key channel for revenue to the organization. Given their need to accept cardholder information as part of their business processes, merchants need to comply with PCI requirements in order to protect the cardholder information stored, processed, or transmitted by the entity. Contrast that with a third-party processor (TPP). A TPP's primary role is to process card payments. The TPP receives cardholder information from multiple merchants (source) and routes the transactions with cardholder information to the appropriate payment brand and the appropriate issuer bank (or issuing processor that the TPP might also be). The TPP's business requirement is to process and route cardholder information, providing settlement and other secondary services relating to card issuance (in the case of an issuing TPP), PIN mailers, and the like. We can see here that the merchants and TPPs have the need to store, process, or transmit cardholder information, but they are at different sides of the payment-processing cycle. This brings a change in their business functions, thereby changing their approach to PCI compliance in a significant way.

6.1.1.2 Cardholder Information Touch Points

We will explore this concept in greater depth as we move forward in this book, but the concept of cardholder information touch points is critical to determine the enterprise approach to PCI compliance. *Touch points* refer to the specific areas of the enterprise where cardholder information is either stored, processed, or transmitted. For instance, at a merchant enterprise, a key touch point for cardholder information (among several others) may be the point-of-sale (POS) billing system,

from which cardholder information is stored and/or transmitted to the acquirer. This system might consist of workstations (terminals), an application server, and a database. The touch points of cardholder information are all three of these systems, as cardholder information "touches" them at some point in time, even if ephemerally and/or in transit.

The number and the nature of the touch points change an enterprise approach to PCI compliance. Typically in the case of medium- to large-scale merchant organizations, the touch points of cardholder information are very high in number. While each of these systems may only have momentary access to cardholder information, the enterprise (and subsequently the PCI-QSA) will have to dedicate significant efforts to identify the effects of these touch points on the enterprise's PCI-compliance status and assess them for security. The larger the number of touch points, the greater the difficulty in identifying, implementing, and assessing the security measures for them.

On the other hand, the nature of the touch point is also a key determinant of the enterprise's approach to PCI compliance. For instance, in the case of an acquiring TPP, the key touch point of the organization would be the organization's payment switch that is used to process and route the transaction based on specific transaction parameters to different payment brand networks and different issuer banks/acquirers. The payment switch is a critical touch point in the case of the TPP. While the number of touch points across the enterprise may be lower as compared to a merchant organization, implementing security and assessing security for the touch point may be a challenge.

6.1.1.3 The Organization Itself

Sometimes, the greatest challenge for an organization to achieve PCI compliance is the organization itself. Let me explain with an example. Let us imagine a large multinational corporation with management distributed across the world and operations spread across multiple countries and verticals. Let us imagine that the PCI-compliance effort in said organization only amounts to a single operational unit within the organization. A password policy has been initiated across the organization such that passwords to the organization's systems would be a maximum length of six characters, with alphanumeric and special characters, and the policy has been implemented organization-wide, across all of its units, in all of its geographies. However, the PCI requirements mandate a minimum password length of seven alphanumeric characters. This sounds like a trivially simple example, where said company would amend the enterprise-wide password policy and implement a minimum seven-character password length requirement for the PCI-scoped environment. However, the personnel in charge of PCI compliance in the organization say that change in any enterprise-wide policy would take an unduly long time, requiring hours spent on meetings, discussions, and deliberations for this seemingly simple requirement, thereby delaying the entire PCI-compliance effort.

Believe me, such things happen. In such cases, the organization might decide to add a separate set of policies and procedures for the areas covered under the PCI scope and add an addendum to its enterprise-wide policies and procedures. This is typically an unconventional route to compliance, but a necessary one to achieve it. The enterprise's approach to PCI compliance might undergo a sea change because of the organization's structure, budgetary constraints, business operations, hierarchy, management style, etc.

6.1.2 Merchants

Merchants are one of the primary target organizations for PCI compliance, as they are organizations where cardholder information is typically handled in great volumes. Large merchants process millions of card payments across countries all over the world. In such cases, merchant PCI compliance is of utmost importance to protect customers' cardholder information against a data breach that could cause heavy losses to the payment-card industry at large.

PCI compliance for merchants is quite a challenge, simply because of the number of cardholder-data touch points that are present in a merchant environment. For instance, touch points would be the POS terminal at the billing counter for merchants, card payment kiosks, e-commerce servers, internal billing systems, financial reporting systems, workstations, and POS system log files. These are all viable and highly probable areas where cardholder data is not only transmitted or processed, but more dangerously persists in storage.

The most recommended approach to PCI compliance for any entity is to create the right scope. However, in the case of merchants, this has a greater bearing. The merchant organization must really spend a great deal of time before its PCI-compliance effort into drawing out the most appropriate scope. We will explain scoping in later sections, but the merchant organization needs to understand all the touch points of cardholder data as well as the applications and systems being used as touch points of said data, and then start identifying data owners or process owners who have taken responsibility for said data points. This can be done as part of an effective PCI risk-assessment activity. The process of scoping will broadly flow for a merchant organization as follows:

- Create a core PCI-compliance team that drives PCI compliance in the organization.
- Understand effectively all the cardholder-data touch points through the following methods:
  - Identify all the critical cardholder-data sets.
  - Identify systems and areas across the organization that store *or* process *or* transmit said information and identify the touch point.
  - Identify the nature of the touch point. Is it storage only? Is it a processing and storage system?
  - Examine in detail all the inputs and outputs to said systems that store/process/transmit cardholder information. Examine databases, log files, system traces, etc.
- Discuss the need to store/transmit information from said touch point with core team members, system owners, and management. In the effort to try and reduce touch points of cardholder information, the core PCI team at the merchant organization must question the need for each cardholder-data touch point. Over time, several touch points can form purely by drift rather than the result of a business strategy.

Merchants use a smorgasbord of applications that are part of their payment-processing system, including POS systems, e-commerce systems, fraud-management systems, kiosk software, and mobile applications, all forming an integral part of the merchant's payment channels. If these applications inherently do not support PCI compliance, it is a great challenge for the merchant to become PCI-compliant. Therefore, it is essential for merchants to deploy PA-DSS (Payment Application Data Security Standard)-validated applications in their environments, thereby simplifying and facilitating their PCI-compliance efforts.

Merchant organizations also have to spend a significant amount of time identifying estuary storage locations of cardholder information. These are areas where cardholder information is not conventionally meant to be stored but, due to software configurations, human intervention, and force of habit, become viable and expansive storehouses of cardholder information.

These estuary sources of storage are the most dangerous for an organization. They are usually back-end systems or linked servers or log servers that provide supporting functionality to the operations. These are usually provided with basic protection and are not meant to store highly sensitive information like cardholder data. For instance, an application logs sensitive information like the complete PAN (primary account number), cardholder name, CVV (card verification value), etc., and these application logs are pushed into a centralized log server. In this instance, the log server is not conventionally meant to be a viable storehouse of sensitive information. However, it accumulates a large amount of cardholder data because the application is constantly feeding it with this information. If an attacker is able to compromise the log-management server, she gets access to an incredible scale of confidential information that shouldn't have been there in the first place.

Another classic example is a merchant's business-process outsourcing locations, where tele-calling executives use the customers' card numbers to place orders, handle chargebacks, etc. In such cases, the call-center executives might input these details into a text file or document file and store it permanently on their hard drives, even though they are not meant to. They might just be storing it for the sake of convenience and not due to malicious intent. In the event that the endpoint is compromised, confidential cardholder information would have been breached by the merchant and/or its partners.

6.1.3 Service Providers

Service providers may be categorized in different ways. The easiest reference to the term *service provider* from the standpoint of PCI compliance is that of a third-party processor (or TPP). The TPP is a critical service provider in the payment-processing cycle. TPPs perform acquiring functions and issuing functions on behalf of banks. Banks that do not want to set up their own acquiring and issuing functions contact TPPs to perform these operations on their behalf.

The TPP is fundamentally required to route transactions to the right payment brand networks and perform issuer authorization for transactions where the TPP is the issuing processor. The TPP also performs additional functions like bill mail services and integrating with enhanced security services like Verified by Visa or MasterCard SecureCode/3DSecure.

As in the case of a merchant organization, the TPP's approach to PCI compliance will always hinge on the creation of a scope. While, in the case of the TPP, the cardholder-data touch points may not be

as many in number as in the case of a merchant, the volume of transactions being handled by the TPP will be much greater and is a major factor for consideration. There are also several differences in approach for issuing TPPs and acquiring TPPs.

6.1.3.1 Issuing TPPs

Issuing TPPs have a greater risk of cardholder information storage. Their systems contain the cardholder's file along with information like the PAN, cardholder's name, credit limits, and other details. In fact, in some older payment-processing facilities for acquirers, the CVV/PIN is also stored with the cardholder-data file. The acquiring processor also has multiple related operations with respect to issuing, like card manufacture and embossing, where the processor also generates the physical cards and ships them to the bank's customers along with the PIN mailers, and so on. These operations of the issuing processor increase the touch points for cardholder data significantly.

As with the merchant, a core PCI-compliance team has to be constituted within the TPP's operations. This PCI-compliance team needs to conduct a risk assessment (oriented toward PCI) to identify cardholder-data touch points. The compliance team also needs to identify estuary points of cardholder-data storage. In the case of an issuing processor, they may be as follows (but not limited to):

- *Switch logs*: The payment switch used by the issuing processor is an all-important aspect of the organization's issuing operations. The payment switch routes transactions to and from the issuer and is used to authorize or decline transactions. In the case of some switches, the logs of the switch log the full track data in clear text, or at least some portion of the track in clear text, thereby creating an automatic barrier to PCI compliance.

- *FTP servers*: One of the most common areas of cardholder information storage is the FTP (or other transmission servers) of the issuing processors. These servers are used to upload and download data from the bank relating to card applications or embossed card lists. These FTP servers, while they may be protected from external and internal attacks, may be storing data without a defined retention period or against the organization's data-retention policies.

- *Linked servers*: In many cases, linked servers can present a great challenge to PCI compliance. This is due to the fact that linked servers to the TPP's operation perform some critical aspects of the payment-processing cycle. For instance, many issuing TPPs send out text message (SMS) alerts to the bank's customers when a transaction has been performed/authorized on said customer's card. This application might be storing cardholder data, even though it is unnecessary.

6.1.3.2 Acquiring TPPs

TPPs that perform issuing functions also oftentimes perform acquiring functions, owing to the obvious business benefit. However, this is not always true. Acquiring TPPs may perform only acquiring functions, in which case they are not required to maintain systems relating to issuing, such as card-embossing applications, mailing applications, etc. However, they have other equally critical systems and applications that would be subject to the requirements of the PCI-DSS. For instance, the acquiring processor might provide an interface to their systems for e-commerce merchants through an application programming interface (API) or through a payment gateway set up by the acquiring processor. Additionally, acquirers also provide payment equipment to the merchant, such as electronic data capture (EDC) machines and terminals to swipe payment cards to be acquired by the acquiring process on behalf of the merchant. However, the most important system for an acquiring processor would be the payment switch that is used to perform acquiring for all the transactions.

Acquiring processors typically use payment switches that are commercially available applications, although some of them choose to develop their own payment switches in-house with an application development team. The payment switch would provide the all-important functionality of routing merchant transactions to the right payment brand network and receiving authorization/decline status of the transaction back to the point of sale (whether it be card-present or card-not-present transactions). The payment switch would also provide billing-related information to the acquiring processor. This information is used by the acquirer for settlement with the merchant and in the case of disputed transactions, where specific transactions are pulled up for analysis and confirmation.

6.1.4 Banks

One would expect a bank's payment-card operations to be gargantuan and highly complex. However, the bank's card operations are those of the acquiring and issuing processor. Most banks outsource their card processing operations to the acquiring and issuing processors and these entities handle all of the card operations to the bank. However, in the event of a bank maintaining its own card-processing function, the functions would mirror those of an acquiring and issuing TPP. The ATM network of a bank also works with the same flow. The ATM transaction of a bank is acquired by said bank or its processor, and subsequently the transaction is authorized by said bank if the card-issuing bank and the acquiring bank are the same. The transaction also has to be authorized by an issuing bank.

6.1.5 Other Service Providers

There is a class of service providers beyond the typical TPPs that are also under the purview of PCI compliance. These entities are those that provide support functions to merchants, TPPs, banks, and so on. For instance, let us assume that a merchant organization has outsourced its customer service department to a call center in India. If this call center handles all incoming and outgoing customer-related communication for said merchant, then the merchant organization would be required to track and monitor the PCI-compliance program of this organization.

Let me illustrate this with an example. Panthera Water Company is a utility company that provides water to residents of a particular town in the United States. Panthera has outsourced its customer-service division to ServiceOne, a business-process outsourcing organization (BPO) in India. The BPO organization handles all incoming and outgoing customer-service requests for Panthera. The utility's customers can contact the call center and pay their utility bills by providing their credit card/debit card details to the call-center agent handling the service request. Through such operations, among others, Panthera shares its payment-card information with ServiceOne. Requirement 12 of the PCI-DSS requires the organization to track and monitor the compliance status of the service provider with whom the entity shares cardholder information or to provide technology that is part of the entity's payment-processing operations. ServiceOne would ideally have to become PCI-compliant and report its compliance status to Panthera.

Another example of service providers would be in the case of software development. Let us assume that RightProducts, a large retailer of consumer appliances in the United States, is having its customized e-commerce application designed by InfoBean Technologies in Israel. A significant part of its e-commerce application relies on being able to accept card payments from customers and transmit said details to the payment gateway. Infobean also manages production support for RightProducts' e-commerce site. The site is a customized Web application that is under the purview of the PCI requirements. Therefore, by extension, the development environment is also subject to certain requirements of the standard. As a result of this arrangement, InfoBean's development environment and the application will be under scope for PCI compliance. Even if RightProducts does not share cardholder data with InfoBean, the application that is in scope for PCI and part of the payment-processing cycle of RightProducts will extend the PCI compliance to InfoBean as well.

In the case of such service providers, the concept of *scope* becomes exceedingly important to PCI compliance. Many of these service providers work in semi-isolated environments for each client requirement, only drawing on certain common resources for specific functions and technology. For instance, ServiceOne would have a specific process and operation designated for Panthera's requirement. In the event that Panthera is undergoing PCI compliance and requires ServiceOne to get PCI-compliant as well, then ServiceOne can perform PCI compliance on a specific scope, that is, the Panthera process in its organization. This can be similarly applied to software development companies.

Hosting companies are also considered service providers. However, the standard specifically details the PCI-compliance process and applicability of PCI to the hosting providers.

6.2 ENTERPRISE CHALLENGES: PCI COMPLIANCE

6.2.1 Information Overload: A Perspective

One of the greatest challenges and a constant barrier to enterprise PCI compliance is information overload. From a PCI-compliance standpoint, however, information overload has a slightly modified meaning from its traditional one. Information overload really has to do with the amount of data that has to be sifted through for an organization to become compliant. This affects the uninitiated and the unprepared, as with any other challenging project.

An organization's PCI-compliance effort always begins with identifying a scope. This in itself requires a great deal of analysis that is proportional to the scale of the organization and its exposure to cardholder information. Identification of the scope is of great importance, as it will provide the boundaries for the implementation of PCI requirements and allow the organization to address different risks to cardholder information differently as identified in the scope. Specific methodology needs to be adopted in creating a scope and drawing out its risks and impact on the PCI-compliance process. Organizations with a mature risk-management process would be able to handle PCI scope creation better than organizations that do not pay a great deal of attention to their risk-management framework.

The other source of information overload is from the requirements themselves. Internally, the company has to compile a great deal of data to meet the requirements of PCI compliance. This data, if not managed appropriately, can result in several critical security areas being overlooked, resulting in a posture of lowered information security as well.

6.2.2 Knowledge of the Team

The PCI requirements are quite specific and granular in nature. However, organizations implementing PCI compliance usually have issues with understanding and interpreting the requirements of the standard, since the PCI requirements consist of dimensions ranging from physical security to application security and comprise multiple subrequirements that are highly specific in nature. If the organization's knowledge of PCI is poor or nonexistent, the implementation effort would potentially be a long-drawn-out affair with several iterations of gaps in the requirements. Furthermore, in the event of low awareness and knowledge of PCI within the organization, then the compliance process may also be derailed or paused indefinitely for want of more information.

I usually suggest conducting a PCI orientation workshop or equivalent to a client who is undergoing PCI compliance. This would provide some clarity on the PCI standards and requirements while also providing insight into the implementation aspects of different requirements of the standard.

In the case of large companies undergoing PCI compliance, it is always advisable for one or more representatives of the organization to become a PCI-ISA (internal security assessor). The PCI-SSC conducts ISA training programs for organizations so that representatives can gain an in-depth understanding of the requirements of the PCI and help his/her company meet the requirements.

6.2.3 Management Impetus

In some cases, where a large company is undergoing PCI compliance, management is disconnected from the PCI-compliance effort, seeing it as an "IT security requirement" having little or no bearing on its business. This could not be further from the truth. PCI is an industry-wide compliance requirement that is essential for entities that store, process, or transmit cardholder information. Sooner than later, organizations of this nature will have to comply with the standard, given the security incidents occurring against the payment-card ecosystem and the need for security evolution across the payment-card ecosystem.

It is well known that management impetus is required to drive a critical standard like PCI within the organization. Therefore, management disconnect for the standard would be a major challenge in its successful implementation.

6.2.4 Budgetary Constraints

The PCI requirements are highly specific and granular in nature. As the result of their vast application on the security infrastructure of the organization, there would be some requirements that require a great deal of capital investment and operating expenses to maintain. Depending on the organization, there may be several expenses incurred toward procuring new hardware and software in order to meet and maintain compliance. Additionally, there may be increased manpower requirements to administer and manage these components. Therefore, it is highly advisable to have a budget for PCI frozen beforehand by a single team responsible for PCI compliance. This team should be knowledgeable and be able to freeze any procurements that need to be made at the initiation of the compliance effort.

Additionally, there are several open-source technologies that may be adopted by entities to meet different aspects of the PCI-compliance requirements. Open-source applications ranging from log-management solutions to file-integrity-monitoring applications are available, thereby eliminating the need to pay for software.

6.2.5 Technical Constraints

Technical constraints are perhaps the most important challenges against an organization's PCI-compliance efforts. Technical constraints specifically refer to barriers imposed by technology or technological legacy that prevent an entity from becoming PCI compliant. For instance, if a POS application deployed by a merchant organization only encrypts card numbers with a 56-bit DES cipher, then there is a technical constraint against PCI compliance. The standard specifically requires that card numbers be rendered unreadable during storage. If encryption is used, strong encryption standards have to be adopted for an entity to comply with Requirement 3 of the PCI-DSS. Such constraints, among others, might pose serious challenges to an organization's meeting the requirements of the PCI-DSS.

Technical constraints have to be dealt with, with a strong understanding of risk. If the constraint can be overcome with an ideal implementation of the requirements, then the barrier imposed by the constraint may be overcome.

Additionally, there is also the option of a compensating control. However, compensating controls also have to meet the intent and rigor of the original PCI requirement. Any single other requirement that is already a PCI requirement cannot be used as a compensating control to overcome a technical constraint.

6.3 GOOD PRACTICES: TO GET PCI-COMPLIANT

6.3.1 PCI Taskforce

Any project that requires action and decisiveness should be driven by a task force. PCI compliance is no different. PCI compliance is a significant standard to pursue. An organization should pursue it with all its might and focus. The task force should ensure that all of the functional departments involved

with PCI compliance or under the scope of PCI compliance should work in tandem and ensure that the project is successful. The task force should not only be in effect until the initial compliance is achieved, but should continue to exist for as long as the company remains PCI-compliant, as PCI is a continuing and evolving compliance standard.

The task force would ideally comprise senior members across multidisciplinary departments. This would ensure that the organization is committed to the PCI-compliance effort. This would also ensure that decisions requiring expeditious approvals and actions can be taken without delay.

The PCI task force in an organization should ideally perform the following roles:

- Be trained in PCI compliance requirements and their implementation across the organization
- Consist of individuals from multidisciplinary departments
- Conduct PCI risk assessment for the organization to identify the scope
- Create road maps and plans both operational and financial to achieve PCI compliance
- Liaise with multiple departments relating to or under the scope of PCI compliance to ensure that their operations meet the intent and rigor of the PCI requirements
- Conduct internal audits and assessments (with assistance from information security and/or audit and risk departments)
- Create budgets and obtain approvals from senior management for PCI compliance
- Oversee the PCI-compliance efforts to ensure that it happens with the least amount of interference and friction

- Engage with a PCI-QSA (if required) to ensure that an audit is carried out and that any gaps found are closed before the final audit is performed

6.3.2 Create a Defined Scope

I have already discussed the need for defining a scope for PCI compliance at some length. I reiterate it here only because it is critical to compliance. However, as with other standards or projects, the scope of PCI compliance cannot always be defined by the organization's choice. Unlike self-driven standards like ISO-27001, PCI is an industry-driven standard that has a certain mandatory requirement when it comes to defining the scope.

Very simply, the scope is defined based on the areas of the organization where cardholder information is stored, processed, or transmitted. Therefore, touch points of cardholder information and operations around these touch points are in scope for compliance. However, the scope in some ways can still be defined. This can ideally be done by pruning the amount of cardholder information touch points in the organization. For instance, if an e-commerce merchant is able to disallow the storage of cardholder information in the database by having the user mandatorily enter card information on a payment gateway's portal, then the e-commerce site can effectively go completely out of scope on PCI compliance, as long as the organization does not store, process, or transmit cardholder information anywhere else.

Another example would be that of a merchant back-office operation, where the merchant's customer service representatives would record calls for quality, etc. This system would also capture cardholder information by the customer. If the merchant organization finds that storing said information is very risky, decides to delete the recordings and discontinue the process, then the system and its related operations could potentially be out of scope, thereby reducing the scope and the risk of cardholder information being exposed.

6.3.3 Don't Focus on PCI Compliance

This may seem like counterintuitive advice. After all, if an entity wants to achieve PCI compliance, surely it must focus on achieving it? In my opinion, PCI compliance is a by-product of a mature security posture for any company. Based on the risk for a company that is handling payment-card information, the company must look to implementing controls that are commensurate with the scale and risk of the exposure of the payment-card information. Security should be the ultimate motivation for any organization intending to become PCI-compliant, because a data breach to organizations handling cardholder information can have devastating consequences on the organization's finances and reputation. PCI compliance is a benchmark that attests to the achievement of a certain level of security. However, given a sound understanding of risk, compliance should be considered a by-product of security implementation.

6.3.4 Understand Risk—Always

Risk is the foundation of all security. Security in itself is a derivative of the concept of risk. However, in matters of compliance, risk is oftentimes overlooked at the peril of the organization. An entity handling cardholder information needs to understand the specific risks of dealing with said information. Based on these risks, the entity needs to frame controls that are commensurate with the risk of a cardholder-data breach as well as the scale of the organization's operations. This will ensure that the controls implemented by the organization, by way of security measures, will be optimal to the risk and scale of the organization.

Organizations need to perform structured risk assessments to ensure that they comprehensively identify cardholder-data touch points, identify specific vulnerabilities and potential threats, rank them based on a qualitative or quantitative risk evaluation criteria and, finally design and implement controls that manage the risk effectively. While the PCI controls remain a constant, the organization's risk is always subject to change. Organizations have to constantly evolve their controls based on current risks.

We have already discussed the difference between security and PCI compliance. My take on this is as follows. Security measures implemented by the organization should always be based on a sound understanding of risk. This provides a comprehensive and holistic view of the organization's security requirements. PCI compliance is a standard that helps drive and attain a higher security posture through specific controls. However, the standard is not, in and of itself, a panacea against all types of security incidents. It is a standard that is to be considered a minimum benchmark for an entity that is storing, processing, or transmitting cardholder data.

6.3.5 Pick the Right QSA

An audit by a PCI-QSA is required for Level 1 merchants and service providers. However, many organizations at lower levels choose to employ the services of a QSA to get them certified and compliant.

The PCI-QSA's position with reference to the compliance and certification process is unique, because the QSA can consult with and also certify the organization. This sort of arrangement is not seen as a conflict of interest by the PCI-SSC. However, several PCI-QSAs and QSACs misuse this position of trust. They use this as a front for marketing their products and forcefully make the entity adopt them, citing that compliance is not possible without these applications that they market. This is prohibited by the QSA under the PCI-SSC terms of ethics. The PCI-QSA is allowed to market products to clients, but the consultant should not tout that the only way to achieve compliance is by use of said product(s).

Knowledge of the PCI-QSA is a very important matter. PCI-QSAs must be security professionals who should be highly knowledgeable about the requirements of the standard as well as matters of information security. However, in special cases, QSAs may not have adequate knowledge to assess specific types of systems or environments. For instance, auditing mainframe environments requires a different set of skills that the QSA might not possess, owing to the low frequency of mainframe environments. In such cases, the PCI-QSA must be able to call on the services of a subject-matter expert to assess the said environment and given infrastructure component.

6.4 GOOD PRACTICES FOR APPLICATION VENDORS: PA-DSS

6.4.1 Security from Incipiency

One of the greatest challenges for an application to be validated for PA-DSS is the application development life cycle. Application vendors uninitiated in information security practices and application security practices do not pay attention to the application development life cycle to their own peril.

One of the basic requirements for a secure application is to ensure that security is integrated with the application at every step of the life cycle. Right from requirements gathering to the completion of the application development life cycle, security requirements have to be comprehensively covered with a structured application risk-management process. We will detail a risk-management process when we discuss Requirement 6 of the standard in Chapter 13.

Security from inception will ensure that the application meets a certain security benchmark right from the outset. In fact, having the PA-DSS requirements as an initial benchmark will expedite the validation process for PA-DSS.

6.4.2 Document, Document, Document

The PA-DSS has quite an extensive set of documentation requirements that need to be followed. One of the most important documents in the PA-DSS requirements is the PA-DSS Implementation Guide. The implementation guide is an exhaustive document that details the security implementation, deployment, and configuration guidelines for customers, resellers, and integrators of the application. This document needs to contain detailed functionality of the application with respect to security required by the PA-DSS.

Applications also have to follow a document-change control process to ensure that changes that are defined are rolled out and rolled back only after document change-management procedures are followed.

6.4.3 Scope Out

Several PA-DSS applications are those that have limited card-management operations but primarily perform a different function. For instance, a POS application's primary behavior is to provide point-of-sale capabilities for a retail organization. As part of the application's capability, card processing and management might be a functionality that is provided by the application vendor. In such cases, it may be challenging and unnecessary to subject the entire application to PA-DSS compliance. If the component handling cardholder information can be separated and logically isolated from the rest of the application, the component by itself can be validated under the PA-DSS as opposed to the entire application. This is especially useful for applications that typically do not require a great level of information security implementation in sections excepting the card-processing and -management section of the application.

6.5 SUMMARY

This chapter was oriented toward understanding an enterprise approach to PCI compliance. We began by discussing some of the key aspects of PCI compliance from the viewpoint of different industry verticals, such as merchant, service provider, etc. We then detailed some of the key industry verticals and identified typical key systems and processes in their organizations that would be within the scope of PCI compliance. We next delved into some of the key challenges faced by enterprises when undergoing PCI compliance and some of the practices they can adopt to overcome these challenges. Finally, we detailed the best practices that can be adopted by application vendor organizations within the scope for a PA-DSS validation.

7

Scoping for PCI Compliance

Scope is a very important aspect of a PCI-compliance project. PCI compliance is a technically rigorous standard that requires a great deal of focus and implementation. If an organization undertakes PCI compliance with a poor understanding of scope, then the compliance effort would potentially be misguided and incomplete.

In this chapter, we will focus our energies toward learning the first and most important aspect of PCI compliance: scoping. We will understand the fundamental need for scoping a PCI environment. We will also delve into the cardholder-data environment, referring to the environment on which PCI-DSS (Payment Card Industry Data Security Standard) controls are implemented and applicable. We will also explore different dimensions of scope creation by understanding scoping practices for the network, servers, operating systems, and applications.

7.1 SCOPING FOR PCI COMPLIANCE: A PRIMER

Scope can be defined as "the extent of the area or subject matter that something deals with or to which it is relevant." For any project, scope becomes an important consideration. The scope provides an understanding of the type of effort that needs to be undertaken to complete the project and apply it to a scope. Scope may be referred to in terms of human effort or in terms of the area/environment of a particular deployment or implementation.

Let us imagine this scenario. A merchant is identifying all of the cardholder touch points* within the merchant environment. The merchant identifies the following systems as cardholder-data touch points:

---

* Defined in Chapter 6, *touch points* refer to the specific areas where cardholder information may be stored, processed, or transmitted.

- *The POS system*: Because customer cardholder information may be stored at the POS terminal and the POS server.
- *The e-commerce system*: Because the customer uses cardholder information to shop on the merchant's site. The cardholder details are stored in the database connected to the e-commerce system.
- *The finance team*: The finance team members at the merchant's organization generate reports based on the cardholder-data billing that has happened at the merchant's location and perform settlement functions with the acquiring bank for the payments rightly due to the merchant.

Along with these touch points, the merchant organization identifies other cardholder-information touch points. However, the merchant's analysis misses a key area. The merchant has recently deployed self-payment kiosks for a retail business across multiple locations in different shopping malls across the country. These kiosks allow a customer to use his/her credit/debit card to make payments for transactions or for goods and services booked through the kiosk.

We can clearly see through this example that the merchant's scoping process is less than satisfactory, simply because the merchant organization has completely missed a critical system that is typically in scope as a cardholder-data touch point. If the merchant's scoping process were a structured and thorough one, it would not have overlooked a critical system like the kiosk system, which is a viable cardholder-data touch point.

Such issues have widespread repercussions. For instance, during the PCI-QSA's assessment at the merchant's location, the QSA (qualified security assessor) identifies the kiosk system as a cardholder-data touch point, finds stored cardholder information, and renders the merchant noncompliant with certain requirements based on the assessment of said systems. This would effectively hinder the merchant organization's ability to get certified under the PCI-DSS. Worse, attackers could identify vulnerabilities with the kiosk system and be able to extract thousands of customer card details along with personally identifiable information of customers, thereby causing a significant data breach of the merchant's environment. Such effects could exist simply because the merchant organization did not include the system in its cardholder-data scope and ignored security implementations for the same.

It is very important to create a defined scope for PCI compliance, as the controls that are applied based on the PCI requirements will be focused on the scope. This scoped environment will be the environment that handles the storage, processing, and transmission of cardholder information.

7.2 THE CARDHOLDER-DATA ENVIRONMENT (CDE)

7.2.1 Defining the Cardholder-Data Environment

The cardholder-data environment (CDE) is one of the most important concepts in an organization's PCI-compliance effort. I will also refer to this as the PCI environment throughout this book for ease of understanding. The CDE or the PCI environment refers to the processes or business activities in the organization that are touch points for cardholder data. This includes supporting functions and infrastructure like networks, applications, and shared components that are necessary for the PCI environment or CDE.

The PCI controls are stringent and technically rigorous; therefore, the organization would do well to define a specific scope within the organization, called the CDE or PCI environment, where these controls are focused and managed. This is done to ensure that the scope of managing continuous PCI compliance is managed effectively and efficiently. Also, some business activities, processes, and units have no relationship with cardholder data. In such cases, including them in the CDE and subjecting them to the same controls may be wasteful and not commensurate with the risk of cardholder-data security. For instance, I was recently working with a business-process outsourcing (BPO) company that had multiple client processes. Among these client processes were some bank-client processes where customer service departments for multiple banks and financial institutions were set up. The organization created a scope to include only these companies in the CDE by physically and logically separating them from the rest of the company. This ensured that the CDE was focused on a specific scope and not extended to the rest of the organization, e.g., the customer service department for an automobile company that did not require these security controls.

However, for some companies, such as merchants where many departments in the company would handle cardholder data, the CDE must be created based on the "in-scope" departments or business units. For instance, the marketing department of the merchant organization might be removed from the scope, as it doesn't handle cardholder data. Using physical/logical segmentation, the departments like legal, marketing, human resources, and so on, may be removed from the CDE. Removing these departments from the scope does not necessarily mean that some shared services from these departments can never be availed by the "in-scope" departments, but for technical controls like network security, system security, application security, and so on, they are not included in the same environment as the CDE. These services might still have some requirements in scope. For instance, the human resources department must maintain employee records, perform security-awareness training, and maintain background checks for employees. However, as it doesn't store, process, or transmit cardholder data, it may be removed from the cardholder-data environment.

7.2.2 Cardholder-Data Flow

The first activity to be performed in establishing the CDE or PCI environment is to create a cardholder-data flow diagram. The cardholder-data flow diagram highlights the flow of cardholder data into and out of the organization. For instance, a merchant might handle cardholder data from the following business activities:

- *In-store point-of-sale (POS) billing*: Cardholder information received from a customer during an in-store billing process. The cardholder data is swiped on the merchant's POS terminal, which interfaces with its internal billing server and the payment gateway.
- *E-commerce site billing*: Registered users on the merchant's e-commerce site can

pay for the products on the merchant's site using their credit/debit cards.

Mail-order billing: Customers can order items by sending mail orders to the merchant. These mail orders are handled by the merchant's outsourced customer service department. Subsequently, these are fed into the merchant's order-management system, which is linked to the billing server.

Telephone-based billing: Customers can place orders through the phone, where the customer's card details are captured over an IVR (interactive voice response) system and transmitted to the organization's billing server.

Transaction reconciliation services: The merchant's accounts department performs transaction-reconciliation services, which reconciles payments made to the merchant organization with the transactions from the acquiring bank.

Chargeback and returns: Customers who want to return their products or, in the case of product flaws, may submit their products to the in-store or e-commerce customer service department for chargebacks.

Similarly for issuers and acquirers (processors), cardholder-data flows may be from a variety of sources, including ATMs, POS terminals, payment gateways, and so on (see Figures 7.1 and 7.2). For acquirers, cardholder data comes in from these sources and is transmitted to the organization's

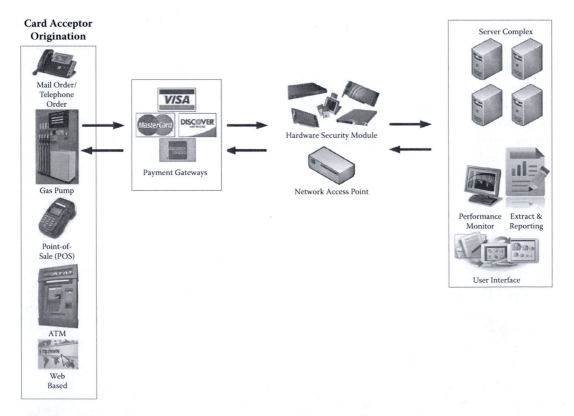

FIGURE 7.1
Issuer cardholder-data flow.

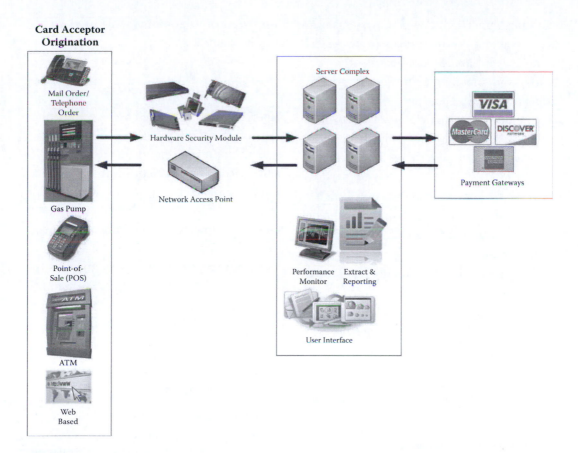

Card Acceptor Origination

Mail Order/ Telephone Order

Gas Pump

Point-of-Sale (POS)

ATM

Web Based

Hardware Security Module

Network Access Point

Server Complex

Performance Monitor

Extract & Reporting

User Interface

Payment Gateways

VISA

MasterCard

DISCOVER

FIGURE 7.2
Acquirer cardholder-data flow.

payment switch, which routes the transaction to a payment brand network like Visa, MasterCard, and so on. For issuers, the sources of receiving cardholder data are usually the payment brand networks like Visa and MasterCard, or their own ATM and POS networks (if issuer and acquiring functions are the same), and the transaction is routed to their card-management-system for authorization. Issuers and issuing processors might also have card-issuing functions that include embossing, PIN (personal identification number) mailers, cardholder account management, cardholder account customer service, and so on. In such cases, the cardholder-data flows will increase to these departments and business activities.

7.2.3 Cardholder-Data Matrix

The cardholder-data matrix (CDM) is a single-sheet approach and key input in identifying the cardholder-data environment or PCI environment. The objective of the CDM is to identify all areas, business processes, and units within an organization where cardholder data is stored, processed, and transmitted. The CDM must also capture whether the cardholder data is encrypted or whether other protection strategies have been applied on the cardholder data.

The focus of this exercise is to find the touch points of cardholder data across the organization, categorize these, and ultimately define the CDE and the PCI environment. Let us examine the CDM with an example. SuperTech Payment Systems is an acquiring and issuing processor. Supertech acquires and issues on behalf of several banks and merchants in North America. SuperTech has identified some flows of cardholder data as part of its business operations. It has the following business operations where cardholder-data flows exist:

- *ATM card processing*: Acquisition
- *Card issuing*: Embossing, cardholder account management, PIN mailer, and so on
- *POS acquiring*: Acquiring retail transactions from merchants
- *Fraud-management services*
- *Cardholder customer service management*: On behalf of client banks

7.2.3.1 ATM Card Processing: Acquiring

SuperTech sets up and manages ATMs on behalf of its member banks. For instance, Bank National, one of SuperTech's major customers, has contracted with SuperTech for setting up its ATM branches across the United States. All transactions from the ATMs will be acquired by SuperTech. If the cardholder swipes a debit/ATM card that is not issued by a nonmember bank, then SuperTech purely behaves as an acquirer. The transaction is routed to the payment brands to an issuing bank. However, if the cardholder swipes a Bank National ATM/debit card, SuperTech will handle both the acquiring and the issuing function. SuperTech manages the ATM operations of 30 such member banks across the United States. The network traffic from the ATM is encrypted and routed directly to SuperTech via a dedicated line. SuperTech decrypts the cardholder data and routes the transac-

tion based on the issuing card used by the customer at the ATM.

7.2.3.2 Card-Issuing Function

SuperTech manages the card-issuing function for thirty member banks. The banks send the applications for customer credit/debit cards. Banks deposit this information to SuperTech over SFTP (Secure File Transfer Protocol) to SuperTech's server. SuperTech downloads the information, sets up cardholder-data accounts for the applicants, generates the card, and embosses the cardholder data onto the card. SuperTech also generates the PIN and mails the PIN to the cardholder separately (PIN mailer).

7.2.3.3 POS Billing and Merchant Acquisition

SuperTech has over 500 merchant establishments that rely on it to perform their acquisitions. SuperTech provides POS billing machines and a payment gateway API (application programming interface) for merchants to accept card payments from their customers. Merchants can opt for POS machines provided by SuperTech. Merchant POS applications and billing servers can utilize SuperTech's API for in-store card transactions. Merchants can also integrate their e-commerce applications with SuperTech's payment gateway (API) for card-not-present transactions.

7.2.3.4 Fraud-Management Services

SuperTech has an active fraud-management team to track potential payment card fraud for its acquiring and issuing functions. It has procured a fraud-management application that performs transaction-based analysis of the cardholder's transaction history, and transaction patterns. SuperTech also has a fraud-management team that is in charge of rules for fraud management, customer authorization, and so on.

7.2.3.5 Cardholder Customer Service Management

Most of SuperTech's member banks have also outsourced their cardholder customer service operations to SuperTech. SuperTech has an active inbound customer service team that handles customer queries, complaints, and requests on its credit, debit, and ATM cards. Members of this team help customers for any services related to their card accounts, including reward points, and so on.

7.2.3.6 Identifying Cardholder Data

The organization is aware of several cardholder-data touch points and areas of storage. However, it often happens that cardholder data may be present in more areas and touch points in the environment than imagined. This presents a great deal of risk. We already know that the higher the storage of cardholder data, the higher the risk of exposure and, consequently, the higher the risk of data breach for the organization. Sometimes the organization may not even know that cardholder data may be captured and stored in multiple locations, increasing its risk of data breach. Apart from the risk of data breach, unnecessary storage of cardholder data may necessitate the inclusion of areas into the PCI environment (CDE) even though it may not be necessary. The organization must take active efforts in identifying such areas where cardholder data is likely to be stored.

For instance, I was working with a leading telecom merchant recently. Some of its stores, unknown to the head office and compliance departments, had started to take photocopies of users' credit/debit cards that were used to make payment. This form of recordkeeping was a dangerous practice. Thousands of cards had been scanned (along with the CVV2 shown fully) and kept in files in stores that were secured only with some basic physical security controls like a locked cabinet. Once we identified multiple instances of cardholder data across at least 20 stores, it was decided to incinerate said copies. The merchant issued strict instructions to all of its store managers to *not* make photocopies of customer cards.

Another time, I was working with a leading bank for PCI compliance. Its Web application was handling customer cardholder queries and requests. To its shock, it discovered that it was logging the full PAN (primary account number) in clear text into a log server that was not well protected. Its developers had included system console statements in the code that logged the customer card number along with the customer's name and other details to the application logs/console. Once this was discovered, the developers were instructed to remove all log statements capturing customer card data, and the existing logs were encrypted and stored off-site.

The organization must direct its efforts to discover cardholder data in all systems that store, process, and transmit cardholder data. While systems that store cardholder data would typically contain said data, processing systems and transmission systems might also contain traces of said data as part of log files, debug files, history files, traces, and so on. For instance, customer service departments for processors and banks might have cardholder data in their e-mails. This may be dangerous, as e-mails are not a secure form of communication.

There are tools available for cardholder-data discovery. Some of them include:

- SENF
- Cornell Spider

7.2.4 The Role of the PCI-QSA in the CDE

The PCI-QSA has an important role in the cardholder-data environment or the PCI environment. The QSA must ensure that the CDE framed by the organization encompasses all cardholder-data touch points within the organization. The QSA must examine the PCI environment or the scope prepared by the organization and prepare a CDM based on the assessor's assessment or preassessment with the organization. The assessor must use multiple techniques like risk assessment and data discovery (identifying cardholder data in different areas) to arrive at the scope. If the scope does not match the organization's scope, then the assessor must ensure that the necessary additions and amendments are made to the scope to frame a cardholder-data environment or PCI environment.

Assessors must note that this is a *critical* activity. If the scope signed off by the assessor is not reflective of the actual scope of the CDE, and the organization suffers a cardholder-data breach or if the PCI-SSC audits the assessor, then the assessor is likely to be subject to sanctions for negligence in the assessment.

7.3 TIPS FOR SCOPE REDUCTION

7.3.1 Why Reduce Scope?

PCI compliance is based on the risk of cardholder-data exposure and breach. Therefore, the natural corollary of this concept is: "Don't handle cardholder data unless absolutely required." While the organization may not be able to rid itself of every trace of cardholder data, it can use some techniques to ensure that cardholder-data management is kept to the minimum in some specific business activities and processes where management of cardholder data (storage, processing, and transmission) is absolutely required. It is highly recommended that the organization look at reducing the scope of the cardholder-data environment through multiple techniques and practices, some of which include:

- Network segmentation
- Application-related scoping
- Tokenization and other data-protection techniques

7.3.2 Network Segmentation

Network segmentation is a highly effective and useful scoping and demarcation practice. In most companies, only specific departments handle cardholder data; otherwise, most of their other business operations do not handle cardholder data. In such cases, network segmentation is a great way to reduce the scope of the cardholder-data environment or PCI environment. If the PCI environment is logically segmented from the rest of the organization, then the areas where cardholder data is handled are limited to the segmented area. However, if the network is not effectively segmented, system components and business processes that are not required to be a part of the CDE would also be included in the CDE. This is unnecessary, expensive, and not commensurate with the risk of the rest of the environment. You can read about network segmentation in detail in Chapter 8 of this book.

7.3.3 Scoping Out E-Commerce Applications

E-commerce has become a major force on the Internet today. E-commerce is ubiquitous and appealing only because it allows users to make payments using simple instruments like their credit/debit card, bank account, and so on. However, many e-commerce companies do not have the size, scale, or ability to support and undertake PCI compliance. Often, the only source of a company's cardholder-data inflow is the e-commerce site. For instance, let-seat.com is a small diner that has introduced an online ordering service for its sandwiches. It set up a simple Web application that allows customers to select the sandwich they want and fill out the delivery address. Once the customer clicks on the order page, the website redirects the customer to a payment gateway site, where the customer's credit card details are filled out and the order is completed. Here, letseat.com has no cardholder-data storage, as the cardholder data is not filled out on its site, and cardholder data is not even transmitted through the site. While it has to protect its site and ensure that it has agreements with its payment gateway for protection of its customer cardholder data, it has effectively scoped out the need to achieve PCI compliance, as it does not handle any cardholder data.

Similarly, several payment gateways provide i-frames that can be embedded in the application's payment page upon customer checkout. There is also an option where the merchant site can directly post to the payment gateway over an API. In such cases, the e-commerce portal does not handle any cardholder data. They have effectively scoped out of the PCI compliance because they don't handle cardholder data.

7.3.4 Tokenization and Other Data-Protection Techniques

Tokenization is a technique where the organization handling cardholder data transmits the data to an acquiring processor. The processor generates a same-length token that is not the PAN to take its place within the organization. In such cases, the organization, while transmitting cardholder data, is not actually storing cardholder data at all. This effectively reduces the organization's scope of PCI requirements. Other data-protection strategies to reduce scope include encryption where the keys are not present with the receiving organization, and so on.

7.4 SYSTEM COMPONENTS IN THE PCI SCOPE

7.4.1 Network and Network Components

Networks and network components constitute a key aspect of the scope for PCI compliance. Network security is also a key requirement as part of Requirement 1 of the PCI-DSS. When I say *networks*, there is a certain distinction that you must understand. Internet service providers provide communication facilities for companies and users. Sensitive data like cardholder information and other information is transmitted over these networks. In this case, a natural question would be, "Is my ISP within my scope of PCI compliance?" The short answer is "No." The ISP is a service provider to you or your company. The ISP provides the network communication to you for you to communicate and does not dictate or take responsibility for the data that is transmitted over this communication channel. The ISP might have to undergo PCI compliance for its role as a merchant, but a network is in your company's PCI scope only if it is managed by the company.

Network devices are within the scope of the PCI-DSS. Requirements 1 and 2 deal extensively with the security over network devices. Wireless networks are also part of the PCI scope. Organizations can choose to reduce the scope of their PCI-compliance effort with network segmentation, but the network devices connected to the PCI environment (CDE) are within the scope.

7.4.2 Servers and OS Components

The operating-system layer is essential for the operation of the PCI environment. Operating systems for servers, workstations, and mobile devices undeniably influence the security of the PCI environment. Requirements across the PCI-DSS state multiply security controls and monitoring requirements for operating-system components, files, and applications. People have a misconception that mainframes are not included in the PCI environment because they are largely immune to attacks. This could not be further from the truth. While mainframes present some technology challenges to an attacker, they are computing devices that can be compromised. Additionally, they handle critical and highly sensitive information like cardholder data, and so on. Therefore, mainframes are definitely in scope for the PCI-DSS requirements.

7.4.3 Applications

Applications are the lifeblood of any organization. PCI environments usually have several applications—APIs, services, and so on—that they depend on heavily. Some applications directly handle cardholder data, such as POS applications, e-commerce applications, fraud-management applications, and so on. However, some applications—SMS gateways, e-mail applications, workflow applications, and so on—support the operations of the PCI environment. Applications that operate (or are operated) in a CDE are within scope. These may be custom applications, commercial applications, or payment applications (custom or commercial). Requirement 6 of the PCI-DSS deals heavily with applications, as do some of the other requirements of the PCI-DSS.

7.5 SUMMARY

The objective of this chapter is to introduce the highly important facet of scoping for PCI compliance. As PCI requirements are highly stringent and technically challenging, they need to be focused on an environment within the organization that deals with cardholder data. We learned that to effectively develop a PCI-scoped environment, we need to understand the flow of cardholder data. Understanding the flow of cardholder data provides us information about cardholder-data touch points. These touch points are areas that store, process, or transmit cardholder data. Creating a frame around the touch points and shared services constitutes the cardholder-data environment. We explored some of the different touch points for different industries that are targets for PCI compliance. We explored the cardholder-data landscape for merchants, service providers, processors, and so on. We also focused our energies on identifying measures to reduce PCI scope, including Web-application development practices for e-commerce companies, use of tokenization, and so on. Finally, we explored system components that would be essential for the PCI scope or the cardholder-data environment.

8

Requirement 1: Build and Maintain a Secure Network

The network is the first logical bastion of an information security framework in an organization. The network connects the organization internally and with its partners, customers, and so on. A compromise of said network could cause a great deal of financial damage both by loss of reputation and by diminished productivity. In the event that the network transmits cardholder information, a heightened implementation of network security becomes a basic essential. The PCI-DSS has several requirements that focus on network security. Throughout this chapter we will discuss the PCI Requirement 1 and its implementation strategies in a PCI environment.

8.1 NETWORK SECURITY: A PRIMER

8.1.1 Network Security Architecture: Enterprise

Network security in enterprises has taken a great leap forward. From the time where TCP (Transmission Control Protocol) flood attacks and basic network attacks used to cripple enterprise networks, modern enterprise networks have a host of protection mechanisms that have rendered such attacks obsolete. However, network security occupies a critical place in the world of enterprise security. Network security teams understand that if an attacker is able to compromise the network in any way, either internally or externally, critical information assets could be breached, with devastating results.

Organizations today deploy a host of tools and appliances to guard the network, from firewalls to intrusion prevention systems (IPSs) to unified threat-management solutions. In addition to network security components, organizations heavily deploy routers, switches, VLANs (virtual local area networks), and other networking technologies, including wireless networking components, to simplify network-manage-ment operations.

Over the course of the last 10 years, network security has matured greatly in organizations. Organizations are able to implement higher quality protection mechanisms for the network, and the tech-nologies available have also facilitated the organization into building a secure network infrastructure. However, organizations continually face a network-configuration-management challenge. With a wide array of network device deployments within the organization, configuring network devices for security is a challenge.

For example, consider a telecom opera-tor that has deployed thousands of net-work devices in their environment. While deploying an Internet-facing router, the network administrator does not change the SNMP (Simple Network Management Protocol) default community string* from "public." An attacker who is looking to compromise the telecom operator's network finds the router and starts enumerating vul-nerabilities. The attacker discovers that the router's SNMP community string is set to a default value of "public." The attacker enu-merates a great deal of information from the router, including some of the interface information, hardware information, and so on. The attacker now looks to enumer-ate the read/write community string from the router and attempts a brute-force attack against the router. The (private) read/write community string happens to be a simple value "password." The attacker uses the community string to download the router's

configuration file, thereby obtaining the password for the router. Now the attacker has been able to compromise the router. Using the compromised router as a pivot, the attacker is able to gain access to inter-nal network resources of the organization, compromising the organization's critical information assets.

In the previous example, the organiza-tion's network deployment is not at fault; it is the configuration of said network com-ponents that was nonsecure, thereby caus-ing a data breach. Organizations have been able to bring network security practices to a greater level of maturity through better security tools and technologies for network security, but configuration of the network devices is a critical facet requiring a great deal of focus as well.

Organizations that take information secu-rity seriously take a great deal of care with network security. They go by the concept of *defense in depth*.[†] Figure 8.1 is an example of a network that has followed the principles of the defense-in-depth philosophy.

8.1.2 Network Architecture: Scoping Out

In Chapter 6 (Enterprise Approach to PCI Compliance), we discussed a key concept called *PCI-scoped environment* or PCI environment. The PCI-scoped environ-ment consists of all the operations of the organization that are under the scope for PCI compliance. In many cases, the entire organization may not have to be under

---

* The SNMP protocol is used to manage network devices. SNMP is accessed using its community strings. If the community strings are easily enumerated, network device information and configurations can be gleaned by an attacker.

† Defense-in-Depth is a concept of security where security controls are implemented by an organization with a lay-ered approach, i.e. one layer of controls is always supple-mented or complemented with controls in a subsequent layer, thereby ensuring that an attack is exponentially difficult to execute or succeed.

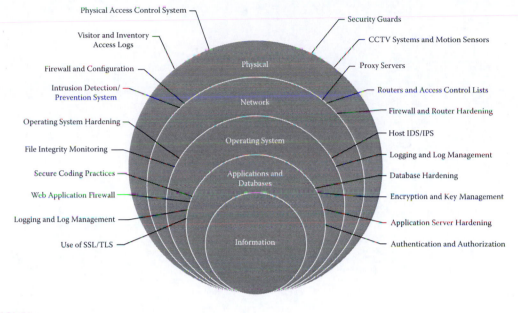

FIGURE 8.1
Network security: defense-in-depth network architecture.

the purview of PCI compliance for all its operations.

For instance, BancoAmerica, a commercial bank in the United States, is undergoing PCI compliance, and one of the key areas of compliance is an application that is handling cardholder information. This application is being developed by Panthera for Banco's card-management operations. In addition to developing the application, Panthera also provides production support to Banco for this card-management application. As a result of this relationship, Panthera is Banco's service provider and is in scope for PCI compliance. According to Requirement 12.8.4 of the PCI-DSS, BancoAmerica has to track the PCI compliance state of their service providers. Panthera is a software development company that provides software solutions to multiple industry verticals like manufacturing, insurance, and banking. Banco instructs Panthera to achieve PCI compliance for their organization.

However, Panthera understands that only a single development center of its operation handles cardholder information (that is one of Banco's). No other operation in Panthera's operations handles cardholder information. Panthera has divided different projects into different development centers; however, they are not logically segmented over the network. Panthera decides to perform adequate network segmentation to ensure that all other development centers of Panthera are out of scope for PCI compliance, and only the BancoAmerica Development Center is in scope for the PCI-compliance effort. Panthera realizes that the other development centers do not need to put in the scope for PCI compliance because

- They do not handle cardholder information in any way.
- They are not subject to the same security requirements as those specified by the PCI-DSS.

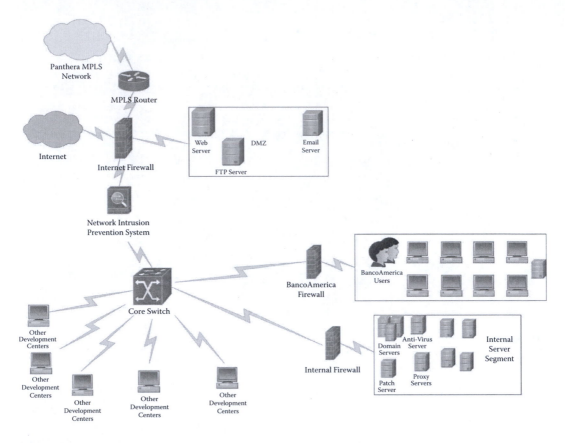

FIGURE 8.2

Panthera's network segmentation for PCI compliance.

Figure 8.2 highlights the network segmentation approach adopted by Panthera with the use of a high-level network diagram.

In the previous example, I discussed a network segmentation strategy for an entity that was different from the one that was undergoing the primary PCI-compliance effort. However, an organization might have several reasons for segmentation internally within its departments as well. For instance, BancoAmerica might decide to segment its core banking operations, marketing department, and its finance departments from the PCI scoped environment, as they do not handle cardholder information and they in no way need to interact with the cardholder environment for their operations. In such cases, segmenting the network effectively will ensure that departments or functional operations that do not handle cardholder information may be effectively put out of scope, and controls need not be applied unless they have a bearing on the security of the PCI scoped environment.

8.1.2.1 Benefits of Scoping Out with Network Segmentation

PCI compliance is a technically rigorous standard. The standard has been designed keeping in mind the risks of handling critical data like cardholder information. The organization should spend time and effort ensuring that these requirements are addressed to areas that require these controls based on the risk of critical data. However, an organization might find it difficult and unfeasible to implement these controls on less critical information assets that are typically low risk (in the view of the organization). In such cases, it is always prudent to segment the organization's network to ensure that only areas requiring PCI compliance are segmented away from those areas that do not need to be under these controls.

Additionally, network segmentation reduces the risk of cardholder data exposure. If a network is segmented and the PCI scoped environment is logically segmented from the rest of the organization, security incidents that might affect the organization's network should not permeate to the PCI scoped environment if properly implemented. For instance, if malware targeting Microsoft SQL server databases is propagating across the network, the chances that the PCI-scoped environment in the organization will be shielded from this attack are greater if the PCI-scoped environment has strong access-control rules that prevent external traffic on certain ports from the network to access the PCI-scoped environment.

8.1.2.2 Common Resources

There are several common resources for an organization when it comes to its IT deployment. For instance, in the previously discussed case of Panthera, common resources include the patch server, antivirus server, active directory server, e-mail server, and so on. In such cases, the common resources must also be subject to the requirements of the PCI-DSS, as they are being used in or by the PCI-scoped environment. Access to common resources to and from the PCI-scoped environment should be restricted with strong access-control lists (ACLs), firewall rules, MAC restrictions, and so on. The PCI-QSA (qualified security assessor) or the assessment team would actually have to measure the network segmentation by examining these ACLs or other rules that have been laid down to segment the network from the PCI-scoped environment.

8.1.2.3 Technology: Network Segmentation

Today's technologies allow network segmentation through a variety of technological implementations. We will delve into multiple ways of performing network segmentation to meet the PCI requirements.

The PCI-DSS does not by itself require network segmentation. The standard, however, recommends network segmentation, as it has multiple benefits highlighted in Section 8.1.2.1. The standard does not require any specific method of network segmentation. However, the standard has mentioned that network segmentation can be achieved with firewalls, routers with strong access-control lists, or other technologies. The effectiveness of network segmentation is really up to the discretion and risk perception of the organization and the PCI-QSA who is assessing the organization for PCI-DSS compliance.

Firewalls are probably the best way to perform network segmentation. A stateful-inspection firewall with strong firewall rules, providing only required access to and from the PCI-scoped environment, is an undeniable measure that, if properly implemented, will provide assurance as a network segmentation measure. In some cases, I have seen hardened Linux deployments with IP (Internet Protocol) tables acting as firewalls, segmenting the network from the rest of the organization network.

Virtual LANs (VLANs) are a popular mechanism for network segmentation. Virtual LANs are actually different LAN segments that may be set up on a single switch. VLANs are a popular way of having multiple broadcast groups on the same switch, as opposed to having physically separate network infrastructure (switches) for different broadcast groups. This creates a segmented network where different LAN segments are typically the equivalent of multiple switched networks. One of the chief drawbacks of VLANs is that they were not created with security in mind, but mostly to isolate LANs. Therefore, VLAN-hopping attacks and ARP (Address Resolution Protocol)-spoofing attacks[*] can render VLANs compromised, as one LAN would be able to communicate with another. However, with Layer 3 switches and access-control lists, VLANs can be configured to block access from other VLANs and networks on the same Layer 3 switch.

Additionally, Cisco's VRF (virtual routing and forwarding) technology and other specific network segmentation technologies from various network component vendors can be used to segment networks.

8.2 NETWORK SECURITY REQUIREMENTS FOR PCI

8.2.1 The Network Security Documentation

The PCI-DSS has several controls that are centered on network security. We will explore all of these controls in greater depth in this chapter. However, as Charlton

Heston says in the famous film, *The Ten Commandments*, "So it shall be written. so it shall be done." Information security controls have a very similar relationship. The organization needs to document extensively all its security controls to provide (a) clarity for their employees and stakeholders as to their stance on information security and (b) procedural guidance in implementing these security practices across the organization. We will first delve into the documentation required for the organization with respect to the network security requirements of the PCI-DSS.

8.2.1.1 Requirement 1.1: Firewall and Router Configuration Standards

The first requirement of the PCI-DSS is for the entity to create firewall and router configuration standards. These standards should be implemented across the organization's PCI-scoped environment for all the network components in said environment.

The firewall and router configuration standards are meant to act as a base document that provides the network-security-management personnel in the organization with specific procedures to follow that are required for the organization to be compliant with the PCI-DSS.

8.2.1.1.1 Requirement 1.1.1: Approval and Testing Requirement

The firewall and router configuration standards have to mandate a process of approval and testing of all network connections and changes to the existing network components. The verbiage must be part of the firewall and router configuration standard or may even refer to the organization's change-management procedures that require approval before any changes are made to critical

---

[*] Such attacks have been detailed: http://rikfarrow.com/ Network/net0103.html.

infrastructure, especially like the network. I have observed several firewall configuration standards that tie into the organization-wide change-management procedures.

8.2.1.1.2 Requirement 1.1.2: Current Network Diagram

The network diagram is one of the primary ways of understanding the organization's network connectivity. The network diagram highlights internal and external connectivity. High-level network diagrams provide details of connectivity into and out of an organization, highlighting all of the specific services and areas that the organization connects to. A high-level network diagram seldom identifies endpoints and the like. The high-level network diagram identifies specific areas of connectivity like the demilitarized zone (DMZ), the server segment of the network, firewalls, IPSs, specific servers, external connectivity, and internal WAN (wide area network) connectivity (through MPLS [multiprotocol label switching] or so). Figure 8.3 is an example of a high-level network diagram.

A low-level network diagram contrasts with the high-level network diagram in terms of granularity. A low-level network diagram is one where the specific systems and their names and IP addresses are highlighted. Multiple low-level network diagrams may be required to capture the specific details of a given environment, especially in the case of organizations that have vast operations. Figure 8.4 is an example of a low-level network diagram.

From a PCI standpoint, a network diagram is more than just a typical network diagram. Imagine if a network diagram highlighted the flow of cardholder information through the network and indicated specific connectivity to sensitive information, like cardholder information. Such a diagram would be immensely helpful for an organization as well as its assessors in identifying and zeroing in on these information assets. This would behave like a powerful focus area for cardholder information. Said network diagram would behave as a diagrammatic representation of the organization's risk-management program manifested in the network. The PCI-DSS has stated that a current network diagram highlighting the flow of cardholder information into and out of the network as well as highlighting specific connectivity to cardholder information must be maintained.

I find it simple to highlight network flows of cardholder information using a network connectivity indicator of a different color. This would specifically highlight cardholder data flows into and out of the organization. Low-level network diagrams can be used to specifically highlight connectivity to cardholder information. This would likely require some kind of documented addendum to the network diagram to specify specific devices connecting to the cardholder-information repositories with business justifications for said access. Figure 8.5 is an image of a small e-commerce environment depicting the cardholder data flow in the network.

8.2.1.1.3 Requirement 1.1.3: Internet Connectivity and the Demilitarized Zone

The firewall and router-configuration standards should require a firewall at each Internet connection and in between the demilitarized zone (DMZ) and the internal network. Organizations run several external-facing components as part of their infrastructure, including Web servers, mail servers, DNS (domain name system)

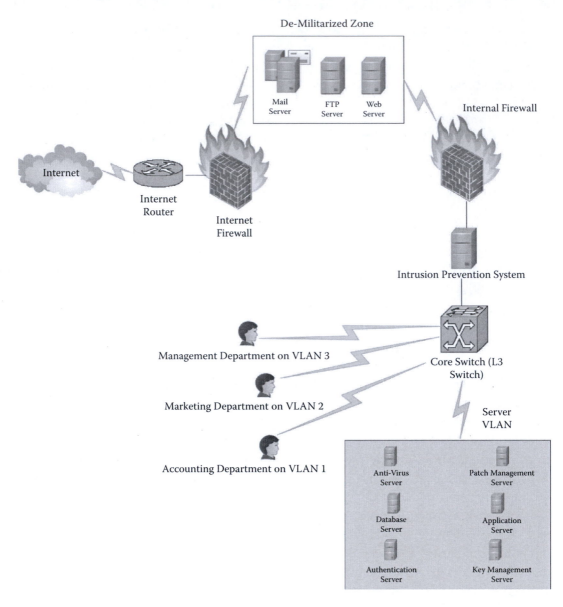

FIGURE 8.3
High-level network diagram.

servers, FTP servers, VOIP (Voice Over Internet Protocol) servers, among others. These components are subject to a great deal of traffic that emanates from outside the network. By nature, these components have to be made available externally, as their primary purpose is to communicate externally. By extension, external-facing devices are subjected to a higher risk of attacks from malware and traffic from individual attackers that are constantly attempting to penetrate the defenses of these components and compromise the internal network. Placing these servers in an internal network zone would be very dangerous, as the compromise of one of these servers would be a pivot point for compromising all the other servers in the network zone that can

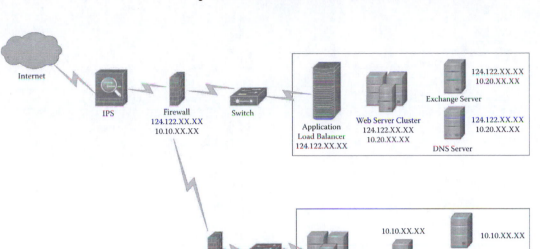

FIGURE 8.4
Low-level network diagram.

be accessed by the attacker. The DMZ is a specialized network zone that is separated from the internal network zone. The DMZ houses servers that serve as public-facing devices. As necessary, these servers communicate with the internal network zone to provide services to internal users.

The PCI-DSS requires organizations to maintain a firewall in front of their DMZ and a firewall separating their DMZ from their internal network zone. This, in essence, means that all of the Internet connectivity to and from an organization must pass through a firewall and terminate in the DMZ (for public-facing services). Additionally, there needs to be a firewall, as the DMZ connects into the internal network zone. This requirement emanates from the potential security hazard introduced by the

DMZ and highlights the need to separate the DMZ from the internal network zone.

For instance, let us imagine a scenario where an attacker has compromised a Web server of an organization. The attacker has root-level privileges on the Web server and is looking to pivot the existing access into a higher level access. In the event that the DMZ is not separated from the internal network zone, said attack can be easily perpetrated by a determined attacker. However, in the event that a firewall with well-configured access restrictions is present, then the attacker would find it difficult to compromise the rest of the internal network zone. This also highlights another requirement of the PCI-DSS, which stipulates that the internal communication to the Internet must terminate at the DMZ. This is most likely achieved with a proxy server,

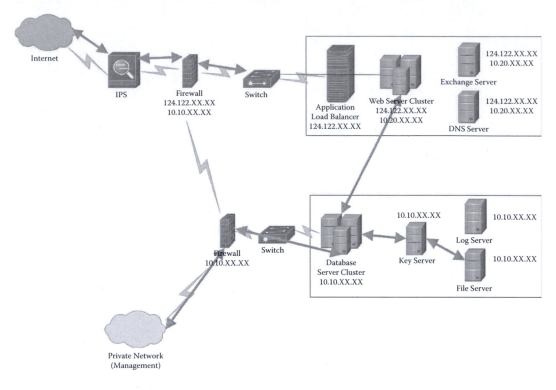

FIGURE 8.5
Network diagram highlighting cardholder-data flow in the organization.

and so on. This requirement additionally ties into Requirement 1.3.3, which specifies that all traffic from payment-card applications or from the cardholder-data environment must terminate at the DMZ and must never be allowed direct connectivity to the Internet.

8.2.1.1.4 Requirement 1.1.4: Groups Roles and Responsibilities for Network Management

In any organization, it is essential that the network be managed as a discipline. This would usually entail a hierarchy and privileges, as with any other management structure. Network management is no different. There are usually different people in the organization performing different roles in the management of network components. There may be an administrator (manager) for the network as well as a team under her that performs routine operations on the network components. PCI requires that there be specific groups, roles, and responsibilities for users managing the network and, in relation to that, these roles and privileges need to be reflected in the configuration of said network components. For instance, if a network engineer is able to make administrative-level changes to a network device, then it would be a potential violation of her privileges as well as a potential security incident. Additionally, this would also result in lack of accountability for users in management of the network.

The ideal way to achieve this requirement is to lay down an access-control list for the network-management team. This access-control list should define the role and the privilege of that user on various network components.

For instance, a network engineer may be able to effect changes of access-control lists on a router or a switch but not on a firewall or IPS. Rules may be more granular. For instance, a network engineer may only be allowed to view routing information for troubleshooting purposes, and her privileges on said network device may be highly restrictive owing to her role in the organization.

This documented "procedure" in the network-management team and network-security-management team (if both are separate) must serve as the template document for all network devices within the organization. It is also required that all network-management users be identified with unique usernames, to ensure that there is accountability, and in the event of their termination, these credentials can easily be deleted or changed.

This documented list of users and roles must be replicated on the network components themselves. Most network devices have capabilities where user roles can be defined to the most granular level possible. For instance, you can configure up to 16 privilege levels on a Cisco router, 0 being the most restrictive, to 15 being the most privileged access. Other network devices like SonicWall also provide multiple privilege levels for user access.

8.2.1.1.5 *Business Justification for Ports, Services, and Protocols*

For me, this requirement is a massive value-add for an organization's security posture. Rules or access-control lists (ACLs) for network components are a key requirement to provide security assurance in a network environment. For instance, if the organization does not want Internet users connecting onto their Web server over FTP, then they restrict access through the firewall and disable public access to port 21 or any other port that may be running the FTP service. Network components like routers, switches, and so on, are replete with such rules, and these rules are updated based on new needs and requirements of the organization. For instance, consider an organization that has recently procured a new application that communicates over port 9000. In response, the network-security-management team might have to create a firewall rule allowing traffic from specific IP addresses on port 9000.

Insertion of new entries into the rule set is a constant scenario in every organization. However, it is often seen that deletion or updating of these rules is not. Organizations rarely relook at existing rules in firewalls or other network components, thereby potentially leading to security vulnerabilities being introduced into the system. For instance, for testing or debugging, the application team of an organization might request the network-management team to open up the TFTP service from the internal network. TFTP is a highly nonsecure protocol that allows for file transfers without authentication of any kind. The application team is using TFTP only as a test requirement for a single day. The network team opens up the TFTP service on a server but does not complete the loop by closing the nonsecure protocol as soon as the application team is done testing its application. As a result of this, vulnerability has been introduced. An internal attacker identifies the open TFTP port and is able to overwrite system files or upload malware that provides the user access to the system and, potentially, access to connected systems as well. The service was not required beyond the initial business justification of the application team. However, the network-management team did not close the access as soon as the team's work was completed, thereby leading to a data breach. Although this is a fictional scenario, I have personally seen most organizations create self-inflicted vulnerability states because of improper network rule review and improper change management (which we will discuss later).

PCI requires all the services, ports, protocols, and addresses that are allowed by each network component to have a documented business justification. For instance, if the network-management team accesses the network components from IP addresses 192.168.1.4 on port 22 (SSH), then the rule has to be documented with the business justification being that the network-management team has to access the network component over SSH (secure shell) to perform routine administrative functions and operations.

I would highly recommend having a master list of documented business justifications for rules with the network-management team. This can be replicated in the remarks section of the rules for each device.

8.2.1.1.6 Biannual Firewall and Router Reviews

Firewall rules and router access-control lists (ACLs) constantly undergo change. Requirements might change from time to time because of new technology being implemented by the organization or old technology being transitioned out of the organization. New requirements might crop up from human resources, where a person or group might require higher-privilege access or access to some special ports or IP addresses. Especially in a large organization, firewall rule sets and ACLs on network devices like routers and switches undergo change. Let's imagine a scenario. The organization is

experimenting with new applications for its workflow-management operations. It has loaded multiple test apps on different virtual machines, and the applications team has requested the network-management team to open up a bunch of ports to access these apps. Over the course of the next month, the organization evaluates these applications, decides to procure a single application, and completes the procurement and deploys the application in their environment. However, the test servers with several unnecessary ports open are still running with the firewall rule also being open. If left without review, this rule will last for a very long time and potentially introduce several vulnerabilities in the network.

Firewall and network device ACLs (rules) have to be reviewed on a biannual basis to mitigate these types of vulnerabilities from being introduced in the network. When performing a review of network components, there are multiple perspectives that a reviewer has to take into account. Some tips for conducting a network device review are as follows:

- The existing configs (ACLs) have to be copied onto a working file for the review. This can be done manually or using automated scripts.
- The review is best done with a view of the latest network diagram. Both the high- and low-level network diagrams must be maintained for the review to be effective.
- Configs from previous reviews should also be available to ensure that the changes can be closely monitored from review to review.
- A reviewer can also gain insight into the effectiveness of the change-management process by randomly identifying change tickets and approvals for

about 20 percent of the rules (sample) identified during the review. This will identify the effectiveness of the change-management process for network management.

- A reviewer has to identify whether the rules are restrictive and unambiguous. The rules ideally should be restrictive on specific ports and specific IP addresses, except in cases like public-facing server components, where the IP restriction cannot be present.
- The reviewer has to identify any obvious risks introduced by certain rules in the devices. For instance, telnet access on switches and servers is a certain risk that has to be flagged in a review.
- The reviewer can also perform a simple but powerful check of the rule by diving into the logs. The reviewer can open up the device's logs and identify whether the rule has been in use or otherwise. If the rule has not been used for a considerable period of time, it is more often than not indicative of an obsolete rule, which can be removed after consulting with the business unit requiring said rule.
- The reviewer must also identify obsolete rules by asking the business unit if these rules are required for the applications that are being run in these business units. Several obsolete rules may be identified through such a process.

The review of the firewall rules and network component ACLs is an activity that has to be supplemented with documentation and evidence. During the PCI assessment, the documentation of these activities being carried out is essential for PCI compliance.

8.2.1.2 PCI Assessor's Notes: Requirement 1.1

The PCI assessor needs to pay special attention to Requirement 1.1, as it establishes the entire network security practice of an organization. The firewall configuration standard is a critical document for network security effectiveness in the organization.

Requirement 1.1 is a documentation requirement. The assessor must ensure that all the points covered in the Firewall and Network Component Configuration Standard or Hardening Guide contain the following requirements and cite specific forms and sections for reviewing when performing a technical review of the implementation of the security controls. I would pay special attention to the network diagram, as several organizations fall short on the network diagram. Outdated and obsolete network diagrams that do not reflect the current state of the network cannot be considered for the assessment.

Another area that has to be emphasized is the business justification for ACLs and rules. Organizations need to provide justification for the firewall rules and router ACLs that are in operation. The assessor has to review the configuration to understand the true ramifications of these rules.

8.2.2 Network Components: Firewalls, Routers, and Other Network Components

8.2.2.1 Firewall and Router Specifications and Configurations

8.2.2.1.1 Requirement 1.3.6: Stateful-Inspection Firewalls

A stateful-inspection firewall is a firewall that keeps track of the connection state of the network connections that are being transmitted through the firewall. These firewalls are also commonly known as deep-packet inspection firewalls. To understand stateful inspection, we need to understand some history here.

Before the advent of stateful-inspection firewalls, there were packet-filtering firewalls. These firewalls operate on the network layer (L3) and look at the header and the packet, namely, information relating to the protocol, source IP, destination IP, and source port. However, these firewalls did not keep track of the state of the connection. As part of a typical TCP three-way handshake, the client first sends a SYN packet to the recipient. The recipient responds with a SYN/ACK, and the client responds with another ACK to complete the handshake and establish the connection. Packet-filtering firewalls do not maintain the state of the network connection to identify whether the connection is established or part of an established connection. For instance, if an attacker sent ACK packets to a packet-filtering firewall, the firewall would assume that it was part of an established

connection, as a client would only typically send an ACK packet if the connection was about to be established. This caused the firewall to "leak" packets unnecessarily and cause a potential network security breach.

Stateful-inspection firewalls are different in that they maintain the connection state for each and every connection that is passing through the firewall. Only connections that are allowed as part of an established connection are permitted by the firewall. Also, the firewall performs deep packet inspection. Stateful-inspection firewalls can inspect a packet at the application layer to verify the packet being transmitted. Today, most firewalls are stateful-inspection firewalls (Figure 8.6), ranging from Linux's IP tables to Cisco ASA firewalls.

The PCI assessor must verify that the firewall actually performs stateful inspection. The PCI-DSS requires that the assessor not only verify through observation, but by technical testing, to ensure that the firewall is stateful inspection. The assessor can utilize the popular network security testing tool NMap to verify the stateful-inspection

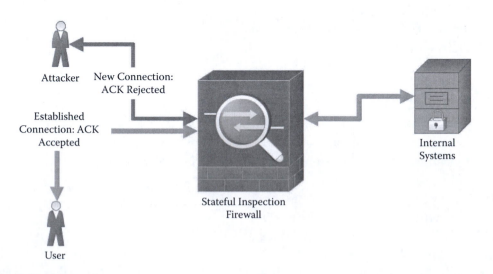

FIGURE 8.6
Stateful-inspection firewalls.

capabilities of a firewall. Some of the NMap queries for stateful inspection are as follows:

```
nmap -sA -PN <IP Address(es)>
nmap -sP -PA <IP Address(es)>
```

8.2.2.1.2 *Requirement 1.2.1: Traffic Restriction for Cardholder Environment*

Typically, firewall configurations must be written to be very specific, i.e., port-to-port and IP-to-IP rules that are specific as to the IPs that can communicate and the ports that these IPs communicate on. These are the firewall rules that restrict inbound and outbound traffic to and from the network. However, this is seldom practiced in several organizations. They adopt a very generic set of firewall rules, which may have port restrictions without specific IP restrictions, and other rules, which may have IP restrictions without port restrictions, thereby rendering several services or IP access to the cardholder environment unnecessary.

The assessor should perform a detailed review of the firewall rule base to identify rules that are generic and not restrictive. While every rule cannot be specific by mapping specific ports and IPs, the assessor must exercise discretion while reviewing the rule base. The assessor must watch out for the firewall stealth rule. This rule is usually at the top of the firewall config, which prevents the firewall from being accessed by unauthorized hosts or entities, thereby preventing the firewall from being attacked, as an unauthorized host can not even communicate with the firewall in the first place.

The assessor also needs to watch out for the cleanup rule in the firewall configuration. The cleanup rule is like a default in a programming switch-case statement. Let's examine this with an example:

```
!ftp tcp 20 & 21
access-list 122 permit tcp any host
<ftp-host> eq 20
access-list 122 permit tcp any host
<ftp-host> eq 21
!secure shell (ssh) tcp 22
access-list 122 permit tcp any host
<ftp-host> eq 22
!smtp 25
access-list 122 permit tcp any host
<email-server> eq 25
!DNS 53/53
access-list 122 permit tcp any host
<dns-server1> eq 53
access-list 122 permit udp any host
<dns-server1> eq 53
! tcp 80 http
access-list 122 permit tcp any host
<web-server> eq 80
access-list 122 permit udp any
<ntp-server> eq 123
! else deny (default anyway)
access-list 122 deny ip any any log
```

This is an example of a Cisco PIX firewall configuration for an Internet-facing firewall. Multiple rules have been configured for access to different servers in the DMZ. The final rule is the cleanup rule that essentially means that any rule from IP source or port that is not specified in the above configuration must be denied and logged. In the event that the firewall encounters traffic that has not been specified in the rules mentioned above, then the firewall will explicitly deny that traffic and log that information in the firewall logs. This serves multiple purposes. First, it adheres to the concept of defense-in-depth and provides a *deny-all* functionality that is necessary for the firewall. Second, by logging the dropped packets, network security teams can identify the kind of attack traffic or anomalous traffic that is hitting the network.

8.2.2.1.3 Requirement 1.2.2: Secure and Synchronize Router Config Files

This requirement is in conjunction with Requirement 1.1, which details firewall and router configuration standards. Routers have a startup configuration and a running configuration. Naturally, the startup configuration is one that is provided to the router at the initial deployment time. The running configuration is one where network administrators make changes to the configuration based on business requirements. For instance, if the organization has procured a new application that requires communication over port 9000, the network administrator has to provide a router ACL for a particular IP on a particular subnet on port 9000. This change occurs due to needs of the organization and not at startup. However, oftentimes, router configurations might be erroneous or, in the event of a reboot, might have to revert to the startup configuration. In such an event, it is essential that the startup configuration and the running configuration are secure and that the router does not revert to a nonsecure state after the synchronization. Most routers have automated synchronization capabilities, not only for a particular device, but across similar devices on the network as well, thereby synchronizing all running configurations to startup configurations in the event of a reboot or other business requirement.

Before deploying the router on the network, the network administrator must ensure that the startup configuration is robust and secure. Router configurations must adhere to the security best practices specified in the organization's router configuration standard. The administrator must make a copy of the startup configuration for application in the event of a reboot

or rollback of router configurations. The network administrator should ideally have "snapshots" of router configs at different points in time, thereby ensuring that the latest configuration would be applied in the event of a rollback requirement.

TFTP was a common protocol used by routers for synchronization of config files. However, TFTP is not a recommended protocol today because of its obvious vulnerabilities.[*] Routers today support secure protocols like SCP (Secure Copy Protocol),[†] and it is recommended that the network administrators utilize secure protocols for the upload/synchronization of sensitive configuration files to the router.

8.2.2.1.4 Requirement 1.3.8: Disclosure of Private IP Addresses and Routing Information

One of the most common ways to achieve this requirement is with the use of network address translation (NAT), depicted in Figure 8.7. NAT is a relatively simple concept that was actually not designed for network security, but somehow acquired status as a security practice, as it enabled obscuration of the IP addresses.

Network communications consist of the internal networks and hosts and external networks and hosts. For instance, a local area network (LAN) in an office would count as an internal network, whereas google.com as a host is a publicly available

---

[*] Trivial File Transfer Protocol (TFTP) is a protocol that is used for transfer of files (akin to FTP). However, TFTP is a highly insecure protocol, as it does not provide for authentication and authorization (access control) of any kind to transfer files to and from a system.

[†] Secure Copy Protocol (SCP) is a protocol that is based on the BSD RCP protocol. This is meant as a file transfer protocol that is built on the SSH protocol for file transfers and access control. SCP runs on port 22 by default. Currently, SCP does not have an RFC specification.

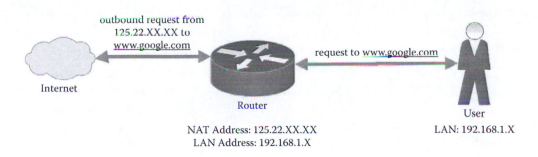

FIGURE 8.7
Network address translation.

host. The IANA (Internet Assigned Names Authority) has reserved IP addresses for the internal IP space, namely 10.X.X.X, 172.16.X.X, and 192.168.X.X. The rest of the IP addresses were reserved for public IPs. However, if internal networks were to communicate with external hosts, they required a public IP address. This was the reason for the advent of NAT.

In Figure 8.8, IP address 192.168.1.2 is connected to google.com through the router 192.168.1.1, which translates the internal IP (192.168.1.2) to a public IP address (122.166.145.111) to communicate with google.com. Google responds to 122.166.145.111, and

the router internally translates the same to the internal IP for communication.

NAT was actually created because the world was running short of IP addresses. As the Internet grew larger in size, the availability of public IP addresses grew limited for companies the world over.

Over time, NAT has morphed into port address translation (PAT). Earlier, each internal IP address required a different public IP address to communicate over the Internet. However, this was an unfeasible solution for organizations with limited public IP space. PAT is a concept where the same (set of) public IP addresses are used

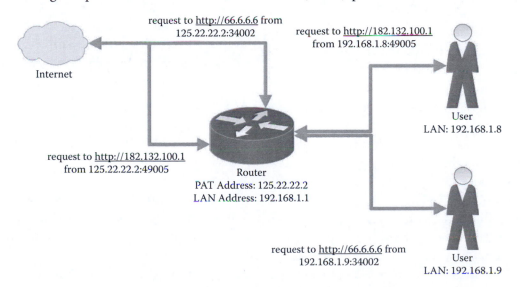

FIGURE 8.8
Port address translation.

for different internal IP addresses. However, they communicate externally over different ports. Following is an example of the PAT.

In several cases, public-facing servers like e-mail and Web have to possess a single static IP address for communication with the outside world. In such cases, they have to be configured with static NAT, where a single IP address internally is translated to a static IP address externally.

From a security standpoint, NAT/PAT provide obscuration to the internal IP space. Internal IP addresses do not directly communicate with the external world, hence identifying or enumerating these internal hosts proves to be a difficult task for a determined attacker.

PCI-DSS does not specifically mention NAT as a singular method to prevent disclosure of IP addresses. The standard also mentions that servers containing cardholder data should be behind firewalls/proxy servers.

8.2.2.1.5 Requirement 1.4: Personal Firewall for Mobile or Employee-Owned Computers

Several attacks today rely on compromising vulnerable endpoints to launch attacks against the organization. At the time of this writing, my team was working on a security test, where we were supposed to gain access to the organization's R&D Information. Our key success areas in achieving this objective were through compromising vulnerable endpoints, such as laptops, desktops, and so on, to gain access to a particular endpoint and use that access as a pivot to penetrate deeper into the organization. Personal firewalls, aka host-based firewalls, are an effective way of protecting endpoints against data breaches. Effective host-based firewalls and prevention systems (HIPS)

add an additional layer of security and prevent OS-layer attacks from executing on the system. Additionally, in the event that the OS (operating system) is not patched, an updated host-based antivirus will be able to recognize attack signatures and prevent an attack from being perpetrated against the system and, subsequently, the organization.

Recently, we were performing an internal security test against an organization. We found that several workstations in the organization's environment had not been patched in a very long time. A pernicious vulnerability called MS-08-067 rendered several Windows XP systems vulnerable to an attack, where an attacker could send crafted code and gain access to execute code remotely on the Windows system. The attacker can completely compromise the target system by exploiting this vulnerability. However, to our surprise, the antivirus application on the target systems was behaving like a host-based intrusion-prevention system, recognized the signatures of the attack, and prevented the attack from executing in memory, thus rendering the attack useless.

PCI-DSS mandates the use of personal or host-based firewall solutions to protect endpoints in the cardholder-data environment. On Windows hosts, well-configured antivirus solutions along with the Windows firewall serve as an adequate defense, and on Unix hosts, IP tables is a popular host-based firewall to prevent unauthorized access to the target hosts.

PCI also requires that the host-based firewall be configured in such a way as to prevent a user from deactivating the firewall on the host system. Several users, if given an opportunity, choose to disable their host-based firewalls or antivirus solutions to gain an edge in performance, or simply to bypass certain security controls that are offered by these applications.

8.2.3 The Demilitarized Zone (DMZ)

8.2.3.1 PCI Requirements Relating to the DMZ

8.2.3.1.1 Requirement 1.3.1: Limit Inbound Traffic to System Components

The primary role of a DMZ in a PCI environment is to ensure that systems containing cardholder information are not directly accessible over the Internet. Requirement 1.3.1 mandates that the rules at the firewall or the router only allow inbound access to systems that have a requirement to communicate on authorized ports, protocols, and services. For instance, the firewall rules must ensure that all Web traffic must be directed to a particular server in the DMZ on port 80, 443, or any other port that carries HTTP/HTTPS traffic.

Assessors have to verify this requirement and document it as part of their findings during the assessment. One of the most effective ways for an assessor to verify this requirement is to communicate with the servers from outside the scope of the firewall (where the interface is connected to the DMZ). The assessor must review all of the firewall/router/device rules and the business justification for those rules and run Nmap scans with specific ports to test and identify the veracity of the rules.

This rule can be read in conjunction with the Rule 1.3.2 that mandates that all inbound external traffic must terminate in the DMZ. The DMZ is meant as a termination point for all the public-facing services of an organization, therefore ensuring that all inbound traffic from the Internet termi-nates on the DMZ is merely an extension of this rule.

8.2.3.1.2 Requirement 1.3.3: Restrict Direct Inbound or Outbound Traffic between the Internet and the CDE

The cardholder-data environment (CDE) is meant to be highly confidential and highly secure owing to the risk of data breach that is carried with the presence of sensitive payment card information being stored, processed, or transmitted from the environment. Direct access to the CDE would result in a potential exposure of the data in question. Any inbound traffic from the Internet must terminate on the DMZ, and the information required from the CDE must be initiated by the servers in the DMZ, and outbound communication must also terminate on the DMZ. For instance, let's examine the scenario in the case of a Web application. Let's suppose that a proxy server has been placed in the DMZ for inbound and outbound Web requests. The users communicate with the proxy server, which in turn communicates with an application server, and that communicates with a database, both present in the CDE. In this case, the proxy server is initiating the request to the application server, and in several cases, security measures may have been implemented at the proxy server level, adding an additional layer of security.

8.2.3.1.3 Requirement 1.3.4: Internal Addresses Passing through the Internet to the DMZ

This requirement has been developed to protect against spoofing attacks. Attackers commonly try to masquerade as a legitimate internal IP to bypass the firewall and get unauthorized access to the network. For instance, let's assume that the attacker guesses an IP address 10.10.10.10 (internal IP Address). He decides to craft a packet to the firewall that is seemingly emanating from internal IP address 10.10.10.10. If the firewall does not perform strong filtering, the firewall assumes that it has come in from an internal IP address and would allow the packet into the network, where an attacker could potentially compromise the systems in the network with crafted attack traffic.

Network-ingress filtering prevents the occurrence of such scenarios by ensuring that traffic that is spoofed by the attacker that is seemingly emanating as internal traffic gets dropped by the firewall, as it does not adhere to the rules or ACLs of the firewall. The firewall is intelligent enough to divide the IP space into internal and external IPs, and the internal IPs trying to contact servers from outside the firewall will be blocked.

8.2.4 The Role of Managed Services

Several companies opt for managed-services providers to handle the organization's end-to-end IT management. In some cases, they might only handle specific instances of the organization's IT environment, like applications or networks. In the event that the organization is supported by a managed-services provider (MSP), the requirement to maintain a secure network applies all the same.

In the event that the MSP has deputed resources at the client's location for managing their network/IT, then the PCI assessment needs to be carried out as normal, where the assessment would be performed against the network being owned by the organization but managed by the MSP.

However, in some cases, this is not always true. On occasion, organizations outsource their entire network-management operations to an MSP, which not only manages the network, but also owns the network components. Additionally, the MSP might manage the network out of a separate network operations center (NOC). In this case, the assessment for PCI needs to be carried out on the network operations that are being owned and managed by the MSP.

With reference to network access, the MSP has to adhere to the same rules as an internal network administrator/network security team would have to manage. Business justification, firewall-configuration standards, hardening templates, and configs must be available for assessment.

8.3 SUMMARY

This chapter has focused on Requirement 1 of the PCI-DSS, which deals with building and maintaining a secure network. We began with an exploration of enterprise network security management. We then identified how we could develop a scoped network environment, where PCI controls could be applied. We identified that network segmentation was the ideal way of logically segmenting the environment based on the requirements of the PCI-DSS.

Subsequently, we delved into Requirement 1 in detail, where we began with an understanding of the documentation requirements that are present for PCI-DSS Requirement 1. Subsequently, we explored the meaning of each of the requirements under Requirement 1 of the standard and explored implementation practices for the same.

9

Requirement 2: Vendor-Supplied Defaults, System Passwords, and Security Parameters

Vendor-supplied default passwords, or default passwords by any margin, are the cause of multiple security vulnerabilities in an organization. System components like servers, network devices, etc., have default credentials and default security parameters. These default credentials are known publicly, as the component vendor publishes them along with default security parameters. These configurations are meant to be changed by an organization upon deployment. However, often these configurations are not changed, and attackers are able to execute powerful attacks against these components and, consequently, the organization and its cardholder-data environment.

In this chapter, we will discuss the PCI requirements for vendor defaults and parameters. Additionally, we will also identify PA-DSS (Payment Application Data Security Standard) requirements that deal with vendor-supplied defaults and security parameters for the payment application deployed in an organization's cardholder-data environment, part of the payment-processing life cycle.

9.1 VENDOR-SUPPLIED DEFAULT PASSWORDS

9.1.1 Configuration Standards and Vendor-Supplied Default Passwords and Security Parameters

Vendor-supplied default passwords are present for most system components by default. For instance, the default credentials for an Oracle database are *scott* and *tiger*, respectively, as username and password. For a Cisco router, it is *cisco* for both the username and the password. However, these default credentials are common knowledge. Using a simple Google search, default credentials for all of these components are identified and found.[*] During a vulnerability assessment or penetration test, we commonly look for systems with default credentials available on the network. Such devices provide instantaneous access to the component and consequently to other components in the network, thereby making it simple for an attacker to perpetrate a data breach.

Additionally, security parameters are an important measure of control for system components. For instance, in the case of the network components, which are governed with Simple Network Management Protocol (SNMP),[†] if the public and private SNMP strings are not changed from the defaults—being "public" and "private" or any other vendor-supplied default SNMP string—the attacker is able to glean useful information about the network device, thereby being able to launch more-sophisticated attacks against the system to effect a compromise. In the previous chapter, we discussed hardening and configuration standards for network devices. It is equally if not more important for organizations to harden their servers and workstations to ensure that attackers are not able to easily enumerate the system, identify vulnerabilities, and attack the system.

9.1.1.1 Requirement 2.1: Change Vendor-Supplied Default Passwords

The organization must ensure that all vendor-supplied default credentials are

changed or disabled. This is best performed by including a practice as part of a system configuration guideline or checklist and implementing the practice in real life.

An assessor needs to verify the absence of vendor-supplied defaults by actual verification of the same. The assessor needs to sample devices in the environment and attempt to log in to all of them to identify if vendor-supplied default credentials are enabled on said devices. If the results contain anomalies, then the assessor can recognize that the configuration standard and the security parameters used by the administrators of the system components is flawed.

Additionally, the assessor can review vulnerability assessment reports of previous quarters or years, where vendor-supplied defaults have been featured as a finding for the system component.

9.1.1.2 Requirement 2.2: Configuration Standards for System Components

Vendor-supplied default passwords/credentials are one aspect of security configuration for a particular system component. There are also several aspects of security configuration that an organization has to handle before deploying a server or workstation in the cardholder-data environment. Some aspects of security configuration include the following (but are not limited to):

- Identifying and disabling services that are not necessary for operation of said system component
- Identifying and disabling known non-secure services to ensure higher levels of information security

---

[*] A comprehensive, collated guide to system default credentials can be found at http://www.cirt.net/passwords.

[†] SNMP is an application-layer protocol that is used to manage network components. SNMP has public and private strings that are used to manage the network device. Using the right public string provides access to monitor and read the network device config, and the private string provides write privileges to the device.

- Restricting user-access control to privileged services in the operating system (OS)
- Identifying and disabling nonsecure or unnecessary services on virtualized hosts and virtual machine infrastructure
- Enabling security parameters, features, and functionality on said servers and workstation components to ensure that security for the components is working at an optimal level

There are several guides available from OS vendors and organizations like SANS and NIST on specific guides to secure operating systems and applications. Specific guides are released by the Center for Internet Security (CIS),* SANS (SysAdmin, Audit, Networking, and Security),† National Institute of Standards and Technology (NIST),‡ and specific vendor security guides can be followed for optimum security for these components. The organization must use these guides and standards to harden existing systems, including network components, mainframes, servers, and workstations. In some cases, a configuration image or a master set is taken by the administrator and rolled out for all the systems across the network. This makes a great deal of sense for workstations at the very least. Even for network components, configuration files can be uploaded by an administrator to form the running config for the network component. The configuration standards or hardening guides of the organization for system components should detail the following:

- Specify one primary function per server.

---

* CIS: https://benchmarks.cisecurity.org/downloads/multi form.
† SANS: http://www.sans.org/score/checklists.php.
‡ NIST: http://csrc.nist.gov/publications/PubsFL.html.

- Enable necessary protocols, services, and daemons.
- Establish system security parameters to prevent abuse.
- Remove unnecessary scripts and drivers.

9.1.1.3 Requirement 2.2.1: One Primary Function per Server

This requirement has been quite controversial within PCI-compliance circles. The organization should be implementing individual servers for services that require different security levels. Let's explore that in detail. For instance, if a Web server and database (DB) server were housed in the same server, it would be a violation of the PCI-DSS requirement, because

1. The Web server performs a different function than the DB server.
2. The DB server has a different security level than the Web server, in that it is not meant to be directly accessible to the user or required to be accessible on the same server, because the Web server and DB server have multiple security levels and different security requirements.
3. From a risk standpoint, if the security of cardholder information is influenced by the server being on the same box, then the requirement is valid. For instance, in this case, if an attacker is able to gain access to the Web application and compromise the server, he/she also gets access to the DB server, because it is on the same server. However, if the DB server is in an internal network zone, behind the firewall with restricted access, then the likelihood of attack diminishes.

This requirement, however, tends to be taken too literally. In fact, I had a client ask me once if it was alright to have an internal DNS (domain name service) and WINS* on the same server. In such cases, where the presence of a similar service with a similar security level has little bearing on the security of cardholder information, attack vectors for the same are unlikely.

The requirement also applies to virtualized hosts. If an organization is virtualizing its environment, and the services are

1. Not on the same security level,
2. Perform different functions, and
3. Influence the security of cardholder information,

then it is essential to separate the servers over different virtualized hosts. Additionally, it is essential to ensure that the virtualized hosts are subjected to similar security parameter configurations, such as

- Separate access control for the virtualized system
- Hardening of the virtual machine component
- Encryption of virtual machines containing cardholder information, apart from other PCI controls

For an assessor, the first input for verification of this requirement is the network diagram. This will provide an overview of the servers and services that are present as part of a network environment. Based on the

network diagram, the assessor has to verify the physical/virtual state of these servers based on interviews with the administrator or tests performed by the assessor to specifically identify these virtual hosts. There are several tools and reconnaissance techniques that identify the Web virtual host environment; however, that is not typically the requirement for us. We need to be able to identify hosts in virtualized environments.

9.1.1.4 Insecure Protocols and Services

Operating systems, applications, and network components oftentimes come with a set of nonsecure default services and protocols. For instance, most network devices come with a default HTTP server for configuration changes, and an HTTPS service has to be enabled by the administrator after initially logging into the application. It is important to note that organizations have to ensure that only secure protocols and services are used to access these system components. For instance, if a server administrator needs to perform routine maintenance and patching for a Unix server, then the administrator must use SSH (secure shell) to log in to the server, as opposed to Telnet, which is a nonsecure protocol. Nonsecure protocols are rampant in the management of network devices. Far too often, administrators telnet into network devices, use basic HTTP with noncomplex credentials, or use SNMPv2 or lower with no cryptographic controls. For mission-critical systems, this presents a great security risk, because credentials can be sniffed over the network, and any vulnerabilities in the implementation of the protocol might also result in compromise of said system. PCI requires that organizations mandate a more secure alternative for network protocols that are known to

---

* Windows Internet Name Service (WINS) is a name-service implementation for NetBIOS used to translate system names for computers that communicate with each other over a Windows network. It is a preferred alternative to DNS in a Windows environment and is used extensively in active directory.

be nonsecure, for instance, SSH for Telnet, HTTPS for HTTP, SCP/SFTP for FTP, SNMPv3 for SNMPv2 or lower, and so on.

However, in several cases, provisions for secure protocols cannot always be used in some environments. There may be several constraints in using secure protocols from a technical standpoint. For instance, I was working with a third-party processor (TPP) who was performing both the issuing and acquiring functions for banks. Before it achieved PCI compliance, its client banks would upload and download cardholder information over their processor's FTP server. This was obviously a highly nonsecure practice. However, as the processor moved toward PCI compliance, they set up an SFTP* server, where they were to upload and download credit card information and embossing information from the banks. Surprisingly, this move was largely resisted by its client banks. Although the move was made to achieve compliance with PCI and ensure that the security of its client (bank) information was secure, the very clients requiring this security feature resisted it. Several banks did not adopt the practice, and this was a cause for concern for the TPP. It could not make its clients forcefully adopt it. We decided to solve this problem as follows.

The banks that were agreeable to perform file transfers over SFTP were allowed to do so. Access to the SFTP server was highly restricted to specific Internet Protocols (IPs) from these banks.

For the banks that did not adopt the SFTP way of doing things, their data was encrypted into a compressed container like a ZIP file (with AES-128 bit encryption and a preshared key [password]) and stored on the FTP server, with a script for automatic deletion within 24 hours of the file being placed in the FTP server. The access to the FTP server was, again, highly restricted to specific IPs originating from these banks only. This ensured that the transmission was confidential, as the information, if not the transmission channel, was encrypted. In the event that the organization does use nonsecure protocols, the assessor must ensure that there is a documented business justification for the same with a management sign-off. Additionally, the assessor must ensure that there are controls to overcome any weakness created by the use of these insecure protocols.

9.1.1.5 Requirements 2.2.3 and 2.2.4 Security Parameters: To Prevent Misuse

System hardening is primarily about security parameters. System administrators have to ensure that nonsecure and unnecessary services are disabled before the system is deployed in a cardholder-data environment. This applies equally to test systems. Often, organizations roll out test systems for applications and products that are in testing. However, I have noticed that these test systems are seldom hardened, usually running with default credentials. While these test systems may themselves not be a great asset to the organization, compromising said systems may give an attacker access to the rest of the network, thereby creating a viable (and dangerous) entry into the organization.

The system-hardening and configuration guidelines of the organization must specify and require the system administrators to:

---

* SFTP is nothing but secure FTP, which is an extension of the SSH protocol to provide secure file transfer and secure remote file management operations.

- Disable services that are known to be nonsecure services
- Enable services and controls that are known to be secure
- Install services and applications that enhance the security of the existing system
- Define an access-control implementation that prevents regular users from disabling security services or enabling nonsecure and unnecessary services

The concept of an unnecessary service needs to be explored before we proceed. What is unnecessary? Who defines it? What if it becomes necessary? These questions are best answered by users and data owners. For a developer, running a Web server with a database server in his/her workstation is a necessary service. However, the same service for a billing clerk at a merchant establishment is definitely unnecessary, as she would not be writing any code or doing application development on her system. The organization should have defined required services or applications from a business standpoint. This requirement drives the services to be available or unavailable to the user. The business management needs to define and justify the use of applications and services, and system administrators, network administrators, etc., need to be able to implement controls based on the required services for the organization.

I was consulting with an organization recently that had deployed a new help desk ticketing system. When installed on users' desktops, this ticketing system would also automatically install an Apache Web server on the local system. When my team was performing an internal vulnerability assessment on this organization's workstations,

they found Web servers and SQLite databases running on all the systems. When we spoke to the system administrator, he was completely unaware and was quite sure that there was no possibility of a Web server being deployed on the systems. The organization ran four or five Web servers, but that had nothing to do with the users. When we reviewed our scan reports and connected to IPs over port 80, we found that they were indeed Apache Web servers that hadn't been patched. The organization had gone from four or five Web servers to running about 2000 Web servers!

There are several cases like this in the world today. System administrators must ensure that only those services required for business requirements, and those not posing a security concern, need to be deployed on the systems. Some systems running Windows OS come with a default install of Internet Information Services (IIS), which needs to be disabled for users who do not require IIS or any other Web service to run off their systems.

Assessors must verify these requirements with the following:

Interviews with SysAdmins: One of the most effective ways of verifying this requirement is by interviewing or discussing it with a SysAdmin. The assessor should read the system-hardening standards in detail and interview the administrator about how she implements the hardening controls for the cardholder-data environment. Identify any deviations from the hardening standard.

Sampling of systems: The assessor also must assess a sample of the systems to identify whether the hardening requirements have been performed

FIGURE 9.1
Lynis results of a test Mac OS X system.

against the system. In several cases, the assessor can have the system administrator run certain scripts on the sampled system to identify any security misconfiguration or weak defaults. One that comes to mind is the Microsoft Baseline Security Analyzer[*] that is provided by Microsoft to identify missing security updates and flaws in security configuration of the system. This is an effective tool, as it is provided by the company and provides a detailed analysis of the nonconformances of the system against the best practices. There are similar tools for Linux- and Unix-based operating systems like Lynis[†] and Bastille,[‡] which are particularly effective in identifying and implementing hardening best practices. Figure 9.1 is a screenshot of Lynis against a test Mac OS X system.

9.1.2 Nonconsole Administrative Access

Requirement 2.3 of the PCI-DSS deals with secure nonconsole administrative access. Network and system administrators have to constantly manage devices and system components. Changes in configuration, updates, rollback of previous configurations, and maintenance activities are among the reasons that administrators would access these components. Often, these components are enabled with nonsecure defaults. For instance, several modern firewalls come with a Web-based management console. However, the access to this console is over HTTP, which is an unencrypted protocol that can be sniffed over the network. This scenario is especially dangerous if an attacker gains access to a network administrator's credentials. The network component would be compromised, leading to a potential data breach.

PCI mandates that all nonconsole access to system components must happen with strong cryptography. Therefore, common protocols like Telnet, SNMPv2, TFTP, HTTP, etc., are considered nonsecure due to the fact that data is not

---

[*] Microsoft Baseline Security Analyzer is available at http://www.microsoft.com/en-us/download/details.aspx?id=7558.

[†] Lynis is available at http://www.rootkit.nl/projects/lynis.html.

[‡] Bastille is available at http://www.bastille-unix.org/.

cryptographically secure during transmission. Examples of secure protocols would include (but not be limited to) SSH, SCP, SNMPv3, HTTPS, or over a VPN (virtual private network) connection.

The other interesting concept is *strong cryptography*. We will discuss strong cryptography, both from the point of view of data in transit and data at rest, in the upcoming chapters. For now, understand that nonconsole access to system components in the cardholder-data environment must always happen with encryption.

From an assessor's standpoint, there are multiple ways in which this requirement can be verified. The assessor may observe an administrator logging into the system component. If the administrator logs into the application over a secure protocol like SSH or HTTPS, it is highly likely that the administrator would be using encrypted channels to communicate with the system component.

Another way of verifying this requirement is by inspecting the configurations of the system component. For instance, in a firewall configuration, if Telnet access to the firewall is enabled, it can be assumed that the administrators use Telnet to access and manage the firewall. In certain cases, if SNMPv2 or lower is enabled with default community strings, then it can be assumed that the network administration team has not hardened the device and is utilizing nonsecure protocols to manage the device.

Another way of verifying this requirement is to run a network sniffer specifically looking for traffic emanating from the network administrator's host on the network. This can be achieved by connecting

to a SPAN[*] port that might have been set up by the network administration of an organization.

9.1.3 Wireless Security Consideration: Vendor-Supplied Defaults

Wireless security has always been a potential red flag in view of the creators of the PCI-DSS, and rightfully so. There have been several successful attacks against wireless networks, which has proved to the world that wireless networks still have to mature a great deal with reference to security. Additionally, the fact the one of the world's largest data breaches[†] was through a nonsecure wireless access point does not make a very good case for wireless networks.

Nevertheless, wireless networks are popular all over the world today, and they are heavily in use, especially in merchant establishments where they might have wireless billing machines and storefront systems that might run off wireless networks. In such cases, Requirement 2.1.1 of the standard is applicable to any environment with wireless networks.

It must be noted that when PCI-DSS makes a reference to wireless, it also encompasses Bluetooth (802.15) networks. There are several billing systems and handheld commercial devices that use Bluetooth to

---

[*] SPAN (switch port analyzer) is a term used to describe the practice of port mirroring on a network switch. Port mirroring is an implementation where all packets on the network switch are copied onto a single SPAN port on the network. This is used for traffic monitoring, intrusion detection, and so on. The term SPAN is a term coined by Cisco, but it is used commonly to refer to the implementation of port mirroring.

[†] The T.J. Maxx data breach was perpetrated through a wireless access point at a single store.

communicate with a back end machine. This is, again, largely used in merchant organizations.

At this point, I would like to make a suggestion that if the wireless network is not required for an organization in its cardholder-data environment, it is prudent that it be removed. It is a helpful way of lowering the attack surface.

Requirement 2.1.1 of the standard specifies that the requirement for vendor-supplied default passwords and security parameters must be followed for wireless access points as well. They include the following:

- Wireless access points must have their SNMP community strings for both public and private changed before being deployed. It must be ensured that if SNMP is required for the network, then SNMPv3 should be utilized, but if it isn't, then SNMP should be disabled on the wireless access point.
- Wireless access points should have encrypted access over WPA2 Personal. While WPA-Enterprise is preferred, a minimum security requirement of WPA2 is a mandate. The preshared key (PSK) that is used to authenticate to the network and encrypt communications over the network must be a minimum of 13 characters in length and must be complex, preferably with alphanumeric and special characters. It is recommended that the AES mode be used for encryption.
- The default administrative password must be changed for the wireless access point. The default password must be a

minimum of seven characters and be an alphanumeric password.
- The firmware on the wireless access point needs to be upgraded to the latest based on the release cycle of the vendor.
- Additionally, other security measures that may be taken by the entity to protect wireless networks (802.11) are to:
  - Create SSID names that cannot be easily understood. For instance, an SSID* called "WAP-Richmond-Sector1" would be easily understood that a merchant's wireless network at their Richmond store in Sector 1 is in use. As opposed to this, an SSID called "FSRICS1" would be less comprehendible to an attacker.
  - Disable unnecessary protocols and services, such as Telnet, TFTP, and, if required, SNMP.
  - Ensure that the administration of the wireless access point happens over an encrypted transmission line. Most wireless access points come with an HTTPS connectivity or SSH connectivity. This ties into Requirement 2.3 of the PCI-DSS
- Another dimension of security of wireless communication relates to Bluetooth (802.15) networks. Certain security requirements that are to be kept in mind for securing Bluetooth networks are as follows:
  - The PINs for the Bluetooth network are to be long and random. The size of a Bluetooth PIN is anywhere can be 1–16 bytes in

---

* SSID is an abbreviation for service set identifier.

size (8–128 bits). However, most of the Bluetooth PINS are four characters.

- All devices utilizing Bluetooth must have mutual authentication.
- Encryption standards for Bluetooth should be set to the maximum possible.
- Pairing should be performed occasionally. Pairing must be done in a secure area that is unlikely to have attackers, including areas where attackers can observe passkey entry over the shoulder.
- Users should never respond to PIN requests unless they has been initiated by the user from one of the user's other devices.
- Bluetooth Security Modes 3 and 4 should be utilized. These modes ensure that security procedures are in place before the physical link is established. Mode 4 utilizes the Elliptic Curve Diffie Hellman key exchange algorithm, replacing key agreement for link key generation. Modes 1 and 2 are nonsecure and subject to man-in-the-middle attacks.
- All Bluetooth profiles except the serial port profile must be disabled at all times.
- Users should not initiate or transmit messages from unknown or suspicious devices. For instance, in some stores, Bluetooth connections are automatically requested and users connect to them without knowing the device they are connected to.

9.2 PA-DSS: APPLICATION REQUIREMENTS FOR VENDOR-SUPPLIED DEFAULTS AND SECURITY PARAMETERS

9.2.1 Payment Application Vendor-Supplied Defaults

Commercial payment applications that are deployed in a PCI environment have to ensure that the applicable PCI requirements are to be adhered to as well. This will ensure that companies deploying these applications in a production environment as part of their payment-processing life cycle will not run counter to or be noncompliant with the PCI requirements.

9.2.1.1 Requirement 3.1b of the PA-DSS

Requirement 3.1b of the PA-DSS mandates that the payment application should not require the use of default usernames and passwords on third-party software components. For instance, let us assume that a point-of sale (POS) application only connects to an Oracle database over default Oracle credentials like *scott* and *tiger* for username and password, respectively. Then the application would ensure that the environment would be forcibly vulnerable because of a design flaw in the application (of having to use the default credentials on the third-party component). Additionally, the payment application should not be using the default credentials of third-party software components.

9.2.1.2 Requirement 5.1.3 of the PA-DSS

In the event that the payment application has default usernames and password credentials or default credentials that are used during testing or debugging, it must be ensured that the default usernames and credentials are removed from the application before being shipped to customers. Additionally, if the application requires the use of default usernames and password credentials, then the application must initiate a forced change of credentials by the administrator upon completion of the installation and must also remove the default credentials from the application.

9.2.2 Secure Network Implementation: Payment Applications

9.2.2.1 Requirement 5.4 of the PA-DSS

In line with Requirement 2.2.2 of the PCI-DSS, the payment application must ensure that it uses only secure protocols to communicate, and these protocols and services must be activated as a default feature of the application "out of the box." For instance, in cases where the application provides for an interface over HTTP, then the default implementation must be over HTTPS. This requirement extends to all the components and hardware specified and used by the payment applications. These components should only be used if necessary for the application to function effectively, and the communication protocols and services should also be enabled only as necessary.

In the event that the payment application supports nonsecure protocols like Telnet, FTP, and so on, it must be ensured that secure implementations of said protocols is enabled by default for the payment application. For instance, if an application allows access over Telnet, HTTP, HTTPS, and SSH, the default implementation should enable HTTPS and SSH out of the box and not to nonsecure defaults like HTTP and Telnet.

The documentation of the protocols, services, and components used must be documented in the PA-DSS implementation guide, including the details such as secure defaults, etc.

9.2.2.2 Requirement 8.1 of the PA-DSS

One of the essential requirements of the PA-DSS for successful implementation of a commercial payment application into a PCI-compliant environment is that the application must not interfere with the PCI-DSS security requirements of the components in the environment. For instance, the application should not disallow the application of patches in the environment. Several applications are only designed to work on specific operating systems at specific service-pack/patch levels, and any change of patches or service packs would render these applications unusable. I have seen several POS applications that run only on Windows XP SP1 unpatched. This presents a serious problem with regard to the PCI-DSS and the security of the organization and its data at large. An unpatched system is open (and extremely inviting) to an attack, and the presence of an application that can only run in an unpatched system is a serious flaw on the part of the application's developers and implementers. Similarly, some outdated applications may not function unless the antivirus software is turned off, which obviously increases the access for an attacker.

I have also come across applications that interfere with firewall configurations that require several nonsecure services to be open. Several applications also "jump ports," where imposing such firewall rules would render the application unusable. These applications, among others that run counter to PCI-DSS requirements, cannot be allowed for a PA-DSS–validated commercial payment application.

9.2.2.3 Requirement 6 of the PA-DSS: Wireless Security Requirements

The PA-DSS requirements specify that the assessor should verify in the test environment that wireless security practices are deployed for applications that use wireless products in the payment-processing cycle. The wireless security requirements are the ones mentioned in Section 9.1.5 of this chapter. In the event that the application is bundled with wireless hardware, the application developer has to ensure that the hardware supports the highest levels of wireless encryption, namely WPA2 Personal or Enterprise, given the requirement of the organization. The wireless security practices have to be documented in the PA-DSS Implementation Guide of the Commercial Payment Application.

9.3 SUMMARY

The focus of this chapter was on Requirement 2 of the PCI-DSS. This requirement specifies the treatment for vendor-supplied default credentials and security parameters for system components in the cardholder-data environment (CDE). One of the first and most important aspects of this requirement is to maintain a System Hardening and Configuration Guide that drives the implementation of these requirements across the CDE. The rule of thumb is to disable/delete vendor-supplied default credentials, as they are widely known and are vulnerable to an attacker, who can use default credentials to compromise the system and, potentially, the entire environment. The other aspect of Requirement 2 is to harden existing systems against the use of nonsecure and unnecessary services. Nonsecure protocols include FTP, Telnet, and so on. These must be replaced with secure protocols like SSH, SFTP, SCP, and so on. Operating systems and network components need to be hardened based on best practices provided by institutions like SANS, CIS, NIST, and so on. The requirement also delves into wireless security practices, including hardening of wireless access points that are used in the cardholder-data environment. Wireless security practices include practices for both 802.11 (WiFi) as well as 802.15 (Bluetooth) networks, for which security practices differ—but both share a common objective from the point of view of the PCI-DSS. Finally, we detailed some of the requirements from the PA-DSS applying to commercial payment applications that are to be followed for applications with reference to vendor-supplied default credentials, network protocols and hardening, as well as wireless security practices.

10

Requirement 3: Protect Stored Cardholder Data

Requirement 3 is the crux of the PCI-DSS. It deals with the storage of cardholder information. For organizations that handle cardholder information extensively, like merchants, processors, and banks, this is a challenging requirement that must be adhered to, with detailed and meticulous implementation. In this chapter, we will explore this requirement in detail. The chapter initially focuses on the motivation to store cardholder information, with special emphasis on the fact that there may be several unnecessary touch points for cardholder information storage. Subsequently, we explore the security requirements of the standard relating to cardholder information storage and display. We also discuss specific implementations, such as cryptography for cardholder information storage, and identify the specific security requirements when implementing said solutions in an organization. This chapter provides several examples and anecdotes that provide a great deal of insight into Requirement 3. Finally, we close with the PA-DSS requirements for storage of cardholder information by applications. This is tightly bound to the PCI-DSS requirements for storage of cardholder information.

10.1 STORAGE, RETENTION, AND DESTRUCTION OF STORED CARDHOLDER DATA

10.1.1 Do You Really Need to Store Cardholder Data?

Before getting any further into this chapter, there is a question that I would like to revisit, only because of its sheer importance to the overall PCI-DSS and specifically to Requirement 3. That question is, "Do you really need to store cardholder information?" This question does not apply to the overall need to store cardholder data; rather, it refers to the practice of storing cardholder data in locations that are unnecessary.

At the time of this writing, I am performing an application security code review project for one of the largest card processors in the world. It has a customer-facing Web application that its customers can access to get info on balances, payments, and so on. As an issuing processor, it is storing cardholder information in several areas. However, one of the key areas that came up as a possible red flag was the storage of cardholder information in log files. Its application has been developed to log all sensitive cardholder information, including the PAN (primary account number), expiration date, and so on. One of the first questions I asked the developers was, "Do you really need to be logging cardholder information to the log files?" The response to that was, "Not really sure, it's just for troubleshooting and debugging. Maybe we can stop logging the PAN." In this case, the cardholder data was being logged as a debug log to the back-end log server. This was unnecessary; moreover, it was also potentially nonsecure simply because log systems may not be secured with the same technical rigor as servers and other production systems.

This is one of several instances where organizations should look at reducing their cardholder information storage only to information that is absolutely required. We also discussed in Chapter 7 how an organization can potentially take systems out of scope by reducing the number of touch points for cardholder information storage in their environment. This must be done as part of framing the scope for the PCI compliance and framing the boundaries for the cardholder data environment.

10.1.2 Policies and Procedures around Storage of Cardholder Data

Requirement 3.1 of the PCI-DSS requires that data retention and destruction policies and procedures of the organization be in place for the protection of cardholder information.

10.2 REQUIREMENT 3.2: SENSITIVE AUTHENTICATION DATA AT REST

A major concern for the payment card industry is the security over sensitive authentication data. Sensitive authentication data refers to the CVV/CVC/CAV, CVV2, CVC2, CAV2, PIN, PIN block, and full track data of the card. The primary reason for concern is that these details can be used to completely duplicate the card and perform card transactions, both CP and CNP. One of the basic requirements for the PCI-DSS is that sensitive authentication data should *never* be stored by an entity. Requirement 3.2 specifically describes the nature of the prohibition for entities against storage of sensitive authentication data.

Before we delve into Requirement 3, let's review the flow of sensitive authentication data and its purpose in the card transaction process. For instance, a shopper goes to an electronics store, buys a TV, and pays for it with his card. The cashier swipes the customer's card on the terminal and enters the amount, and that commences the process. The customer's information, namely the track data, traverses through the payment channel and finally reaches the issuer, where the track data has to be authenticated and subsequently authorized before the transaction is accepted or declined in the event of a failure of the authentication and authorization process.

10.2.1 Authentication Parameters: Concept Overview

Card transactions (either debit or credit) must be authenticated and authorized before the approval of the payment. These authentication parameters form the key components of sensitive authentication data. Let us explore these concepts and their authentication techniques for a better understanding of sensitive authentication data

- CVV/CVC/CAV1&2
- PVV/PIN Offset
- PIN/PIN Block

10.2.1.1 CVV/CVC/CAV1&2

The card verification value (CVV) is referred to as the card verification code (CVC) by MasterCard and the card authentication value (CAV) by other companies. However, its objective is the same. The CVV is used as an authentication parameter for credit card transactions the world over. There are two CVVs in the card. One is the CVV that is embedded into the magnetic stripe track, invisible to the eye. This passes through as part of the payment-processing cycle to be authenticated by an issuer/issuer processor and get authorized or declined as the case may be. The CVV2 is used for CNP transactions like e-commerce and IVR (interactive voice response), where the card is not present (CNP). The CVV2 is entered along with the other cardholder data fields. Upon successful authentication, the transaction is authorized.

The CVV/CVC is authorized by an issuer with a generated CVV. Let's assume that the CVV is sent over a network for a CP (card present) transaction that a cardholder has physically performed at a merchant location. At the issuer's end, when the transaction is received, the CVV/CVC is calculated on the fly. The PAN, expiration date, and service code of the cardholder are encrypted with a DES algorithm using two data-encrypting keys or two MAC keys, where a 1–5-byte value is generated. The CVV is generated using this method and then compared with the CVV/CVC sent by the transaction and, if they match, the transaction is authenticated.

This method is usually supported by the hardware security modules deployed by issuers, as it involves key management and the generation of multiple values based on certain algorithms. This effectively ensures that the CVV/CVC values (both 1 and 2) do not have to be stored by an issuer/issuer processor.

10.2.1.2 PIN Verification Value (PVV) and PIN Offset

The PIN verification value (PVV) is a four-character numerical value that is encoded in the magnetic stripe of the card. The PVV is a cryptographic signature of the card along with other information. When a user enters his/her PIN on an ATM terminal or in a POS (point of sale) environment, the PVV is sent over the network to the issuer. The issuer generates a PVV on the fly and verifies the authenticity by comparing the two PVVs (generated and transmitted); if they are the same, the card is authentic.

The PVV is a Visa method to authenticate the PIN value provided by the cardholder. The verification algorithm of the PVV is based on the following: The first parameter required by the PVV for the verification algorithm is a 64-bit Transformed Security Parameter (TSP). The TSP is derived from the leftmost 11 characters of the PAN, a key selection value, and the PIN to form the TSP. For instance, if the PAN is 1234 5678 9012 3456 and the PIN verification key indicator (PVKI) is 1 (single-digit value encoded on the card) and the PIN is 2345, then the TSP would be 5678901234512345. This TSP is enciphered multiple times with the PVV generation key, and the PVV is derived from this process.

The PIN offset is also called the IBM 3624 PIN algorithm. The PIN offset is the difference between the generated PIN by the issuing bank and the PIN chosen by the cardholder. The offset is identified by subtracting the generated PIN from the customer-selected PIN using mod10.

The PIN is verified with a process wherein the PIN is derived using an encoded (padded) PAN value, which is encrypted multiple times using a triple DES algorithm with a PIN verification key. The leftmost digits of the resulting value are added with a mod10 to the offset value, and the customer-entered PIN is derived from this. If the derived PIN and the customer-entered PIN are the same, the transaction is said to be authentic.

Although the PVV is a Visa-created PIN generation and verification scheme, it is followed by other payment brands as well and is known to be more popular than the IBM 3624 practice, which is older in comparison and has been attacked successfully, for example the decimalization table attacks in 2002 and 2003.

10.2.1.3 PIN/PIN Block

When the cardholder enters his/her PIN on an ATM or at a POS location, the PIN is first encoded in the machine as a PIN block value. The PIN block consists of the PIN as well as a portion of the PAN. This is in plaintext. Subsequently, this block is encrypted using algorithms like DES and triple DES, based on the format, and transmitted over the network.

There are multiple standards and formats that are used to generate a PIN block, including ANSI, ISO, IBM, and VISA formats that differ based on the verification methods and the parameters used by these verification methods to authenticate the card and, subsequently, authorize the transaction.

10.2.2 Authentication Parameters

Authentication parameters are critical for an issuer to successfully validate a transaction. Similar to the user authentication process, the PAN acts as the identification parameter (like username), and the CVV/PIN acts as the authentication parameter. Only upon successful validation of the authentication parameter, and the adherence to authorization rules by the issuer, does a transaction successfully validate.

The CVV2/CVC2, as it is popularly called, is also a parameter for authentication, very much like the CVV in the magnetic stripe or the smart chip in the card. However, CVV2 is printed on the back of the card and is used largely in CNP transactions, where the user cannot view the CVV1. It must be noted that the CVV2 and the CVV(1) are not the same value.

For debit cards, the authentication parameter is known as a PIN. The PIN is usually a four-digit number that the customer enters at an ATM before performing actions like "balance verification" and "cash withdrawal" from the bank. Debit cards are widely used for POS and CNP transactions as well.

Apart from these common authentication parameters, certain networks such as American Express utilize an additional authentication measure called the address verification service (AVS), where the billing address of the card provided by the cardholder in a CNP transaction is matched against the billing address registered against the cardholder's file on the issuer's system. If the addresses match, the transaction is successfully authenticated.

With reference to the PCI-DSS, it is imperative to understand that all these authentication measures, with the exception of the AVS, are termed as *sensitive authentication data*.

10.2.3 Issuers and Storage of Sensitive Authentication Data

Issuers face certain challenges with the storage of sensitive authentication data. One of the most important challenges is that of legacy applications. Several issuers utilize payment applications (switching applications) that store the PIN/CVV/CVV2 as part of the cardholder's file. The transaction is authenticated and authorized by comparing the CVV sent as part of the transaction with the one that is in the card file of the cardholder. As you can see, this process requires the storage of the cardholder's CVV and CVV2, thereby going against the requirement of the PCI-DSS. Earlier versions of the PCI-DSS required any organization to not store sensitive authentication data post authorization, i.e., once the transaction was

authorized by the issuer and executed, the sensitive authentication, including CVV/PIN/track, could not be stored under any circumstance, even encrypted by any of the entities involved in the transaction. However, in PCI v 2.0, issuers with a valid business justification may store sensitive authentication data. Additionally, the standard requires that said data be stored with same level of protection as provided to the PAN.

As mentioned previously, several issuers have technical and business constraints with reference to the storage of sensitive authentication data, the principal one being legacy software. However, modern payment applications—especially ones in switching—perform authentication in a different way. For credit cards, the hardware security module of the issuer generates a CVV on the fly as the transaction hits the issuer. The CVV generated is compared with the CVV sent as part of the transaction. If the two values match, the transaction is authenticated. With reference to debit cards, modern card-management systems store the PIN offset. The PIN offset is the difference between the original PIN that is generated by the system for the card and the PIN chosen by the cardholder. The PIN offset is generated by a hardware security module (HSM) and stored in the database along with the cardholder data.

However, for issuers who are constrained from storage of the sensitive authentication data like the CVV and PIN, it must be ensured that the justification is documented and signed off by management. Additionally, it is essential that said data be protected on the same lines as the protection of the PAN in storage. Protection measures include:

- Encryption/tokenization
- Access control based on roles and job requirement
- Logging access to said data on the lines of the logging requirements for the PCI-DSS

10.2.4 Requirement 3.2: Assessment Notes

For an assessor who is assessing an issuer environment, it is imperative that extreme caution be taken while assessing Requirement 3.2. The issuer has to first understand the payment infrastructure being used to process the cardholder data. The payment switch or processing application is a critical aspect of this requirement. Oftentimes, the payment switch would not allow the entity to prohibit the storage of sensitive authentication data. I have also come across issuers or issuer processors who are in the process of migrating from one payment switch to another, where cardholder data from their previous switch are still present. Even if their newer switch allows for generation of the CVV or authentication based on PIN offset, the details stored in the older payment switch would not allow them to be fully compliant with the requirement until they have transitioned all their existing accounts to the new payment switch.

The assessor may sometimes be faced with a unique challenge where the organization might have the capability not to store the sensitive authentication data, but they may be storing for reasons of convenience rather than a legitimate business justification. In such cases, the assessor must explain the benefits of adhering to the original requirement and stand firm on the stance that he/she has taken. Change is never handled easily by an organization, and it holds true for this as well.

10.3 DISPLAY OF THE CARD PAN

Another key PCI-DSS control is the masking of the PAN wherever displayed. The PAN is considered cardholder data by the standard, and it has to be protected wherever it is stored, processed, displayed, and transmitted. With reference to display, the PCI-DSS requires the PAN to be masked wherever displayed, except in areas where there is a valid business justification for employees and other third parties to view the entire PAN. The PAN may be displayed in several areas across the organization, especially in the case of merchants.

Merchants have POS terminals, card-processing terminals and machines, and e-commerce software, and the PAN is used heavily for settlement and back-office processing. There are several areas where masking must be implemented, for instance in the case of POS receipts or card-terminal charge slips, the PAN must be masked. However, in some cases, it is not possible to mask the PAN, especially in the case of mail-order transactions or customer service scenarios where the PAN is provided by the customer and employees need to see the PAN in order to successfully process the transaction or the query, as the case may be. For instance, issuing processors need to have access to the full PAN in order to process a request on behalf of the cardholder. In several cases, customer service representatives for banks and other issuing entities need to have the customer's PAN in order to process requests for the customer. I have seen that personnel performing card settlement operations on the acquiring and issuing side prefer having the full PAN, as a truncated PAN might lead to more confusion.

However, even if the PAN must be masked, the PCI requirement states that a maximum of the first six and last four digits may be displayed to be compliant with the requirement. This has become a standard practice now, where most POS terminals, applications, card terminals, and applications mask the PAN except for the first six and last four digits. The first six digits form the BIN of the card, which is also known as the issuer identification number.

10.4 REQUIREMENT 3.4: RENDERING THE PAN UNREADABLE WHEREVER STORED

10.4.1 An Overview of Techniques to Render the PAN Unreadable

The PCI-DSS (and the PA-DSS) has mentioned a few techniques to render cardholder data unreadable when stored. The choice of these techniques is highly dependent on the need for cardholder information management in the organization. For instance, an acquiring processor may not require cardholder information to be stored, as much as a merchant might require. The techniques mentioned by the SSC in the standard are as follows:

- Use of strong cryptography to protect stored PANs
- Use of one-way hashing algorithms to protect stored PANs
- Use of truncation to render PAN unreadable
- Use of index tokens and pads

10.4.1.1 Use of One-Way Hashing

One-way hashing, as the name suggests, is a one-way process. It is irreversible. The plaintext is passed through a hashing algorithm to provide a fixed-length string that is cryptographically secure. For instance, the word *PCI-DSS* produces an MD5 hash value of a60ee1ea2069e8f8568e4de0cff9476b. Obviously one cannot identify the plaintext value from the hash value generated here. However, with one-way hashing, the hash value also cannot be regenerated to form the string *PCI-DSS* once again. One-way hash functions are largely used when the original (plaintext) data does not have to be regenerated but does have to be compared with another value. It is popularly used for storage of passwords. When a user registers into a system, he/she generates a password. Most likely, this password is passed through a one-way hash function and is stored in a database. Every time a user logs into the system, the system performs the one-way hash against the user-supplied password and matches it with the one in the database. If the hash values match, the user is identified as an authenticated user and is granted access to the system.

Hashing is also widely used for message verification. For instance, if I change the string *PCI-DSS* to the value *PCIDSS*, the value of the MD5 hash also correspondingly changes to 8991ef43ed4c61f79b-336f4870cf0046, thereby ensuring that even a perceivably small change to the text or to a file would result in a change of the hash value generated. This is a very useful feature for message verification or file verification. One can identify whether the integrity of said data is maintained during a transmission or otherwise. The hash values can be compared and, in the event of a change of hash values, it can be assumed that the integrity of the transmission was affected. Figure 10.1 is an example of how one-way hashing works.

10.4.1.2 One-Way Hashing Algorithms and Security Considerations

When considering a one-way hashing function for cardholder data, it is essential to consider the following:

- Strength and complexity
- Salt (and pepper)

A one-way hash function (algorithm) should provide a cryptographically secure random string as an output. However, hashing functions may be subject to preimage attacks or collision attacks. A preimage attack is an attack where the attacker possesses the hash h and would like to generate the message m from the hash h, where h is essentially the hash(m). Preimage attacks have been successfully attempted against hashing algorithms like MD5 and SHA-1.

A collision attack is one where the attacker attempts to find the message by attempting to replicate the same hash value of the message m. For instance, if an attacker generates two identical messages $m1$ and $m2$ by replicating the hash($m1$) and hash($m2$), the hashes would have collided, and the message of the original hash would be known to the attacker. Collision

attacks have been widely attempted against popular hashing algorithms like MD5 and SHA-1. MD5 has been badly broken with collision attacks. For example, in the year 2000, security researchers were able to generate false X.509 certificates with collision MD5 hash values. It is widely known that MD5 and SHA-1 are both broken algorithms. In fact, as recently as 2012, the Flame malware targeting Microsoft systems used MD5 collisions to replicate Windows code signing certificates.

From a PCI-DSS standpoint, the strength of the hashing algorithm is very important and highly pertinent as a security consideration. For instance, if an attacker compromises an application, gains access to the application database, and finds that PANs are hashed with MD5 hashes, it is only a matter of a short time before the attacker can crack the entire set of PAN hashes and gain access to the plaintext PANs.

Enterprises today are largely in a state of flux with reference to the hashing practice of PANs. It is mostly because the two most popular hashing algorithms, namely MD5 and SHA-1, are broken. These algorithms have been the most popular hashing algorithms in recent times, and the fact that they have been broken causes a great deal of concern to any organization that is hashing sensitive information with these algorithms. I would certainly *not* recommend using MD5 and SHA-1 for hashing PANs.

Another important security consideration for one-way hashes is the concept of a *salt*. A salt, in the case of a hash value, is very different from its culinary implementation. A salt or a nonce is meant to add greater complexity to the hash value. The reason for a salt to be included is to prevent similar hash values from existing in the system. For instance, let's assume that

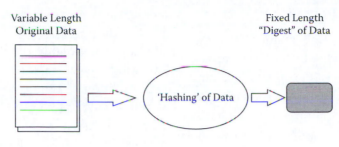

Variable Length
Original Data

Fixed Length
"Digest" of Data

'Hashing' of Data

FIGURE 10.1
One-way hashing process.

Bob has a password "password" (not a very strong password, but a password nevertheless) to authenticate to an application. Alice has the same password to authenticate to the same application. Both the passwords are "password." In the event that the organization is using MD5 to hash passwords, the hash value of Bob's password would be 5f4dcc3b5aa765d61d8327deb882cf99, and Alice's password hash would be 5f4dcc3b5aa765d61d8327deb882cf99 as well. Given enough users having similar passwords, an attacker would be able to enumerate the hash values and guess the plaintext values based on the hash. However, a salt or a nonce is a value that adds another parameter in the hashing process, along with the plaintext and the hashing algorithm, to provide a hash value that is different from the value generated when the same value is passed through a hashing algorithm.

I have used OpenSSL libraries to generate multiple hash values from the same initial plaintext value. I have also utilized a different eight-character salt for each hashing process. The differences are quite self-explanatory.

```
openssl passwd -1 -salt 19z6NXvp
password
$1$19z6NXvp$42LeLrgNC8E5r59DNFhSM0
openssl passwd -1 -salt 20x5MZwq
password
$1$20x5MZwq$I9EX7VaUXoiDXnx84Yp1J.
```

```
openssl passwd -1 -salt rAjTvKuL
password
$1$rAjTvKuL$QOIMsLvmDdJdPttAUHgTE0
```

In this example, you can see that I am using OpenSSL to generate a password hash of a given password, which in this case is the value *password*. The given salt is the eight characters following the option −*salt*. You can see that the hash values generated are quite different from each other, even though the plaintext value is the same.

The salt may be stored with the hash value and by itself is not sensitive. It is simply used to add complexity and randomness to the hash value generated from the plaintext and the hashing algorithm.

PCI-DSS and PA-DSS do not require a hash value of a PAN to be salted. However, in the interest of higher levels of security and subject to the perception of risk to an organization, salting of hashes is definitely a good practice to follow.

For an assessor, it is imperative to identify all the cardholder data touch points where hashing of the PAN is being performed. The assessor has to identify the hashing algorithm being used as well as the complexity of the hashing process (with salt or otherwise). I would really urge assessors to identify cases where nonsecure hashing algorithms like MD5 and SHA-1 are being used.

10.4.1.3 Use of Truncation

Truncation is, in my opinion, the most effective way to render the PAN unreadable. Truncation is the practice of stripping away characters in the PAN to replace them with null characters or characters that would render cardholder information unreadable. For instance, a PAN bearing 4147XXXXXXXX4107 renders the card information completely unreadable. Indeed, one might have difficulty even identifying that the truncated number is in fact a card number. Truncation is a practice that is heavily utilized at point-of-sale (POS) environments at merchant locations where the cashier swipes the card number or reads the card number with a reader and the PAN is truncated on screen. This practice is carried over to the charge slips, where the PAN is also truncated. This practice is popular with ATMs as well, where the PAN on their slips is truncated for purposes of security.

Truncation is also quite an effective practice when the PAN has to be seen to an extent, but not completely. Truncation is utilized heavily by processors who do not have to see the complete PAN, but prefer having evidence of transactions being performed. For instance, in the case of acquiring processors, storing a truncated PAN as part of their transaction processing activity is quite an effective process and ensures that there is evidence of the transaction, without the concomitant card details being displayed or stored in full.

We will deal with truncation as a measure of display control a little later in this chapter. However, it must be noted that when the PAN is stored in a truncated manner, it should ideally not be regenerated as a complete PAN. For instance, if a company truncates the card number during

storage and encrypts some digits of the PAN excluding the first six and last four digits, it is not highly effective, as the PAN can still be regenerated using a decryption key. Additionally, the truncated PAN and the hash value of the PAN should not be correlated. In the event that an attacker is able to obtain a hash value of the PAN and the truncated value of the PAN, it becomes quite simple for the attacker to be able to use brute-force against the other characters of the truncated PAN to obtain the complete PAN.

Requirement 3.6 of the PCI-DSS mentions that the first six digits and the last four digits of the PAN may be displayed, and the rest of the PAN is to be truncated. The requirement may be utilized for truncation of the PAN for storage as well, where the characters in the middle are stripped away and the first six and last four digits may remain.

10.4.1.4 Use of Tokenization

Tokenization as a practice has become popular in recent times, especially with merchants. Tokenization is, at its core, data substitution, and while one can draw parallels to encryption, it is quite different. For instance, there is a PAN 4111 1111 1111 1111 that a merchant is accepting for payment for goods and services. This PAN is accepted on the system and transmitted to a token server. The token server stores the PAN in its data vault and provides a random token number 9281 1209 4512 3489 as the token for the PAN. This token is stored in the database of the merchant's POS application.

Here we can see that a token that has no value externally has been stored in the database of the merchant. The token replaces the card number in the application and has no value to an attacker, as opposed to the PAN, which does. The token is randomly generated and has no way of being regenerated to the original PAN. When the merchant organization requires access to the customer's PAN, the application queries the token server with the token, and the original value (PAN) is returned.

Tokenization is different from encryption, in that tokenization does not rely on keys to perform encryption. Encryption also represents the data (PAN) in a completely unreadable format with characters that do not even remotely resemble a PAN. However, with tokenization, the PAN is represented in a similar format, and the original value is stored in a token server and data vault. While it is imperative to secure the vault and the token server, the organization does not have to worry about securing encryption keys.

Tokenization works quite comprehensively, where the information is first routed to the token server, and then the token (provided as output from the token server) is stored in all of the areas that store cardholder information, for instance databases, file systems, CRM systems, and so on.

Several providers also offer a SaaS (software as a service) model of tokenization, where the token server and data vault are with the service provider company, and the client company requests that the SaaS provider supply tokens for PANs provided by the client organization. This saves a great deal of cost for the client organization, as it does not have to invest in software and equipment for the tokenization process. Figure 10.2 is a depiction of the tokenization process and implementation.

10.4.1.5 Use of Strong Cryptography

Cryptography is one of the most common yet feared practices in information security. From a PCI standpoint, several workshops, talks, white papers, and so on, have been dedicated to the topic. One of the measures that can be used to render the PAN unreadable is the use of strong cryptography.

Cryptography or *cryptology,* as it is sometimes referred to, can be defined as the practice and study of hiding information. This is derived from two Greek words, *krypto* (hidden, secret) and *grapho* (to write). Cryptography involves rendering plain text into an unreadable, undecipherable format through a method that only the intended recipient of the message can, using the same method, convert the message from the unreadable format back to the plain text.

The practice of cryptography dates back to over 4000 years ago. It has long been used extensively for exchange of secrets during wartime by generals and the military. One of the famous users of cryptography was Julius Caesar, who developed his own encryption system, now popularly known as the Caesar cipher.

Encryption became an important requirement for nations during the two world wars. Just after World War I, Germany developed an encryption system, a machine known as Enigma. The Nazis used this machine extensively in World War II. With the advent of computers, cryptography saw great advancement, as complex mathematical algorithms remain one of the prime elements of cryptography, and computers are capable of processing complex mathematical operations. The most well-known encryption system was a project entitled Lucifer, developed by IBM. This system was later adopted by the National Security

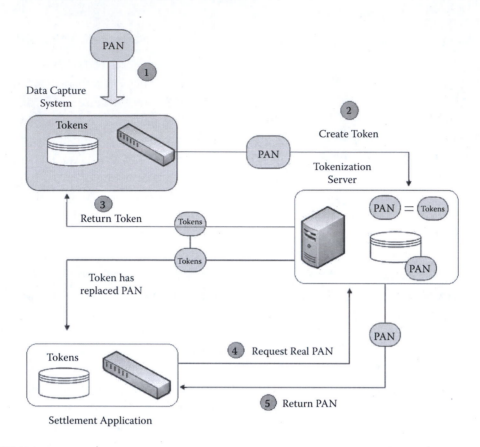

FIGURE 10.2
Tokenization process.

Agency and named as a data encryption standard (DES) in 1976.

Encryption is a process by which readable data, called *plaintext*, is rendered as incomprehensible data, called *ciphertext*. The process of encryption ensures that the data cannot be read and processed until it is decrypted. The plaintext is passed through an encryption system and consequently is rendered incomprehensible. Decryption is a process where the same incomprehensible ciphertext is passed through an encryption system and is rendered readable and comprehensible, i.e., plaintext.

The process of encryption involves three important elements, namely, the plaintext string/message, the encryption algorithm, and the key. The plaintext message is processed by the encryption algorithm in conjunction with a key to be converted into ciphertext. The process of encryption and decryption is highlighted in Figure 10.3.

The use of cryptography to render the PAN unreadable requires multiple additional security measures to be considered and implemented. Organization will have to consider the following:

- Use of cryptosystem/encryption algorithms
- Strength and randomness of the cryptographic process
- Key management

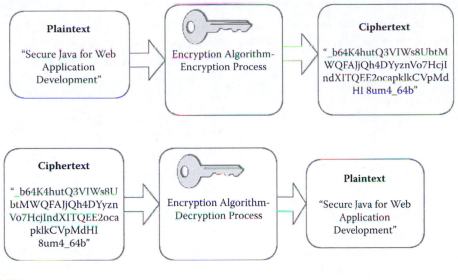

FIGURE 10.3
Encryption and decryption process.

These topics are covered in detail in the latter sections of this chapter.

10.4.2 Rendering the PAN Unreadable *Everywhere* It Is Stored

Requirement 3.4 of the PCI-DSS contains the following statement: "Render PAN unreadable *anywhere* it is stored." This statement is a critical element in an organization's PCI compliance, and it ties back to the cardholder data matrix that we had described in detail in Chapter 7.

For certain entities the PAN is stored in multiple areas, sometimes unnecessarily. Therefore, the cardholder data matrix is the primary activity that provides a detailed view of the storage of the cardholder data in the environment. Areas that can be eliminated as storage areas must be eliminated. The rest need to be evaluated in detail for Requirement 3.4.

Cardholder information may be stored in databases, file systems, log files, trace files, debug files, e-mails, voice recordings, and so on. There may be several ways to render the PAN unreadable on these diverse storage media. For instance, TPPs might be logging the PAN in their application logs. In this case, truncation may be the best way to render the PAN unreadable, as the TPP might require maintaining logs but not the full PAN as part of the application logs. If the PAN is truncated with only the first six and last four digits, the requirement would be met for that medium. Similarly, all other cardholder data touch points need to be identified, and the PAN must be rendered unreadable through one of the measures mentioned in Requirement 3.4.

10.5 CRYPTOGRAPHY: TERMINOLOGY AND CONCEPT REVIEW

Before we go further into cryptography and its role in the encryption of the PAN, let's discuss some key concepts and terminologies that form the basis for our understanding the topics presented in the rest of this chapter. The terms are as follows:

- Cryptosystem
- Key and keyspace

10.5.1 Cryptosystem

The system that provides encryption and decryption is known as a cryptosystem. It can be created either using hardware components (please refer to the example of the Enigma in the previous section) or using software program code. The cryptosystem uses an encryption algorithm along with its keys and necessary components. An encryption algorithm is a complex mathematical function that is designed to convert plaintext data to ciphertext data and vice versa. The algorithm can be succinctly summarized as the rules and boundaries that govern the encryption algorithm, which also involves the use of a string of bits, commonly referred to as a *key*. An encryption algorithm is also sometimes referred to as a *cipher*.

10.5.2 Key and Keyspace

The key in a cryptosystem is supposed to be the most secret aspect of that cryptosystem. Most encryption algorithms today are public, and the only element ensuring the secrecy of the ciphertext is the key. In this case, the key is a long sequence of random bits that is used in conjunction with the encryption algorithm to render the data incomprehensible. The key is what is used to decrypt the data when it is to be read by the intended recipient of the message.

A keyspace is the range of values that can be used to create a key for an encryption algorithm. The greater the size of the keyspace, the greater the complexity of the key and, ergo, the greater effort necessary for an intruder to break the key and render the data readable. For instance, the key "APPLE" will be much less complex than the one "i@mg0ing2DmArKet4groCeries." The attacker would find it difficult to break the second key because the encryption algorithm provides for a larger keyspace. Strong encryption algorithms of today generally provide for a keyspace of 128 bits and above. Keyspace is expressed as follows: For instance, if the keyspace for an encryption algorithm is 128 bits, then the key size would be 2^{128}, which means that there could be 2^{128} combinations for an attacker to try in order to find the key.

10.5.3 Initialization Vector

Ordinarily, when a specific message is encrypted with a particular encryption algorithm repeatedly, it produces the same ciphertext in every single instance. During World War II, the repetitiveness of the encrypted messages of the Japanese-enabled American cryptanalysts to infer and decrypt the messages. Initialization vectors are random values introduced into the encryption process to ensure that two identical plaintext messages, when encrypted with the same encryption algorithm and the same key, do not produce the same ciphertext. Initialization vectors are mostly adopted in stream ciphers, which require more randomness to the encryption process and consume higher processing power. Initialization vectors, when used in stream ciphers, utilize a *keystream* to perform the encryption and decryption process.

A keystream is a combination of random or pseudo-random characters (the key) that are used to encrypt the cleartext message. Initialization vectors add a greater degree of randomness to the keystream and thus provide an extra layer of complexity to the encryption process. Current software implementations for initialization vectors are based on initialization vectors being generated from pseudo-number generators, which generate numbers based on a certain degree of randomness required for cryptography. The initialization vector should vary with each data record encrypted in the process of encryption, and the initialization vector should also not be paired with the same key. However, initialization vectors may be stored in plaintext, as they do not have to be rendered a secret, as opposed to the key. The concept of an initialization vector is illustrated in Figure 10.4.

10.5.4 Symmetric and Asymmetric Cryptography

Symmetric cryptography is one of the methods of cryptography whereby plaintext is passed through an encryption algorithm with a key to generate the ciphertext. The same key is used with the encryption algorithm to decrypt the data

as well. For instance, Bob wants to send a message, "Hi, I will be coming to your office on Friday," and he wants to encrypt it with a symmetric encryption algorithm using a particular key. He encrypts it and sends it to Scott. Scott has the same key that Bob has used to encrypt the message and decrypts it using the key to read the message and brace himself for Bob's visit to his office on Friday. Figure 10.5 depicts a process of symmetric encryption.

As we can gather, the key is the most important aspect of a symmetric key encryption method. The key used to encrypt the data is the same one that is used to decrypt it. Therefore, it is important that the secrecy of the key be maintained to the fullest possible extent. The recipient must have the same key that was used to encrypt the data, which means that the key has to be delivered to the recipient in such a way that the key is protected.

Asymmetric cryptography is also known as *public-key cryptography*. Public-key cryptography consists of two keys, namely a public and a private key, which is known as a *key pair*. The public key may be given to anyone under the sun. It may even be written on a park bench, but it is imperative that the private key be retained only by the individual or organization to which the key

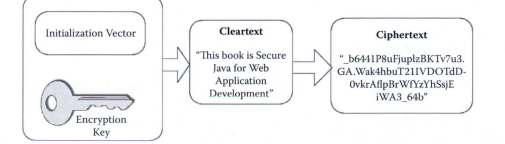

FIGURE 10.4
Initialization vector in the encryption process.

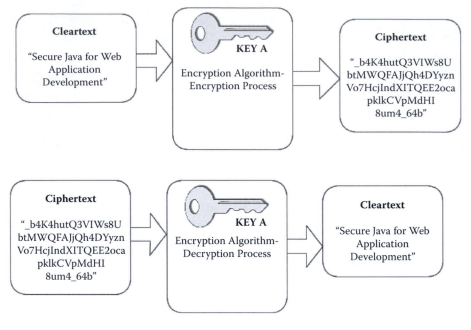

FIGURE 10.5
Symmetric key encryption: Use of the same key for encryption and decryption.

belongs. Data encrypted with one key in the key pair can only be decrypted by the other key of the same key pair. The private key may not be disclosed to anyone. Public-key cryptography involves the use of one key to encrypt data and a different key to decrypt the same data.

For instance, Bob wants to send a message, "I am coming to your office on Friday" to Scott. He will encrypt the message using Scott's public key and send it to Scott. This message can only be decrypted by Scott, with his private key. Therefore, Scott uses his private key to decrypt the message. This example shows us that public-key cryptography can be used to ensure the confidentiality of data. Bob encrypts the message with Scott's public key. This process ensures that the message can only be decrypted with the use of Scott's private key. Asymmetric cryptography can also be used for nonrepudiation. For instance, if Bob had encrypted the message with Bob's private key instead of

Scott's public key, then Scott could decrypt the same message only with Bob's public key. While this implementation does not ensure confidentiality (as Bob's public key is public), it ensures nonrepudiation and authentication, which means that there is no doubt that the message came from Bob. This is so because only Bob would have access to his private key. Figure 10.6 illustrates the use of a public–private key-pair for encryption.

There are some differences between symmetric and asymmetric cryptography. They are as follows:

- Symmetric cryptography is much faster (as much as 1000 times faster) than asymmetric cryptography. This makes asymmetric cryptography impractical for the encryption of a large quantum of data.
- Symmetric cryptography does not provide authentication and

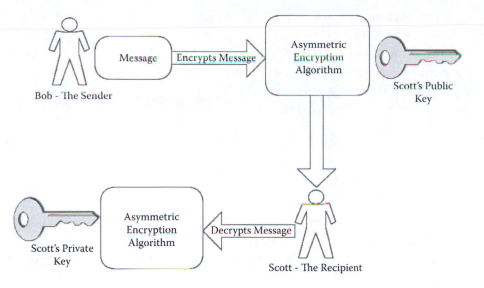

FIGURE 10.6
Asymmetric encryption: Use of public-private key-pair for encryption.

nonrepudiation, unlike asymmetric cryptography. It is only meant to preserve the confidentiality of the data encrypted.

- Symmetric cryptography requires a secure method of key distribution. As there is only a single key for encryption and decryption, the chances of loss of data confidentiality are high during the key exchange, as the keys can be intercepted by an attacker, who could use it to decrypt the data. This problem is not one that would be associated with asymmetric cryptography. The public key may be distributed to anyone, but the individual's private key needs to be kept secret.
- Symmetric cryptography suffers from the drawback of scalability. Several complications arise in trying to maintain secrecy over multiple keys that are present in a system, as opposed to asymmetric cryptography.

- Asymmetric cryptography is not only slower, but also needs to have a much larger key size for it to be as effective as a symmetric algorithm of a much lower keyspace.

Several cryptographic implementations are based on a hybrid method of cryptography that combines a symmetric and asymmetric cryptographic system. We already understand that asymmetric cryptographic algorithms are not suitable for encryption of large chunks of data, and we are aware that symmetric cryptography has the disadvantage of the need for a secure transport and scalability factor. The hybrid encryption system addresses these problems. The hybrid encryption system is explained in the form of an example:

- Bob obtains Scott's public key.
- Bob generates a symmetric key and encrypts his message, "Please don't come to my office," with the symmetric encryption key.

- Bob then encrypts the symmetric key with Scott's public key.
- Bob sends both the encrypted symmetric key (encrypted with Scott's public key) and the message (encrypted with the symmetric key) to Scott, who reads it.

10.5.5 Block Ciphers and Stream Ciphers

Symmetric key ciphers consist of two types of ciphers: block and stream ciphers. Block cipher is the one where the message to be encrypted is split into fixed-length blocks of data. These blocks will pass through the encryption algorithm, where several mathematical functions are performed for substitution and transposition. For instance, if a data block of 256 bits in plaintext is being encrypted by a block cipher of 128 bits, then the block cipher would split the data block into two blocks of 128 bits and encrypt these blocks. DES was the earliest block cipher developed by IBM in the 1970s. Block ciphers have several modes of operations while encrypting and decrypting data, some of them adding a higher degree of complexity to the encryption process, thereby making it difficult for the attacker to break the encrypted data. Block ciphers are ideal for files and database encryption, as the data can be split into blocks of data to be encrypted and decrypted.

Stream ciphers, on the other hand, are quite different from block ciphers. Stream ciphers do not handle the data or the message as a block, but as a stream, where each bit of the stream is subjected to encryption. Stream ciphers use what is known as keystream generators, which is nothing but the stream generated based on the key given for encrypting and decrypting the data. Stream cipher is ideal for encrypting voice traffic, streaming media, etc., where the data cannot be split into chunks of data for encryption.

10.5.6 Block Cipher Modes of Encryption

Symmetric block ciphers have modes of encryption that govern the way the algorithms function. Each algorithm has different modes, which may be developed based on the implementation in hardware/software. These modes also vary with the level of protection provided by one mode of encryption vis-à-vis the other. The modes of encryption and their characteristics are as follows:

- Electronic code book
- Cipher block chaining
- Cipher feedback
- Output feedback
- Counter

10.5.6.1 Electronic Code Book

The electronic code book (ECB) mode of encryption is quite simple to understand. The encryption algorithm and the key process the data block to produce a block of ciphertext. In the ECB mode, for the same block of data, with the same key, the same block of ciphertext is always generated. While the ECB is the fastest mode, it is also the least secure. The reasons for that are quiet obvious: The ECB does not provide any randomness to the process of encryption, thereby causing the problem of patterns developing if identical cleartext is encrypted with the same encryption algorithm and the same key. ECB is the only block-cipher mode of encryption that does not require the use of an initialization vector. If the cleartext block provides the same ciphertext on every single occasion, patterns in a data block are not hidden very well, and it is easier for a cryptanalyst to be able to decipher the cleartext. The functioning of the ECB is highlighted in Figure 10.7.

There is a funny story about the ECB. The popular online game *Phantasy Star Online: Blue Burst* used Blowfish as the encryption algorithm and ECB as the mode of encryption. Cheaters often used the "monster killed" encrypted Blowfish data block to gain experience points in the game quickly, because the message had the same ciphertext every single time.

10.5.6.2 *Cipher Block Chaining*

Cipher block chaining (CBC) is a block-cipher encryption mode that provides a greater degree of randomness to the encryption process than the ECB mode. The CBC utilizes a system where the ciphertext of the previously encrypted block of data is used along with the subsequent block of plaintext block of data that is to be encrypted. The combination of the ciphertext of the previous block and the plaintext of the subsequent block acts as an initialization vector to add randomness to the encryption process. The ciphertext from a previous block

is XORed with the plaintext of the subsequent block to add more complexity and randomness to the encryption process. This process is repeated for all the blocks of data encrypted by the algorithm. To ensure that the first block of data is encrypted with adequate randomness, an initialization vector is introduced to the process to fill the void that would have been created for the first block of data being encrypted. Figure 10.8 depicts the working of the CBC mode.

10.5.6.3 *Cipher Feedback*

Cipher feedback (CFB) mode is quite an interesting block-cipher mode of encryption, as it allows block ciphers to act as stream ciphers. Implementations involving data transfer like e-mail and instant messaging cannot employ block-cipher modes, as this would involve data being chunked into blocks and sent over the wire, which would result in delays and reduced quality of service. Cipher feedback mode provides an answer to this problem of encrypting large blocks of data by encrypting smaller blocks of data (for example 8 bits). CFB works in a similar manner as CBC. An initialization vector and the key are used to generate

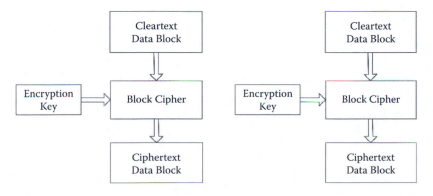

FIGURE 10.7
Electronic code book mode of block cipher encryption.

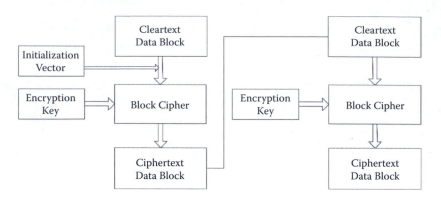

FIGURE 10.8
Cipher block chaining: Block cipher mode of encryption.

a keystream. The cleartext is encrypted with this keystream and converted to ciphertext. The ciphertext from the first block is used along with the key to produce a second keystream, which is used to encrypt the second block, and so on. CFB mode can be used to encrypt blocks of any size. The CFB mode is illustrated in Figure 10.9.

10.5.6.4 Output Feedback

Output feedback mode (OFB) is very similar to CFB. In the case of CFB, the first block is encrypted with the keystream generated from the key and the initialization vector. For subsequent keys, the keystream is generated with the key as well as the ciphertext from the preceding block. In OFB, the first block is encrypted in a similar manner as that for CFB, but the subsequent blocks are encrypted with the combination of the previous keystream and the key, forming another keystream to be used to encrypt the subsequent block. It must be noted that for both CFB and OFB, the size of the ciphertext for the CFB and the size of the keystream for the OFB need to be the same bit-size as that of the cleartext being encrypted, thus providing optimal security. The OFB mode of block-cipher encryption is illustrated in Figure 10.10.

10.5.6.5 Counter

The counter mode of encryption is also quite popular as a block-cipher mode of encryption. The counter mode also allows block

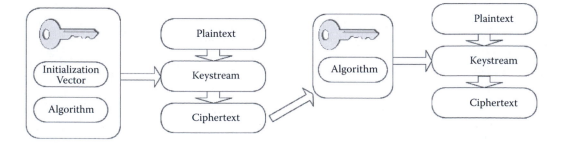

FIGURE 10.9
Cipher feedback mode: Block cipher mode of encryption.

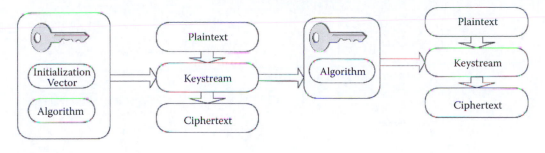

FIGURE 10.10
Output feedback mode: Block cipher mode of encryption.

ciphers to be used as stream ciphers and perform encryption. The counter mode is, in many ways, similar to the CFB and OFB, but in the counter mode, there is no initialization vector used to generate a keystream to add randomness to the encryption process. Instead, the counter mode employs an incremental counter for every block of data encrypted. Since the encryption of the subsequent block of data does not depend on the ciphertext or the keystream of the previous block, as it does in the case of CFB and OFB, the counter mode is quite fast, and the encryption of the blocks can be performed in parallel, resulting in significant performance benefits. The counter mode has been depicted in Figure 10.11.

10.6 REQUIREMENTS 3.5 AND 3.6: KEY SECURITY AND KEY MANAGEMENT

10.6.1 Key-Management Considerations: Enterprises

Key management differs greatly based on the type of organization that is undergoing PCI compliance. For instance, banks and acquiring and issuing TPPs will have to implement more detailed and complex key-management processes and procedures. These entities would have to manage keys not only for the encryption/decryption process of the PAN, but for multiple operations involving the keys for CVV and PIN verification, and so on. The key-management process for these keys is critical, as it involves the cryptographic operations for sensitive authentication data.

However, for an organization like a merchant or an e-commerce vendor, it is highly likely that the encryption operations involving PCI compliance are largely centered on encrypting and decrypting the PAN. Such organizations would not need the cryptographic processes involving sensitive authentication data, either for its generation or verification, as these activities are completely unrelated to their business needs.

Other service providers, such as software development organizations and business process outsourcing (BPO) companies, would have application-driven encryption requirements to protect the PAN in multiple storage areas. However, the specific approach needed to understand these different perspectives is highly dependent on the organization type.

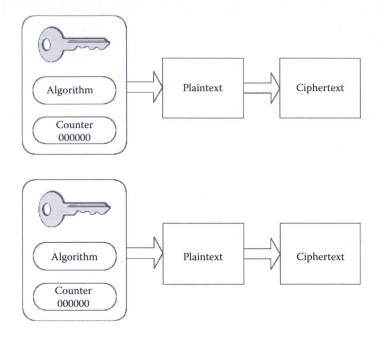

FIGURE 10.11
Counter mode: Block cipher mode of encryption.

10.6.2 Key-Management Practices for Banks and Acquiring and Issuing TPPs

Banks and acquiring and issuing processors that handle and manage payment card transaction operations have extensive cryptographic operations that require detailed key-management processes. Given the criticality of these operations, key management is one of the most important aspects of security for their organizations. We'll have to explore several concepts to understand how banks and acquiring and issuing processors manage their cryptographic key-management operations. We will discuss the following topics:

- Hardware security module
- Local master key
- Zonal control master keys
- PIN encryption keys/working keys
- PIN verification key

- Message authentication keys
- Card verification keys
- Derived unique key per transaction

10.6.2.1 Hardware Security Module (HSM)

The HSM forms an important aspect of key management, especially for banks and acquiring and issuing processors. The HSM, as the name suggests, is a hardware appliance or a device that manages the cryptographic operations of the organization. It can be used to perform multiple operations from key generation to key storage, key distribution, and so on. They are used to protect high-value cryptographic keys. For banks and acquiring and issuing processors, HSMs perform a host of additional functions, such as key generation, key verification algorithms and operations, key loading, key storage, key management, key authentication, and so on. HSMs might store keys in other media-like databases, but they often manage the storage of keys from within encrypted wrappers in the operating system. HSMs often utilize smartcards and tokens to store keys.

In the case of banking and acquiring and issuing processors, the HSM acts a centralized key server. The HSM is used to not only store the keys and manage their ingress and egress functions, but the HSM also interacts with the payment switches and payment-processing solutions for POS transactions, ATM transactions, and so on. Popular HSMs in the market include SafeNet, Thales, and others. Figure 10.12 is an image of an HSM.

10.6.2.2 Local Master Key

The local master key (LMK), as the name suggests, is the master key for the HSM. This is a symmetric key that is used to encrypt all the other keys stored and managed by the HSM. The key is also known as the key-storage key (KSK) by some HSM vendors.

As the key is highly critical (it secures every other key in the HSM), it is generally recommended to be created of triple length by key custodians to ensure the best possible security for the key. Typically the key generation process is as follows:

- Key custodians prompt the HSM, which provides a hexadecimal value (32 bits) along with a key check value.
- The clear value that is generated must be maintained by a key custodian. This process is repeated three times for the triple-length process of the key to be achieved.
- The clear values held by each custodian must be entered three times into the HSM.
- The HSM prompts the users for the insertion of a blank smart card. Upon loading the blank smart card, the HSM writes the key information onto the device, and the device must subsequently be stored in a secure location.

The LMK is never meant to be available outside the HSM. The LMK is the master key and, as such, it is not supposed to be removed from the HSM by any user. The LMK is also

FIGURE 10.12
Hardware security module image.

called the master file key (MFK) because it is the master key that derives and encrypts any keys that are stored externally in files as well.

10.6.2.3 Zone-Control Master Keys

The zone-control master key (aka zone master key) (ZMK) is the key that is generated by the payment brands that are interfacing with the bank (and processors as well). This is a key generated by payment networks like Visa and MasterCard that is shared with the member banks (and processors). This key is used to encrypt various keys for the CVV, PVV, and so on. This is called to action when the PIN blocks, CVV, etc., are to be passed from one bank through the network to a remote member bank that is required for authorizing a transaction. This is also called the key-encrypting key (KEK), as it is used to encrypt keys that are used for distribution across the payment life cycle.

This key is encrypted with the local master key.

10.6.2.4 PIN Working Keys

The PIN working key (KWP) is a session key that is used in ATM and POS transactions involving debit cards. When an ATM terminal goes online for the first time, it is loaded with a terminal master key (TMK). The KWP is used to transmit PIN blocks from the ATM/POS terminal to the bank (or processor). This is a session key that is changed often based on regular intervals. The PIN entered by the user is translated to a PIN block (explained previously), encrypted with the KWP and sent to the bank, and is subsequently part of the complete payment-processing life cycle. The KWP is exchanged using the terminal master key.

10.6.2.5 PIN Verification Key

We previously learned about the concept of the PIN verification value. Let me reiterate that PINs are not (and should not) be stored in a persistent form of storage like a file system or a database. They are verified on the fly with VISA's PVV method. The PIN verification key is used by a bank (or processor) to generate a PIN value from the cardholder's PVV sent as part of the transaction along with the PIN verification key indicator/index (PVKI). The PVKI is a single-digit value that identifies which pair of keys must be used for the PVV computation. The PVKI is an index of numbers 0–6 for single-key configuration and 1–6 for group key configuration. The PVKI is both encoded on the card's magnetic stripe as well as stored in the bank's (processor's) database.

Based on the PVKI and the PVV sent by the cardholder's card as part of the transaction, the PVV is generated using the PIN verification key, and if the PVV transmitted and the PVV generated a match, then the transaction is authenticated.

As you can see, the PIN verification key is meant as a key for derivation and not for protection. The PVV key is shared by the payment brands (networks) with the member banks (and processors). It is generated as a pair.

10.6.2.6 Message Authentication Keys

Message authentication keys are used for transaction integrity verification in a transaction. The message authentication key is exchanged between two payment-processing switches. The message authentication key is generated and exchanged using the zone master key (ZMK or KEK). The message authentication key and the message data are used to derive a 4-byte message authentication code, which is stored in the message. Once the message reaches the recipient, the MAC is derived from the message authentication key and the message and then compared with the MAC that is transmitted. If they match, the transaction has not been tampered with or has suffered no loss of integrity during the transmission process. Message authentication keys are usually encrypted with a 3DES–CBC cryptosystem.

10.6.2.7 Card Verification Keys

Similar to the PIN verification, the authentication of a credit card transaction is done with CVV verification. CVV is a part of sensitive authentication data that should not be stored in the organization's databases. The CVV is generated on the fly as part of the transaction and is compared with the CVV that has been transmitted as part of the transaction. If there is a match, the transaction is authenticated.

The CVV is usually a DES algorithm key that is loaded into the HSM. The HSM will generate a CVV value based on the transaction that has been transmitted for processing. The card verification key will generate a CVV, and if the generated value matches the transmitted CVV value, the card transaction is authenticated.

The Card verification key is used for verification and not for confidentiality. The card verification key is generated and issued by the payment brands (networks) to the member banks.

10.6.2.8 Derived Unique Key per Transaction (DUKPT)

The concept of DUKPT is a diversion from the master key concept of PIN encryption.

DUKPT refers to the key-management scheme that has a unique key generated/used for encryption for every transaction, derived from a fixed key. It is used for POS transactions. There are two popular systems of DUKPT, one being the Visa DUKPT system and the other being the initial PIN encryption key (IPEK)-derived DUKPT system.

The key that is used to derive the unique keys is called the base derivation key (BDK), which is usually stored in the HSM (or sometimes in the payment-processing application) as well. In the IPEK-derived system, the IPEK is preloaded into the POS terminal/device and is used to encrypt the message. Subsequently, a key sequence number (KSN) is generated from the device's unique identifiers. The encrypted message and the KSN are then forwarded to the acquiring bank, where the decryption process happens and the transaction is processed further.

On Visa's DUKPT system, the IPEK is generated with the combination of the BDK at runtime to ensure that the IPEK is not preloaded into the system.

10.6.3 Principles of Encryption and Key Management for Protecting the Stored PAN

In the previous section, we described in great detail the multiple types of keys and their functions in the generation and protection of sensitive authentication data. However, the section largely applied to practices followed by banks and TPPs that handle cardholder data extensively as part of the payment-processing life cycle. Key-management practices are also required when the PAN is subjected to cryptography.

There are a few best practices to follow when the PAN is being subjected to cryptographic controls. They are as follows:

- Strong key generation
- Single-purpose encryption keys
- Secure key storage
- Secure key distribution and exchange
- Cryptoperiod and key changes
- Secure key destruction

10.6.3.1 Secure Key Generation

Cryptographic controls are only as effective as the key used to encrypt/decrypt data. It is imperative that the key used to encrypt/decrypt critical information like the PAN is a strong key that is not easily identified by even a determined attacker. A strong key refers to one that provides a high degree of randomness and complexity that even upon time-consuming brute-force attempts, the key is still unknown to the attacker. Ideally, the key must be generated using a random number generator (RNG), which is a physical device that is used to generate truly random numbers and characters that are difficult to enumerate and guess. However, with the coming of age of computational algorithms and the power of computer programming, there are pseudo-random number generators (PRNGs) that can be used as a RNG to generate almost-true random numbers and characters to be used as keys for cryptographic operations. In the event that an organization is using an HSM for key management, the key can be derived from the master key of the HSM, which is also generated with a RNG.

In the event that manual key generation processes are used with key custodians generating a master key (or any other key), it is required that no single custodian has the entire key that is used for encryption and decryption. Split knowledge of keys ensures that the key is not fully disclosed even to the key custodians. For one application I was reviewing, the company had provided an additional executable that behaved like an HSM. The application would output random eight-character strings for every key custodian, and every key custodian would enter the key into another screen, where the concatenated string would be the key that would be the master key for the application.

The quality of the key generated is especially more important for a symmetric key, as the same key is used for encryption and decryption. Therefore, the quality of the key will absolutely determine whether the cryptographic control applied is effective or otherwise.

It is highly recommended that keys be generated from a strong cryptographic module like an HSM. However, there are several libraries, modules and API that can be used to generate equally strong keys. They include OpenSSL libraries, Java JCA/JCE, PKCS#11 (RSA), Microsoft CAPI, and so on. It is recommended that the key be generated with a FIPS 140-2[*] compliant cryptographic module.

In the event that multiple cryptographic keys are used to encrypt PAN—for instance, if the organization utilizes a data-encrypting key (DEK) for encrypting/decrypting data and uses a key-encrypting key (KEK) to encrypt the DEK—then the quality of the KEK should at least be equivalent if not more than

---

[*] The Federal Information Processing Standard is the US government standard for the validation and accreditation of cryptographic modules. It is seen as a standard for high-quality cryptographic modules. The full list of validated Is available at http://csrc.nist.gov/groups/STM/cmvp/documents/140-1/140val-all.htm#1747.

the quality of the DEK. Therefore, for instance, if the KEK utilizes asymmetric cryptography and the DEK utilizes symmetric cryptography, and the DEK uses an AES 128-bit cryptosystem and the KEK uses a RSA cryptosystem, then the key size for the RSA cryptosystem of the KEK should be at least 3072 bits, as it is considered equivalent to the 128-bit key of the AES cryptosystem used by the DEK.

10.6.3.2 Single-Purpose Cryptographic Keys

An important, but oft-ignored best practice in cryptography is the use of a single key for multiple functions. For instance, if a key used for data encryption is also used as a session key, then the potential for key compromise (and consequently data compromise) is much higher owing to the fact that the same key can be used to decrypt both communications and data at rest. Therefore, it must be ensured that a single key is used for a single purpose only. This is also evident with the key-management concepts for banking and TPPs covered previously. It is essential to make a distinction between KEKs, DEKs, session keys, derivation keys, and so on, when they are used in the cardholder-data environment.

10.6.3.3 Secure Key Storage

It is a no-brainer that keys that are used to secure critical information assets like the PAN should be stored securely. An initial measure of access control to the key is to use DEKs and KEKs, where the KEK protects the DEK, which protects the data. However, it is also imperative that the KEK be protected against access by unauthorized entities. One of the popular ways of protecting keys is to use protected wrappers in the operating system or application server (in the case of applications). It is also important to note that if HSMs or central key servers are not used, then the keys must not be stored in the same location as other keys. For instance, the DEK should not be stored with the KEK in the same location. Some systems rely on external devices like a USB drive attached to the server to store keys. Some systems rely on smart cards to store keys securely.

In the case of application-driven encryption, it is highly recommended that keys be stored in a key-manager file/object that provides access to keys to the rest of the application as required. The access to this object (and consequently the file) should be highly controlled to only authorized users who require the keys to perform encryption and decryption operations.

In the event that unencrypted/single keys are used to protect the PAN, the keys should be stored away from the data in an area like a protected or access-controlled config file.

10.6.3.4 Secure Key Distribution and Exchange

Key distribution is a very important consideration, as keys are usually compromised when they are transmitted or distributed to other entities. A simple attack like a man-in-the-middle attack, with an attacker sniffing network traffic, could compromise keys if transmitted over a network with no/inadequate encryption.

Keys must be transmitted and distributed over secure channels. These channels include secure physical distribution and logical key exchange.

10.6.3.4.1 Secure Physical Distribution

When keys are distributed physically to one or more key custodians, the document containing the key must be sealed and packaged. The key must also be delivered by a reliable entity and tracked closely. In the event that multiple key custodians are present, it is always ideal to have a split knowledge of a single key to ensure that no single custodian can perpetrate a breach. Similarly, distribution of multiple keys to these custodians is also protected due to the split-knowledge effect, thereby ensuring that the entire key is never completely in the hands of a single individual.

10.6.3.4.2 Logical Key Exchange

One of the most common ways of key distribution is to exchange them over a logical channel like a network. However, this is also fraught with danger, as attacks are much easier to perpetrate on this channel. There are, however, some ways to overcome this issue with the use of public-key cryptography, key-exchange algorithms, usage of encrypted transmission channels like SSL (secure socket layer) and TLS (transport layer security), or password-authenticated key-file exchange.

With public-key cryptography, the sender can encrypt the key with the recipient's public key and transmit the key to ensure that only the recipient can access the key with his/her private key. Key-exchange algorithms (e.g., Diffie Hellman) are used to ensure secure key exchange. Another popular method of key exchange is the use of PGP*/GPG keys (web of trust), where users

exchange each other's keys and certificates. The messages can be encrypted with these keys and sent to the user.

Applications typically utilize SSL/TLS to transmit keys to other applications or other components of the application. However, note that keys must be transmitted over an encrypted channel even on a local network. It is also highly recommended that, even over an encrypted channel, keys must be encrypted and not passed in cleartext. The concept of master and session keys may be utilized for such implementations.

We will cover detailed aspects of secure transmission in Chapter 11.

10.6.3.5 Cryptoperiod and Key Changes

Keys that are used to protect critical data need to be changed over periodic intervals. It is recommended that keys be changed every one to three years based on the organization's security requirements. The reason for key changes is essentially because keys used over an extended period of time could be compromised due to attempts by attackers, both internally and externally. It might also happen that the keys could be subject to inadvertent disclosure to multiple entities. The practice of a defined cryptoperiod ensures that the keys used to encrypt the PAN are changed periodically. However, the implementation of a key change has to be carefully executed. Entities that store large volumes of cardholder information often have major challenges in implementing key changes and managing cryptoperiods. Applications have to be able to support a change of cryptographic key, where the data is decrypted with the old key and reencrypted with the new key.

---

* PGP is 'Pretty Good Privacy,' a data encryption program which uses public private keypairs. The sender generates a random key for data encryption and encrypts the key with the receiver's public key. The receiver can decrypt the message and the key using his/her private key. GPG is GNU Privacy Guard which is the Open Source Implementation of PGP.

10.6.3.6 Dual-Key Management for Manual Cryptography

Cryptography is a practice that can have far-reaching consequences for an organization. If the organization does not design its cryptographic practices to be both secure and available, it would suffer a great deal of adverse consequences. Confidentiality is the obvious objective in cryptography. However, there may come a time when highly automated and so-called fail-safe cryptography might disallow the organization access to its own data. In such cases, organizations opt to use some amount of human intervention with a manual key-management process.

In a payment application I was reviewing, the key-management process was driven through two key custodians. The key custodians would generate the key-encrypting key for the application, which had a separate executable where one-half of the key was generated by a single custodian, and the other half of the key was generated by the other. When the key was to be replaced or used to decrypt the data-encrypting key, the executable was used. One custodian would provide half of the entire key, and the other custodian provided the other half. Manual key-management operations are sometimes used for key management in devices like an HSM or a key-management server. However, manual key-management operations are cumbersome when systems are highly dependent on encryption keys. When manual key-management operations are used, key custodians are entrusted with the task of protecting keys. In such cases, Requirement 3.6.8 requires that the key custodian must acknowledge his/her responsibility as a key custodian in writing to the organization.

10.7 SUMMARY

This chapter deals exclusively with Requirement 3 of the PCI-DSS. The chapter also details the cryptographic requirements for payment applications as required by the PA-DSS as well. We began with a very important question, "Do you really need to store cardholder data?" The organization needs to take enough action and effort to reduce the storage of cardholder data to the minimum. It automatically reduces the scope of PCI and the risk of cardholder data breach.

We then explored the sensitive authentication data parameters of a payment. We learned about the CVV, CVV2, PIN block, pin verification key indicator, and other parameters that constitute sensitive authentication data. Subsequently, we explored the all-important Requirement 3.4, which states that the PAN has to be rendered unreadable wherever stored using techniques such as encryption, one-way hashing, truncation, and so on. We explored all of these concepts in depth. Next, we delved into cryptography, exploring some cryptographic concepts like symmetric and asymmetric cryptography. We also explored multiple modes of block-cipher encryption like ECB, CBC, and so on. We focused a great deal of effort on the key-management practices as required under Requirements 3.5 and 3.6 of the standard, including the need for multiple keys like key-encryption key, data-encryption key, and other keys required for banks and payment processors who are an integral part of the payment-processing life cycle.

11

Requirement 4: Securing Cardholder Information in Transit

Apart from the security for the data at rest, it is equally important to ensure that cardholder information that is transmitted is secure. Attackers have relied on being able to intercept/read traffic that is being transmitted over a network to be able to perpetrate a number of attacks. In fact, some of the major cardholder information breaches occurred due to attackers being able to sniff network traffic and gain access to sensitive data based on said traffic.

Requirement 4 of the PCI-DSS deals with the transmission of cardholder information over open, public networks. In this chapter, we will discuss Requirement 4 and its implementation guidance. We will also briefly delve into how assessors must address this requirement and how developers of commercial applications must develop and implement payment applications that adhere to the requirement.

11.1 REQUIREMENT 4.1: SECURE TRANSMISSION OF CARDHOLDER INFORMATION OVER OPEN, PUBLIC NETWORKS

11.1.1 Open, Public Networks: A PCI Viewpoint

Requirement 4.1 of the PCI-DSS requires that cardholder information be encrypted when it is transmitted over open, public networks. However, it is prudent for us to understand what the PCI defines as open, public networks in the first place.

One of the simplest examples of an open, public network is the Internet. Any traffic to and from the Internet, unless secured with encryption, is in plaintext. Any traffic to or from the organization's cardholder data environment (CDE) over the Internet, containing cardholder information and/or sensitive authentication data, must be encrypted with strong ciphers. This includes Web traffic (over HTTP) and other protocols that are utilized with the Web. Another popular mode of data transmission is the File Transfer Protocol (FTP). I have personally come across several banks and third-party provider (TPPs) that utilize FTP to transmit cardholder details. FTP, without any additional encryption or protection, is a protocol that transmits data in plaintext, which is not recommended, especially with cardholder data being transmitted.

Another example of an open, public network is slightly confusing to many people. The PCI defines any wireless network as an "open, public network." This is largely owing to the fact that wireless networks tend to be inherently weak and vulnerable to exploitation.

We have already seen that the PCI requirements have been specifically stringent on wireless communications in both Requirement 1 and Requirement 2. You will also notice that the creators of the standard have expressed the same level of "progressive paranoia" with reference to wireless networks over all the 12 requirements. Even if the wireless network is an internal network, the PCI requires certain mandatory encryption controls over the wireless networks transmitting cardholder information.

Mobile technologies have been on an upsurge in the last decade and, as a result of the recent smartphone revolution, mobile payments have become a major class of applications that are available to users in the market. Mobile payment applications, or any other application that transmits cardholder data, therefore are also specifically at risk with reference to "man-in-the-middle" attacks. Mobile applications usually transmit information from applications over global packet radio service (GPRS) networks or third-generation (3G) networks. Therefore, these communications contain-ing cardholder data must be encrypted with strong ciphers.

The PCI-DSS has specified all of these network types as open, public networks. However, the list may not be exhaustive, as there may be multiple implementations of networks that might be open, public networks.

With the advent of cloud computing, the concept of public networks has become even more important. In most cases, utilization of the cloud would require transmission of cardholder data over encrypted connections, as the cardholder data is transmitted over a public network. Even in the case of cloud providers like Amazon with its Virtual Private Cloud, where users can completely configure network configurations and gateway settings, connectivity must be established over a virtual private network (VPN) or similar technology, as the transmission is over the Internet.

Networks like MPLS (multiprotocol label switching) or private cloud networks are not considered open, public networks, as they are part of the organization's network.

11.1.2 Secure Protocols

Requirement 4.1 of the PCI-DSS requires the transmission of cardholder information over open, public networks to happen over encrypted communications. There are multiple protocols and implementations of protocols that can be used for encrypted communication. Some of them include SCP/SFTP, HTTPS with SSL/TLS, SSH, IPSec VPN, and so on. However, there are some customized implementations where data is encrypted at the sender's end and decrypted at the recipient's end with a preshared key or a public-private key pair. Let's explore some of these protocols in greater depth.

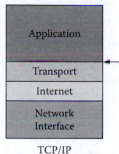

FIGURE 11.1

Representation of SSL/TLS in the TCP/IP stack.

11.1.2.1 HTTPS with SSL/TLS

One of the most popular implementations in the world is the use of Secure Socket Layer (SSL) over HTTP. This implementation is used by thousands of sites all over the world to encrypt transmissions between the HTTP server and the browser.

The abbreviation *SSL* has been replaced by Transport Layer Security (TLS), which is an upgraded and more secure protocol than the SSL. However, since SSL was the first, the abbreviation *SSL* almost always means TLS, which is the latest protocol.

The SSL/TLS exists somewhere in between the transport and application layers of the TCP/IP stack, with services extending to both levels of the stack. Figure 11.1 is a representation of SSL/TLS in the TCP/IP stack.

SSL version 1.0 was developed by Netscape, and version 2.0 was released in 1995, but was found to be flawed in several aspects, leading to the creation of version 3.0 in 1996. The Internet Engineering Taskforce (IETF) took over SSL, and it was called the TLS, which was adopted as a standard. In 1999, all the major payment brands like Visa, MasterCard, and Amex, as well as several financial institutions publicly declared that SSL/TLS would be adopted as a security measure for e-commerce transactions.

Traffic that is protected with SSL/TLS for access to a website/application will occur over Hypertext Transfer Protocol–Secure (HTTPS) instead of over the regular HTTP protocol, which is unencrypted.

To provide secure transport of information over a network, SSL/TLS uses a combination of cryptographic processes. SSL/TLS is essentially a secure enhancement to the standard TCP/IP sockets protocol used for Internet communications. The latest version of TLS is version 1.2.

The benefits of TLS vis-à-vis SSL include the following:

- TLS protects against a downgrade of the protocol to a less secure version like SSL 3.0 or a weaker cipher suite.
- The use of message digests is enhanced with the key.
- TLS has a stronger pseudo-random number generator (PRNG) function.

SSL/TLS uses many different cryptographic processes for secure data transportation and at various stages. For example, SSL uses (a) public-key cryptography to provide authentication and (b) secret-key cryptography and digital signatures to secure information and privacy. Communication over SSL/TLS essentially begins with a series of exchanges of information between the client and the server. This series of exchanges of information is called the SSL handshake. The SSL/TLS handshake ensures negotiation of the cipher suite, authentication, and agreement on encryption algorithms for establishing the information security.

A sequence of messages is exchanged between the two systems, viz., client and server, in the SSL mode of data transfer.

11.1.2.1.1 Acquiring the SSL/TLS Certificate

The Web application vendor or organization will obtain a certificate from a certificate provider with a Certificate Signing Request. This request contains the name of the Web application/website, contact e-mail address, and company information. The certificate provider would sign the request after scrutiny of the same, which produces a public certificate. When a user connects to the Web application/website, the public certificate is provided to the browser during the handshake process. The certificate contains details of the website/Web application that the certificate has been issued for, the organization name, certificate serial number, the class of certificate, the certificate provider, and the dates of validity of the certificate.

In recent history, there has been a rash of attacks against certificate authorities, such as Comodo, GlobalSign, and DigiNotar. DigiNotar was one of the largest breaches against certificate authorities in recent times, because it was a complete compromise of the company. Hackers were able to penetrate DigiNotar's defenses and started issuing rogue certificates to domains like google. com, Skype, and Mozilla add-ons. The attack was used to spy on Iranian Internet users. With fake certificates, the attackers were able to perpetrate man-in-the-middle attacks against Internet users in Iran.

Upon investigation of DigiNotar's security defenses, it was found that they had displayed an amateurish and shockingly negligent execution of security. Public-facing Web servers were not patched, intrusion-prevention systems (IPSs) were not in place, and antivirus applications were not present on critical servers. Centralized logging and log management had not been implemented. There was a major backlash against the company by the security community, and this negative publicity drove the company to bankruptcy. One of the sub-requirements of Requirement 4.1, namely 4.1b, requires trusted certificates and tokens to be used. Therefore, SSL certificates that are self-signed or signed by a known vulnerable certificate from a certificate authority are not to be deployed for applications and servers in the CDE.

The process of client–server handshake and data exchange for SSL are as follows:

Step 1. Client initiation: Client initiates a SSL/TLS request that includes the SSL version and list of supported cipher suites. This step is usually referred to as "ClientHello" in the SSL/TLS parlance. The cipher suite information also includes cryptographic algorithms and key sizes. For instance, TLS_RSA_WITH_RC4_128_MD5 is a cipher suite. The algorithm used for key exchange and certificate verification is the RSA algorithm. The encryption algorithm used for encrypting messages in this case is the RC4. The MD5 algorithm is used to verify the contents of the message.

Step 2. Server acknowledgement: Upon receipt of the client request, the server chooses the highest version of SSL/TLS and the best-suited cipher suite that both the client and server support and returns this information to the client. This step is referred to as "ServerHello" in the SSL/TLS parlance.

Step 3. Send certificate: Optionally, the server sends the client a certificate (or even a certificate chain). In the case where a certificate chain is being sent, it begins with the server's public key certificate and ends with the certificate authority's root certificate. This step becomes essential if the server requires authentication. This step is referred to as "Certificate" in the SSL/TLS parlance.

Step 4. Request certificate: This is an optional step. However, if Step 3 is mandated due to authentication requirement, then the server needs to authenticate the client, and it sends the client a certificate request. This step is referred to as "Certificate request" in the SSL/TLS parlance.

Step 5. Server key exchange: The server sends the client a server key exchange message when the public key information sent in Step 3 is not sufficient for key exchange.

Step 6. Server ready: Now the server indicates to the client that its initial negotiation messages have been successfully completed. This step is referred to as "ServerHello done" in the SSL/TLS parlance.

Step 7. Send certificate: If the server had requested a certificate from the client, as in Step 4, the client sends its certificate chain, just as the server did in Step 3. This step is referred to as "Certificate" in the SSL/TLS parlance.

Step 8. Client key exchange: The client will generate information used to create a key to use for symmetric encryption. For RSA, the client then encrypts this key information with the server's public key and sends it to the server.

Step 9. Certificate verification: This message is sent when a client presents a certificate as described in Step 7, and this is optional, as it depends on Step 3. Its purpose is to allow the server to complete the process of authenticating the client. When this message is used, the client sends information that it digitally signs using a cryptographic hash function. When the server decrypts this information with the client's public key, the server will be able to authenticate the client.

Step 10. Change cipher spec: In this step, the client sends a message directing the server to change to an encrypted mode.

Step 11. Handshake establishment on server side: In this step, the client notifies the server that it is ready for secure data communication to begin.

Step 12. Change cipher spec: Now it is the server's turn to send a message to the client asking it to change to an encrypted mode of communication.

Step 13. Handshake establishment at the server side: The server tells the client that it is ready for secure data communication to begin. This indicates the completion of the SSL handshake.

Step 14. Encrypted data exchange: Henceforth, the client and the server start communicating using the symmetric encryption algorithm and the cryptographic hash function negotiated in Steps 1 and 2, as well as using the secret key that the client sent to the server in Step 8.

Step 15. Close: At the end of the communication process, each side will send a close_notify message to inform the peer that the connection is closed.

Figure 11.2 shows the handshake and key-exchange process of the SSL/TLS.

It's a common misconception that SSL/TLS can only be used with HTTP. SSL/TLS can be used with other protocols like FTP, also commonly referred to as FTPS. Mail protocols like IMAP can also be used over SSL. SMTP is also available over SSL/TLS with the STARTTLS extension.

There are some considerations while implementing SSL/TLS for websites and Web applications, especially ones that are in scope for PCI compliance, or commercial applications that are in scope to be validated for PA-DSS. Some of them are:

- Cardholder data has to be transmitted over HTTPS. In any instance of the website or Web application, it must be ensured that the cardholder data is not transmitted over an unencrypted connection, or that the HTTPS is applied selectively only in authentication screens, but not for transmission of cardholder data.
- Certificate authority selection is critical. Certificate authorities are supposed to perform multiple verifications before the certificate is granted.

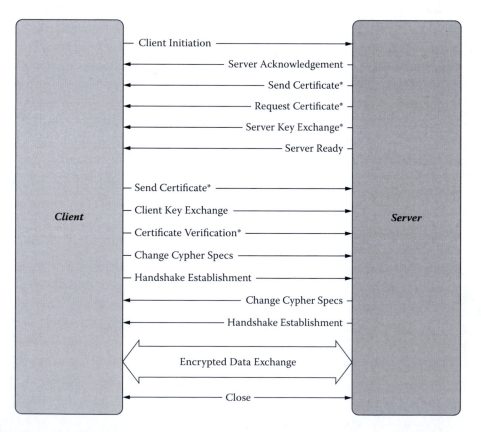

FIGURE 11.2
SSL/TLS handshake and key-exchange process.

- SSL v 3.0 and below are not to be implemented. TLS has to be deployed for all certificates.
- Utilize TLS certificates with strong cipher suites. Strong cipher suites include those that are FIPS (Federal Information Processing Standard)-compliant. Please refer to Chapter 10 for an understanding of FIPS-compliant cryptosystems, including AES, 3DES, SHA-1, and so on.

11.1.2.2 Secure Shell (SSH)

Secure Shell (SSH) is one of the most popular protocols on the Internet. SSH is used predominantly for management of systems over a network. It utilizes public-key cryptography (asymmetric) for authenticating and encrypting sessions between the client and server. The latest version of the SSH protocol is the SSH v 2.

SSH works on public-key infrastructure where a public–private key pair is generated by the user. The user generates a public–private key pair on the server. The server's public key is added to the client's list of authorized public keys (authorized hosts). The client might also generate a passphrase that is to be used for manual login (recommended) as opposed to automated key-pair-based authentication.

The client connects to the host system using the SSH protocol. The password is encrypted with the server's public key. The packet is received by the server and decrypted with the server's private key. Based on the validity of the password/passphrase provided, the user is authenticated to the host and is allowed to access it subsequently.

SSH is used for multiple actions and activities. It can be used for system administration, and it can also be used for tunneling connections through proxies. It is also used extensively for file transfers, and so on.

SSH works on the TCP/IP for transport and network services. The transport layer manages authentication, sets up encryption, compression, and integrity verification. The User Authentication Layer handles user authentication based on multiple authentication modes. SSH might utilize password-based authentication, public-key authentication, or API-based authentication (SSO).

Figure 11.3 is an image of SSH layers, and Figure 11.4 is the communication chain between client and server in the case of an SSH connection.

11.1.2.3 IPSec VPN

IPSec is one of the most popular protocols that is utilized for creating virtual private networks (VPN). VPN is a popular way of connecting remote computers over public network connections in such a way that the remote computer becomes part of the local network of the network that the remote computer is connecting to. For instance, I would like to access files in my office from my home. However, my office and my home are separate networks. I can log in to a VPN server/device in my office, authenticate, and the VPN server/device makes me part of the office subnet and gives me access to my system/files. IPSec is a suite of protocols that is used to establish VPN connections by providing protection at the IP data packet level. Therefore, it can be the network vehicle for other transport and application protocols. IPSec provides the following functions with reference to security:

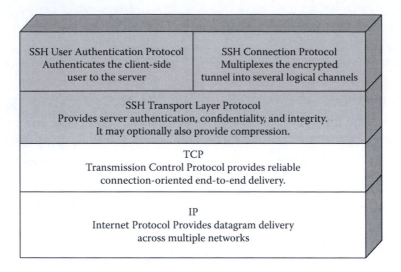

FIGURE 11.3
SSH protocol stack.

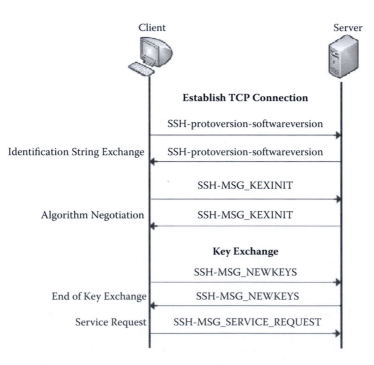

FIGURE 11.4
Communication between client and server—SSH.

Authentication: Ensures that the packet received is from the claimed/legitimate sender

Integrity: Ensures that the packet is not modified by an unauthorized entity

Confidentiality: Ensures secrecy for the message content through encryption over public networks

IPSec works in two modes, namely the transport mode and the tunnel mode. In the transport mode, only the payload of the IP packet is encrypted and/or authenticated. The IP header remains unchanged. As the IP header is not protected, the attacker can learn the source and destination of the IP packet. The tunnel mode provides more comprehensive security, where the entire IP packet, including the header, is encrypted and/or authenticated. The new IP header contains two IPSec gateway addresses. The gateways that send and receive packets perform encapsulation and decapsulation. Use of the tunnel mode prevents an attacker from identifying the source and destination of the IP packet.

The following elements of the IPSec provide the following facets of security:

- Authentication header
- Encapsulating security payload (ESP)
- Internet key exchange

Authentication header (AH): The AH provides authentication and integrity using industry-standard algorithms. The AH is inserted between the IP header and the message contents. It does not provide data confidentiality, as that is provided by the ESP. The AH ensures that the packet's origin, destination, and contents are not tampered with.

Encapsulating security payload (ESP): The ESP provides authentication, integrity, and confidentiality. It is mostly meant to provide message content protection through encryption. It utilizes industry-standard algorithms to perform encryption. It can perform both authentication and encryption operations. In the event that the ESP is used for authentication, it provides authentication and integrity for the payload and not for the header.

Internet key exchange (IKE): VPNs utilize a concept called "security association" for the security functions into the IP. The security association is a suite of algorithms and parameters that provides encryption and authentication in a unidirectional flow. In normal, bidirectional traffic flows, IPSec traffic is secured with a pair of security associations. Security associations are implemented with the Internet key exchange. To decide the level of security for a packet, IPSec utilizes the security parameter index (SPI), which has an index to the security association database (SADB) that is configured. Based on the inputs from the SPI based on the SADB, the traffic on IPSec is protected accordingly. Security associations may be set up from group to group. There may be more than a single security association per group.

11.1.3 Requirement 4.1.1: WiFi Security Practices for Cardholder Data Transmissions

In the previous section, I briefly mentioned that the PCI-DSS considers wireless networks as open, public networks, where the encryption of cardholder information for wireless networks in the cardholder data environment (CDE) is mandatory.

Wireless protections include encrypted and authenticated transmissions to and from a wireless access point. The first type of protection introduced for wireless encryption and authentication was the wired equivalent privacy (WEP). The WEP is based on encrypting the communications with an RC4 stream cipher with a CRC32 utilized for message integrity. However, by 2001, it was confirmed and demonstrated that WEP was easily broken.

Owing to the obvious security flaws and deficiencies of the WEP, the WiFi Alliance introduced the Wi-Fi-protected access (WPA) as a security specification. The WPA utilized a Temporal Key Integrity Protocol (TKIP) to ensure that keys were changed for every packet transmitted across the network. The WPA also utilized a larger key size as opposed to the WEP. Whereas the WEP utilized a 40-bit or 104-bit key, the WPA generated 128-bit keys for encrypted transmissions across a wireless network.

In 2004, the WiFi Alliance introduced the WPA2, which is currently the security standard for protected wireless communication. The WPA2 added greater strength to the previous security features of the WPA. It supports an advanced encryption standard (AES) and is eligible for FIPS 140-2 compliance.

WPA2 has two modes, namely the personal and the enterprise mode. The personal mode is used for homes or small offices. The personal mode utilizes a preshared key, where the user uses a shared key to authenticate to the network. The WiFi access point generates a 256-bit key from the passphrase or the preshared key to encrypt the traffic between the clients and the WiFi access point. A pre-shared-key authentication system is usually not recommended or scalable for an enterprise, as keys generated by users tend to be weak and subject to brute-force attacks.

The WPA2 personal can also be set up to utilize the TKIP that was utilized with WPA. The TKIP was actually first introduced during the WEP era to offset some of the security issues surrounding WEP. TKIP uses a key-mixing function that uses a secret key and an initialization vector before being passed through an RC4 cipher. This was a departure from WEP, which just concatenated the initialization vector and the secret key and passed it through an RC4 cipher.

Additionally TKIP also uses a sequence counter, and packets that are not received in order will be rejected by the WiFi access point. The TKIP also uses a rekeying mechanism that ensures that every single packet that is transmitted contains a unique key that is used for encryption.

I would definitely rely on the WPA personal with preshared key, as it has AES encryption, provided that the encryption key is generated with a pseudo-random number generator (PRNG).

The WPA2 enterprise, however, is focused on enterprise deployments of the WPA2. Home and small-office users usually do not possess authentication servers that can be used in conjunction with the WiFi access point. The enterprise must deploy an authentication server like a RADIUS, LDAP, OTP, or active directory server to utilize the WPA2 enterprise. This ensures that a unique key is generated for every individual using the WiFi, thereby being scalable without compromising on the security, as every user has his/her own key to access the WiFi access point. The WPA2 enterprise utilizes Enterprise Authentication Protocol (EAP) for authentication to the access point. The WPA2 can also be run in TKIP or AES. Of course, AES is preferred, as it is a stronger cipher, and combined with the EAP and unique key per user, it is definitely a secure solution for an enterprise.

The EAP has multiple modes that can be utilized for enterprise deployment, like the Protected Extensible Authentication Protocol (PEAP), which is the EAP with an encrypted TLS tunnel. Another mode is the EAP TTLS, where the EAP extends the TLS for encryption and authentication. However, in both these modes, the servers need to have certificates installed, and the clients authenticate over passwords or a one-time password (OTP). The most secure mode is said to be EAP-TLS, where the EAP implements TLS for encryption and authentication. However, the main difference here is that the client as well as the server must possess certificates to perform authentication, thereby making it more secure but more difficult to implement as well.

Wireless networks are largely present in merchant environments, especially for POS and billing. The PCI-DSS mandated the discontinuity of WEP as a security measure for wireless points on June 30, 2010, subsequently mandating the use of WPA2 for wireless access.

11.2 REQUIREMENT 4.2: UNPROTECTED PANS OVER END-USER MESSAGING TECHNOLOGIES

Requirement 4.2 is quite a simple requirement. It extends the transmission of cardholder data over messaging technologies. For the PCI-DSS, messaging technologies

include e-mail, instant messaging, communicator applications, chat applications, and so on. These technologies are used extensively in customer support departments and in banks and TPPs when they are communicating card disputes, and so on, over e-mail.

If card information must be sent over these technologies, it must be encrypted. The encryption provided must be with the same rigor of encryption of cardholder data as specified in Requirements 3 and 4. E-mail encryption methods like PGP (pretty good privacy) and GPG (Gnu privacy guard) may be used to encrypt primary account numbers (PANs) before sending them to recipients over e-mail. Additionally, an encrypted ZIP file with an AES 128-bit key or higher might suffice as well.

Organizations must have written policies in their acceptable-usage documentation explicitly stating that PANs must never be sent over end-user messaging technologies like e-mail, and so on.

Assessors have to identify all areas of messaging technologies utilized in the CDE. Tools exploring IMAP servers, Outlook PST and OST files, Jabber servers, and so on, may be in order. Many organizations have started adopting data-leakage prevention software at the gateway. These appliances perform deep packet inspection and file parsing to identify traces of plaintext cardholder information sent over an open, public network. I was recently performing a security-code-review project for one of the payment brands, and they had deployed a DLP (data loss prevention) application to handle such instances of policy violation. They might have to run tools to discover PANs in e-mail attachments and the message body if required. Instances of e-mailing cardholder information is the largest at merchant customer service operations, banks, and TPPs.

11.3 SUMMARY

Requirement 4 has been the focus of this chapter, where we have explored the requirement precluding cardholder information from being sent in plaintext over open, public networks. We first defined the meaning of open, public networks. We then noted that PCI-DSS includes wireless networks and GSM/GPRS networks within the purview of open, public networks. We then delved into protocols and implementations that can be used to implement encryption of data in transit. Multiple protocols like the SSL/TLS, SSH, and IPSec were explored, with the focus on protocol details. We also discussed wireless security requirements of PCI-DSS Requirement 4.1.1, where WPA/WPA2 must be utilized to secure wireless authentication and encryption. We detailed some of the implementations of WPA2 and various authentication and encryption techniques.

Finally, we closed with Requirement 4.2, which mandates that cardholder information must never be sent unencrypted over e-mail or other messaging technologies. We also briefly explored some techniques that assessors can use to identify traces of cardholder data transmitted over plain text.

12

Requirement 5: Use and Regularly Update Antivirus Software

Malware is one of the most common and pernicious threats to security in the modern enterprise. Malware has devastating impacts on operating systems, software, and applications, causing large environments and mission-critical infrastructure to fail or be compromised. One of the key defenses against malware is to use antivirus software and virus-management applications to thwart the intrusion and subsequent propagation of malware within the environment. PCI-DSS Requirement 5 deals exclusively with antivirus management for the PCI-compliant organization.

12.1 REQUIREMENT 5.1: USE OF ANTIVIRUS PROGRAMS TO PROTECT COMMONLY AFFECTED SYSTEMS

12.1.1 Antivirus Deployment within the PCI Environment (CDE)

Requirement 5.1 should have been the simplest requirement in the PCI-DSS. However, it is often the most debated requirement in the standard, not because the requirement per se is complex to execute, but because it is puzzling to many experienced IT managers and security professionals. The requirement goes like this: "Deploy antivirus software on all systems commonly affected by malicious software (particularly personal computers and servers)."

An antivirus application has become an enterprise staple requirement today. Most organizations have a centralized antivirus console and have an instance of the antivirus application installed on all systems within the environment. The administrator accesses the console to perform routine virus-management tasks, such as scanning systems, updating antivirus signatures as they are released by their principal, taking corrective action in the event of a virus outbreak, and so on.

However, the cause for controversy is the phrase, "systems commonly affected by malicious software." Further, Requirement 5.1.1 specifies that the antivirus program must be capable of removing and protecting against all kinds of malware, including viruses, worms, trojans, rootkits, spyware, adware, and so on. This causes a great deal of flutter among users of the non-Windows variety of operating systems, typically, Unix-based operating systems (OS) like the multiple flavors of Linux, BSD, Mac OS X, and so on.

I believe that the intent of this requirement (why it has been worded this way) is that the PCI-DSS does not want to exclude any class of operating systems from the scope of requiring an antivirus application. Over the years, Linux and Mac systems have also been affected by malware. However, while this malware is largely in the form of worms[*] and not viruses or trojans, etc., the fact remains that they are still not above the requirement. Therefore, this requirement is to be interpreted as saying that if there is a viable antivirus solution available for these operating systems (Unix-based OS), then the organization must deploy an antivirus solution. For instance there are antivirus applications available for the Mac, Ubuntu, RedHat, and some other Unix-based and Linux distributions. Antivirus applications like AVG, ClamAV, and

Symantec come to mind. However, for operating systems like mainframes and other distributions where no viable antivirus product/application exists, organizations are not required to deploy an antivirus application.

This requirement is also largely based on the interpretation and discretion of the qualified security assessor (QSA), especially regarding the requirement specifying commonly affected systems. In the event that the QSA sees that the remedy to malware for Linux/Unix-based OSs is in hardening, patching, and continuous monitoring, then an antivirus application would not be deemed necessary. Additionally, both hardening and patching are separate PCI requirements that are duly addressed.

Let us return to the requirement now. The requirement states that the antivirus application should also serve as a protection not only from viruses, but from worms, trojans, spyware, and so on. Most antivirus products today provide multiple protections for all these malicious instances of code. However, I firmly believe that many antivirus applications do not possess a great capacity to detect and contain worms that are based on operating system/application vulnerabilities.[†] Therefore, antivirus efficacy always has to be viewed in conjunction with patching and patch management and/or host/gateway-based firewalls.

---

[*] Worms are independent programs that are designed to exploit a specific flaw in a system. They can be controlled remotely, unlike viruses. They do not attach themselves to executables like viruses. They usually act on memory and CPU and possess capabilities to self-replicate and spread across a network. Examples include the Code Red Worm and Conficker, among others.

[†] During penetration tests that my organization performs, we are able to trigger exploits and escalate privileges several times, even with a fully functional and updated commercial antivirus application running on the system. I would not like to name specific brands or products, but there are many ways that attackers are able to exploit system vulnerabilities to gain privileged access to a system.

12.2 REQUIREMENT 5.2: MANAGING THE ANTIVIRUS APPLICATION

12.2.1 Managing and Monitoring the Antivirus Application for PCI Compliance

Antivirus applications have to be configured and managed optimally for PCI compliance. As mentioned previously, antivirus applications are usually managed at a centralized level across the enterprise. However, in the event that a centralized management cannot be implemented, the administrators must put in a little more effort to ensure that they are continuously protected. The following are the PCI requirements for the management of an antivirus deployment within the PCI environment or the cardholder data environment (CDE):

- *Logging*: The antivirus application should be capable of generating logs of all of the antivirus application-driven events and malware-driven events affecting the system.
- *Updates*: The antivirus application must be configured for automatic updates on a regular basis. Most antivirus products are configured for updates on a daily basis from the antivirus server. The antivirus server is the centralized server deployed by the organization that receives its updates from the server that is maintained by the creator of the application.
- *Scanning*: The antivirus application must be configured for periodic and automated scanning. In most cases, full-system scans are run on a weekly

basis. Other than that, the antivirus application is configured to perform continuous protection at the network layer, memory layer, and the application layer of the operating system.

Figure 12.1 is a screenshot of a popular enterprise antivirus console.

12.3 COMMERCIAL APPLICATIONS: ANTIVIRUS REQUIREMENTS

One of the requirements of the PA-DSS that is in conjunction with Requirement 5 of the PCI-DSS is that the payment application should not interfere with the working of the antivirus software. For instance, some applications require the antivirus software on the system to be turned off for them to function properly. Such applications are in violation of the PA-DSS, and an organization cannot hope to get compliant by deploying such commercial application in the PCI environment, which mandates the need for antivirus applications.

12.4 SUMMARY

This chapter focused on Requirement 5 of the PCI-DSS. The requirement relates to the deployment of antivirus software on all of the systems and servers within the PCI environment (CDE). We also learned about the controversy involving antivirus deployments for all systems within the environment, regardless of the type of operating system. Finally, we explored some aspects

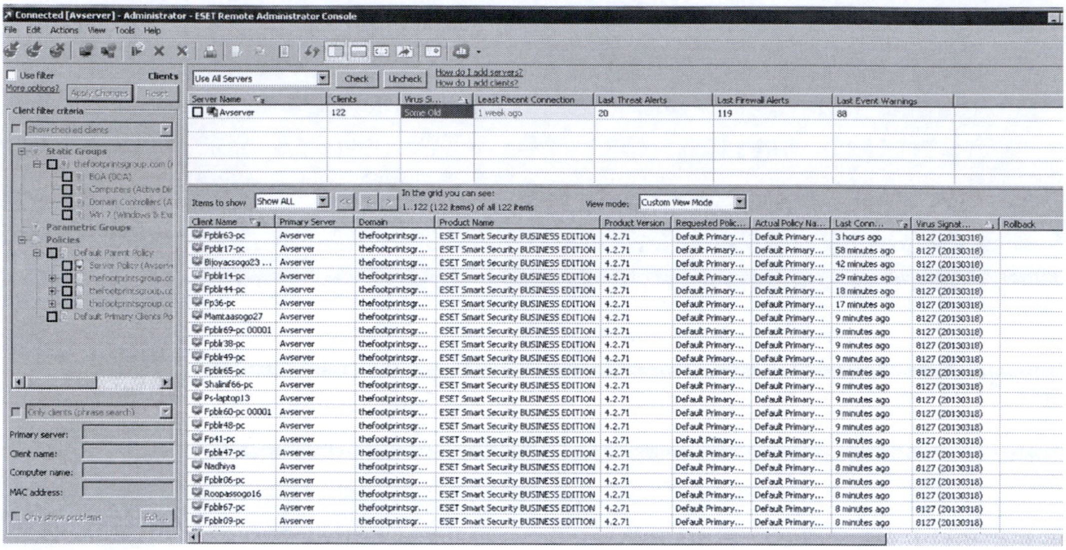

FIGURE 12.1
Antivirus console.

of management of the antivirus application through logging, regular updates, and automated scans for all of the machines deployed within the PCI environment.

13

Requirement 6: Develop and Maintain Secure Systems

Applications are the lifeblood of any organization. This is true of organizations in the payment-card industry as well. Applications are an indispensable entity for organizations like merchants, TPPs, e-commerce merchants, service providers, and so on. Requirement 6 deals heavily with the security of applications. The requirement begins with the process of patching and patch management across operating systems (OS) and application components in the PCI environment. Subsequently, the requirement dives deep into application security practices for organizations developing/deploying applications in the PCI environment, including vulnerability management and secure coding practices for said applications. This requirement addresses the all-important aspect of Security in the Software Development Life Cycle (SSDLC).

13.1 REQUIREMENT 6.1: PATCH-MANAGEMENT PRACTICES FOR PCI COMPLIANCE

Security is always going to be a cat and mouse game because there'll be people out there that are hunting for the zero day award, you have people that don't have configuration management, don't have vulnerability management, don't have patch management.

Kevin Mitnick

I recently had a candid conversation with an experienced security consultant, and we discussed information security challenges, problems, compliance, and so on. I asked him what he believed was one of the greatest security challenges that organizations faced today. One would normally expect an answer on the lines of the latest technologies and practices like advanced persistent threats (APTs), cloud security, secure cloud deployment, securing Web services, and so on. However, his answer was on the lines of my personal experience when he said, "Organizations still do not patch their systems."

Patch management is an essential aspect of security that few organizations get right. The negative effects of this can be devastating in terms of a data breach. At the time of this writing, a Java flaw has been found that allows an attacker to exploit Java's Runtime Environment (JRE), a platform that runs on pretty much every single system and can execute commands on the system by bypassing Java's security sandbox. It is interesting to note that five weeks after the exploit had been released, my team was performing a penetration test at a client's location that was to be certified for PCI-DSS, and this flaw was found on all of its production servers and most of its desktops. Figure 13.1 is an article at ArsTechnica about the Java exploit.

13.1.1 Patch Management for PCI Compliance

Requirement 6.1 of the PCI-DSS requires that all system components and software must be updated with the latest patches for known vulnerabilities.

Let's explore one of the primary aspects of this requirement, which is the aspect that focuses on patching being required for all system components and software. This requirement essentially means that all network devices, operating systems, and software/applications that run on these operating systems need to be patched with security patches as and when they are available to address known vulnerabilities.

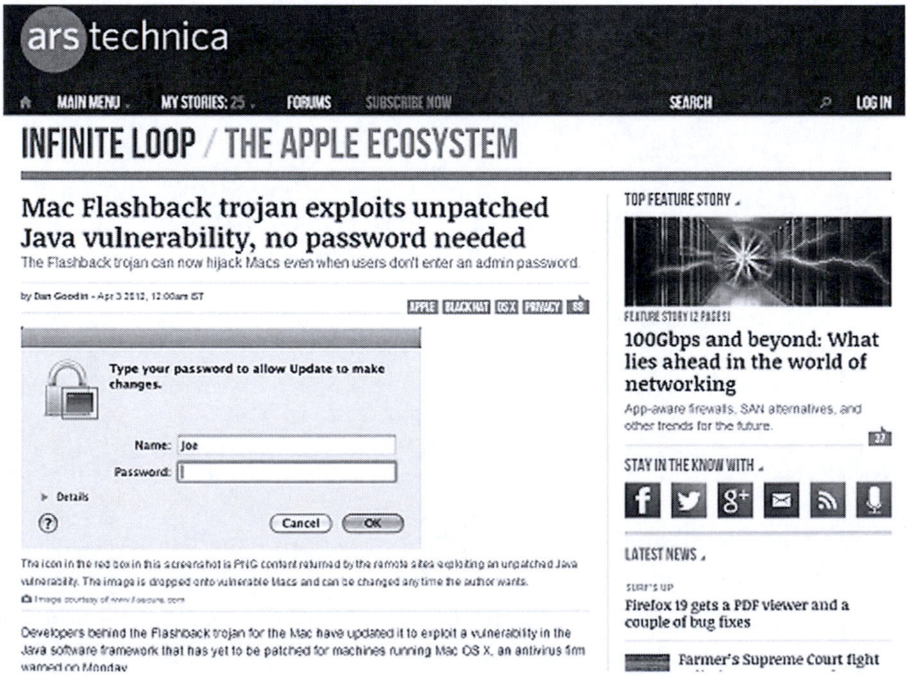

FIGURE 13.1
News article on Arstechnica.com on the Java exploit.

It is a common practice to patch operating systems, especially Windows operating systems. In a typical Windows environment, the organization would run a Windows server update services (WSUS) server or its equivalent, and the patching would be driven from the WSUS server to all of the servers and desktops within the environment through the active directory, thereby ensuring a uniform deployment of patches across all systems within the environment.

Some of the real challenges to patching involve third-party software and applications that run on the operating system, such as Adobe Reader, Microsoft Office, Java, and browser patches (Mozilla, Chrome, and so on), aside from the myriad applications that run on end-user systems. Servers present a different challenge because they contain a veritable Pandora's box of software and software components that may not be able to be patched because of the server's criticality.

If applications present a challenge, network devices are equally challenging. Network devices usually have firmware updates. Network device vendors such as Cisco routinely release firmware updates for their routers and firewalls that perform general bug fixes as well as security bug fixes. These patches are tougher to deploy, as they require downtime that must be scheduled for said devices, and the patch must be applied carefully without hindering the existing configurations and functionality of the device. Imagine installing a firmware update on the organization's Internet router and the router crashing. The organization would be without Internet access until the problem was fixed. Fortunately, these firmware updates are not as common as updates for OSs or software/applications.

Unix/Linux-based systems are often considered challenging to patch for several organizations. These servers usually power the organization's critical production servers, which are the organization's "purveyors of services." Scheduling downtime for these servers is highly challenging and is sometimes impossible owing to the critical nature of their services.

13.1.2 Approaches to Patching and Patch Management

Automated patching and patch management is one of the most common approaches. The organization deploys a patch server, which runs WSUS, SCCM, IBM's Tivoli Endpoint Manager, Desktop Central, Solarwinds, or other applications on a particular server. This server aggregates patches for multiple operating systems, software, and applications and, based on the administrator's schedule, deploys these patches on the system components and applications within the environment. These applications also have sophisticated consoles that provide administrators with in-depth and up-to-date information about the patch levels across the organization, allowing them to identify noncompliant systems, systems where patches have failed, and so on. Figure 13.2 is a screenshot of the dashboard of a popular patch-management product.

The patch-management solution that the organization deploys must ideally be able to address third-party software patches like Adobe, Java, and so on, apart from operating-system patches. The PCI standards require the organization to roll out patches, especially critical security patches, within a month of their release. This means that all patches that have been identified as a critical security patch by the vendor must be deployed across all systems in the PCI environment within a month. Thus

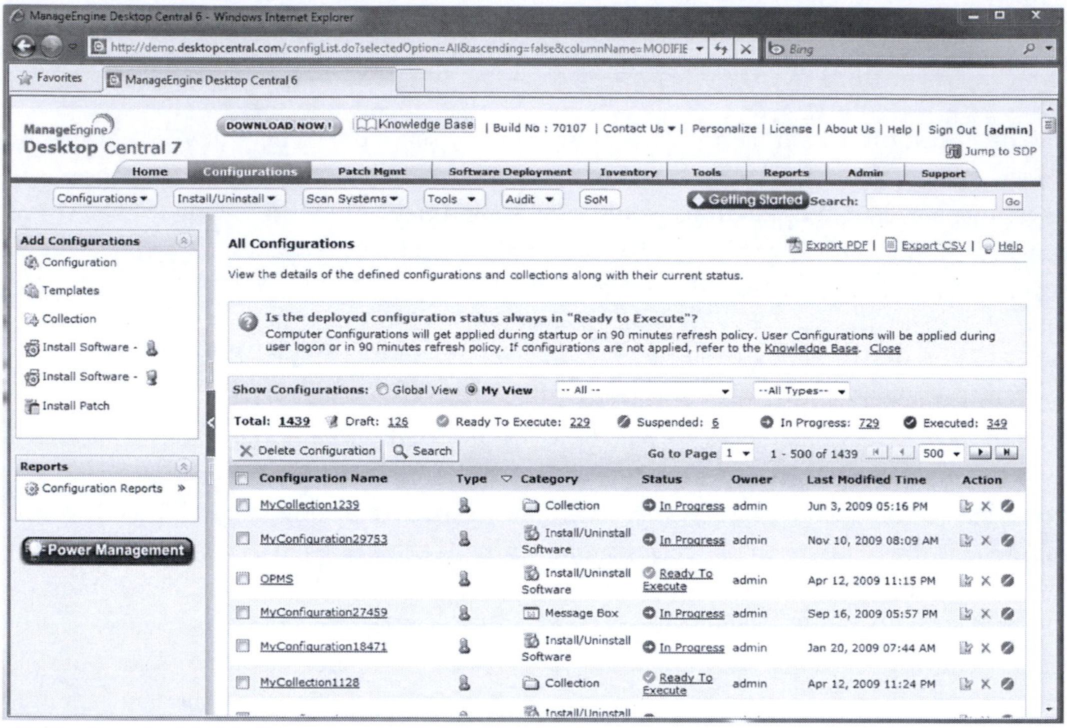

FIGURE 13.2
Dashboard of a popular patch-management application.

the organization must follow a complete change-management cycle for patching systems to ensure that critical security patches are rolled out into the organization's systems within a month of their release. The patch-management process is described in the following subsections and is the subject of Requirement 6.4.5 of the PCI-DSS.

13.1.2.1 Change-Management Process of System Patch Deployment

System patches have to be applied carefully. This is essential because system patches affect the behavior of systems, sometimes in a negative way. For instance, in 2010, some security patches for Microsoft Office® 2007 rendered some PowerPoint Compatibility View features unusable, thereby hindering essential functionality of the application.

Therefore, there has to be a proper change-control and change-management process planned for the deployment of system patches in the PCI environment. These consist of the following processes:

13.1.2.1.1 Establishment of Controlled Patch Process

One of the key patch-management strategies is to have a controlled patch-management process that involves approvals and sign-offs from relevant stakeholders. This is especially important because once patches are deployed, the systems usually need to be restarted, thereby causing downtime for the involved business. Usually, the request is raised by the system admin or the IT department. These approvals should usually be obtained from the head of the department (IT or IT security) and involve key stakeholders, including the business owners (project managers or heads of business units, etc.) to account for downtime. The request is usually in the form of a change request or a change ticket that is part of the organization's ticketing system. Sometimes, organizations utilizing patch-management software raise it via the software as well. Often it is just an e-mail detailing the following:

13.1.2.1.1.1 Documentation of Impact

The impact of the patch is documented by the system admin or the personnel deploying the patch across the systems. The impact could occur due to downtime caused by installation of the patch.

13.1.2.1.1.2 Patch Testing Procedure

The patches deployed within an environment need to be tested in a staging environment. The staging environment is a test environment created by the system admin or personnel in the IT department that reflects some or most of the systems within the target environment. The patch is deployed in the environment for a while, usually a week or so, and observed for any adverse impact. In the event that the patch does not cause adverse impacts and behaves without instability on the test environment, it is rolled out to the entire environment, subject to the patch-management process approvals, and so on. System admins may use virtual machines to simulate multiple types of systems in their environment. For instance, let us assume that they use CentOS servers with JBoss application servers, CentOS with Oracle DB, and Windows 7 in the environment. They can simulate these conditions on multiple virtual machines and observe patch impact. In the event that the patch does not impact

the environment adversely, then the patch can be rolled out.

13.1.2.1.1.3 Back-Out Procedures

Sometimes, even with due diligence exercised with patch testing and studying the patch, the patch can prove to have adverse impact on the system. It might hinder essential functionality or create a denial-of-service condition. In such cases, back-out procedures have to be prepared to roll back the patch or take corrective action against the adverse effects of the patch.

13.1.3 Risk-Based Approach to Patch Management

Often it is not possible to patch even critical security patches in a month for organizations with large IT operations. The size and scale of several enterprises, supplemented with several variables like operating-system type, software applications deployed, and so on, can present a challenge to several IT departments for patching. For instance, patching a production DB server running a Linux operating system and a MySQL database might present a challenge, as downtime cannot be scheduled for the application of the patch. Additionally, let's assume that the server is one of 100 such servers, and it becomes clear that application of the patch manually is likely to take some time. In such cases, a risk-based approach to patch management can be taken, where the organization deploys patches to critical systems like public-facing systems and servers and deploys patches to less critical systems (e.g., internal systems and servers) within three months of the release of a critical security patch. Figure 13.3 is a visual representation of elements in a change-management process.

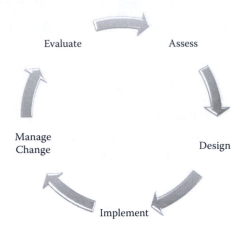

FIGURE 13.3
Visual representation of elements in a change-management process.

13.1.4 Assessor's Notes for Verifying Patch-Management Practices

Patch management can be a tricky aspect of assessment. However, it is essential that an assessor delve deeply into the organization's patch-management practices and its effectiveness hitherto. Most organizations of a certain size and scale should possess automated patch-management solutions that roll out patches at a scheduled interval. However, this is not always the case. In the event that the organization is utilizing an automated patch-management system, the assessor should look into the console of the system to identify the presence of patches across systems in the enterprises. In some cases, applications have a tendency to stop functioning due to a security patch. In such cases, the organization usually ceases to patch these applications. In such events, the assessor has to verify the presence of some kind of compensating control that is over and above the requirement of the standard.

It must also be noted that *all* systems in the PCI environment need to be patched. Several sys admins and organizations cite criticality of the server/resource as a prime factor for not patching said system. However, the requirement is very clear, and there is little subjectivity to it.

The assessor must also consider running tools like the Microsoft Baseline Security Analyzer and Lynis (for Linux systems) to identify the patch levels of the system. Another focus area for the assessor must be the security update process for network devices. Network devices that need to be manually updated with firmware tend to be the most ignored, as administrators do not take them offline to apply a patch. However, unpatched network devices might be an open invitation to multiple attack types based on the vulnerabilities in the firmware.

13.2 REQUIREMENT 6.2: VULNERABILITY-MANAGEMENT PRACTICES FOR PCI COMPLIANCE

One of the key considerations for a patch-management practice is the criticality of the patch or the security update. The standard requires that critical security patches and updates must be applied to the systems and software components in the PCI environment.

There are several questions that come to mind. How do we know which update/patch is critical? How do we know whether a critical update for one is a medium-severity update for another? Where do we exercise subjectivity in this process?

The good thing is that PCI does not require the exercising of subjectivity with reference to patching and security updates for critical systems and software components in the PCI environment. The PCI standard requires the use of common vulnerability measurement metrics to define critical severity vulnerabilities in the PCI environment.

Vulnerability metrics have become a very important aspect of identifying and ranking vulnerabilities in different applications. The use of common metrics has made it easier for organizations to be uniform in their ranking of security vulnerabilities, thereby ensuring that enterprises do not need to exercise subjectivity in remediating or treating a risk incorrectly based on assumed parameters and incorrect perceptions. One of the most popular metrics for vulnerability management is the Common Vulnerability Scoring System (CVSS). The CVSS is a scoring system that is calculated based on multiple parameters for a given vulnerability. Based on the scores on the individual parameters, a base score is derived that is used to measure the severity of the vulnerability in question. The parameters used by the CVSS are as follows:

Access vector: The access vector is essentially a measure of remoteness of the attacker with reference to the target. It can either be local network access (part of the same LAN), adjacent network (which includes the exploitation of a local network and gaining access to the target via a given vulnerability), or a remote network, where an attacker could be across a remote network to exploit the given vulnerability.

Access complexity: The access complexity parameter measures the complexity of the attack vector required to carry out the exploit on the target system. The complexity of the attack can be classified as high, medium, or low. High complexity indicates that the attack is complex to successfully execute. Medium and low are indicators of the complexity of the attacks.

Authentication: The authentication parameter measures whether the attacker requires authentication to the target system to perform the attack. For instance, to execute certain Microsoft SMB (Server Message Block Protocol) exploits, the attacker has to have authentication credentials on the target machine. The measures of authentication are multiple, single, and none. Multiple authentication means that the attacker has to be authenticated multiple times before being able to exploit the vulnerability. Single authentication is when an attacker has to be authenticated once to the target system to exploit the given vulnerability. None refers to an unauthenticated attacker being able to perform the attack against the vulnerable target system.

Impact on CIA: The last three parameters measure the impact of the exploit by an attacker on the target system for a given vulnerability on the Confidentiality, Integrity, and Availability of the system. The impacts are measured in terms of high, medium, and low severity.

Based on the parameters, a base score is calculated, called the CVSS base score. This base score determines the level of severity of the given vulnerability.

The CVSS is a key metric for vulnerability measurement, as it is used extensively by the PCI-DSS in more than one instance. The PCI-DSS requires all vulnerabilities with a CVSS base score of 4.0 and higher to be categorized as a high-severity vulnerability. In the event that the vendor has categorized the security update/patch as a "critical" patch, the same has to be taken into consideration as a critical security patch.

The organization has to define a structured process that involves identifying and ranking vulnerabilities discovered through the patching process or the vulnerability-management process. The vulnerabilities of a high severity and critical nature have to be ranked as such by individuals identifying said vulnerabilities. This was a best practice until June 30, 2012; after that date, it became a requirement of the PCI-DSS.

13.3 SECURE APPLICATION DEVELOPMENT PRACTICES FOR PCI-DSS AND PA-DSS

13.3.1 Requirement 6.3: Secure SDLC for Application Development

This requirement is in scope for organizations that develop software applications. This refers to organizations developing software applications for their use or when an entity has outsourced custom application development to a company that develops software solutions. For instance, a merchant Panthera might have their own software development department that develops custom apps that they deploy in the PCI environment. Alternatively, Panthera may outsource custom app development to Tiger Inc., which develops custom applications to be used in Panthera's PCI environment. In the latter case, several requirements relating to application development, and so on, will be in scope for the outsourced service provider under their compliance process.

A secure application is best secured from the ground up. The reason for this is that an application that is secured from inception is more comprehensively and more effectively secure than an application where security is an afterthought and where security controls are implemented based on specific reactive findings, rather than being integrated into the design from the ground up.

The practice of infusing security requirements from an application's inception is called the Secure Software Development Life Cycle (SSDLC). Simply put, an SSDLC is said to have been followed when an organization takes security into consideration at every stage of the SDLC.

Typically, an SDLC begins with the requirements for the application. The requirements are finalized and designed based on the needs and objectives of the application. The design is finalized and, subsequently, the design is translated to code and the application by development. Once the application has been developed, it is tested. Finally, it is deployed and maintained in an environment. Figure 13.4 is a representation of the stages of a typical SDLC process.

This is a very simple and typical SDLC. There are multiple models and standards for the SDLC, such as Waterfall, Agile, etc. However, the parameters of the SDLC remain the same regardless of the model followed. Design, requirements gathering,

Application Development Lifecycle

FIGURE 13.4
Stages of a typical SDLC process.

development, and so on, are universally present in any SDLC model. A secure SDLC (SSDLC) is one where security is infused into every stage of the SDLC. For instance, while considering requirements for the application, security requirements must also be considered, documented, and finalized. Security requirements must be designed into the application along with the rest of the application's design. The secure design of the application must be developed securely as per a secure specification, with secure coding practices and processes.

There are several techniques and processes that people use to integrate security into the SDLC, including the following:

- Application risk assessment
- Threat modeling
- Informal secure SDLC practices

This is a critical requirement not only for the PCI-DSS, but for application security itself. However, I have seen very few companies with the ability to infuse security into the SDLC. Most of the security provided to the application is based on an unstructured process of client inputs, informal meetings by designers and architects, and allusion to some security standards.

Oftentimes, I find that organizations implement basic security measures and start considering security only after they are rejected by a client organization on account of poor security or after their application is involved in a security breach. I was

reviewing code for a custom application developed by a reputable software development vendor for a merchant organization. While I cannot delve into the technical details of the review, suffice it to say that the presence of gaping holes for security would be an understatement. Only after multiple rejection cycles and failed security tests did the organization develop an application that was relatively robust from the point of view of security.

13.3.1.1 The Risk-Assessment Approach to Secure SDLC

Risk assessment is the process where risks are identified, assessed, and evaluated based on the threats, vulnerabilities, and the impacts of threats exploiting those vulnerabilities. Although, there are several standards and methodologies to assess enterprise or organizational risk, there are no specific methodologies to assess Web-application risks. The methodology that has been expounded in this book is a unique standard that we at my company have implemented. This aims to be a practical and effective methodology that helps the organization perform a comprehensive risk assessment of the application, which then becomes the security requirements for the application. This security requirement subsequently feeds into the SDLC and integrates into what ultimately is known as a SSDLC. This is a structured methodology for assessing Web-application risks by imbibing some of the best concepts from several structured risk assessment methodologies like the OCTAVE (operationally critical threat, asset, and vulnerability evaluation), the NIST SP800-30 (a methodology for performing risk assessments for the system during the software development life cycle), and also using the DREAD methodology used for threat modeling Web application security attacks. A brief overview of Web application security risk assessment is as follows:

- System characterization
- Threat profiling and threat modeling
- Risk-mitigation strategy: formulation of detailed security requirements for the Web application.

The processes of the risk-assessment phase are highlighted in Figure 13.5.

13.3.1.1.1 Overview of the System Characterization Process

The first step in a Web-application risk assessment is to characterize the system being designed and developed. The system-characterization process includes the subprocesses of identifying the critical information assets that need to be protected. Critical information assets are those without which the application would be adversely affected. These information assets, which are indispensable to the organization, are stored, processed, or transmitted via the Web application. Identification of critical application data/information assets is imperative, as it would be the sole determinant of the controls and risk-mitigation plans that are drawn up later for the protection of the application data. The rationale is simply this: How do we know what to protect and how much? The answer clearly lies in identifying critical assets and understanding the impact of a breach of confidentiality/integrity/availability of the same.

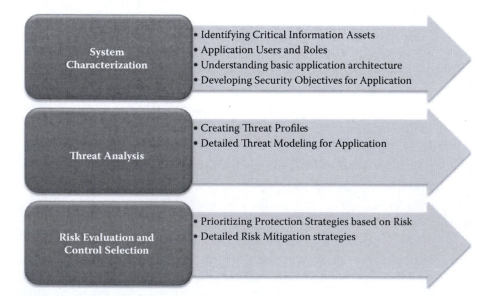

System Characterization
- Identifying Critical Information Assets
- Application Users and Roles
- Understanding basic application architecture
- Developing Security Objectives for Application

Threat Analysis
- Creating Threat Profiles
- Detailed Threat Modeling for Application

Risk Evaluation and Control Selection
- Prioritizing Protection Strategies based on Risk
- Detailed Risk Mitigation strategies

FIGURE 13.5
Web-application security risk-assessment overview.

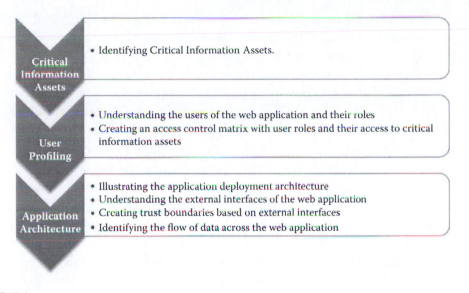

FIGURE 13.6
The system-characterization phase and its subprocesses.

Another aspect of system characterization is to understand the various users of the application and their access to critical information assets. This provides a great deal of clarity about the types of users and their interactions with the critical information assets. For instance, a Web application with users constituting the general public would be more at risk than an application only constituting the employees of an organization. Finally, system characterization involves understanding the basic application architecture and its deployment environment (see Figure 13.6). Network diagrams are used to understand the deployment environment of the application. Application architecture diagrams are used (a) to understand the system interfaces of the application and the systems the application interacts with and (b) to formulate the levels of trust to be established with each interface of the application.

13.3.1.1.2 Identifying Critical Information Assets

An organization in today's world is a giant storehouse of information. Financial information, marketing information, production information, and customer information are some types of information, among several others. A quote from the 1987 movie *Wall Street* rings true. The movie is about the stock market and its players. The protagonist, Gordon Gekko, says, "The most valuable commodity I know of is information." Information, without doubt, is the lifeblood of any organization. However, critical information is the most valuable type of information and needs to be treated as an asset.

For a bank, customer account information, customer records, and the like would be extremely valuable information. Without such information, the bank wouldn't be able to function. For an architecture firm, the designs of its buildings are probably its most critical piece of information. These are assets that are extremely valuable to the entity. The firm would not be able to do business without their building designs. In a similar vein, every organization would have its set of information assets that are critical for their business, and the organization would like to ensure that their business is not hindered because of a loss of confidentiality, integrity, or availability of the asset, depending upon its sensitivity. A nation's defense is deeply dependent on its key defense secrets, and any breach of confidentiality of this information could result in a great loss of national security. The price quoted by a vendor to a potential customer is a critical information asset, and any modification of the said information (breach of integrity) could result in a major loss of revenue for the vendor. For an e-commerce merchant, the Web application (the information transacted over it) is a critical asset, and if the website is unavailable for a long period of time, such organizations would suffer debilitating losses of revenue.

As part of a security risk-assessment exercise, it is always important to identify critical information assets. With reference to Web applications, the critical information assets constitute the information assets that are being stored, processed, or transmitted via the Web application. Different information assets have different security requirements as part of the CIA triad. For instance, in the case of defense secrets, confidentiality is the most important attribute that needs to be maintained. While availability and integrity may also be secondary considerations, confidentiality is the primary attribute of focus. In the case of financial information like stock quotes, integrity would be the most important attribute, as even a slight change in the figure of the stock quote could result in several millions of dollars lost or gained.

Identifying critical information assets is one of the most important phases of a risk-assessment activity, because a flawed identification of assets would result in the misapplication of the risk-assessment activity or would result in the activity being rendered ineffective. Several risk assessments go off course because of faulty identification and evaluation of information assets. If a vulnerability-scanning activity were to be conducted for 3000 servers, of which only 500 servers contained the critical asset, then the activity would be wasteful and ineffective, and the organization would unnecessarily spend precious time and resources trying to mitigate the vulnerabilities in the 2500 servers that do not require that level of protection. That said, it should also be noted that all risks cannot be mitigated. The focus on the critical information assets provides a clear scope for implementation of controls, based on which a protection strategy may be developed. In several cases, critical assets are closely tied to other elements, which may be noncritical. The organization, in its quest to secure critical assets, could unknowingly add a layer of security for these elements as well. While the focal point for protection is the critical information asset, it usually ensures security for the noncritical information elements as well.

13.3.1.1.3 Developing a List of Critical Information Assets

In the first phase of the risk-assessment stage, identification of critical information assets and evaluating them based on their criticality for the organization is important. It is important to appropriately identify the information assets in this phase, failing which, the entire risk assessment will be rendered ineffective and misguided. Let us explore the ways in which one can create a collated set of information assets that are stored, processed, or transmitted by a Web application:

- Workshops
- Questionnaires
- Description sheets

13.3.1.1.3.1 Workshops A workshop is the most effective way of creating a collated list of information assets. The OCTAVE methodology prescribes that senior management, operational management, and staff workshops need to be conducted to gain a detailed insight into the critical assets of the organization. While OCTAVE is a risk-assessment methodology for enterprise risk assessment, its principles may be adopted for a Web application as well. Discussions with management/customers regarding the types of critical information that will be stored, processed, or transmitted need to be understood before formulating the requirements of the application. A workshop facilitated with a brainstorming session will help ensure that the most comprehensive view of critical assets will be revealed during the course of the interactions with management/customers. The workshop leverages on the existing knowledge of the organization. Using the knowledge of a few key individuals ensures that the organizational experience is tapped to the fullest and that a comprehensive view of information assets is achieved.

13.3.1.1.3.2 Questionnaires Questionnaires are an effective medium of eliciting information about critical information assets. In several cases, individuals are spread across different locations in different countries, in which case, workshops may not

be feasible. Questionnaires have questions directed at eliciting the information necessary to determine the types of critical assets that are stored, processed, or transmitted by the Web application. Based on the results of the questionnaire, the risk-assessment team collates the information and prepares a list of critical information assets for which the risk assessment needs to be performed.

13.3.1.1.3.3 Description Sheets Description sheets are similar to questionnaires, but this approach differs in the level of detail. This technique is usually the least effective, as it requires the subjects to pen down a great deal of detail into the sheets, which most people don't do because of either time constraints or lack of motivation. Individuals seldom take the time to fill out proper descriptions of the critical information assets, and the end result of this analysis is usually vague and futile. This is more suited for smaller entities, where the results are not too many to analyze.

13.3.1.1.4 User Roles and Access to Critical Information Assets

User profiling is a very important activity to be performed for understanding the envisaged application. Once the critical information assets for the application have been tabulated, the next piece of the puzzle is understanding the types of users that are likely to exist as part of the application and the level of access these users have to these critical information assets. Users of a Web application have access to create, update, or delete critical application data as the case may be. It is important for the risk assessment to capture who has access to the said critical information asset and what kind of access the individual has to the same. For instance, a customer of an e-commerce application will have access to his/her account information, including personal details, transaction history, order status, and credit card information stored, processed, or transmitted by the application.

In a similar manner, the administrator of an e-commerce application will have access to stock-related information in the Web application. The administrator can insert, update, and delete stock-related information like stock item name, price, and discount.

The ideal way to profile users and capture information about the information assets they can access is through provisioning an access-control matrix that characterizes the privileges each individual (subject) has to the critical information asset (object). In a typical operating system, an access-control matrix would contain information about whether a particular user or user role can read, write, or execute a particular file in the system.

13.3.1.1.5 Understanding Basic Application Architecture

Understanding the application's architecture is an important step in the system-characterization phase. Interfaces between different systems are usually commonplace with a Web application. Any Web application has, as external interfaces, connectivity to a database or a file server. In some cases, Web applications also interact with other enterprise applications such as e-mail and messaging applications. While incorporating security into the Web application, a rough deployment diagram of the Web application and its subsystems and interfaces needs to be created. As the security functionality and capability is formulated, specific details relating to security implementation like authentication and authorization, encryption, and logging need to be incorporated into the application deployment architecture.

The information captured in a basic application architecture diagram for the purpose of risk assessment includes the following:

- Deployment topology
- System interfaces

13.3.1.1.5.1 Deployment Topology Risk assessment is made more effective with an understanding of the network topology in which the application will be deployed. Network diagrams are most effective in understanding the logical environment under which the application will be deployed. Network diagrams should be created to include the layout of servers, network components, and the logical segments that exist as part of the network. Network connectivity into and out of the network needs to be highlighted to provide adequate clarity on connectivity to the Internet or intranet. An understanding of the network security controls implemented by the organization will also help a great deal while developing security requirements for the Web application. Firewall configuration and router configurations may also be considered during the deployment process. For instance, if an organization's perimeter firewalls expressly disallow network traffic on a particular port owing to its nonsecure condition, then the application architects might be able to avert unnecessary configuration time and possible vulnerabilities by developing the application to work on different ports.

13.3.1.1.5.2 System Interfaces Web applications interact with other systems or services as part of their operating environment. They most commonly interface with databases for the insertion, updating, and deletion of data. Apart from databases, present-day Web applications also interact extensively with e-mail and messaging applications for sending and receiving messages, which might form outputs or inputs for the Web application. With respect to e-commerce Web applications, one of the key interfaces for a Web application is with a payment gateway, where the Web application sends credit card or banking information to be authorized and receives information about the approval/denial status of the transaction. Web applications also commonly interact with a file server for file-based operations such as facilitating downloads of files and writing files into the said servers. The most common interface of a Web application is the one where the user accesses the application through the browser. This interface is usually the most public of the interfaces for a Web application.

Understanding system interfaces is vital to the risk assessment, because exchange of critical information assets of the application takes place through these interfaces. Our focus is to understand the flow of information in the application, which can be achieved by studying the data interchange between the interfaces. Knowledge of the information interchange in between these interfaces can be used to gain an insight into the level of trust that one can have for data exchanged over these interfaces. Based on the level of trust, risks may be kept in mind for which security functionality is created subsequently. For instance, one of the interfaces of a Web application is the user interface, and it must be kept in mind that the users may be both genuine users and malicious users. Keeping in mind that users may be malicious, the trust level for the data entered by users would naturally be low, and security functionality may be formulated keeping in mind the low trust level for the data interchanged from the user interface. Security functionality for the interaction between these interfacing elements may be designed keeping in mind the criticality of the data being transmitted and the level of trust that can be expected from the data emanating from or being transmitted to these interfacing systems.

13.3.1.1.6 *Threat Profiling and Threat Modeling*

Understanding threats and their outcomes is an important set of activities to be performed as part of the risk assessment. A comprehensive understanding of threats and their effects is imperative in order to develop a clear and effective protection strategy to counter the multifarious threats that might actively exploit vulnerabilities in a Web application. There are two processes that are essential in gaining a detailed understanding of threats and their outcomes. They are

- Threat profiling
- Threat modeling

13.3.1.1.6.1 Threat Profiling   Threat profiling is the process of envisioning threat scenarios. Usually, this is the only process that is followed when performing enterprise risk assessment, but in the case of Web applications, both threat profiling and modeling yield better results, as they provide a deep insight into the threat and the attack vectors that may be used to compromise the application.

Threat profiling is the activity performed where several threat scenarios are created for the various threat actors for a given information asset. A threat profile usually captures the following details:

- Asset name
- Threat actor/agent
- Threat access
- Threat motive
- Threat outcome

As part of the threat-profiling process for a Web application, we will need to identify the threats from human actors using the network. Let us explore a simple threat profile. A malicious user of an e-commerce application is able to perform actions on behalf of other users of the application. In this scenario, the asset in question is customer login information, which basically means the customer's username and password; his account-specific information forms the constituents of the asset. The threat actor, in this case, is the malicious user, a human outsider. The malicious user accesses the Web application via a browser, over the Internet, essentially meaning that he is using network access, which is the threat access. The threat motive in this case is a deliberate attempt by the malicious user to gain access to other user accounts. The outcome of the threat is that there is a loss of confidentiality, because the malicious user was able to gain access to a different customer's information and have

complete access to the legitimate user's account. It is not always that humans are the threat actors. There are several cases of self-propagating worms and botnets being responsible for Web-application attacks.

As we can clearly see from the example provided here, the threat profile has been created with the basic information about the type of threat that might adversely affect the application. In order to sensitize management and other stakeholders relating to the application, a threat-profiling exercise is very beneficial, as it creates awareness among the nontechnical stakeholders and sensitizes them to the fact that security is an important consideration for the application. The threat profiles may be tabulated for easy reading as given in Table 13.1.

While threat profiling is useful for a preliminary understanding of the type of threat and its outcome, it is far from adequate while assessing Web-application threats. Threat profiling should be done to understand, at a high level, the types of threats that might have an adverse effect on the critical information asset. Management, application owners, and customers who are the key stakeholders in the application development process need to be aware of

TABLE 13.1

Threat-Profiling Table

Asset Name	Threat Actor	Threat Access	Threat Description	Threat Motive	Threat Outcome
Customer information	Malicious application user (hacker)	Over the Internet: human actor using network access	Attacker can use the user accounts of other legitimate users of the application	Deliberate	Loss of confidentiality of customer information

the types of threats that might hinder the smooth functioning of the Web application. A threat profile conveys to these stakeholders the type of damage that can be caused by a particular threat actor. Threat profiling is a useful process to create a preliminary threat scenario, both for the consumption of nontechnical stakeholders in the application-development process and for providing a much-needed input to the next process, namely threat modeling.

13.3.1.1.6.2 Threat Modeling *Threat modeling* is a commonly used term in the Web application security sphere. Threat modeling refers to a formulated scenario in which the threat exploiting the vulnerability is explored in great detail to bring a perspective of realism into the threat analysis exercise. With respect to Web applications, threat modeling is a highly technical exercise. It is recommended that application architects along with security specialists with some experience in Web-application penetration testing be involved to ensure that all possible threat scenarios are considered. This will ensure that the threat-modeling exercise permeates into an effective and comprehensive protection strategy for the Web application.

Let us explore the threat-modeling process for the example used for the threat-profiling exercise (see Table 13.2). What is projected here is a basic threat model. This methodology is quite flexible, and one can plug in multiple dimensions of different risk-assessment practices to form the SSDLC. I would also recommend utilizing the STRIDE* method from Microsoft for the threat-modeling aspect of the SSDLC.

13.3.1.1.7 Risk-Mitigation Strategy: Formulation of Detailed Security Requirements for the Web Application

Mitigation of identified risks is the primary goal of a risk-management process for a Web application. Controls need to be designed, developed, and implemented based on the outcome of the entire risk-assessment phase. The output of the risk-assessment phase is the risk-mitigation strategy and the detailed security requirements for the Web application. The risk-mitigation strategy should not be confused with the risk-mitigation phase, which is the phase succeeding the risk-assessment phase in the risk-management cycle, where the risks to an existing application are mitigated during the development and testing phase of the application development life cycle. Risk-mitigation strategy is the output from the risk-assessment phase, which forms the input for the actual mitigation of risk in the risk-mitigation phase.

The risk-assessment phase identifies critical information assets to gain an understanding of what information needs to be protected. The application environment and deployment architecture is understood to provide more clarity on the type of application and its users. Security objectives are formulated to understand the

---

* STRIDE refers to Spoofing, Tampering, Repudiation, Information disclosure, Denial of service, and Elevation of privileges, which is a Microsoft methodology for threat modeling that I personally find very effective for threat analysis of Web applications. Microsoft has also provided a tool for performing a STRIDE threat-modeling activity for an application. Information on this standard can be found at http://msdn.microsoft.com/en-us/library/ee823878(v=cs.20).aspx.

TABLE 13.2

Threat Modeling for Threat Profiles

Detailed Threat Scenario	Possible Vulnerabilities	Impact of the Exploit
Cross-site scripting attack: The malicious user may find a cross-site scripting vulnerability in the application because of weak/lax input validation and may be sending phishing e-mails to legitimate users of the application, upon the clicking of which the session information of the legitimate user is exposed to the attacker, who can then use this information to perpetrate session-hijacking attacks on users in the system.	Lack of proper input validation scheme for inputs at the server level Lack of output encoding	Medium: The attacker may be able to steal sessions of some users in the system and gain access to their user profiles, passwords, and transaction history and then perform actions on their behalf.
SQL injection: The attacker may craft SQL queries using the input of the application and gain access to the user database containing usernames and passwords, from where all user accounts are exposed to the attacker.	Lack of input validation scheme at the server level Lack of parameterized SQL requests to the database	High: The attacker can compromise the entire database by gaining access to it. Not only is sensitive data exposed to the attacker, but the database is also available for the attacker. This leads to a complete compromise of the database.
Session tampering: The attacker may be able to guess session IDs for different users and thereby gain access to accounts of different users through session hijacking.	Lack of strong random session identifiers	Medium: The attacker may be able to guess the session IDs of the users and gain access to sessions of various other logged-in users. Some of the users will be affected by this attack.
Cross-site request forgery: The attacker may force the logged-on user to execute requests without the user's knowledge, thereby illegally performing actions as the user.	Lack of random request tokens with each request Lack of input validation, thereby allowing cross-site scripting	Medium: The attacker may be able to execute requests on behalf of some users in the system. Some of the users will be affected by this attack.

prime motivations and necessity for implementing security for the Web application. Subsequently, threats that might adversely affect the Web application are understood, and detailed scenarios are created as part of the threat-modeling phase. These detailed scenarios capture the possible vulnerabilities in the Web application and its environment that might enhance the threat scenarios.

There are some factors that need to be taken into consideration while designing, developing, and implementing security functionality. The threat-modeling process has provided a great deal of insight into the several threat scenarios, their impact, and possible vulnerabilities that might have aided the threat scenario. Security controls need to be developed to fix the vulnerabilities that have been identified during the threat-modeling process. Apart from this factor, security compliance and contractual requirements are also an important aspect for consideration. Security compliance requirements as well as contractual and/or regulatory obligations need to be taken care of while designing security functionality for the Web application, as the organization's competitiveness or, in some cases, their very survival, depends upon their adherence to these compliance requirements. In addition to this, industry best practices may also be kept in mind while designing application security controls. Several bodies such as OWASP, NIST, SANS, and so on, prescribe several security best practices for network, host, and Web-application security. These best practices provide a real-world implementation view and would aid greatly in the development of security functionality for the Web application.

Once the controls are selected, it is important to create the final set of detailed security requirements for the Web application. The document containing these detailed security requirements is the final deliverable from the risk-assessment phase. This document must provide specifics about the detailed security implementation and functionality that will be put into service for the application. This is amalgamated with the requirements for the Web application, which is the first phase of the application development life cycle. The requirement phase of the application development life cycle or SDLC focuses on the functional and nonfunctional requirements of the Web application that is to be developed. Functional requirements need to be formulated keeping in mind the type of application, its intended use, its scale and size of operations, and so on. Security requirements constitute the nonfunctional requirements of the application and are based on the type of sensitive data stored, processed, or transmitted by the application and the risk of attacks to that sensitive information. These two sets of requirements form the total set of requirements for the Web application, following which the design for the application is created based on the requirements, and then the application goes into development.

During the course of the application development life cycle, changes are inevitable for any enterprise application. It is, therefore, essential for the architects and developers to revisit the risk assessment for the enterprise application and update the critical information assets, threats, and risk-mitigation strategies, as the case may be. The risk-management process fits in quite well with a typical change-management cycle, where any changes to the application are first discussed, understood, justified in terms of impact and need, and then implemented and tested. Risk management should be built into the change-management process, where the risk-assessment process is active during the period where the need for change is raised, its feasibility evaluated, and its impact understood. Risk mitigation and continuous evaluation come into play when the change is to be implemented, tested, and verified.

While risk management is extremely beneficial for security, there is a single immutable truth that needs to be understood. One can never mitigate every risk. As individuals, we tend to believe that every risk that is present in an environment can be mitigated. This could not be further from the truth. There are certain points where risks will have to be accepted, as there would be several constraints that would be intertwined with its mitigation. It might be cost prohibitive, where the cost of mitigating the risk would be more expensive than leaving the risk unmitigated. It might not be possible to mitigate certain risks because of constraints imposed by third parties, whose involvement is necessary for mitigating a particular risk. It might not be achieved quickly, because it would involve downtime of a critical system. Risk acceptance needs to be understood and utilized as a course of action only in circumstances where it is possible to do so. It is usually seen that organizations choose to address high- and medium-impact threats, as they are usually very severe in nature. Low-impact threats are not mitigated or are mitigated at a later date.

13.3.1.2 Requirement 6.3.1: Removal of Default User Accounts, IDs, and Passwords

Custom applications and commercial applications often have default user accounts. While the commercial ones are usually documented, you are not unlikely to find either default or preconfigured accounts to access custom applications as well. Recently, I was testing a Web application that had multiple types of user roles. The system had just then gone live and we were testing the application in the first week of its release to production. The application had an administrative interface that was accessed with the admin URL, and my thought was to attempt a brute-force attack against the admin interface. However, that was not necessary, as the username was "admin" and the password was "userpass." When we disclosed the issue as part of our findings, the company mentioned that it was a default admin credential that had been utilized during the development and testing phases of the application and the same credentials were

not removed, even though different admin credentials had been created before being deployed to production.

Such scenarios are all too common. Therefore, it is imperative to realize that the intrinsic security measures provided to an application becomes a moot point if default credentials or accounts are present on production systems. Default credentials and accounts usually tend to possess easily enumerable usernames and simple passwords (to facilitate initial login). However, they have no place in a production system. They must be removed from the application prior to deployment.

13.3.1.3 Requirement 6.3.2: Custom Code Review for Security

Requirement 6.3.2 is a requirement that many organizations are yet to get right. The requirement mandates that custom code (for applications in the PCI environment) has to be reviewed for nonsecure coding practices that might introduce vulnerabilities in the application.

It is often seen (and we will detail it in later sections of this chapter) that nonsecure coding practices are one of the leading causes of vulnerabilities in applications. Additionally, nonsecure coding practices are also difficult to fix, especially for organizations that have developed complex applications with a large code base already in production. I am currently working with a company that is undertaking a PCI-compliance effort for its PCI environment. They have developed a merchant settlement Web application for their internal settlement operations. One of the key findings, in both the code review and a penetration test, was that the application had not utilized PreparedStatements for SQL queries to the database. Hence, due to poor input validation and absence of PreparedStatements, the application is vulnerable to SQL injection. This application is a large application that has been developed iteratively over several years. However, as they have utilized nonsecure coding practices for the application, they have to revisit the code and change several aspects of code to ensure that it is a securely coded application. This is hard to achieve (especially with compliance timelines); however, it had to be done for the security of said application.

Some of the considerations and best practices for a code review are as follows: The code review has to be performed by individuals or teams that are different from the code author(s). This has multiple ramifications. Several (in fact, most) organizations engage with external parties to perform code reviews for custom code developed in the organization to be deployed in the PCI environment. While the PCI standards do not mandate any specific type of code-review vendors, it is highly recommended that the external party/entity be specialized in performing code reviews for security. Some organizations have started adopting code-review tools to perform security code reviews for applications. These applications are usually commercial applications that are specialized for the purpose of a secure code review. Some organizations choose to deploy their in-house resources to perform code reviews for security for their applications. In such cases, it must be kept in mind that the reviewer/reviewing team must be different from the author(s) of the code. For instance, code reviews are performed by QA (qualified assessor) personnel or specialized application security experts in the organization. It must be ensured that the individual/team reviewing the code must

have a depth of knowledge in performing code reviews for security.

Another key consideration for performing the code review is to identify the right best practices and benchmarks for secure code. These include secure coding guidelines that have been released by the platform vendors for Java, DOT.Net,[*] Ruby,[†] Python, and so on. Additionally, another great source for secure coding guidelines is the CERT Secure Coding Guidelines that have been released for Java, Perl, C, and C++.[‡] Yet another great source for secure coding guidelines is the Open Web Application Security Project (OWASP), a body that is a leading force in application security and in the spread of application security awareness in the management and development community. The OWASP has released a code review guide and a testing guide, along with its famous OWASP Top 10, which is a detailed compilation of the top 10 vulnerabilities and flaws found in Web applications at the time. Whenever I perform code reviews, I personally like to use a hybrid approach to these best practices, deriving the best of the vendor guidelines, CERT guidelines, and the OWASP guidelines.

One of the critical facets of any testing and/or review effort is that vulnerabilities and flaws identified as part of the code review process be mitigated and fixed as per the risk of the findings. The fixes have to be documented as part of the change-control process of the application, a topic that will be discussed in Section 13.3.2. Additionally, the code-review

---

[*] ASP DOT.Net secure coding guidelines: http://msdn. microsoft.com/en-us/library/d55zzx87(v=vs.71).aspx.

[†] Ruby on Rails secure coding guidelines: http://guides. rubyonrails.org/security.html.

[‡] CERT secure coding standards. http://www.cert.org/ secure-coding/scstandards.html.

results need to be reviewed and approved by management before their release.

The other question that is most commonly asked of me is whether the code review only has to be performed for the code of public-facing Web applications. The simple answer is "No." Code reviews of all custom code for applications deployed internally or externally in the PCI environment have to be performed. Public-facing Web applications have other requirements in addition to this requirement of code review. If the application has been identified as being part of the PCI environment, then a code review for the application has to be performed, regardless of its network location.

13.3.2 Requirement 6.4: Application Change Management and Change Control

13.3.2.1 Requirement 6.4.5: Change-Management Document and the Essentials of Change Control and Change Management

Requirement 6.4 deals with application change-control and change-management practices that are followed by an organization that is PCI compliant. Change control is a process where the changes to any system/application are introduced through a controlled and coordinated process. For instance, a company is developing and deploying an e-banking application for its customers. Naturally, the e-banking application is a critical application that has widespread implications on the company. If developers are arbitrarily making changes to the functionality, there would be a great deal of adverse impact on the application with reference to consistency of the application's functionality and/or with the security of the

application. It is quite easy to understand the motivation for a strong change-control and change-management process, as it makes the entire process of change to a system/application more streamlined and organized.

Typically, a change-control and change-management process consists of the following stages:

- Request initiation
- Request examination and change approval
- Build and test
- Deploy/implement
- Close: gain acceptance

13.3.2.1.1 Request Initiation

Request initiation refers to an individual or group of individuals requesting a change in a particular system or application. This has to be documented in the form of a change-request form or, with more modern software and Web-based systems, a change ticket in a project-management application. The change request should typically contain the following details:

Nature of change: A description of the change and the type of change that is planned for the system.

Reason for change: The reason for making specific changes to the system, for instance, enhancing system security by implementing a request-authentication code to prevent CSRF (cross-site request forgery) attacks (discussed in Section 13.4.9.2).

Complexity of implementing change: The possible complexities of developing and implementing the suggested changes on the target application must be documented.

Impact of change: The impact of the change needs to be documented from multiple perspectives. One of the key perspectives is the downtime of the system/application that will be undergoing the change. Other parameters may be related to other impacts, like security functionality.

Rollback measures: Sometimes, against the organization's best efforts, the changes made to a system adversely affect the operations of the application. In such cases, the organization must have a planned rollback strategy to ensure that the application suffers the least possible impact. For instance, if the developers roll out a new patch that affects some components of the application adversely, then the organization must have detailed rollback measures, such as a backup of the application to the last version, that are ready to be implemented within a specified time frame.

13.3.2.1.2 Change-Request Examination

The change requests are examined by the supervisors/management/business owners of the application after due consideration provided by the change-request form. Sign-offs usually are obtained by multiple stakeholders to ensure that the process has appropriate segregation of duties.

13.3.2.1.3 Change Build and Testing

The change is developed, built, and tested in a testing environment that simulates the production environment.

13.3.2.1.4 Deploy/Implement

The tested and finalized change is then deployed to production. The effect of the change is examined in production to identify adverse effects on the application. In the event of an adverse impact of the change, rollback procedures are initiated. Otherwise, the change is monitored and closed with an acceptance on the change.

13.3.2.1.5 Acceptance

The change-control and change-management procedures need to be documented by the organization in the form of a procedure and/or a policy as part of the overall documented information security practices. The change-control procedure must specify the previously mentioned steps for a change rollout and rollback plans. The change-control procedure must also specify the need for forms and information being captured for a change request. Additionally, the change-control procedure for a PCI environment must document and necessitate the adoption of additional practices mentioned in Sections 13.3.2.2 to 13.3.2.4.

13.3.2.2 Requirements 6.4.2 and 6.4.3: Separation of Production, Development, and Test Environments

The application development environment is an important consideration for any company developing applications or writing custom code for the organization. It is essential that the production, development, and test environments be separate from each other. This is a measure to prevent against unintended changes to each of these environments. For instance, the integrity of the production environment is critical for the organization. If developers are allowed unbridled access to the production environment and make changes directly in the environment, the application(s) might be subject to several security vulnerabilities due to the changes introduced by the developer.

Consider the case of a developer who has designed a new reporting add-on to an existing application and would like to see if it works well in the production environment. The add-on has not been tested for security. Input validation testing and code reviews have not yet been performed, but the developer's idea is to merely test its functionality in the production environment. Let's assume that this developer has complete access to the production environment. He/she includes the add-on into the production environment to examine how well it works in production. An attacker planning his attack against the organization discovers this functionality, which is untested, unverified, and nonsecure. The attacker launches a number of attacks and is able to completely compromise the application leveraging the vulnerabilities introduced by the add-on.

An important reason to separate development and test environments is for fraud prevention. Development and testing are constantly at loggerheads about the application. The primary function of testing is to perform exhaustive tests of the application and identify nonconformances to the intended functionality, security requirements, and so on. Development is usually at the receiving end of their inputs, comments, and findings that would result in more hours spent by developers on the application. It is essential to separate the development and test environments, as the developers might look to influence the testing results, cases, and conditions in the event that these departments are not logically separate. The organization must ensure that these departments are logically separate and unable to access the systems in the other department.

Additionally, the organization must separate the production environment to ensure that production data that contains sensitive information like cardholder information and other data sets should not be intermingled with the systems in the development and test environments.

It is a relatively simple requirement to know that the resources from each of these departments should not be intermingled with conflicting functions. For instance, a developer cannot also be deployed for testing, as it is a serious conflict of interest. The production environment must be controlled by an individual or team that places completely finalized and tested builds in the production environment and provides production support. This is a measure to ensure that there is accountability and traceability in the software development life cycle.

Some points to be kept in mind about development, production, and test environments:

- Test environments must be designed to simulate the production environment, without being the production environment itself.
- Organizations may be tempted to replicate the production environment's databases into a test-and-development environment and consider this as an effective separation of environments. Wrong! Production data contains sensitive information that should not be privy to the development or testing environments. Only test data and sample data can be utilized in these environments.
- While the development and test environments may be physically segregated from each other, it is even more important to ensure that these environments are logically separated.

- People working in development, production, and the test environment have to be kept separate.

13.3.2.3 Requirement 6.4.3: Use of Live PANs for Testing

Primary account numbers (PANs) are required for application testing, especially for testing applications that handle payments, like gateways, POS applications, and so on. However, using live PANs for testing either in the development or test environment is considered a bad practice. One of the critical aspects of PCI compliance is to reduce cardholder data storage to a minimum. Exposure of live PANs for testing would result in a potential exposure of the live cardholder data. The organization can utilize test PANs that are provided by their payment gateways, acquiring banks, and so on, that provide specific test PANs that may be used for testing the application.

13.3.2.4 Requirement 6.4.4: Removal of Test Data in Production

Test data is a common occurrence with several custom applications. Developers and testers use test data furiously before the release of the application and, on most occasions, the application gets rolled out with the same test data. Test data could consist of anything from default accounts, to test accounts, to test data sets in the application that intermingle with legitimate production data. Test accounts are usually the riskiest; as they are usually default accounts like "admin" or "test" with equally simple credentials. Attackers who are determined to breach the system often catch on to such vulnerabilities quickly, gain access to the application, and pivot their way into sensitive data like cardholder information.

It is also a good practice to not include test data sets, no matter how innocuously they seem to exist in the system, as said data is usually not in line with the application's legitimate data and tends to be incorrectly represented in reports and logs. The application must be rolled out to production without the presence of test data.

13.4 REQUIREMENT 6.5: SECURE CODING GUIDELINES FOR APPLICATIONS

13.4.1 Secure Coding Guidelines: References and Best Practices

Nonsecure coding practices result in a majority of application vulnerabilities. Especially with Web applications, nonsecure coding practices tend to be devastating given the public nature of such applications. Therefore, it is absolutely required for an organization to utilize secure coding practices (regardless of the platform) to develop secure applications that are in use in the PCI environment.

There are several guidelines and best practices for secure coding practices, most notably the OWASP (and the OWASP Top 10), where security vulnerabilities for Web applications are detailed to a great extent with examples by some of the leading application security experts in the world. The OWASP has released several guides, tools, and documents that detail implementation of Web application security concepts and practices for different platforms like Java, Dot.Net, Ruby, Python, and so on.

Another great source for application security guidelines and best practices is the SANS. This organization is a treasure trove for information on security, especially the SANS list of top 25 software errors that detail weaknesses in applications relating to specific issues such as insecure cryptography management, missing authorization, and so on. CERT and other application platform vendors have also released a smorgasbord of information for organizations who are looking to build their apps securely.

In sections 13.4.2 to 13.4.10, we will be addressing Requirements 6.5.1 through 6.5.9 of the PCI-DSS that address application vulnerabilities and specific controls to ensure that these high-severity vulnerabilities are not part of applications that are deployed in the PCI environment.

13.4.2 Requirement 6.5.1: Secure Coding to Address Injection Flaws

Injection flaws are one of the most pernicious vulnerabilities that affect Web applications. They are also the most dangerous class of vulnerabilities. Injection flaws refer to vulnerabilities where an attacker can gain access to the back-end data system by "injecting" crafted queries into the application's form fields and parameters. If the application does not have strong input validation and encoding routines, the input is likely to query the back-end data source and provide the attacker with information that was not intended to be provided, or it may leak other sensitive data from the application. There are multiple injection attacks that Web application developers need to protect against. They are as follows:

- SQL injection

- XPath injection
- LDAP injection
- Command injection

13.4.2.1 SQL Injection

SQL injection is by far the most popular type of injection attack. It is also considered widely to be the most dangerous type of attack. SQL injection is an attack where the attacker is able to send crafted SQL queries in the application's form fields and parameters, and if the application is not validating input and/or performing secure database access routines, the input containing meaningful SQL queries runs these queries on the database and provides the attacker with sensitive information from the database.

Let me explain this with an example. Let's take a URL of an e-commerce PHP Web application (http://www.e-commerce.com/item/subcat.php?cat_id=2228). One of the parameters, cat_id, queries the database for the category ID and fetches all of the items in that category. The SQL query at the back end would probably look something like this:

```
SELECT cat_id, cat_name FROM prod-
uct_cats WHERE cat_id = 2228
```

Let's assume that the attacker wants to identify whether the Web link is vulnerable to SQL injection. In this case, the attacker might change the cat_id parameter to

```
cat_id = 2228' OR 1 = 1
```

Now, this query essentially means that the

```
cat_id = 2228 OR 1 = 1
```

(which is an always-true condition) must be fetched, and since 1 is always equal to 1, the entire table product_cats is fetched for the attacker.

I encounter SQL injection on Web applications that we test at least six out of ten times. SQL injection attacks can have a wide array of scary consequences. Suppose, in the previous example, I change the value of the cat_id parameter to

```
2228 AND UNION select username,
password from users;
```

In this case, the query would unite with the users table of the application and fetch the usernames and passwords for the attacker. Or worse, that cat_id parameter could be changed to

```
2228 AND DROP TABLE product_cats;
```

Given the adequate database privileges that are provided to the application (usually high, because most admins configure applications to run with elevated privileges), the attacker can even delete tables from the back-end database.

SQL injection attacks can provide the ultimate tunnel into an organization. In fact, in one penetration test, I found a vulnerable public-facing application that had been deployed by one of my clients. I was able to perform an SQL injection attack against it. Using the access to the database that was running with privileged credentials, I was able to execute commands on the back-end operating system and subsequently tunnel my access all the way to the company's domain server and steal the administrator's tokens to become the domain administrator. All of this was possible while being completely outside the network and simply injecting SQL into a public Web application. SQL injection has been the attack of choice for hackers going after

organizations that process sensitive data such as cardholder information. In fact, the CardSystems breach and the Heartland Payment Systems breach are examples of how attackers leveraged SQL injection to gain access to millions of card numbers and other sensitive data. Figure 13.7 is a screenshot of an MSSQL database that has been enumerated using SQL injection.

The most effective defenses against SQL injection are as follows:

- Use of PreparedStatements/Parameterized SQL queries
- Use of strong input validation routines
- Use of output encoding/escaping to the database

13.4.2.1.1 Prepared Statements/ Parameterized SQL Queries

One of the best defenses for an application against SQL injections is the use of prepared statements/parameterized queries to access the database and perform queries against the database. I am going to call them *prepared statements* for ease of understanding. A prepared statement is a database query statement that takes the form of a template, where additional parameters are added during the execution of the statement. The statement looks something like this:

```
SELECT search_term, search_link
from SEARCH where search_term = ?
```

In a prepared statement, unlike a dynamic statement, the query is not populated with the data, but is bound to the query only later. The DBMS (database management system) parses, compiles, and optimizes the query before storing the query and not executing it. However, a dynamic query would look

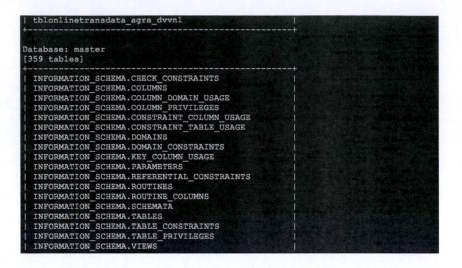

FIGURE 13.7
Screenshot of a SQL injection attack against a Microsoft SQL server database.

something like this (demonstrated with a Java code snippet):

```
"SELECT search_term, search_link
from SEARCH where search_term = '"
+ request.
getParameter("searchTerm") + "'"
```

Here, the dynamic query is only executed at runtime. There is no "preparation" by the DBMS in terms of parsing, compiling, and optimizing the query.

Additionally, the use of the dynamic statement is also highly nonsecure, as the attacker can change the intent of the query. This occurs because the dynamic statement executes the statement as is and does not separate the query from the data.

For instance, let's take the same query and demonstrate a potential SQL injection possibility:

```
"SELECT search_term, search_link
from SEARCH where search_term = '"
+ hello' UNION SELECT
USERNAME,PASSWORD FROM USERS + "'"
```

Here, the user supplied the malicious input and completely changed the intent of the query. Instead of passing a search term into the SQL query, the user performed a UNION with the USERS table querying the usernames and passwords in the table, thereby gaining access to functionality that should not have been exposed to the user. Additionally, the query is executed as is by the DBMS, with no separation of the query from the data. Another major benefit of using the prepared statement is that the query and the data are separated. The query is already running with the results stored, but not executed. Only when the prepared statement binds the data into the already prepared query does the query execute, with the response returned to the user. As the query and the data are not bound, the user cannot modify the intent of the query by crafting appending SQL queries to the original query to gain access to functionality that should not have been available to the user in the first place. Prepared statements are also more efficient than dynamic queries.

Prepared statements are available in all major application development platforms like Java (PreparedStatement), ASP.NET (SQLCommand and OleDBCommand), PHP (PDO with Bind Params), Ruby, Python, and so on.

13.4.2.1.2 *Input Validation*

Input validation is one of the most common and effective ways of protection against not only SQL injection, but other types of injection attacks as well. Input validation refers to the programmatic checking of application input to ensure that malformed and malicious input is not processed by the application. While input validation is utilized heavily to check for consistency of data within the system, its value as a security control is immense. For instance, if a user enters "john OR 1 = 1" in the username section of the application, and the application does not validate the data, a vulnerable application might process the crafted SQL query as data and provide an attacker access to the database. However, if the input was validated to allow only alphanumeric characters as well as limited special characters like underscore, hyphen, and so on, then the attacker wouldn't have been able to inject malformed input or malicious attack strings into the application's input. Input validation is ideally performed with the help of a white list, being that the developers specifically validate input that is known to be legitimate and disallow any anomalies.

Another aspect to consider for effective input validation is to ensure that input validation is performed on the server side. Client-side validations (in JavaScript, and so on) can be easily bypassed by attackers using interception proxies or disabling JavaScript on the browser or sending requests to URLs with parameters. However, if effective validation code is placed on the server side, it will ensure that malicious input is validated at the server side, which cannot be easily accessed, thereby ensuring that the application is secure against SQL injection and other attacks.

13.4.2.1.3 *Output Encoding/Escaping*

Although this is not the best option to prevent against SQL injection, it can be used in conjunction with other defenses like prepared statements and input validation. Output encoding/escaping refers to the practice of converting special characters like ' ' < > into their encoded representation. This applies specifically to special characters, as their representations differ based on multiple encoding standards and practices. Encoding ensures that dangerous characters (special characters) that are used as part of the query are encoded, and this encoded representation does not allow the application to parse and execute the query (special characters are not confused as data). The representation ensures that even malicious requests are not parsed and, therefore, are not executed as SQL queries, thereby preventing SQL injections. For instance, single-quote characters are appended with slashes to perform escaping.

```
\'this is in quotes\'
```

would be the representation of characters in quotes. However, there are attacks that are able to bypass and evade these escaped characters to perform injection attacks.

13.4.2.2 XPath Injection

Just as an SQL query is used to query databases, XPath is used to query XML files. XML files are used by modern applications to store critical information. For instance, XMLs may be used to store page information, display information, usernames and passwords, and other details that are essential for the functioning of the application. XPath queries are developed to access these elements in an XML document. XPath is very similar to SQL in that attributes can be specified and search operations can be performed on the XML document to query information.

XPath injection refers to flaws in the application that are very similar to SQL injection. The attacker injects crafted XPath queries into the application's input. The vulnerable application processes the input and returns sensitive data back to the attacker. XPath injection attacks are similar to SQL injections and are used heavily to bypass authentication that is driven by validation with XML files.

Another danger with XPath injection is that there is no way to perform access restrictions on the XML file being queried. Therefore, if the attacker is able to inject and query information from one set of elements and attributes of the file, the attacker can potentially gain access to the entire file. This is unlike a relational database, where access rights to different databases, tables, and the OS can be restricted based on required privilege levels.

Protection for XPath is similar to prevention of SQL injection flaws, except that there are no parameterized queries for XPath injection. Output escaping is considered a good defense against XPath injection. However, a stronger defense is to use XPath queries using the precompiled XPath queries, where the queries can be precompiled into XPath expressions and variables can be bound separately. This is very similar to the concept of a parameterized query for SQL queries.

13.4.2.3 LDAP Injection

The Lightweight Directory Access Protocol (LDAP) is a popular protocol that is used as a storehouse of ordered, hierarchical sets of information, such as a corporate user list, e-mail directory, telephone directories, and so on. Most popular implementations of this protocol are used for Microsoft Active Directory and IBM Tivoli, among several others.

LDAP is also heavily used in Web applications that have to integrate with these solutions for access control or querying other types of information. For instance, I was recently performing a code review for a banking client that exclusively used LDAP for all user-authentication and user-querying functions. The traditional view of the database was, for me, completely changed by the vision of LDAP being their primary resource for access control, authorization, and other user-driven actions.

LDAP injection is similar to other injection attacks like SQL and XPath injections, in that the attack performed relies on passing meaningful LDAP characters into the application's inputs to gain access to more functionality than required by the user.

For instance, a Java code interfacing with LDAP is as follows:

```
String username = request.
getParameter("username");
String ldapQuery = "(cn = " +
username + ")";
//query code follows
```

In this code snippet, the username value is being sent to the LDAP server to be queried. In the event that the user enters "*" in the application's input, which denotes all the users in the LDAP server, a vulnerable system might potentially fetch all the usernames for the attacker.

Prevention of LDAP injection is not unlike prevention of other injection flaws. Input validation is an essential that I would suggest as a control measure for any Web application. This prevents most attacks across class of injection and scripting flaws. However, output escaping is a very viable control option where LDAP-specific special characters can be filtered. For instance, these characters can be filtered as effective protection against LDAP injection.

```
'\\' = > '\5c',
'*' = > '\2a',
'(' = > '\28',
')' = > '\29',
"\x00" = > '\00'
```

13.4.2.4 Command Injection

Command injection is a deadly but lesser-known attack in the family of injection attacks. Command injection is a flaw where an attacker is able to inject OS commands into the application's input and execute OS commands on the back-end operating system.

The vulnerable application is unable to tell the difference between legitimate input and crafted OS commands injected by the attacker, and therefore execute queries and provides information to the attacker.

For instance, a Web application is designed to perform WHOIS requests on a user-provided domain. The user provides the domain that the WHOIS command will be run on and provides information to the user with the WHOIS results. However, an attacker enters the domain name appended by the ls command, which executes the WHOIS request as well as the ls command that fetches all the directories and files in the current working directory of the application.

The user enters input

```
google.com;ls
```

This input would perform the whois query on google.com as well as provide the attacker with a directory listing of the current working directory. Similarly, the attacker could use the application as an injection point to inject even more dangerous and malicious commands that provide the attacker with elevated access to the application and its back-end OS.

Protection for command injection is quite similar to other injection attacks. Input validation will be the most critical control to ensure that malicious input containing commands are filtered out of the application.

13.4.3 Requirement 6.5.2: Secure Coding to Address Buffer Overflows

Buffer overflow is a common vulnerability condition for languages like C and C++. Buffer overflow occurs when writing data that is written to the buffer exceeds the buffer's boundary and overwrites the adjacent memory. The resulting overflow can result in a variety of nonsecure conditions such as memory access errors, crash of the system, or in some cases, access to change the behavior of the application to benefit the attacker. Buffer overflow is a basis for some of the most dangerous security vulnerabilities discovered in the world today.

A buffer overflow occurs when there is insufficient bounds-checking for the data written to the buffer. Bounds checking is a method of validating if a variable is within its assigned bounds before it is used. It is especially important for a variable that is used as an index to an array to be validated for bounds. For instance, a value 1234567 would be out of bounds to be allocated to a 16-bit integer value that has the bounds −32767 to +32767.

As mentioned earlier, buffer overflow is a major problem with applications developed with C and C++, as the memory and access to memory has to be explicitly managed by the developers in the code, and developers tend to make mistakes and omissions while developing applications.

Some of the ways that developers can prevent buffer overflows in the code are as follows:

Canary defenses: Canaries or canary characters are values that are inserted between the buffer (the area that the user input is written into) and the control data (the data that is influenced by the buffer). In the event that the attacker attempts at overflowing the buffer by increasing the size of the input, then the canary value is overwritten, and the overwritten canary acts as a warning when the verification of the canary value fails. This can be used to invalidate the data.

Nonexecuting stack: Another approach to protection against buffer overflows is to ensure that execution of code is impossible in the stack. However, x86 processors have issues with this. Therefore, an ASCII armor was developed, where an attacker cannot insert an ASCII NUL character that is used typically in buffer overflow attacks. In this case, it becomes impossible for an attacker to make a program return to any address with a 0 in it, thereby making the attack that much more difficult.

Bounds checking: Bounds checking is a compiler technique that adds bounds to allocated blocks of memory at runtime. This is checked against all pointers at runtime.

13.4.4 Requirement 6.5.3: Secure Coding to Address Cryptographic Flaws

Cryptography is an important consideration for any application with user-management requirements and handling of sensitive information. Implementation of cryptography helps ensure continued protection of confidentiality and integrity of data at rest and in transit. Sensitive data stored in databases need to be encrypted to ensure that confidentiality of the data is not compromised even if the database is. User passwords and account information must be encrypted to ensure that user account information is not compromised, even if an attacker accesses the database or the Web server illegally. Cryptography has great benefits and is a robust security mechanism to protect against breach of confidentiality and integrity, but cryptographic implementations can also sometimes go horribly wrong if improperly implemented. Cryptographic implementations for Web applications require several factors to be considered. The encryption algorithm, strength of the encryption key, randomness of the key, storage location of the encryption key, and key management are some of the factors to be considered while implementing cryptography for a Web application. Some common cryptographic flaws, which render data nonsecure due to the wrong implementation of cryptography, are as follows:

Homegrown crypto: Developers sometimes write their own encryption algorithms that are based on poor encryption logic and can be easily broken by an attacker. Industry-standard encryption algorithms like AES (Advanced Encryption Standard) are recommended for adoption, as they have been proven after several years of testing and continuous use.

Use of known weak encryption and hashing schemes: Weak encryption algorithms are those that have been broken within a certain time frame, thus allowing an attacker time to guess or obtain the information in cleartext format. It is unfortunate to note that developers, even today, persist with known weak encryption and hashing algorithms like MD5 and SHA-1, RC3, and RC4 for encrypting the sensitive information.

Nonsecure key management practices: When using encryption for protection of sensitive data, it is imperative that key-management practices and processes be borne in mind. Key management includes the following:

- Generation of strong keys
- Data encryption key and master key
- Storage of keys
- Revocation of keys
- Deletion of encryption keys
- Key custodianship

There are several other instances where cryptographic implementation in Web applications is seriously flawed. In some cases, encryption keys are hard-coded into the Web application, thereby making it easy for attackers to gain access to the key and, from there, gain access to the data. Keys are seldom generated, and the encryption keys usually tend to be of a short length, which makes them easily guessable. Such nonsecure practices while implementing encryption and cryptography are very detrimental to the data stored by the application and for data in transit.

13.4.4.1 Cryptography Essentials

Cryptography is an essential requirement that most applications don't get right. It is very important to ensure the following:

13.4.4.1.1 Choose the Right Cryptosystem

The cryptographic algorithm (cryptosystem) that you choose for encrypting data must be industry standard. Industry-standard encryption algorithms are tested by cryptanalysts for several years before they are considered industry standard and recommended for use in applications. Algorithms like the Advanced Encryption System (AES) are considered industry standard due to their track record of defense against multiple attempts by cryptanalysts.

13.4.4.1.2 Strong Keys

The key is supposed to be the only confidential aspect of the cryptographic process. The strength of the key is paramount for any cryptographic operation. Therefore, it is absolutely essential that keys consist of random characters, thereby providing the entire encryption process with the requisite security. Ideally, it is recommended to have the keys generated by the system using pseudo-random number generators (PRNGs). However, this may not always be possible. In the event that that encryption keys are user generated, it must be ensured that strong keys are supplied by the user. A key that consists of special characters, letters, and numbers along with combinations of upper- and lowercase characters is preferred. Another way of strengthening user-generated keys is to append random characters to the user-generated key to produce a stronger key. However, this is still not the perfect solution, as this value has to be stored in the system, and if the attacker compromises the system and enumerates a weak user-generated key, the decryption process becomes an easy matter.

13.4.4.1.3 Protection of Keys

Encryption keys that are used to protect critical information are to be treated with a great deal of care. An attacker compromising the application might be able to gain access to the data, and at the time, if the keys are available to the attacker along with the data, then encrypting said data might be rendered obsolete. Use of key-encrypting keys and data-encrypting keys must be considered for an application to ensure the security of keys in storage. We discussed key management and key storage in detail in Chapter 8 of this book.

13.4.4.1.4 Hashing Practices

Another aspect of cryptographic storage is the use of hashing, a popular practice that is used to perform a one-way irreversible process to cleartext to render it unreadable. It is essential to use industry-standard, strong hashing algorithms like SHA-256, and so on. Additionally, its also important to use salting for the hashing process, as it adds more randomness to the hashing process.

13.4.5 Requirement 6.5.4: Secure Coding to Address Insecure Transmissions

Applications are constantly plagued by the problem of nonsecure transmissions. Network and Web applications are especially affected because sensitive information is always traveling over a network, and attackers can employ simple interception and sniffing techniques to gain access to highly sensitive information. For instance, let's imagine that you are logging into your favorite social network from a WiFi network at your local coffee shop. Some days later, you see a bunch of messages that you never sent to your friends. You see all of your settings changed and other strange things that have happened with your account on this social networking site. Turns out that an attacker at your local coffee shop was running a sniffer on the WiFi network and sniffing everyone's passwords, session tokens, and so on, to gain access to their websites and steal key information. This is a pretty devastating situation for you personally. Now imagine if an attack of a similar nature happened to an organization handling cardholder data. The situation would be debilitating in the event of an attacker being able to "see" messages transmitted across networks either internally or externally.

One of the most common attacks against applications is the "man-in-the-middle" attack, where an attacker sniffs network traffic between an application and a server, either due to lack of encrypted transmission or poor quality of encryption between the server and the client. Man-in-the-middle (MITM) attacks are especially dangerous when perpetrated against administrative accounts by attackers.

The standard implementation for secure transmission for a Web application is the use of Transport Layer Security (TLS). TLS was formerly known as SSL (Secure Socket Layer). Netscape developed SSL for the purpose of transmitting private information over the Internet. SSL uses two keys for its operations: One is the public key, and the other is the private key. SSL is implemented with the help of digital certificates. SSL provides an encrypted link for the client to interact with the server. SSL version 1.0 was developed by Netscape, and version 2.0 was released in 1995, but several aspects were found to be flawed, leading to the creation of version 3.0 in 1996. The Internet Engineering Taskforce (IETF) then took over SSL, and it was called the TLS, which was adopted as a standard. In 1999, all of the major payment brands like Visa, MasterCard, and Amex as well as several financial institutions publicly declared that SSL/TLS would be adopted as a security measure for e-commerce transactions. Traffic that is protected with SSL/TLS for access to a Web application will occur over Hypertext Transfer Protocol Secure (HTTPS) instead of over the regular HTTP protocol, which is unencrypted.

To provide secure transport of information over a network, SSL/TLS uses a combination of cryptographic processes. SSL/TLS is essentially a secure enhancement to the standard TCP/IP sockets protocol used for Internet communications. The secure sockets layer is essentially added between the "transport layer" and the "application layer" in the standard TCP/IP protocol stack, as exemplified in Figure 13.8. The Web application most commonly used with SSL is Hypertext Transfer Protocol (HTTP), the protocol for Internet Web pages.

13.4.5.1 The SSL/TLS Handshake Process

SSL/TLS uses many different cryptographic processes for secure data transportation and at various stages. For example, SSL uses public key cryptography to provide authentication, secret-key cryptography, and digital signatures to secure information and privacy. Communication over SSL/TLS essentially begins with a series of exchanges of information between the client and the server. This series of exchanges of information is called the *SSL handshake*. The SSL/TLS handshake ensures negotiation of the cipher suite, authentication, and agreement on encryption algorithms for establishing

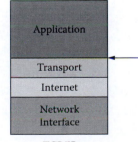

TCP/IP

FIGURE 13.8
SSL/TLS in the TCP/IP stack.

the information security. A sequence of messages is exchanged between the two systems, viz., client and server, in the SSL mode of data transfer.

13.4.5.1.1 Acquiring the SSL/TLS Certificate

The Web application vendor or organization will obtain a certificate from a certificate provider with a *certificate signing request*. This request contains the name of the Web application/website, contact e-mail address, and company information. The certificate provider would sign the request after scrutiny of the same, which produces a public certificate. When a user connects to the Web application/website, the public certificate is provided to the browser during the handshake process. The certificate contains details of the website/Web application that the certificate has been issued for, the organization name, certificate serial number, the class of certificate, the certificate provider, and the dates of validity of the certificate.

> Step 1. *Client initiation*: Client initiates an SSL/TLS request that includes the SSL version and list of supported cipher suites. This step is usually referred to as "ClientHello" in the SSL/TLS parlance. The cipher suite information also includes cryptographic algorithms and key sizes. For instance, TLS_RSA_WITH_RC4_128_MD5 is a cipher suite. The algorithm used for key exchange and certificate verification is the RSA algorithm. The encryption algorithm used for encrypting messages in this case is the RC4. The MD5 algorithm is used to verify the contents of the message.
>
> Step 2. *Server acknowledgment*: Upon the receipt of the client request, the server

chooses the highest version of SSL/TLS and the best-suited cipher suite that both the client and server support and returns this information to the client. This step is referred to as "ServerHello" in the SSL/TLS parlance.

Step 3. *Send certificate*: Optionally, the server sends the client a certificate (or even a certificate chain). In cases where a certificate chain is being sent, it begins with the server's public key certificate and ends with the certificate authority's root certificate. This step becomes essential if the server requires authentication. This step is referred to as "Certificate" in the SSL/TLS parlance.

Step 4. *Request certificate*: This is an optional step. However, if Step 3 is mandated due to an authentication requirement, then the server needs to authenticate the client and it sends the client a certificate request. This step is referred to as "Certificate request" in the SSL/TLS parlance.

Step 5. *Server key exchange*: The server sends the client a server key exchange message when the public key information sent in Step 3 is not sufficient for key exchange.

Step 6. *Server ready*: Now the server indicates to the client that its initial negotiation messages have been successfully completed. This step is referred to as "ServerHello Done" in the SSL/TLS parlance.

Step 7. *Send certificate*: If the server had requested a certificate from the client, as in Step 4, the client sends its certificate chain, just as the server did in Step 3. This step is referred to as "Certificate" in the SSL/TLS parlance.

Step 8. Client key exchange: The client will generate information used to create a key to use for symmetric encryption. For RSA, the client then encrypts this key information with the server's public key and sends it to the server.

Step 9. Certificate verification: This message is sent when a client presents a certificate as described in Step 7, and this is optional, as it depends on Step 3. Its purpose is to allow the server to complete the process of authenticating the client. When this message is used, the client sends information that it digitally signs using a cryptographic hash function. When the server decrypts this information with the client's public key, the server will be able to authenticate the client.

Step 10. Change cipher spec: In this step, the client sends a message indicating to the server to change to an encrypted mode.

Step 11. Handshake establishment on server side: In this step, the client informs the server that it is ready for secure data communication to begin.

Step 12. Change cipher spec: Now it's the server's turn to send a message to the client asking it to change to an encrypted mode of communication.

Step 13. Handshake establishment at the server side: The server tells the client that it is ready for secure data communication to begin. This indicates the completion of the SSL handshake.

Step 14. Encrypted data exchange: Henceforth, the client and the server start communicating using the symmetric encryption algorithm and the cryptographic hash function negotiated in Steps 1 and 2, as well as using the secret key that the client sent to the server in Step 8.

Step 15. Close: At the end of the communication process, each side will send a close_notify message to inform the peer that the connection is closed.

13.4.5.2 Implementation Best Practices for Secure Transmission: Web Applications

The following are some of the important implementation practices that are to be followed for Web applications:

- SSL/TLS needs to be deployed for exchange of all sensitive information like usernames, passwords, credit card information, health-care information, and so on.
- Encrypted transmission needs to be established for the transport and exchange of keys for the Web application.
- TLS v 1.1 or higher should be used for certificates. At the time of this writing TLS v 1.2 is the latest.
- For applications that handle cardholder data in the PCI environment, it is absolutely essential to have high-assurance certificates provided by reputable certificate authorities with strong cipher suites.

13.4.6 Requirement 6.5.5: Secure Coding to Address Improper Error Handling

Attackers don't penetrate Web applications in a single go. Attacking and exploiting Web applications is a detailed and cognitive effort that involves several elements of trial and error and educated guesses and hunches on the part of an attacker, which leads to eventual exploitation of the application. As we can glean from the previous discussions, *information* is the greatest asset for the attacker. The attacker would always look to gain as much information as possible about the application so that its weak points could be exploited when required. The attacker's reconnaissance measures include gaining information about the Web server, the application server, the database, and their versions. Apart from these measures, an attacker can also enter arbitrary input into the Web application to induce error conditions, and if improperly handled, these error messages are publicly displayed to the attacker and the attacker can gain a great deal of insight into the Web application's code, which could lead to an exploit. Figure 13.9 shows a detailed Web-application error message revealing sensitive information.

Upon input of arbitrary code to induce error conditions, detailed stack traces, failed SQL statements, and debug information is displayed as an error page to the attacker. This information can be used to perpetrate SQL injection attacks and other attacks to exploit the Web application.

13.4.7 Requirement 6.5.6: Remediation Measures to Address High-Severity Vulnerabilities

Apart from the vulnerabilities identified by the Application Security Best Practices and Benchmarks like the OWASP Top 10, it is important to understand, appreciate, and address vulnerabilities that are high severity but are identified only in rare cases or in cases where they are not part of a commonly known application security best practice. One of the things that immediately comes to mind is Insecure Direct Object Reference, which has not been mentioned in the PCI-DSS, but would definitely show up as a critical or high-severity vulnerability during a vulnerability assessment effort of the Web

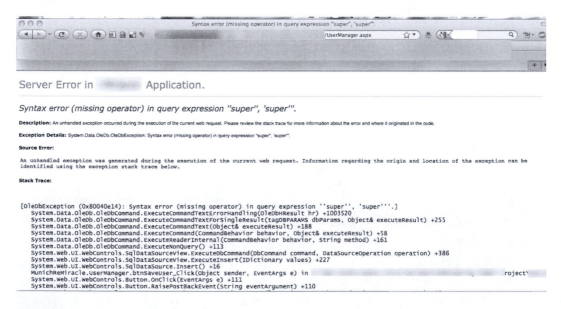

FIGURE 13.9
Detailed Web-application error message revealing sensitive information.

application. Obviously, this has to be dealt with seriously. Even though it has not been mentioned as a specific requirement in the PCI-DSS or the PA-DSS (for commercial applications), in view of the application security, it is essential that such vulnerabilities be fixed. Therefore, it is essential that all critical and high-severity vulnerabilities be fixed without having to cite reasons of compliance (PCI requirements) as an excuse not to.

13.4.8 Requirement 6.5.7: Secure Coding to Address Cross-Site Scripting

Cross-site scripting is an attack where the attacker can inject HTML code or JavaScript code into the Web application. Cross-site scripting originated from the fact that a malicious user could access another website through the use of a window or a frame and then, with the help of JavaScript, write and read data into the other website. Cross-site scripting, popularly referred to as *XSS*, has been named as such so as to not confuse the term with *CSS*, which stands for cascading style sheets. XSS is one of the most prevalent Web-application vulnerabilities identified across all websites and Web applications in the world today. According to the *WhiteHat Security Website Statistics Report* for the year 2011, it was reported that 64% of the websites that were sampled as part of the population were vulnerable to cross-site scripting vulnerabilities. The negative impact of an XSS attack may vary from one application to the other. Some do not consider XSS as a debilitating attack, but that notion is ill-conceived. Recent attacks using cross-site scripting have shown that control over an entire application can be gained

with a cross-site scripting attack.[*] XSS attacks in recent times have reared their ugly heads in the form of XSS worms, which have plagued many Web applications. The two most popular types of XSS vulnerabilities are as follows:

- Reflected XSS
- Persistent XSS

13.4.8.1 Reflected XSS

Among all XSS vulnerabilities, reflected XSS vulnerabilities are the easiest to find and the easiest to exploit. Reflected XSS, as the name indicates, just reflects the user input back to the user. The data sent to the Web server as a parameter is just replayed back to the user in a reflected XSS attack. Let us consider a simple example. A search engine on the Internet allows users to enter search queries and locates pages on the Internet based on those search queries. For instance, we have a variable called searchQuery. Normally, if the user enters the search string *rabbit*, and then the search engine would display all pages containing the key word *rabbit*. Now let us suppose that the user replaces the same search string with

```
<script>alert('This is XSS')</
script>
```

so the URL would look something like this:

```
http://www.mysearchEngine.com/
search?searchQuery =
<script>alert('This is XSS')</
script>
```

Ideally, the server should not accept such arbitrary input, but if the server does due to

---

[*] XSS attacks lead to control over user accounts and applications: http://blogs.zdnet.com/security/?p=3514; http://chirashi.zensay.com/2009/09/how-i-tell-my-clients-that-xss-is-bad/.

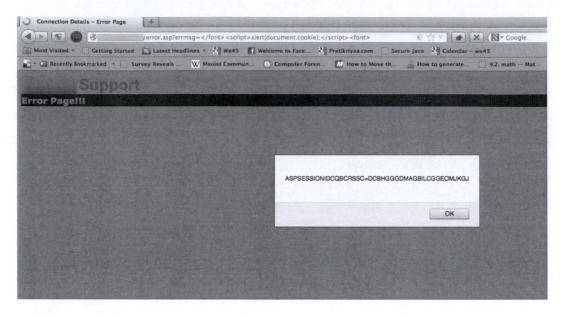

FIGURE 13.10
Reflected cross-site scripting attack.

vulnerability, then the searchQuery entered would process the data in the script tags as HTML and display an alert saying *This is XSS*. Figure 13.10 shows a reflected cross-site scripting attack.

Although reflected XSS looks relatively harmless, it is quite the contrary. XSS attacks are used by attackers of a Web application in attacking the other legitimate users of the Web application. Reflected XSS typically can be used to perpetrate a session-hijacking attack, where a legitimate user's session is hijacked and the attacker uses the session to log on as the user.

13.4.8.2 Persistent XSS

Stored XSS is the type of XSS where the malicious JavaScript entered by one user is stored in the database of the application and then displayed to the other users of the application without being sanitized or padded in any way. Stored XSS is the most dangerous type of cross-site scripting

vulnerability. Stored XSS is also referred to as *persistent XSS*. It is very commonly found on websites that allow end-user interaction. For instance, in a public forum, the message left by a particular user may be seen by other users in the forum. Other users may post replies to the question entered by a particular user in the forum. If a particular user leaves a question with a malicious JavaScript embedded in the message, another unsuspecting user could view the page where the malicious user has posted his question, and then the code would execute and the unsuspecting user's session credentials could be stolen.

Stored XSS can also be used for more devastating types of attacks. The attacker may post the JavaScript to surreptitiously redirect the user to a malicious website, where malware would be pushed out to the user. XSS worms propagate through this method, where the user is maliciously redirected to another site because of the XSS vulnerability on one page, and the site uploads malware to the user through this method.

13.4.9 Requirement 6.5.8: Secure Coding to Address Flawed Access Control

Access-control mechanisms are the perimeter defense for a Web application. Attackers realize that gaining access to an application is the first step toward gaining access to the sensitive information that is stored, processed, or transmitted by the application. Attackers have continually focused their efforts on gaining access to a Web application by circumventing or otherwise defeating Web-application access control. This has also been aided by the fact that most Web applications have poor access-control mechanisms and are generally rife with security vulnerabilities. Attackers have recognized this issue and perpetrated several attacks that have rendered applications accessible by these unwanted elements and have also resulted in the compromise of user accounts of other users in the application. Some of the attacks against access-control systems of Web applications are as follows:

- Session hijacking
- Cross-site request forgery
- Session fixation
- Forceful browsing
- Password attacks

13.4.9.1 Session Hijacking

Sessions are an integral aspect of a Web application. Sessions ensure that the stateless HTTP protocol is able to track the state between multiple connections from the same user. Sessions are created using session IDs, which are used by the server to keep track of the communication between the server and the user of the Web application. Sessions are provided to the user when he/she logs into the system and are destroyed when the user logs out of the system.

Session hijacking is the technique used to capture a legitimate user's session ID while the session is still in progress. Sessions can be hijacked by the attacker brute-forcing random session IDs until he/she reaches a legitimate session of a user. Several Web applications do not generate strong random session IDs and as a result are easily guessable. For instance, some Web applications generate session IDs like 0001, 0002, which are numbers or characters in a series, and this provides an attacker with easy access to another user's session, as the attacker can increment digits to gain access to sessions of other users in the system. Session hijacking can also be performed with other attacks like phishing and cross-site scripting.

13.4.9.2 Cross-Site Request Forgery

Cross-site request forgery, also known as CSRF or XSRF, is a difficult but deadly attack on a Web application. A CSRF attack occurs when an attacker is successfully able to pass a phantom request to the Web application on behalf of the user without the user's knowledge. For instance, a user is logged into his banking Web application and simultaneously logged into his e-mail application. The user receives an e-mail instructing him/her to visit a particular link. The link in reality is a hidden request to the banking application that transfers $1000 from the user's account to the attacker's account. If the banking application is vulnerable to CSRF, this request would be processed, and the banking application would transfer the said amount into the attacker's account. This is successful because the legitimate user is logged into the banking application with a properly issued session ID, and the user would be completely unaware of the request made by the attacker to the banking application. While CSRF is technically not an attack on the access-control system, the attack is made successful because of unauthenticated requests to a vulnerable Web application, resulting in a change of state and possible exposure of sensitive information.

13.4.9.3 Session Fixation

Session fixation is also a popular attack against Web application access control. The attack is carried out when a vulnerable application does not invalidate existing session credentials when the user logs into the Web application. For instance, Bob is an attacker who wants to steal Scott's session and gain access to his e-mail account. Bob accesses his e-mail, for which the e-mail application issues him a session ID. Bob then resets the browser to the login page. Scott notices the open browser window with the e-mail site open and logs into the Web application. The vulnerable e-mail site logs in Scott with Bob's previously existing session (which is still valid), and using that session ID, Bob maliciously gains access to Scott's e-mail account.

A variety of social-engineering options are at the attacker's disposal to carry out a session-fixation attack. Phishing attacks are also used to deliver session-fixation attacks to the victim.

13.4.9.4 Forceful Browsing

Forceful browsing is also a common attack against a vulnerable Web application. Web applications have several links and pages that are not visible to the user or not accessible by the user because they aren't referenced by the Web application. Attackers may be able to manually crawl the Web application for unprotected links and gain access to information through pages that are not referenced by the application. As an example, say the Web application has an admin page called https://www.vuln-app.com/site/admin/admin.jsp. This page is the admin dashboard, which has been not been referenced in the Web application. An attacker can crawl all the directories and files of a Web application and come across this unprotected page, which contains sensitive information, thereby leading to a security breach. Forceful browsing is caused by leaving unprotected links and pages not secured by access control or not defined through strong authorization.

Another example of forced browsing[*] is when the authorization for certain pages and links is enforced through client-side mechanisms like JavaScript. The user can disable JavaScript or use a Web application proxy to easily access restricted links and perform unauthorized actions on the Web application.

13.4.10 Requirement 6.5.9: Secure Coding to Address Cross-Site Request Forgery

Cross-site request forgery (CSRF) is an attack that is popularly pronounced as *see-surf*. CSRF is an attack whereby a user who has logged onto a Web application is directed to send a request to a vulnerable Web application, which then performs an

---

[*] An example of the attack can be found at Abhay Bhargav's blog: http://citadelnotes.blogspot.com/2009/05/overreli-ance-on-javascript-pen-testers.html.

action (through the request) without the user's knowledge. For instance, a user is logged into his e-mail and his online bank account at the same time in two browser tabs. The user receives an e-mail from a source saying that his bank account needs to be updated with specific information, and the information can only be activated by clicking on the given link. Upon clicking the link, unbeknownst to the user, a request is sent to the bank account to transfer funds to another account; all of this is done without the user's knowledge. The request would look something like this:

```
<img src = "http://www.legit-bank.
com/amountTransfer.do?frmAcc =
document.form.frmAcc& toAcct =
123456&toSWIFTid = 22331122&amt =
4025.50">
```

If the banking application processes requests without validation, then it is vulnerable to CSRF. This CSRF attack has gained a great deal of attention in recent times and has proved to be a devastating Web application attack.

13.5 ONGOING VULNERABILITY-MANAGEMENT PRACTICES FOR WEB APPLICATIONS

13.5.1 Web-Application Vulnerability Assessments

The Web-application security threat landscape is constantly changing. Newer and more updated attack vectors are constantly being showcased by exploit developers, security researchers, and hackers all the time. Therefore, unless there are proactive and ongoing vulnerability management

and security practices for the Web application, it is highly likely that attackers may best an enterprise, especially one that is handling cardholder information. The PCI requirements provide two options to organizations for ongoing vulnerability-management practices. The first is to perform Web-application vulnerability assessments for public-facing Web applications. This can be done either manually or by using automated vulnerability assessment tools. Usually, organizations hire external experts to perform Web vulnerability assessments against their public-facing Web applications to ensure that they are validated by external expertise. We will discuss vulnerability assessment and penetration testing for PCI extensively in the latter part of the book, for Requirement 11 of the PCI–DSS. Requirement 6.6 mandates that if a vulnerability assessment of public-facing Web applications is to be done, it has to be performed annually and upon significant changes to the Web application.

13.5.2 Usage of a Web-Application Firewall

Web applications have become complex organisms that are to be governed with equivalent if not more controls than the network layer of an enterprise. The Web-application firewall is one such device that serves as an access-control mechanism for Web applications, in a similar fashion to network-layer firewalls for the network. A Web-application firewall (WAF) is an appliance or a server plugin or filter that acts as an access-control mechanisms against common Web-application attacks like XSS and SQL injection. Web-application firewalls usually come with inbuilt signatures that detect and thwart these attacks against the Web application by inspecting HTTP traffic to and from the application. There are several commercial and open-source products that are WAFs. Some of the notable ones are ModSecurity (open source), Ironbee (open source), and so on. There are several commercial variants that provide a great deal of application security intelligence, apart from just performing the role of the WAF.

A WAF can be used as a substitute for the vulnerability-assessment point in Requirement 6.6 of the PCI-DSS. However, I personally recommend going for both, in the case of critical applications, because there are several attack vectors that can bypass/evade WAFs and perform Web attacks successfully.

13.6 SUMMARY

Requirement 6 was the focus of this chapter. We began with a discussion of patching and patch-management practices required for the PCI standards. We learned that patch management had to be driven with a strong change-management practice to ensure that patches for systems and applications were rolled out in an effective manner, with accountability and plans for rollback in case of failure.

Additionally, we focused a great deal of attention on application-security practices, which are central to Requirement 6. We began with a discussion of security in the SDLC. We also delved deeply into a practical and thorough guide for integrating application security into the SDLC using a strong Web-application risk-management framework. We then explored the specifics of application security and PCI requirements for application security to prevent against attacks like SQL injection, XSS, and so on. Finally, we learned of some requirements of PCI, namely Requirement 6.6, which is required for ongoing vulnerability management and application security assurance.

14

Requirement 7: Restrict Access to Cardholder Data by Business Need to Know

Access control is a primal and fundamental characteristic of any information security program. Access control is the practice of exerting control over individuals or objects that are allowed/disallowed to access a given system. Effective access control hinges on specific concepts and methods that are important to understand and implement access control across diverse systems like operating systems, applications, network devices, physical areas, and so on. Requirement 7 of the PCI-DSS deals exclusively with these concepts of access control and their practice and implementation across the PCI environment.

In this chapter, we will explore Requirement 7 of the PCI-DSS. We will delve into concepts of least privilege, access-control matrix, and so on. Requirement 7 serves as a precursor to a much more detailed Requirement 8 of the PCI-DSS, and a firm understanding of this Requirement 7 provides us with more insight and easier understanding of Requirement 8.

14.1 REQUIREMENT 7.1: RESTRICT ACCESS TO SYSTEMS WITH CARDHOLDER DATA

14.1.1 Access Restrictions across the PCI Environment

Requirement 7 of the PCI deals exclusively with the methodology and the concept of access control for the PCI environment. However, before we go deeper into the requirement, let us explore some access-control requirements.

The PCI-DSS Requirement 7.1 requires access control to be implemented for all system components and cardholder data. This effectively means that all system components in the PCI environment need to be secured with access control. This applies equally to operating systems, network devices, and applications. Operating systems and applications are the most critical, as they are used the most by end users within the environment. Applications tend to consist of multiple layers and linked components. The linked components usually include the database, file servers, linked servers, application servers, and third-party content servers. In such cases, the access-control requirement applies equally to these linked components as well.

14.1.2 The Principle of Least Privilege

Requirement 7.1 (specifically 7.1.1) of the PCI-DSS requires the principle of *least privilege* to be implemented for access control for all system components and cardholder data in the PCI environment. *Least privilege* is defined by the US-CERT as follows: "Least Privilege is the principle of allowing users or applications the least amount of permissions necessary to perform their intended function." This essentially means that people should be provided only with as much access to systems as required for their job/role in the organization or on said system. This extends to all objects, modules, and application functions in the system.

Least privilege also forms the basis for the role-based access control that requires that users should only be provided access privileges that are required for their role in the organization. For instance, a data-entry operator does not need to view financial reports and statements. Therefore, by extension, they should not have access to those resources.

Least privilege can be enforced on the operating systems through practices like disallowing access to root accounts or disallowing access to performing privileged actions for users who don't require

these features and whose job profiles don't require them to perform said functions on the operating system. For instance, the system administration must have the previously mentioned capability on systems if he/she is to manage the systems in the environment.

Modern applications usually have role-based access-control mechanisms built in. Role-based access control (RBAC) is an effective access-control mechanism that works on the principle of least privilege. The access control is driven through user roles, for instance, when a data entry operator is automatically provided access only to raise transaction entries in the system and does not have access to reporting and administration functions.

Requirement 7.1.2 mandates that the organization must assign an individual with privileges on the system that is required for his/her job profile. For instance, a billing clerk at a retail outlet must only have access to make entries and perform billing functions. He/she must not even be able to edit previously raised invoices or alter the rates of products in the system, as that could lead to several errors and potential frauds. This applies across all systems, including network devices, operating systems, applications, and databases in the PCI environment.

According to Requirement 7.2.3, another facet of access control is to ensure that there is a default deny-all setting for users who are not explicitly given permissions to access data within the PCI environment and all its system components. A default deny-all setting works on the concept of "deny until explicit access is provided"; therefore, if the user is not explicitly provided permissions to access a resource, then the system will deny the user access to said resource.

14.1.3 Documentation of Approval: Access Privileges

Requirement 7.1.3 of the PCI-DSS requires that all access to resources in the PCI environment should only be granted based on a documented access-control process and practice. For instance, if a new employee needs to get access privileges on the systems in the PCI environment, the access request must be raised by the human-resource manager, and the request must be reviewed and signed off by the department/business head who is handling the user and/or the IT manager who will be assigning access to the user.

Documentation and sign-off of access control is akin to the change-management process and can be part of the same process. Where an access request is made and only after specific sign-offs by certain users in certain roles within the organization, the user is granted access to operating systems, applications, and devices in the PCI environment for which the user has a business need to access.

14.1.4 Automated Access-Control System

Requirement 7.1.3 requires the access-control system for system components to be driven with an automated access-control mechanism. An automated access-control system is one where the system automatically manages the access control when the user's authentication credentials and permissions are defined in the system. For instance, a billing clerk at the retail outlet must be able to authenticate to the operating system and the billing application, and both of these systems have to automatically drive authentication by rightfully authenticating the legitimate users with credentials and providing them with specific privileges that are required to perform their tasks. Today, access to systems is largely driven with automated access-control systems that handle authentication and authorization out of the box.

14.2 SUMMARY

Requirement 7 of the PCI-DSS focuses on the measurement and assessment of the organization's conceptual implementation of access control. Requirement 7 mostly deals with the implementation of the concept of *least privilege* in the PCI environment. *Least privilege* refers to the practice of allowing users to have access only to the information that is required for them to do their job properly.

Requirement 7 specifies that access to privileged user IDs and credentials can be granted only to users with a specific requirement for privileged access. Requirement 7 also stipulates that approval processes be followed and documented to ensure that there is traceability across the organization's access-control process.

15

Requirement 8: Access-Control Requirements for PCI Environments

Our focus in this chapter will be on access control. In Chapter 14, we had an overview of the access-control concepts that are necessary for a PCI environment. However, in this chapter, our orientation changes specifically to explore access-control implementation requirements for a PCI environment. We will delve deeply into access control and throw light on specific areas of access control such as password management, two-factor authentication, access-control specifics for databases, and so on. We will look at the correlation of access-control requirements to the PA-DSS as well.

15.1 UNIQUE IDS FOR USERS: PCI ENVIRONMENT

15.1.1 Requirement 8.1: Assign Unique IDs to Users in PCI Environment

Unique IDs are widely recognized as an important security feature, and rightfully so. All too often, I have seen organizations missing out on this basic security implementation wake up to horrendous consequences. Let's take a simple example. A major manufacturing company that I was working with was using a very popular enterprise resource planning (ERP) application. The ERP application was the lifeblood of the organization and was the single source of data across the organization. Licensing for the ERP application was very expensive, and as a result of this, the company purchased limited licenses for the application and shared these credentials among all of the users of the ERP. Soon, the company started seeing serious discrepancies in its data on the ERP. Entries seemed to be magically missing. Critical data was modified without reason, and this led to a great deal of financial loss and critical loss of time for the organization. This was all owing to the fact that the company had shared accounts of the ERP application among different users in the company. For instance, three accountants shared a single ID, and all three of them passed entries on the system. The situation was so bad that most people had ID and password information of individuals outside their functional area as well. There was absolutely no traceability in the system, hence leading to a severe breach of integrity.

The use of group or shared user IDs and credentials can lead to a scenario where no single person can be made accountable for changes or adverse impacts to the identified system resource. This is typically seen with enterprise applications where group IDs are provided to users of the application. In the event that a single user deletes or modifies or discloses said data to an unauthorized third party, there is no way of tracing the event back to the specific user who perpetrated the security breach and hold the user accountable for said breach.

The PCI-DSS requires that specific user IDs have to be maintained for every user of all system components and applications in the PCI environment. Unique user IDs must exist for all system components, including operating systems and network devices and any applications in the PCI environment or that provide access to cardholder data.

15.2 FACTORS OF AUTHENTICATION

15.2.1 The Three Factors of Authentication Supplementing User IDs

Authentication is defined as the act of verifying that a person or entity is really who he/she claims to be. Authentication is one of the most basic controls in the world of security. It usually acts a perimeter control for any system, preventing access to unauthorized parties or entities from entering the system or gaining access to critical data.

One of the most popular ways of authenticating users is by way of a password. The user identifies himself/herself with a username/user ID. The user subsequently enters a password that is already stored and accessible by the system. The system verifies the password entered by the user with the user's password stored in the system. If the passwords match, then the user's authenticity is verified, and the user gains access to the system/application. While there are several methods and ways to perform authentication on modern systems, the password remains to be the most popular and prevalent authentication method for systems the world over.

The ways in which authentication can occur falls into three broad categories. They are:

- Something you know: knowledge factors
- Something you are: physical factors
- Something you have

These three factors of authentication are widely recognized as the broad categories against which most authentication methods are driven.

15.2.1.1 Something You Know: Knowledge Factors

"Something you know" factors of authentication rely on knowledge of the authentication parameters. For instance, the user knows his/her password, hence is able to log in to a system that he/she is supposed to have access to. The bank's customer knows his/her ATM PIN, hence is able to perform withdrawals at an ATM. The authentication parameter in this case is the password or the PIN, and since the user knows the password, the user enters the identification parameter (like username or user ID) that identifies the user to the system. It is because the user *knows* the authentication parameter that the user is allowed into the system.

Typical examples of authentication methods of "something you know" are passwords, PINs, passkeys, passphrases, and user-generated encryption keys.

15.2.1.2 Something You Are: Physical Factors

All of us must have used biometric systems to gain access to a computer or to an office or to a data center or other physical environment. Such factors do not rely on anything we know. It relies on who we are. For instance, if I need to scan my fingerprint every day before I enter my office and the door is only open to me if the system identifies me and authenticates me as "Abhay Bhargav," then I gain access to my office. However, this does not rely on a password or anything else I have. It relies on me to be me. The "something you are" factor of authentication does not depend on anything you know or anything you carry. It depends on you. Some popular examples of this method are the biometric systems that rely on fingerprint scanning, retina scanning, facial recognition, and so on.

These methods of authentication are very popular for physical devices, but they are yet to be scaled up to enterprise IT infrastructure. There are obvious challenges, including the cost and deployment of scanners across multiple systems, enrolling, and control of user physical attributes in a central (or distributed) database. There are also concerns about the fail-safe nature of biometric authentication methods, as they tend to be inconsistent with certain specific conditions. For instance, if the user's fingers are dirty or have been malformed due to some development, the biometric system relying on fingerprint scanning may not work. It is seen that pregnant women undergo changes in retinal vascularization as a result of their pregnancy. This serves as an inconsistent measure. Retinal scanners are also rendered ineffective in the event of eye surgeries like cataracts, and so on.

15.2.1.3 Something You Have: Physical Token Parameters

Another important factor of authentication that is gaining vogue, especially with the surge in ownership of mobile phones, is the "something you have" factor of authentication. This factor of authentication relies on something that a user possesses to gain access to a system. Let's assume that the user needs a specific USB dongle that the user attaches to the system to gain access to an application that reads the authentication parameters from the USB dongle. Another popular "something you have" method is the use of SecureID tokens or other password tokens that generate passwords every few minutes (or seconds, depending on the requirements). The user enters the password generated by the token (as a one-time password) to gain access to the system. The one-time password, as the name suggests, is a single-time-use password that cannot be used again to authenticate to the system.

One of the popular ways of performing this method of authentication is the use of a one-time password delivered to the user's mobile phone. Let's assume that I am logging into my bank. I log in with my username and password (something I know), and as soon as I successfully log in, the system requires me to enter my one-time password delivered through my mobile phone as a text message. I receive a one-time password via text message, and I enter the password in the computer to gain access to the system.

Requirement 8.2 of the PCI-DSS mandates that one of these three factors of authentication must be used in conjunction with the identification parameter, which is usually a username, user ID, or something to that effect.

15.2.2 Two-Factor Authentication: Remote Access

As the name suggests, two-factor authentication is where two of the three factors of authentication are used by a system to grant access to a user of the system. For instance, some banks provide SecureID tokens to their customers. Apart from entering their ATM PIN, users must also enter the SecureID password on their token at the time. This adds an additional layer of security, as a single factor does not serve as the only control against a user gaining access to the system. Popular two-factor authentication methods usually include a password and a token. Today, the concept of a one-time password sent to the user's phone is also considered to be two-factor authentication that can be used by the user to gain access to the system. Figure 15.1 is the image of the RSA SecureID that is used for two-factor authentication.

Requirement 8.3 of the PCI-DSS requires that third-party access or remote access to the PCI environment must be verified using two-factor authentication. This is common for several companies that have vendors who are managing their IT infrastructure or some portion of their IT infrastructure. Two-factor authentication using the two factors—"something you know" and "something you have"—are popular for remote access. For instance, network administrators may gain access to the network over a RADIUS* or TACACS† server with tokens. Additionally, network/server administrators can also gain access to the PCI environment with virtual private networks (VPNs) implemented with either a token-based two-factor authentication system or a certificate-driven two-factor authentication system (where the certificate along with the user's password acts as the "something you have" factor of authentication).

The rationale for this requirement is that third-party access to a PCI environment can have serious ramifications. For instance, if your company has outsourced its IT to a service provider and that service provider is careless with passwords, attackers may be able to gain access to your environment with the provider's credentials. However, if there is a two-factor authentication system in place, the chances of such attacks are reduced considerably.

---

* Remote Authentication Dial In User Service (RADIUS) is a protocol that provides authentication, authorization, and accounting services (AAA). It is used for network administrators to access a network remotely for remote management of the devices and the servers. RADIUS is a protocol at the application layer and uses UDP as transport. It can be used in conjunction with tokens for two-factor authentication.

† Terminal Access Controller Access-Control System (TACACS) is a protocol similar to RADIUS that provides AAA services. It is used by remote administrators to manage the network and network devices remotely. TACACS is considered more secure than RADIUS, as it encrypts both the username and password. It also provides provisions for logging admin commands, a feature that RADIUS does not provide. TACACS can be used with tokens for two-factor authentication.

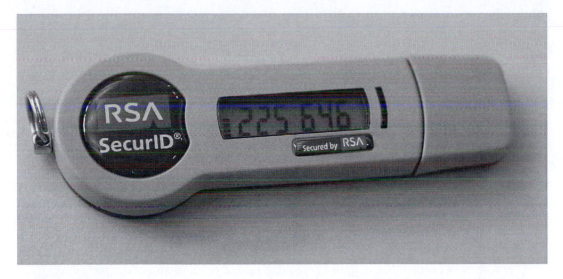

FIGURE 15.1
RSA SecurID token.

15.3 PROTECTION OF PASSWORDS: TRANSMISSION AND STORAGE

15.3.1 Protection of Passwords in Transit

In the event where a password is the only factor of authentication that is being used, which is the case with most systems, applications, and devices, it becomes absolutely essential to protect it during transmission. This is especially true for administrative passwords. Imagine if a malicious insider was sniffing your network and the administrator to a banking application was logging into the application. The transmission of data between server and client is not encrypted or protected in any way. In such cases, the attacker would be easily able to sniff the admin's credentials off the corporate network and gain access to the application as the administrator and cause an adverse impact on the organization.

Encryption of passwords in transit is addressed in PCI-DSS Requirement 8.4.

We have already explained the concept of encrypting information in transit in great detail in Chapter 11. A variety of options are available to organizations for implementation like SSL/TLS, SSH, or other encryption technologies that rely on session keys, public-private key pairs, and so on.

15.3.2 Protection of Passwords at Rest

Apart from being transmitted securely, passwords also have to be stored securely at rest. When attackers are able to gain access to databases, LDAP (Lightweight Directory Access Protocol) servers, or other servers that contain sensitive information, they primarily target passwords and other sensitive data, as that information usually provides them with access to user accounts and all other sensitive information tied to user accounts. Apart from applications, imagine if someone was able to break a poor password encryption scheme on a production database or mission-critical ERP app. The results would be disastrous. Passwords have to be encrypted and stored securely at rest, as they are highly valuable assets not only from the context of a particular device or application, but that of multiple devices and applications, as users tend to use the same password or passwords across multiple systems.

Passwords are usually hashed in most systems today. However, it is not always the case. Encrypted passwords may be in vogue for environments and systems where passwords have to be regenerated and cannot be subjected to a one-way hashing process that renders the password irreversibly unreadable.

We have dealt with encryption of data at rest extensively in Chapter 8, where we discussed multiple encryption algorithms, encryption modes, and so on. There is a great deal of information on effective one-way hashing as well.

15.4 AUTHENTICATION MANAGEMENT FOR PCI ENVIRONMENTS

15.4.1 Access-Control Procedure

I cannot stress the importance of access control enough. Conceptually and practically, access control is usually the first line of defense against attackers, and perhaps the highest number of attempted abuses are against access-control systems. Access control is essential for any system component both inside (private-facing devices) and outside (public-facing devices) the organization. To add to this, with systems growing increasingly complex and access control

becoming discrete across multiple systems, the only way that an organization can make sense of access control in the long run is by documenting it and disseminating it among its employees and other stakeholders.

I have found that a well-documented access-control policy/procedure goes a long way toward clarifying the organization's stance on access-control systems, password policies and management, password resets, and so on. I would always recommend that an organization maintain an access-control policy/procedure before they undertake PCI compliance. It is tremendously beneficial to have a clear deployment and implementation plan of action that is well thought out and discussed, right from the beginning, than to grope in the dark on access-control measures and lose track of the objective. Lacking a clear plan of action, an organization can easily get lost in the maze of multifarious access-control measures that are required for multiple network devices, servers, workstations, and applications in the environment.

An access-control procedure should ideally detail the following:

- Control of addition, deletion, and modification of user credentials in the organization
- Identity verification measures for password resets
- Password issue and enrollment
- Access revocation parameters and procedures
- User reconciliation and account management
- Password policy/practice specifics
  Password length
  Password history
  Password expiration

Password complexity
Password lockouts

15.4.2 Requirement 8.5.1: Control of Operations on Access Control

We have already learned that granting access rights to users is a complex issue, especially in large environments with multiple applications to which people need to be granted access in order to do their jobs. Most organizations implement an access-control form or approval procedure, where a new user who is enrolled into the system must obtain authorizations and approvals from multiple authorities before being granted said access. For instance, in several companies, authorization forms are approved by the human resource personnel, the department head of the enrolled user's department, the IT department, and the application owner(s) that are responsible for executing the user's authorization. Only after specific approvals from these stakeholders should the user gain access into the environment.

This is all the more important for user deletions. When a user leaves the organization, the potential for misfeasance of any kind is elevated to a great degree. In such cases, the user must obtain approvals for a form (like a separation form), where each department or functional area that has granted the user the access during his/her time in the organization is disabled and/or deleted based on the business requirement.

The process of creating, modifying, and deleting user information must be controlled in the PCI environment, as highly sensitive information is involved. When users are created, deleted, or modified in the system, there has to be a set process that includes the key factor of accountability. This factor provides an assurance that

unnecessary user accounts and IDs are not being created and that accounts that are no longer necessary are deleted.

Modification is also a key factor for security consideration. Let's take an example. Bob decides to elevate his friend Scott to the role of an administrator for the e-commerce application that is handled by his company. In the event that this decision was a planned one, with approvals and a clear business need, it would have been perfectly alright. However, without authorization, approval, and due consideration, this decision could prove to be a major security flaw for the organization.

This requirement holds all the more value in this day of cloud applications and diverse and discrete applications, where users in the organizations constantly access multiple resources with different user accounts to do their jobs. It is essential that organizations collate this information in the form of a cohesive practice, where user creation, deletion, and modification is accounted for with a system of authorization and approval.

From an assessment standpoint, it is *very* important that assessors pay special attention to the practice of granting and revoking access to users in the environment, especially ones dealing with a large number of people and multiple systems and/or applications. Assessors must look at multiple samples, dating back to multiple timelines like three months, six months, etc., to the most recent to identify the consistency of the practice of adding and removing users from the systems. It is also *exceedingly* important to look at modifications of user profiles, for instance, if someone gets promoted to a higher position in the company, or if someone changes departments altogether. The assessor must examine the business's need to know and the specific

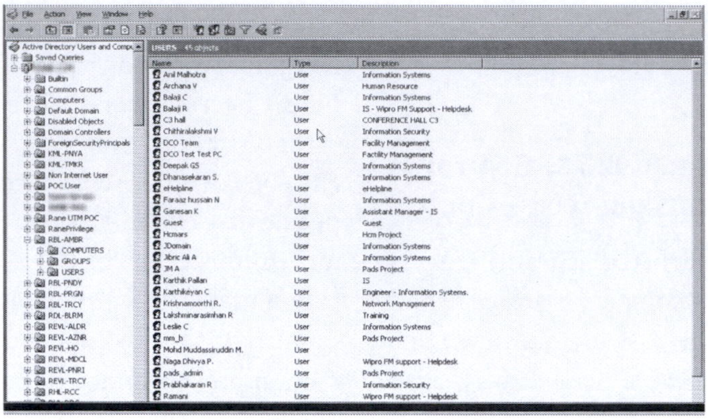

FIGURE 15.2
Different users in the Windows Active Directory system.

rights provided to the user based on that business's need to know. This information should always be corroborated by systemic evidence of the user profiles in the system or otherwise, as the case may be. Figure 15.2 is an image of the user's screen in the Windows Active Directory system.

15.4.3 Requirement 8.5.2: Verification of User Identity (Password Resets)

A common security weakness, especially for large companies, is the fact that user identity is not verified or is inefficiently verified in the case of user-account resets. For instance, an attacker wants to get access to an ID in the organization. He calls the helpdesk and pretends to be Bob from IT. He smooth talks the helpdesk representative into giving him a password. He pretends to have lost his e-mail password and asks the helpdesk rep to provide him with a password or reset the password and tell him the password orally.

Several organizations have been socially engineered into similar attacks by skilled attackers and social engineers who are able to pretend to be legitimate users of the organization and gain access to user accounts and steal sensitive information from the organization.

Therefore, the organization must put in controls to ensure that the user's identity is verified by the admin or the helpdesk rep before the password is reset. For instance, the user's identity can be verified with a series of strong password questions that the user should answer before the admin or helpdesk rep would reset the password. Alternatively, in some companies, the user's manager would send the communication, and the account password would be reset, thereby providing more assurance that another person is involved in the process. Sometimes, the users must physically present themselves to have their account reset by the administrator.

15.4.4 Requirement 8.5.3: Unique Password Value and First-Use Change

Reset passwords are usually weak, especially ones that are assigned by an administrator. Most of the time, it's the company's name suffixed with 12345, or something similar. Some systems provide for the setting of unique passwords or randomly generated passwords for first-time users or users who have their passwords reset. In such cases, the password is something very complex like Xt$48E*u, or something similar, that the user would probably forget or not be able to memorize. In such cases, users might find ways of storing it nonsecurely, like writing on Post-Its attached to their monitors or their desks somewhere, and thereby causing a potential data breach. It is also seen that users who are not forced to change their first-time passwords tend to use the same password over time, as it is just more convenient to do it that way. In such cases, an attacker's job becomes that much easier, as they have to enumerate easily breakable passwords for users that are not changed from a single default.

The organization must enforce a system where a first-time password issued to a user is forced to be changed by the system when the user logs into the system for the first time. This will ensure that the first-time password is *never* the long-term password of the users in the organization. This will also eliminate the use of complicated, randomly generated passwords that have no relation to the user and have little recall value, which tempts users to resort to nonsecure storage mechanisms like writing these passwords in their books, phones, or at their desks. Requirement 8.5.3 requires that the first-time password set for the user by the administrator be a uniquely generated password, with the user being forced to change this password upon initial login to the system.

One of the most common systems that are used for user-access management is the Active Directory service in Windows environments. The Windows Active Directory system allows for administrators to set a first-time password for users and mandate a forced change of the user password upon the first user login. However, the administrator cannot set a unique first-time password. In such cases, the administrator must use a unique password-generation tool to generate the password and force the user to change it upon the next login.

Assessors need to verify this requirement across multiple applications in the environment. Most organizations find this requirement to be a major challenge, especially in the case of card-management applications and banking applications that may not provide for this functionality. However, modern applications of this nature are being driven to become PA-DSS-compliant, as a result of which this requirement is usually addressed. There are ways to manually manage this process, but they are usually tedious and require a great deal of enforcement and discipline on the part of the administrators of such applications.

15.4.5 Requirements 8.5.4 and 8.5.5: Revocation and Removal of User Access Rights

15.4.5.1 Requirement 8.5.4: Revocation of User Access Rights Immediately after User Separation

A user who leaves or is separated from the organization presents an immediate risk of data breach. Even the most harmless of users tend to want to carry certain "useful" information from their previous jobs to their new ones. In fact, I was advising one of my clients against hiring a senior executive on the grounds that he offered to bring sensitive information of great benefit to my client from his previous job with my client's biggest competitor. Therefore, when users are separated from the organization, their credentials to all applications, systems, and devices in the organization must be systematically revoked and disabled. This is exceedingly important in a world that is embracing the cloud in a big way. Some organizations are not even aware of how many third-party apps they use for their daily activities.

This makes me allude to my first requirement under the access-control section, which is to have a cohesive procedure where each user's access to multiple systems, applications, and devices is mapped. When the user is in the process of being separated, the user credentials to all of these applications must be revoked through a systematic method of communication and feedback to all of the administrators of these systems and applications. For instance, if the user is utilizing the organization's mail services, CRM application, billing application, active directory (file access), video communication servers, and so on, the relevant administrators for all of these applications and processes must be contacted for access revocation, and they must respond with feedback in the affirmative for the action to be deemed complete. Even the slightest delays in this process might lead to a data breach; hence, the slightest delays should not be tolerated. Users who are separating from the organizations must have all of their access rights revoked, including physical access, by their last working day, so that they walk out of the organization as third parties.

Many companies have a policy of "absconding employees," where user access is revoked when employees do not report for work for a stipulated period of continuous absence. For instance, one of the banks I was advising had an absconding-employee parameter of three days, after which an employee's access would be temporarily disabled until the employee presented himself to his business unit head and explained the reason for his unexplained absence.

15.4.5.2 Requirement 8.5.5: Disabling User Accounts within 90 Days

Requirement 8.5.5 of the PCI-DSS is an extension of the access-control revocation requirement of the PCI-DSS. This requirement addresses the point of continued user access management over an extended period of time. In several environments, the outgoing user's access is temporarily revoked (either by password change or reassignment) from the system once the user leaves. However, the user's account is not disabled or deleted from the system over a long period of time. This causes a few problems, the most notable being that of management of unnecessary and unused user accounts. Another potential security consideration is that malicious administrators or internal/external attackers can use a revoked user's account to perpetrate fraud and other instances of security breach.

The PCI-DSS requires that old or unused user accounts be disabled or removed at least every 90 days. This task is meant as a measure of pruning of the unused user accounts. A specification of the time frame will also give administrators the time to clear out the user's account of all information and transition to another user. This procedure has to be performed for unused accounts across multiple applications, systems, and devices.

The procedure can be automated or manually performed as well. I highly recommend automating this process with scripts across multiple applications. For instance, Windows Active Directory scripts using Powershell can be used to delete user accounts inactive beyond a certain number of days. Shell scripts can be written for Unix- and Linux-based systems to disable/delete inactive user accounts. Apart from scripts, automation tools are available for multiple systems to perform the necessary functions. Commercial applications to manage access-control systems and applications can perform these activities as well.

Assessors have to look into this practice across multiple systems. They need to perform random-sampling assessments against different systems like Active Directory, network devices, applications, and so on, to identify whether user accounts that are inactive or unused are removed/disabled at least every three months.* This must tied back to the user account forms that are used for separating users from the organization.

15.4.6 Requirement 8.5.6: Vendor Account Access Management

The modern organization relies heavily on vendors and partners, especially for its IT environment. Vendors develop, deploy, and implement applications, network infrastructure, servers, and so on, for the organization, and they are in constant contact with the organization's environment. In such cases, it is imperative that the organization secure the vendor's access to the organization's environment.

PCI-DSS Requirement 8.5.6 requires that all remote vendor access to the PCI environment should only be enabled when there is a need for the vendor to access the organization's environment. Once the vendor is finished with the required task(s) in the PCI environment, the organization must disable said access until it is needed again.

This is primarily required from a security standpoint. In the event that the vendor's environment is compromised or the vendor's systems are not adequately secured, the vendor may be able to gain access to a persistent connection into the organization's PCI environment and cause a data breach for the organization. I was handling an incident recently where a disgruntled vendor employee logged into a client's server using Microsoft Terminal Services and deleted sensitive information on their production server. If the access provided to the vendor was not a persistent permanent access, the incident could have been avoided completely.

Another risk of persistent access with vendors is that of shared credentials. In the event that the organization provides a single credential to a vendor for use, multiple vendor employees might use this access credential to gain access to the client environment, which is a serious problem from the point of view of accountability or in the case of a forensic or incident investigation, where the perpetrator must be identified.

I would suggest implementing a system where the vendor account enabling and disabling are routed through a system of approvals to ensure that there is traceability and accountability. An organization I know utilizes helpdesk tickets to raise vendor access requirements, and once these tickets are authorized by the head of IT and the

---

* Reference to script: http://blogs.technet.com/b/heyscriptingguy/archive/2011/11/30/use-powershell-to-find-and-remove-inactive-active-directory-users.aspx.

business unit head, the vendor account is enabled and then disabled upon completion of the vendor activity.

15.4.7 Requirement 8.5.8: Prohibit Shared, Group, or Generic Accounts

I have detailed this requirement as part of Section 15.1.1 of this chapter.

15.4.8 Requirements 8.5.9–8.5.15: Password Management for PCI Environments

The PCI-DSS has specific requirements with reference to password parameters. In most cases, these password-policy requirements can be defined in the applications or other system components. However, in some cases they must be manually enforced. They are as follows:

Requirement 8.5.9: Passwords must be changed at least every 90 days. Passwords for all system components must be changed at least once every 90 days if not earlier.

Requirements 8.5.10 and 8.5.11: Passwords must have at least seven characters, and they must have alphanumeric characters.

Requirement 8.5.12: Password history of at least the last four passwords has to be implemented for all system components. That is, users should not be allowed to enter the same password used as one of their last four passwords. This requirement has been framed to ensure that users don't easily revert to their older passwords.

Requirements 8.5.13 and 8.5.14: Password lockout must be implemented. In the event that the user enters up to six invalid access attempts, the user's account must be locked out. The lockout duration must be a minimum of 30 minutes or until such time when the administrator verifies identity and grants the user access to the account.

Requirement 8.5.15: Operating systems and applications must be set to enforce a session idle time of 15 minutes, after which the user must be required to log in again to gain access to the system component. The implementation of a session timeout ensures that the user's session, in the event of its persistence, is not misused by an attacker looking to gain access to the said application/system.

Figure 15.3 is an image of the group policy for password management in the Windows Active Directory system. Figure 15.4 is the password-policy-management screen for an Oracle application.

15.5 DATABASE ACCESS REQUIREMENTS FOR PCI ENVIRONMENTS

15.5.1 Requirement 8.5.16: Database Authentication Requirements

Requirement 8.5.16 mandates that all access to the database containing cardholder information should only occur after authentication. Databases have often been the target of internal and external attacks against organizations handling cardholder

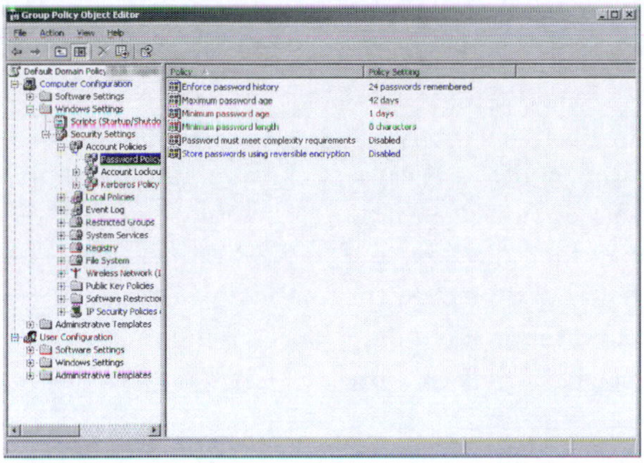

FIGURE 15.3
Group policy for password management for Windows Active Directory system.

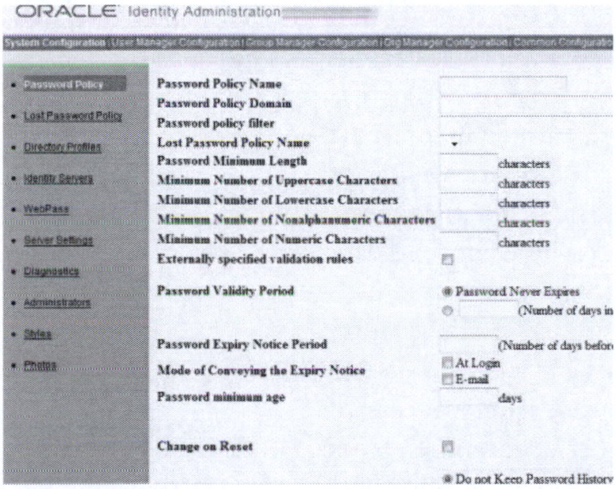

FIGURE 15.4
Password policy management for Oracle.

information. This is simply because the database offers a direct channel to scale. Attackers who are able break into databases gain access to copious amounts of sensitive information that the organization stores. In fact, some organizations route all their data handling to a central database. In such cases, these databases become critical systems that have to be secured with the best possible security practices and measures.

Unfortunately, databases do not get the importance they deserve when it comes to security. Many people still perceive databases to be simple applications that are just supposed to store information. They do not realize that they are complex systems that need to be implemented and configured in several ways for them to be considered secure. The access-control measures detailed as part of Requirement 8, and discussed throughout this chapter, are equally applicable to databases.

Requirement 8.5.16 specifically details the authentication requirement for databases. The requirement states that all users of the database must be authenticated users to the database containing cardholder information. Some organizations do not set authentication requirements for development users or others that tend to connect to the database very often. However, it is required that all users of the database must require authentication before they can gain access to the database.

Another aspect of Requirement 8.5.16 is to ensure that users other than database administrators (DBAs) do not have query access to the database. In the event that regular users have query access to databases containing sensitive information or production databases, it presents a grave security risk, as confidentiality of the data might be breached, integrity of the database might be breached (moving data from tables), or data might be lost (where wrongful queries might result in deletion of critical information). It is required that only the DBA must have query access to the database. The other users must access the database via an application with predefined functions or using stored procedures that perform specific functions without affecting the confidentiality, integrity, and availability of the database and the critical data contained within.

Another key aspect of Requirement 8.5.16 is that the individual users of the database should have their IDs allocated to access the database. Users should not use application IDs (IDs that have been configured for use by the application), as these IDs tend to have higher privileges on the database.

From an assessor's standpoint, this requirement is very critical from a cardholder-data security perspective. Databases are the storehouses for all cardholder data. Therefore, the security for the database of said data should be commensurate with the risk of data breach. Assessors must pay special attention to the following:

Examine database login details. Ensure that database logins are granted to individual users and not to group or shared IDs.

Examine the password policy implementation for the database. All standard database applications have password policy plugins or features that can be enabled and configured to ensure that all users adhere to the stated policy.

Examine transaction logs for specific users other than the DBA to identify the type of queries being performed by the users. Identify if there were any potentially dangerous queries being passed, like DROP tables and UPDATE queries, to ensure that users cannot perform privileged functions on the database. "Select *" queries are also not to be allowed for ordinary users of the database.

Examine the user list of the database-management system to ensure that the users do not have access to application accounts and/or administration accounts.

15.6 PA-DSS REQUIREMENTS FOR AUTHENTICATION

15.6.1 Requirement 8 of PCI and Requirement 3 of the PA-DSS

Requirement 8 of the PCI-DSS, which has been covered in this chapter, has been encapsulated for the commercial payment application in PA-DSS Requirement 3. As the requirements are the same and we have discussed implementation strategies for them in detail, I will not be going into Requirement 3 of the PA-DSS.

One of the changes from Requirement 8 in PA-DSS Requirement 3 is that the application vendor, for a commercial payment application being validated for PA-DSS, must provide a detailed implementation guide that has a comprehensive account of the application's authentication features. The implementation guide must also focus on the authentication requirements for servers, workstations, and databases that are used in the PCI environment that will be used for the payment application as well.

15.7 SUMMARY

Requirement 8 of the PCI-DSS deals exclusively with authentication. The requirement commences with subrequirements that mandate the use of a user ID or username as a unique identifier for an individual or object into the system. The requirement discusses the three factors of authentication: what you know, what you are, and what you have/carry. The requirement details that one of the factors is required to establish authentication for any system component within the PCI environment. Requirement 8 also explores the requirement for password encryption in transit and at rest. The requirement details password policy requirements as well as remote-access requirements for vendors.

16

Requirement 9: Restrict Physical Access to Cardholder Data

In a world that is grappling with application, network, and host security, physical security is an essential requirement for every enterprise information security program. Requirement 9 of the PCI-DSS deals with physical security and media management. The requirement details specific aspects of physical security, including access-control systems, cameras, monitoring, and visitor management, among other requirements. Additionally, Requirement 9 addresses the essential issue of management of physical media in the organization, including hard drives, backup disks, tapes, and so on. The requirement addresses specific physical security requirements for media. The requirement also mandates the need to have strong data-destruction procedures to ensure that unauthorized entities cannot access improperly destroyed information on hard drives and media devices marked for destruction or repair.

16.1 REQUIREMENT 9.1: PHYSICAL ACCESS CONTROLS FOR THE PCI ENVIRONMENT

Requirement 9.1 mandates that all areas containing systems that have access to cardholder data must have physical access restrictions like automated access-control systems with badges and readers or other measures including lock and key. This requirement extends to the PCI environment at large where there are systems (servers and workstations). Typical areas include the production environment, where workstations are usually found, and data centers, where critical servers and network components are housed, among others. Assessors have to verify this requirement by attempting to physically access areas in the PCI environment and identify if said areas are locked before authorized individuals access these areas.

16.1.1 Requirement 9.1.1: Use of Cameras and/or Access-Control Mechanisms

Another physical security requirement is that of cameras and/or access-control systems. The requirement states that areas with systems that store, process, and transmit cardholder data must be protected with video cameras and/or access-control mechanisms that prevent and/or detect unauthorized access to said areas. With reference to merchant establishments with point-of-sale (POS) terminals, this doesn't apply to the areas only with POS terminals. This requirement specifically applies to data centers, server rooms, or any other area with systems that store, process, or transmit cardholder data. Video or other types of cameras should be deployed at all entry and exit points of the area in question. It should also be ensured that the video cameras or access-control equipment is protected from tampering. Recently, I was visiting a facility where the biometric scanner was connected to

a power point. Upon switching off the power point, the biometric access control was also turned off and the control ceased to function. While one might not come across such simplistic ways of tampering, assessors should identify if the physical security components like cameras and access-control systems can be otherwise tampered with by a determined attacker. Figure 16.1 shows some examples of cameras in corporate environments.

Another mandate of PCI Requirement 9.1.1 is to maintain logs or video feeds of data for at least three months from the date of capture. This becomes a little complicated with reference to a video camera. Camera feeds are usually voluminous, and maintaining them for over 21 days or so would require the feed to be archived into another drive/disk to ensure that the feed remains there for the three months required by the standard. Another option for the video feed is to invest in a higher capacity DVR and maintain the feed within the DVR for the mandatory three-month period. One of my

FIGURE 16.1
Cameras in corporate environments.

clients devised a very creative solution. They ran an automated script on an end-of-day basis to copy the DVR feed from the DVR hard drive to a separate file share. The feed would be stored there for three months, after which the script would automatically delete the feed from the file share to prevent against space constraints. However, this remains a challenge, especially for larger companies with more areas of physical security coverage and camera coverage.

This requirement applies equally to all of the other measures used for physical control, including access-control systems, fingerprint scanners, and so on. However, data from said systems are usually smaller in volume and are not difficult to store in the same server.

16.1.2 Requirement 9.1.2 and 9.1.3: Restrict Physical Access to Network Components

16.1.2.1 The Dangers of Visitor Network Access

It is hard to imagine, but visitors may also cause security breaches to the organization. For instance, attackers in the garb of a parcel or pizza delivery person might just hook their laptops or mobile devices to the network and gain access to the organization's network. As I am writing this, I am working on a social-engineering assignment for a bank, where I am masquerading as a telecom maintenance person. I got into their office, pretending to have a meeting with the IT manager. The company escort just dropped me off at the third floor, where the IT department was located, and told me to go to one of the cubicles where the IT manager in charge of telecom equipment was sitting.

The escort left and told me to find my own way. Instead of going toward the cubicles, I went to an unoccupied conference room with a lot of network points. I opened up my laptop, connected an RJ-45 cable and, lo and behold, their DHCP server allocated an IP address for me, and I was officially part of their network. I ran some Nmap port scans, and mapped their entire 10-Series network. I also discovered that their Cisco switch had default credentials on it. I further discovered that most of their systems were running XAMPP with no credentials and a fully featured Apache server with PHP, MySQL, PHPMyAdmin, and so on. I could trigger a host of attacks against the organization now because I had network access as a visitor, and I could use said access to become an "insider" on their network.

As you can probably imagine, this is very dangerous. But the threat is very real. Malicious visitors (knowingly) or visitors whose systems are infected with malware (unknowingly) may cause data breaches in the companies they visit if they are able to gain access to the company's network.

16.1.2.2 Protection Strategies for Visitor Network Access

There are several ways to protect against this. A combination of these measures are highly recommended to provide optimal protections against these threats.

First, it is important for network access-control mechanisms to be in place to ensure that users connecting to the network cannot do so without initial authorization. For instance, in many companies, while there may be open network ports and jacks to connect to, the network connection itself is not done until an administrator enables access to the network on that port with a particular IP. This prevents visitors from directly connecting to the network without authorization. In the case of wireless network connections, it is recommended that a strong WPA2 protection be available for users to authenticate into the wireless access point. Additionally, one can consider implementing MAC ID filtering on the wireless access points, which prevents access from computers/systems that are not registered with the wireless access point. This prevents users from accessing wireless networks in the PCI environment as well.

Second control would be to escort users in the environment at all times and to *not* leave them unattended at any time. This would ensure that users attempting to make physical connections with their systems are thwarted by the escort if the access is unauthorized.

These two measures prevent visitors from accessing the network. However, there are several situations where visitors must be allowed access to the network. I have been an assessor for several companies, and I have had to connect to their network as an internal user with my laptop, with their permission of course. This is not without its risks. Suppose my laptop is infected with malware or is not updated with the latest security patches. The organization's network is now at risk because I have introduced my (unpatched and unprotected) system into the network. Some companies choose to never provide guests with outright access. I often come across companies in banking, insurance, and third-party processing that take such a stance, as their risk of data exposure is very high compared to other organizations in different industries. This is also not a stance that every organization can take. Organizations might have

to provide access to visitors like customers, partners, and service providers to their network with their devices. In such cases, I recommend performing a routine antivirus update scan and a check for unapplied security updates and patches. In fact, I was missing two critical security patches when I had visited a client for an assessment and required access to their network. Their network-management team had both missing updates installed and only then allowed me access to their network.

Many organizations adopt the "sandbox" approach to securing visitor network access. They have a designated network VLAN/segment for visitor network access where the visitors can access the Internet, but they can access nothing else in the corporate network. They are locked down with access-control lists on the firewall, router, or switch, as the case may be.

16.1.2.3 Requirement 9.1.3: Physical Protection for Network Devices

Requirement 9.1.3 requires the organization to ensure that physical access to network devices is also restricted. This is especially dangerous with wireless access points. Wireless access points and switches have to be located on walls and cannot be housed in data centers and server rooms like routers and firewalls. In such cases, visitors may be able to directly connect to these devices and gain access to the network. I recommend placing these devices at an elevated height slightly beyond reach of a human being of normal height. It would also be prudent to have cameras in these areas to detect visitor efforts to access or otherwise tamper with these devices, thereby preventing further damage.

16.2 REQUIREMENTS 9.2, 9.3, AND 9.4: EMPLOYEE AND VISITOR ACCESS

16.2.1 Visitor-Management Procedure

We have already seen some of the possible security-breach scenarios that can arise from improperly implemented visitor management for the organization. Malicious visitors can cause serious security breaches against the target organization. With the advent of several powerful social-engineering tools, it has become extremely easy to masquerade as a legitimate user or an otherwise authorized user like a contractor or delivery personnel.

One of the major challenges with visitor management is that a strong procedure must be developed and disseminated among all the employees in the organization. Requirement 9.2 mandates visitor-management procedures to distinguish between visitors and employees of the organization, especially within the PCI environment.

16.2.1.1 Visitor Access and Employee Access Distinctions

A basic control measure to distinguish between visitors and employees in the organization is to issue badges or identification tags to employees and visitors. Employee identification badges and tags must clearly identify them as employees. In my experience, companies usually issue a different-colored identification badge for the employee that includes a radio-frequency identification card that is used to authenticate the employee at a physical access-control point before entering the environment.

Organizations should consider applying different-colored badges for employees and visitors. Visitor badges must be marked as "VISITOR" in bold, usually with a visitor number or identification number to provide traceability. If the visitor has to be traced back to the source of entry, the identification number or visitor number is essential.

16.2.1.2 Granting Visitor Access

An important consideration of visitor management is the granting of visitor access. A visitor should be granted access only when it has been approved by an employee or authorized member of the company. The standard procedure usually involves the employee sending an e-mail to the physical security officer or the security guard at the perimeter. The guard then verifies the visitor's identity and issues the visitor badge. Subsequently, the visitor may gain access to the environment under supervision or in the escort of the employee authorizing the visitor into the environment.

16.2.1.3 Visitor Access Privileges and Restrictions

Different visitors require different access rights and privileges. For example, if maintenance personnel for the fire-safety equipment of a data center have to perform their routine checks, they must have access to the data center to carry out their fire-safety equipment maintenance. Access for visitors needs to be defined based on the need for said access. For instance, visitors accessing high-security areas or restricted areas in the organization, like the data center, are usually required to have an employee escort or constant supervision throughout their visit to the organization.

16.2.1.4 Revocation of Visitor and Employee Access

When a visitor has concluded his/her visit to the organization, there is no reason for the visitor to have access to the organization or to authenticate with the organization. Therefore, it is essential that said access be revoked by the organization. The organization must ensure that all visitors surrender their access cards/visitor badges and sign out to indicate that they have concluded their visit and that their access to the organization's facility is no longer required. In the event that the visitors have carried their own devices—laptops, mobile phones, USB drives, and so on—into the environment, the organization must check them to ensure that the same equipment is being signed out.

16.2.1.5 Access to Badge System/ Physical Access-Control System

The access privileges to the physical access-control system is an important consideration to maintain the physical security for an environment. If the access to this system is given to personnel who do not require said information, then it is likely to be misused. For instance, a regular employee who has access to the system might register visitors and other users to the environment who may be unauthorized and malicious. In such cases, the organization can suffer massive breaches of data, as unauthorized and malicious visitors can gain access to the environment using a highly legitimate source.

Access to the physical access-control system should lie with the physical security department or the facilities department of the organization. This department only maintains access to the system. Registration and revocation of physical user access rights is controlled by this team/department. This team also receives information from employees about visitors to the environment and is responsible for granting and revoking physical access rights for visitors to the environment as well. In several organizations, I have observed that the physical access-control system is located on a central server, and access is granted by the facilities/physical security team after a user registration process. In the event that the facility requires users to register biometric parameters, the team coordinates with the user to register his/her thumbprint (or other parameter) for access to the environment.

16.2.1.6 Visitor Distinction

In some environments, badges and identification tags issued to visitors are remarkably similar to the ones issued to employees. This can be confusing, especially in large environments, because visitors cannot be distinguished from employees. Such visitors can masquerade as employees and gain a deeper level of access into the organization. We have already noted that visitor access badges must be differentiated from employee access badges for this very reason.

16.2.1.7 Visitor Access Records

We have often come across environments where visitor log books are maintained. Every visitor to the facility must enter his/her details into the visitor log. Additionally, log books are also maintained at data centers and server rooms apart from the entry to the premises of the facility. This is because these are considered high-security zones, and visitors entering said zones must register as a visitor into the visitor log. Visitor logs are ideally meant as a measure of traceability. In the event of a security breach or an investigation where a visitor is in question, the company should be able to trace back the entry and exit of the visitor, and be able to verify certain details about the visitor as well. For instance, in most facilities, the visitor must enter his/her name, the organization they are visiting from, the purpose of their visit, the person in the organization who the visitor is to meet, details such as phone or e-mail, and the entry time to mark the visitor's entry into the organization. In some cases, this entire process is automated, and visitors are given access cards similar to those issued to employees.

PCI requires that these visitor logs be maintained for at least a period of three months. Additionally, visitor logs should also be maintained for sensitive areas *inside* the organization where cardholder data is stored, processed, or transmitted. For instance, when I was performing an audit of a payment processor, I was made to enter a second visitor log when I was visiting their card personalization and embossing section, which was considered to be a high-security zone, considering the sensitive information being processed in the facility.

16.3 REQUIREMENTS 9.5–9.10: MEDIA MANAGEMENT AND SECURITY

16.3.1 Requirement 9.5: Physical Security—Off-Site Media Backup Location

16.3.1.1 The Need for Off-Site Backup

Backup is one of the most effective controls to ensure the availability of critical information assets of the organization. The organization cannot afford to lose mission-critical data, as its customers and internal processes are highly dependent on this data. In most cases, organizations handling data and applications for the financial industry, such as banking, payment cards, and so on, cannot go down for even a minute. In such cases, organizations usually plan to have multiple sites where data is replicated to account for high usage and loss of individual sites due to attacks and security breaches. Aside from such scenarios, organizations must back up their data to manage historical data as closely as possible to current data.

The PCI-DSS does not specify a frequency for the backup process. Ideally, a strong risk-assessment process would be used to determine backup requirements and frequencies. The management, as part of the risk assessment, must identify backup frequencies and an acceptable risk of loss of data. Backup relies on two important concepts of *recovery point* and *recovery time*. For instance, the organization suffers a data breach where its critical data is lost or destroyed. In such a scenario, how quickly should the organization be able to recover its lost data? And till what point should the organization be able to recover its data? Let us imagine that the organization in question is a bank; therefore, they might need to recover all their data within 10 minutes, and data up until the last minute might have to be recovered. In their case, they may need more than just a backup. They might require multiple sites, where servers are available with the most updated data sets, which will ensure that their business continues as usual even if their data from one server/cluster is lost or destroyed.

Assuming that the organization in question is a back-office data processing organization, they may need to be able to recover data until the previous day within four hours to ensure that their business operations are not hindered or adversely affected in any way. In such cases, they may need to maintain an off-site backup that can be restored to the previous day within four hours.

Organizations must maintain off-site backups. Let us assume that there is a fire in the primary data processing facility of the operation. The fire destroys the servers and the backup server that is placed in the same data center. In this scenario, the organization's efforts to take backups of their data are rendered futile, as they cannot restore their data back to acceptable levels. The backup has also been destroyed along with the servers.

Apart from physical threats, there is also a constant threat from attackers. Backup applications tend to have a great deal of access to the target operating system and its file system/database. It is quite obvious that backup systems need to be configured with privileged access control to these systems for the system to effectively and comprehensively carry out backup operations. However, during tests, I have come across several backup applications that were highly vulnerable to code execution flaws, buffer overflows, and so on. On occasion, I have also come across backup systems configured with vendor-supplied default passwords like "password" or "admin." In such cases, attacking the backup along with the server is a trivial matter. An attacker determined to cause damage to the organization might not only be able to gain access to the data in the backup system, but might also destroy the backup data and cause a highly aggravated data breach to the organization.

Due to such issues and many other possibilities, an organization must have an off-site backup location in addition to on-site backup. This backup should be located in a separate location that is away from the organization's primary processing environment. In the event of a breach that affects the local backup system, the off-site backup would act as the secondary backup source for the organization and prevent the organization from suffering data loss due to a data breach.

Off-site backups can be implemented in multiple ways. A modern implementation is the use of a cloud backup service. The backup of the critical data is regularly transported to a cloud backup provider. The backup of data resides in the service provider's servers and can be restored by the users using an application or other service provided by the service provider. This implementation of off-site backup is gaining acceptance in the industry, as the backup resides in a cloud service provider's servers. The organization does not have to invest resources in maintaining a specific off-site location that may prove to be expensive and possibly inefficient. Modern cloud backup service providers are equipped to handle backup encryption with AES 256-bit ciphers and enhanced security for transmission of data to the cloud service as well. While cloud backup is gaining popularity as an off-site backup mechanism, it is bandwidth intensive and tends to be very demanding on the organization's network connectivity.

Another popular off-site backup mechanism is the use of a physical server into which the organization backs up data on a regular basis. This is somewhat similar to a cloud service; however, the server and the infrastructure is managed by the organization. In some cases, organizations rent servers from hosting providers and perform this function. This is even more similar to a cloud backup service provider, except that the server is dedicated and the organization controls the hosted server.

Where data volumes are large, some organizations utilize tape or network-attached storage (NAS) solutions for off-site backup. Backup tapes are used as media for backup applications. The backup tapes are physically transported to the off-site location and maintained in a secure cabinet to ensure that the backup tapes cannot be physically compromised. Organizations with heavy data requirements use tapes to this day. An organization that I was consulting with performed a daily incremental backup and a weekly full backup only with tapes. On a daily basis, authorized personnel from the primary processing facility would load the tapes into a locked box that would be sent to the off-site location where backup tapes were stored and archived. On both sides, there would be an authorization process and registers placed for the outgoing and incoming tapes. The tapes were stored in a fire-safe cabinet in the off-site location that was 3 miles away from the primary processing facility. Figure 16.2 is an image of a NAS device, and Figure 16.3 is an illustration of backup tapes and a tape drive.

16.3.1.2 Security Controls: Off-Site Backup

Requirement 9.5 of the PCI-DSS requires that physical security for the off-site backup location be maintained. This is to ensure that backup tapes or media cannot be stolen or destroyed due to some physical security event. I would recommend at least the following security controls for off-site backup management:

- Some form of access control should be present to access the off-site backup location. Automated or physical access-control mechanisms like locks must be used to protect the facility from data breach possibilities. In the

FIGURE 16.2
NAS device.

FIGURE 16.3
Backup tapes and tape drive.

event that physical security controls are used to protect the facility, the keys must only be available to designated key custodians.

- The off-site backup location should have registers to record incoming and outgoing media to and from the location. Entries in a register should be enforced, either by a security guard or other personnel managing the location. Additionally, it can be done with automated systems and the use of technologies like bar-coding, RFID, and so on. This measure ensures that there is traceability of the backup media and that control over the media is maintained. Lack of such controls might result in backups going missing or being unavailable at a critical time, when restoration is required. The removal of backup media must be authorized by the responsible team/individual and accompanied by a form or documentation stating the same (Requirement 9.8).

- The backup media must be kept in locked, firesafe cabinets or containers. It is recommended that these cabinets be immobile (fixed to the wall or otherwise embedded into the construction). Unauthorized individuals can steal cabinets that can be carried. Only designated individuals or custodians who are made accountable for management of the said cabinets should maintain keys to these cabinets (Requirement 9.9).

- Inventory logs of the backup media stored in the off-site backup location must be maintained. This should contain details of issued media and details of individuals/teams that the media was issued to as well. While the PCI-DSS recommends that a media inventory (media reconciliation) be performed at least annually, I would recommend a quarterly reconciliation process, especially for locations with large media archives (Requirement 9.9.1).

- Backup media must be secured in transit as well. When the backup media is sent via courier, it must be packed adequately to protect against any damage in transit. In the event that backup media is transported by a member of the organization, it must be secured in a container that is preferably locked. The container must be strong enough to withstand possible damage to the equipment contained within. Media must also be capable of being tracked in transit, especially if sent over courier services. Most couriers today provide online tracking capability and the status of the shipment can be determined using a tracking number (Requirement 9.7.2).

- Another important factor to consider with off-site backups is the sensitivity of the data that is contained in the media. For instance, database and file-server backups are highly sensitive and critical. In such cases, media drives containing said backups must be clearly marked as "highly confidential" or similar to ensure that this backup media is distinguished from other types of media. I would also recommend storing highly critical media devices in a separate cabinet/container that can be protected with additional controls to reflect the sensitivity of said data (Requirement 9.7.1).

16.3.2 Requirements 9.9 and 9.10: Media Destruction

An increasing problem with today's IT-guzzling environment is secure disposal. Several incidents have been reported where critical information like passwords, card numbers, financial information, and so on, have been recovered from hard drives and media that have been marked for destruction or have been disposed of by the user. Even if the user takes care to format the drive or the media container, there are several free and commercial tools that can be used to recover information from these media devices.

With the increasing influence of mobile devices on the corporate landscape, this problem is only increasing. People use smartphones and tablets for shorter periods of time before they are disposed of. These devices contain sensitive corporate data that can be recovered quite easily using a variety of readily available tools.

Secure destruction is a highly critical but oft-forgotten consideration for data security. An organization generates a great deal of e-waste or repairs for equipment. There's not a day that goes by where a sizable organization does not send faulty hard drives or computer equipment for repair or where old equipment is sold off or otherwise disposed of. In such cases, it is imperative that the potentially sensitive data on these hard drives/media devices be destroyed completely. It is an ill-conceived notion to assume that formatting that hard drive or media device would suffice. A "delete" or a "format" does not remove the data, but simply removes pointers to the file. A determined attacker, using tools, could easily gain access to the hard drive or media device and gain access to the files stored in said systems. This can be especially dangerous for server equipment and storage equipment sent for repairs or for disposal.

Another consideration is secure disposal of hard-copy documents. Several of these documents contain sensitive information that, if made available to attackers or unauthorized individuals, could result in embarrassing data breaches. I remember walking out of a bank that I was auditing when I found a sheet of paper on the sidewalk. This sheet of paper contained the credit card numbers and names of several bank clients. Someone had obviously not disposed of said data appropriately.

Another time, I was working with a manufacturing company. The CTO of the company often took a quick break in the evenings. His favorite snack was roasted groundnuts sold by a cart standing outside the manufacturing plant. In India, roasted groundnuts are often served in paper containers. These paper containers are usually old newspapers or magazines that the cart vendor can get for free. So, the CTO went out for his usual roasted groundnut snack at the cart in the evening and ate the groundnuts. To his horror, he saw that the paper being used as a container for the groundnuts was actually the machine drawings generated by his R&D department worth millions of dollars. Someone had obviously not taken care to dispose of these drawings correctly, and they had ended up with the cart vendor. He immediately had cross shredders installed and ensured that all paper documents lying around at people's desks would be shredded at the end of the day.

The organization must utilize secure destruction tools or techniques to ensure that data present on media or hard drives is unrecoverable. Some techniques to do this are as follows:

The simplest and most effective way of data destruction on media/hard drives is to physically destroy said media devices or hard drives. The drives must be completely destroyed such that it is not possible for anyone to recover data from them. A company that I was working with used a hammer to completely break hard drives and tape drives that were marked for destruction.

With paper documents, the ideal way to destroy them is to incinerate, pulp, or shred said documents. Figure 16.4 is an image of a shredder.

Another way to destroy data on hard drives and media drives is to use a degausser. A degausser is a physical device that is used to eliminate a remnant magnetic field. Data is stored on hard drives, disks, and so on, by making small magnetic domains. By using a degausser on these drives, one is effectively removing all of the magnetic domains, ensuring that data remnants cannot be recovered using these domains. However, the degausser renders these drives unusable after the degaussing process. Figure 16.5 is an image of a degausser.

Most of the options that I have mentioned so far irreversibly destroy data on the disk and the disk itself. However, in many cases, the objective is not to destroy the disk, but just the data. For instance, when a hard drive is sent outside for repair, the intention is to repair the drive and not destroy it, without compromising the data that might be on that drive. In such cases, one should consider using hard-disk wipe tools that perform a secure wipe on the hard drive or media device. There are certain applications like Darik's Boot and Nuke that can be used to securely wipe data from the hard drive and ensure that unauthorized individuals cannot regenerate the data from the hard drive. The technique involves performing multiple passes of binary overwriting of data. This ensures that all the data that remains on the disk is completely purged and cannot be regenerated by an unauthorized individual. Multiple tools like Disk Wipe, Eraser, Darik's Boot, and Nuke can be used to perform hard-drive purging using multiple algorithms like the Gutmann algorithm and others.

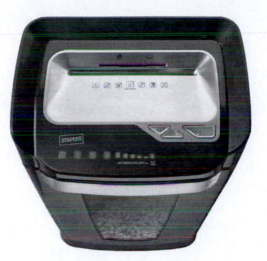

FIGURE 16.4
Paper shredder.

16.4 SUMMARY

Requirement 9 of the PCI-DSS deals extensively with physical security. Requirement 9.1 stresses the need for physical access-control systems in the PCI environment. Physical access-control systems include any automated access-control systems (physical ID-based, biometric systems, and so on). Physical access-control systems also include cameras. PCI requires physical access-control systems to be placed specifically in areas in the PCI environment to protect against physical threats to the cardholder data environment. The logs from cameras or other physical access-control systems must be maintained for a

FIGURE 16.5
Degausser from Verity Systems.

minimum of three months. Requirement 9.1.2 deals with restricting physical network access points or jacks. This measure ensures that visitors to the PCI environment cannot automatically plug their systems into the network and potentially compromise them. Requirements 9.2 and 9.3 deal with visitor and employee physical security measures. Requirement 9.2 states that employees should be distinguishable from visitors. This measure is to prevent against a visitor masquerading as an employee to gain physical access to sensitive areas in the PCI environment. Organizations can achieve this by providing different badges or physical access cards to employees and visitors. Requirement 9.3 emphasizes the need to maintain security over visitor entry into the PCI environment. Visitor entry to the PCI environment must be authorized by a member of the organization. Visitors must have distinguishing physical tokens for their entry into the facility.

Visitor logs must be maintained for at least three months, with all the visitor names and contact information for traceability. Requirements 9.5, 9.6, 9.7, and 9.8 deal with the security over physical media like backup tapes, drives, and so on. Requirement 9.5 states the security requirements for secure storage of physical media devices in off-site and on-site locations. The storage area for the physical media devices must be locked and preferably fireproof to ensure that physical media drives are protected against physical theft and natural events like fire, and so on. The effectiveness of storage security needs to be verified at least annually. Requirement 9.6 deals with security of other media items like physical documents, copies, and so on. The requirement states that these media abstractions pertaining to cardholder data must be secured as well.

Requirements 9.7 and 9.8 specify the security requirements for internal and external distribution of media. Media must be transported based on authorization, with adequate documentation of authorization. The recipients of the media must acknowledge the receipt. A secure courier or a company representative authorized to do the same must transport the media securely. Reconciliation must be performed to ensure that the media transported in and out of a location is recorded and actually reflects the media count that is stored.

Requirement 9.10 deals with the physical destruction of media and physical documents. Data breaches often occur because of data remnants being available on a disk that is disposed of or marked for resale. In such cases, organizations must utilize degaussing techniques, physical destruction, or software-based secure wipe processes to permanently remove all data on the disk and ensure that it cannot be regenerated.

17

Requirement 10: Logging and Monitoring for the PCI Standards

Audit trails are the first and usually the only way to identify security flaws and breaches. Audit trails are meant to provide useful and relevant information about the usage of a system. If this information is captured effectively, it can tell system owners and stakeholders how the system is being used, identify its users, and indicate whether there are any anomalies in the system. Additionally, audit trails are required as evidence in legal proceedings in cases of fraud where the company has to prove the wrongdoing of a person or group of individuals against the system. This chapter focuses on Requirement 10 of the PCI-DSS, which exclusively addresses issues regarding logging, log management, and audit trails, all of which are required for a company that is pursuing or attempting to maintain PCI-DSS compliance. We will also address logging practices that are required not only for commercial applications that will be validated under the PA-DSS, but for custom applications that are developed by PCI-DSS-compliant companies that need to address the important issue of logging.

17.1 AUDIT TRAILS: PCI REQUIREMENTS

17.1.1 The Need for Audit Trails and Logs

Requirement 10 of the PCI-DSS details the implementation and practices that should be utilized by an organization for logging and log management. Audit trails are required by every major compliance standard, regulation, and best-practice recommendation all over the world. However, I have rarely come across a logging and monitoring system that is up to par. I think that the greatest problem here has mostly to do with perception. Most companies perceive logging to be unnecessary overhead on the organization's IT resources. There is a great deal of data generated from system logs, which the organization either ignores or manages poorly because of the sheer volume of the data. Another major issue with the perception of logging has to do with the fact that monitoring logs is an arduous task that is mundane and exhaustive. Unfortunately, both of these perceptions are true. However, companies cannot absolve themselves of the logging requirement, because it is exceedingly important from a security and accountability standpoint.

A log or an audit trail provides invaluable information about the usage of a system. In the event of an anomaly or a potential security breach, these logs capture critical details that allow an organization to prevent security breaches in the future or even when they are in progress. Let me give you a scenario.

I was performing a penetration test in an internal network, where I was to behave exactly like an internal attacker. Therefore, nobody knew who I was, including the IT manager of the company. I was engaged by the IT security management department, and my job was to perform a penetration test. Consequently, the penetration test was also supposed to test the company's incident response processes to identify if they were up to the mark. I started firing port-scan requests by the millions using Nmap (hardly subtle). I performed OS identification, enumerated several services on the servers and some sampled desktops, and launched vulnerability scanners against these devices. In fact, by the end of the penetration test, I was even able to gain OS-level access to their database server running MS-SQL 2005 and drop a temporary backdoor that I could access persistently. I was expecting that at least one single network or sys admin would walk up to me and ask me what the hell I was doing! Unfortunately, it was not

to be. The sys admins and network admins were shocked when I released the results of the penetration test in my presentation. They asked me how I had achieved it without being caught. How stealthy did I have to be to achieve such results? I told them that I had been the opposite of stealthy. I had brazenly launched direct attacks against their systems, and since I was an insider on a relatively flat network, there were no stringent access-control mechanisms to prevent me, or even raise an alert. But there were tons of logs generated. Each system that I had accessed or attempted to attack had captured a great deal of log information. Managed network switches that I was using to connect to these systems captured a boatload of log data. However, all that went to waste, because there was no monitoring or log event management or correlation. If they had an effective log management, monitoring, and alerting practice, they probably would have detected my activity and prevented further damage to the environment.

An audit trail[*] is defined as a security-relevant chronological record, set of records, or destination and source of records that provide documentary evidence of the sequence of activities that have affected at any time a specific operation, procedure, or event. Audit trails are required to establish accountability and evidence for a particular event. In my previous example, suppose I really was a malicious internal attacker and my attacks against my organization were successful. Perhaps audit trails would be the only evidence of said breach happening because of me. The audit trail establishes accountability and evidence. Accountability is especially important in the case of financial systems and reservation systems like

---

[*] See http://on.wikipedia.org/wiki/audit_trail

airlines, and so on, where an individual or user group can cause a great deal of loss to the organization due to inadvertent or purposeful errors of omission and commission.

For the payment-card industry, the need for audit trails is no different. Organizations handling payments (merchants, TPPs, and so on) have myriad applications, multiple systems, distributed databases, and complex network infrastructure. In such cases, an attack against a single vulnerable system or application can lead to a complete compromise of the system. Logging is the first step for an organization of this nature to detect and prevent against attacks. Logging is also extremely important from the view of establishing accountability and nonrepudiation on a payment system. Administrators of a system have highly elevated privileges on applications and systems. Their actions, if not made accountable, can have a devastating impact on the organization, especially if said administrator has malicious intent.

17.1.2 Challenges: Log Management

We have learned that logging and log management are important concepts. However, they are usually very flawed in a typical organizational deployment. Log management presents several challenges for the organization. Some of them are:

- Distributed event logs
- Volume of log entries
- Nonstandard logging practices
- Multiple tools
- People intensive

17.1.2.1 Distributed Event Logs

All devices generate logs and log entries: servers, workstations, network devices,

applications, databases, and so on. In a large organization, these devices are often distributed across multiple locations. In such cases, retrieving system logs from these geographically diverse and multifarious systems becomes a major challenge for administrators to perform manual log analysis.

17.1.2.2 Volume of Log Entries

Systems in an enterprise environment tend to generate a large volume of log entries. Perimeter systems like network devices and public-facing servers generate a large volume of log entries, as they are accessed very often by users. In the event of an attack, log entries are generated at a faster pace and at immense volumes. For most organizations, this is overwhelming, and they are not usually prepared to handle the volume of log entries generated. Additionally, when log entries are generated at such high volumes, and being collated in a centralized log server, organizations do not handle the network-management operations effectively and do not create adequate network capacities for the same.

Most often, there are several trivial incidents that are generated as log entries, and these are usually very high in number. In cases where there is centralized log collation, the trivial or unnecessary log entries are not filtered in any way. This also adds to the challenge of searching for and identifying specific log entries in a veritable sea of device information from various devices across the organization.

17.1.2.3 Nonstandard Logging Practices

I have come across nonstandard logging practices in most environments that I have assessed. This is highly relevant for any environment running custom or customized applications that do not utilize standard logging practices. Several custom apps that organizations develop (or have developed for them) write "log" statements to a file in the form of console information. This is hardly relevant on most occasions, and is highly insecure on some occasions, as logs capture highly sensitive information like passwords and card numbers. Once, I found a custom app that was not only logging the customer's password in cleartext, but also logging the customer's card number as part of its transaction records. This was being logged as concatenated string statements with no severity level, standard format, or template defined for the logs. They were just print statements that were being logged in the console logs of the application server. As a result, these arcane statements could never be collated and managed from a centralized log server/repository.

17.1.2.4 Multiple Tools

Another challenge that I see with logging is that most administrators have or develop tools to review or extract logs from a single type of system like Windows servers or Cisco network devices, and so on. In such cases, several administrators would be utilizing several tools across several devices and never having a centralized picture of a security incident or being able to generate a viable audit trail from the same. Imagine that an organization is investigating a potential security breach or is performing a forensic investigation after a known security breach. Let us assume that admins for the network devices, databases, application servers, firewalls, IPSs, and so on, utilize discrete tools to extract information and collate said information in a meaningful

chronological sequence of events (audit trails). Such exercises would take a really long time, which would probably render the investigation meaningless or, at the very least, mostly ineffective.

17.1.2.5 People Intensive

A common misperception for log management is that it requires too many people to manage it. Yes, that is absolutely right, if the organization's logging strategy is flawed and relies on discrete tools and technologies to extract and collate logs in a meaningful way. However, modern tools and technologies have made it infinitely simpler to achieve high-quality logging and log management to constitute informative events and audit trails. These are mostly automated and require only a few skilled administrators or security professionals to understand, interpret, and take action on the logs generated or alerts received.

17.1.3 Access-Control Link: Audit Trails

Monitoring access is one of the most important reasons for logging and log management. Security incidents mostly involve breaching of access control or tracing back a security incident to the access to a system by an entity. Logging for access control establishes that a system was accessed by an entity that performed certain actions on the systems that might have been erroneous or malicious. In other cases, attackers usually look to exploit weaknesses in access control to gain access to the systems and perform actions on the same.

Requirement 10.1 mentions that all access to systems or components must be logged and linked to a specific user. For instance, if an administrator logs into a database server, his/her access must be logged in the system as an access by the administrator, bearing a username and a valid password. In the event of a security incident involving said user, logs, if available, would be immensely helpful in investigating a possible security breach comprehensively.

The presence of logs linking user accounts to access (and other functions) also prevents users from attempting potential security breaches. In such cases, users might be aware that their actions are logged by the system and that they could be traced back to a specific user in the event of a security breach.

Most operating systems, network devices, and infrastructure components like databases, FTP servers, and Web servers are capable of logging user access and other actions on said systems. In several payment-card environments, mainframes are a norm, especially with merchants, banks, and third-party processors (TPPs). IBM mainframes have the Resource Access-Control Facility (RACF) that not only performs the tasks of authentication, authorization, and enforcing access-control rules, but also performs the function of logging user access and unauthorized access attempts to the system.

However, I have seen several custom applications incapable of providing effective user access logs, because these systems are not designed to log user access information or other functions effectively (refer to my points on the challenges for logging). However, applications that have been designed with security, traceability, and nonrepudiation in mind perform logging of user access. Table 17.1 is a list of common log files and their paths for the Linux operating system. The assessor must verify that user access information is logged by systems in the PCI environment.

17.2 DETAILS: AUDIT TRAIL CAPTURE

17.2.1 Audit Logs: Details

For an organization handling payment-card data, it is critical for logs to capture certain events. Owing to the sensitivity of the data in question, system logs must capture and provide audit trail information to protect the confidentiality, integrity, and availability of payment-card data. Requirement 10.2 of the PCI-DSS focuses on the details and events that have to be captured by companies handling said data and undergoing PCI compliance. This is equally important for commercial applications that are being validated against the PA-DSS standard.

- Individual access to cardholder data
- Actions by root or administrative users
- Access to audit trails
- Invalid access attempts
- Use of identification and authentication mechanisms
- Initialization of audit logs
- Creation/deletion of system-level objects

17.2.1.1 Individual Access to Cardholder Data

Cardholder data is a critical information asset for any company that handles payment-card data. From the perspective of the PCI-DSS and the PA-DSS for commercial applications, security of cardholder information is an absolute necessity. In that light, any access to cardholder data must be logged.

Let me explain, with an example, why logging access to cardholder data is critical. I was performing a Web application penetration test on a client that was a famous

TABLE 17.1

List of Common Log Files and Paths in a Linux Operating System

/var/log/messages: Contains global system messages, including the messages that are logged during system startup. There are several things that are logged in /var/log/messages, including mail, cron, daemon, kern, auth, etc.

/var/log/dmesg: Contains kernel ring buffer information. When the system boots up, it prints the number of messages on the screen that displays information about the hardware devices that the kernel detects during boot process. These messages are available in kernel ring buffer and whenever the new message comes the old message gets overwritten. You can also view the content of this file using the dmesg command.

/var/log/auth.log: Contains system authorization information, including user logins and authentication mechanisms that were used.

/var/log/boot.log: Contains information that is logged when the system boots.

/var/log/daemon.log: Contains information logged by the various background daemons that runs on the system.

/var/log/dpkg.log: Contains information that are logged when a package is installed or removed using the *dpkg* command.

/var/log/kern.log: Contains information logged by the kernel. Helpful for you to troubleshoot a custom-built kernel.

/var/log/lastlog: Displays the recent login information for all the users. This is not an ascii file. You should use lastlog command to view the content of this file.

/var/log/maillog/var/log/mail.log: Contains the log information from the mail server that is running on the system. For example, send mail logs information about all the sent items to this file.

/var/log/user.log: Contains information about all user-level logs.

/var/log/Xorg.x.log: Log messages from the X.

/var/log/alternatives.log: Information by the update-alternatives are logged into this log file. On Ubuntu, update-alternatives maintain symbolic links determining default commands.

/var/log/btmp: This file contains information about failed login attempts. Use the last command to view the btmp file. For example, "last -f/var/log/btmp | more".

/var/log/cups: All printer and printing related log messages.

/var/log/anaconda.log: When you install Linux, all installation-related messages are stored in this log file.

/var/log/yum.log: Contains information that is logged when a package is installed using yum.

/var/log/cron: Whenever crondaemon (or anacron) starts a cron job, it logs the information about the cron job in this file.

/var/log/secure: Contains information related to authentication and authorization privileges. For example, the *sshd* command logs all the messages here, including unsuccessful login.

/var/log/wtmp or **/var/log/utmp:** Contains login records. Using wtmp, you can find out who is logged into the system. The *who* command uses this file to display the information.

/var/log/faillog: Contains user failed login attempts. Use *faillog* command to display the content of this file.

e-commerce company. This company would process the cardholder data as part of the payment transaction and store the primary account number (PAN) and the expiration date in its database. The PAN was encrypted with a 3DES cipher. Using an SQL injection attack, I was able to gain access to some of the tables in the database that contained customer card numbers. I discovered that they were encrypted. I downloaded five entries of encrypted PANs onto my testing virtual machine and sought to gain access to the key or crack the encryption key. To my surprise, further enumeration of other database tables led me to find the symmetric key used to encrypt the database. It was stored in cleartext. Using this, I decrypted the five PANs that I had egressed and successfully gained access to the system. To my disappointment, my client had never discovered this incursion and was clueless about my access to its system.

Now let's imagine if there was an active logging mechanism and event monitoring on its application and/or database. It would have probably discovered that several events relating to the application and the database correlated and were displayed on the console of the SIEM (security information and event management) application. Administrators monitoring these events could have proactively raised an alert and blocked access of my IP or taken other action to thwart me from gaining access to applications and/or the database.

In fact, in several high-profile cardholder data breaches, the most significant observation was that the companies that were breached didn't have active logging and monitoring mechanisms to alert them in the event of a data breach. They could have deployed event logs that captured all access to the database tables containing cardholder data. This can be configured both as part of the database or application logging.

From another viewpoint, logging access to cardholder information becomes essential, even when internal users are accessing the system. If a malicious administrator is stealing cardholder data from the organization, then it is essential to have monitoring over the administrator's access to data sources that contain cardholder data. Monitoring access to cardholder information also serves to detect access by users who might be masquerading as legitimate users to gain access to cardholder information.

17.2.1.2 Actions by Root or Administrative Users

Root or administrative users tend to possess a great deal of control over any system that they manage, and their actions tend to have a great impact on the system. In such cases, organizations must exercise a great deal of diligence and care in logging their actions. For instance, let's assume that the administrative user with control of a card-management application has malicious intent: He/she could create dummy card accounts, use them to run up expenses and reset them to zero or some minimum amount, tamper with credit limits, and so on. I recall a situation in which a disgruntled application administrator for an organization's customer relationship management (CRM) application sent key contact info, customer data, and sales numbers to a competitor over e-mail. This scenario could apply to all other components such as network devices, databases, applications, operating systems, and so on.

Admin credentials or root credentials are coveted by attackers. They are constantly looking to compromise administrative accounts to gain access with highly elevated privileges into the system. Administrative or root access is also oftentimes the route to gain access to other components on the network. For instance, if an attacker were to gain administrative access to an SQL server, the attacker could perform multiple functions using this access, including performing port scans on the target environment, writing into the back-end operating system, and so on. In such cases, monitoring an administrator's or root user's activities is immensely useful to detect the attack and prevent it from becoming persistent and more dangerous. It also provides an opportunity to establish an effective corrective-action process to identify specific security flaws within the organization.

17.2.1.3 Access to Audit Trails

Audit-trail information contains highly sensitive data about the organization's IT environment. Details such as user accesses, invalid access attempts, access to sensitive data, attack attempts, successful attack incidents, and so on, are captured as part of the organization's logs and audit trails. Only authenticated and authorized users with a business need to know should be able to view the logs for the purposes of monitoring, and so on. If unauthorized users are able to access the system due to some vulnerability in the system or due to other issues like a social-engineering attack, then they can glean valuable information about the IT infrastructure and potentially launch attacks against the organization's infrastructure.

In the event that the organization is using a SIEM application, the application must be configured to capture audit trails of users who access the system to view audit trails and related information.

17.2.1.4 Invalid Access Attempts

Brute-forcing is one of the most common techniques of breaching access control and gaining access to a system. It is also a simple technique, wherein the attacker runs multiple password attempts against the system or application. Attackers often use popularly available word lists or dictionaries to gain access to accounts using brute-forcing techniques. One of the controls to prevent such attacks is to have password-lockout mechanisms that block a user account after an invalid password is entered continuously

multiple times. Another viable security control is to log invalid access attempts by a user. This serves as an additional control against brute-forcing and other access-control attacks. Let's take the following scenario. A malicious employee wants to gain access to his supervisor's account to change some values. He attempts multiple access attempts on the supervisor's ID. The system is configured to lock out user accounts for 30 minutes at a time. The malicious employee attempts wrong passwords over a period of time, despite the lockouts, and finally gains access to the supervisor's account. In this case, there is even a defined lockout; however, since the malicious employee had a great deal of time, the account lockouts were nothing more than a brief inconvenience that had to be overcome over time (by waiting 30 minutes before trying again, in this case). There was no other measure of control to detect the malicious employee's attempts at accessing the supervisor's account.

In this example, if the invalid access attempts were logged and captured as audit trails, the team monitoring the audit trails could have noticed the multiple invalid access attempts, investigated the issue, and possibly prevented the malicious employee from gaining access to the supervisor's account over time. This is a typical example of defense-in-depth, where a combination of preventive, detective, and corrective controls are utilized to provide optimal security for the organization.

17.2.1.5 Use of Identification and Authentication Mechanisms

We have already discussed the imperative requirement to log and capture access-control-related events across the organization.

Capturing user access to the system provides evidence of the user's presence (or absence) on a system and is one of the first points of consideration during a forensic investigation. Especially during fraud and misfeasance investigations, the first thing to be identified is the access of a user into the system at a particular time using a particular IP address or machine identification, as the case may be. In some cases, certain users are only required to access systems during certain times of the day. For instance, a purchase manager might only require access to the system between 9 a.m. and 5 p.m. on a daily basis. If an audit trail captures a login by the purchase manager at 11 p.m., it indicates anomalous behavior that might have to be looked into as a security incident or event.

We have already learned that *identification* refers to the practice of establishing the user's identity to the system using some form such as username, user ID, customer number, and so on. *Authentication* refers to establishing that the identified user is indeed the user using a parameter that the user has, knows, or is. This, in most corporate systems and applications, is what the user knows, i.e., the password or passphrase that is used to authenticate and gain access to the system. It must be noted that while the log and audit trail must capture the user identification parameter (username or similar), it must never capture the authentication parameter (password or similar), even if the authentication parameter is encrypted/ hashed. A security breach of the log system or a malicious log administrator might be able to compromise all user accounts by just gaining access to application or system logs.

I find that this weakness is rampant in customized payment applications. I have performed application security assessments for multiple banks, TPPs, and merchants that have developed customized applications. In several of these applications, I find that there are logging statements capturing highly sensitive information like PANs and passwords, all in cleartext! This is specifically important for customized applications. This serves as an important security consideration for PA-DSS applications as well.

17.2.1.6 Initialization of Audit Logs

Just as it is important to capture audit-trail information for the system, it is important to capture the initialization of audit logs, i.e., the time and point where audit trails are being generated for a given system. In many cases, systems might have to be replaced or reinstated. Sometimes systems might not have been configured to log audit trails and events. In such cases, organizations would find it useful to know from what points audit trails have been generated by the system.

17.2.1.7 Creation of System-Level Objects

System-level objects are events and objects that are generated when an operating-system event is triggered by an application. The creation and deletion of such objects in the operating system must be logged, and events must be recorded. This can also be achieved with a file-integrity monitoring solution, which is another mandate under Requirement 10 of the PCI-DSS.

17.2.2 Audit-Trail Entries and Records

Audit trails and logs must capture information that is useful as a detective control. I have come across several log systems that are nothing more than console statements that provide basic information in the most incomprehensible way. For instance, I found the following in a Java payment application to "log" user access.

```
System.out.println("User: " +
username + " has logged into the
system");
```

This does not convey the required information in an intelligible way. This just logs a statement into the server console, which says that a user has logged in. It does not address several key questions, such as:

- When did the user log in?
- Which system did the user log in from?
- Was the login successful or not?

Logs have to capture information in a way that provides adequate information about the event. Additionally, logs have to be captured in formats that can be parsed and interpreted by log-management applications, SIEM applications, and so on.

The PCI-DSS, as part of its Requirement 10.3, requires that the following information must be captured as part of an audit trail or log statement. For a commercial application being validated under the PA-DSS, the following fields need to be captured:

- User identification
- Type of event
- Date and time
- Success or failure indication
- Origination of event
- Identity of affected data, system component, or resource

17.2.2.1 User Identification

The user's identity parameters—username, user ID, user code, and so on—need to be captured in the log statement. This is the first parameter that is required to be logged for the purposes of accountability. Access control consists of three key facets: authentication, authorization, and accountability. Accountability is the process of linking the user to a set of actions or events performed on a system. In the event of an anomaly or a security breach, these events or actions are captured and are nonrepudiable and are traced back to the user, thus making the user accountable for his/her actions on the system.

17.2.2.2 Type of Event

The type of event refers to, but is not limited to, the events covered in Section 17.2.1. An application could consist of multiple events like user login, data creation, deletion, update, user access to specific resources and components, disabling user access, invalid access attempts, and privileged user access, among others. The type of event has to be captured in the event logs or audit trails generated by the system. For operating systems, network logs, and infrastructure component logs, they are usually standardized and consist of useful information about the type of event. The type of event is very important, especially from a security standpoint, because it provides information about any anomalies or security breaches. For instance, if the organization wants to identify specific information based on the type of event, such as disabling users from the system, then they can specifically investigate the issue by filtering the type of event. Capturing the type of event in the logs and audit trails also provides the capability to easily gather information when required. Figure 17.1 is an image of an event-monitoring tool called OSSIM (open source) that

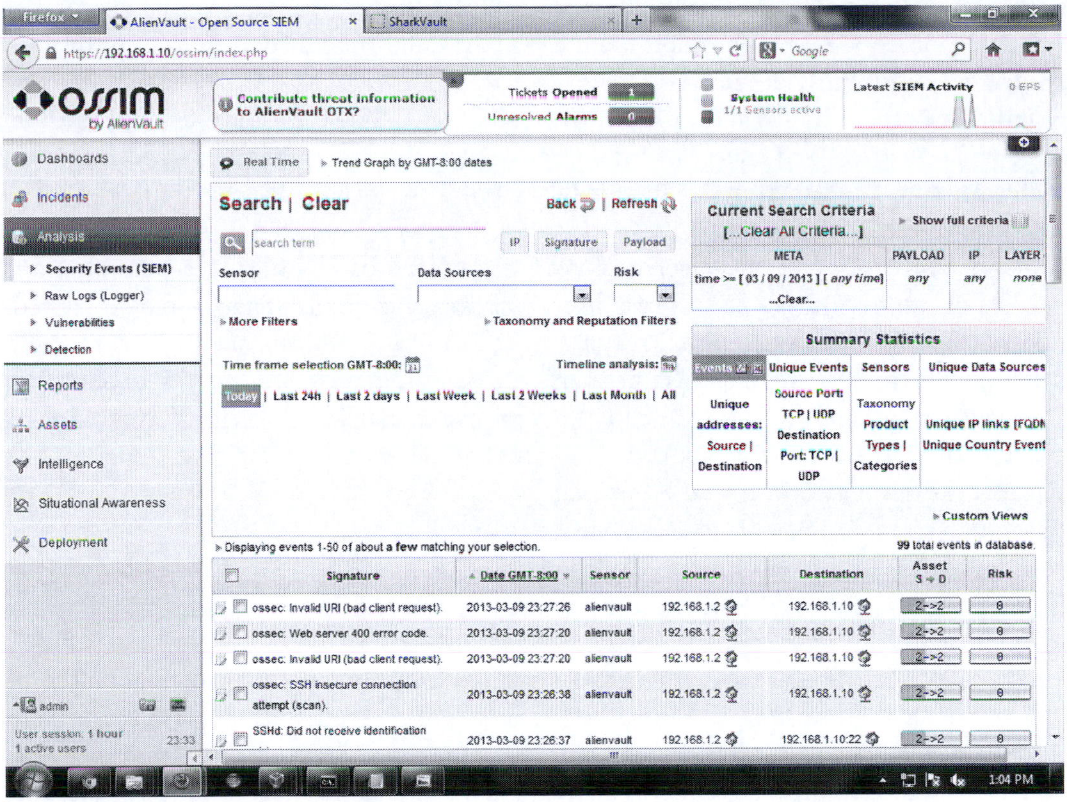

FIGURE 17.1
Event logging in the OSSIM SIEM console.

can be used for log and event correlation, intrusion prevention, and so on.

17.2.2.3 Date and Time

An audit trail cannot be remotely complete without the date and time of the event. Usually, systems capture time stamps to log events. Time stamps refer to a sequence of characters of a certain event, providing date and time, most often right down to the smallest fraction of a second. A time stamp is used by most systems for their logs and event captures. The date and time is essential to convey the specific time at which a particular event occurred. This is absolutely essential for analysis, investigation, and correlation, as a series of connected events forming audit trails can be formed, and anomalies and security breaches can be detected efficiently, with a larger set of useful information.

17.2.2.4 Indication of Success or Failure

Indication of success or failure is a very useful parameter to capture in log events and audit trails, but it is seldom captured in systems and custom applications. Success or failure events capture whether a user action or other event was successful or not. In the event that a particular action or event was successfully performed, then a success indication records that the event was successfully completed as required. However, in the event that there is some exception or error in a process, event, or action, then a failure indication provides useful information that the process failed at the event, process, or action level. While success or failure indications are useful from a functionality perspective, logging said information is also useful from a security perspective. Success or failure indications are very useful to identify the workings of security functionality in systems. For instance, an antivirus server is downloading updates on a daily basis. These must be applied to all systems on the network. In the event that the updates are not downloaded properly, and there is no failure indication logged in the log entries and audit trails, the organization might be missing critical updates for the latest malware, possibly leading to a security breach. For instance, if an authentication system logs failure indications for a user-authentication process, then it is likely that the user is entering invalid credentials to access the system. Multiple failure indications and a subsequent success indication for user authentication might indicate that an attacker has potentially gained access to a system using a legitimate user's credentials.

17.2.2.5 Origination of Event

Information about the origination of an event is highly useful for security analysis. The origination of an event refers to the source of the action or event that led to the eventual action or event performed on a system—the origin process, resource, referring page, and so on. For instance, consider the case where a PID 1596 on a Linux system attempts to communicate with a Web server to provide certain information about a user's system. In this case, the origination of the event is from PID

1596, with a program name that executes at a particular time, attempts to communicate with a server X to transmit crash reports, and then debug information about the host system. From a security perspective, identifying the origin of a particular event is critical when one is investigating a security breach or identifying a possibly nonsecure condition that needs to be reviewed. The origin provides a start in establishing the legitimacy and efficacy of an action or an event that led to certain conditions or assignments in a system (see Figure 17.2).

17.2.2.6 Identification of Affected System, Resource, or Component

It is important to establish the source or origin of an event, but it is also essential to establish the target of the action or event. An event usually affects change in the state of a particular system, resource, or component. For instance, a new sales transaction has been entered into a billing system. This affects change in the system in many ways. Its inventory information is affected; its accounts information is affected; its sales transaction table is affected; and its asset table and customer balances are possibly affected as well. A single transaction or event has an effect on one or more target resources or components. Information about an affected resource, system, or target must be logged as part of a system's audit trail as well as the organization's collated (and possibly correlated) audit trails. For instance, I was recently performing an audit of a newly deployed card-management application. The application was being accessed by multiple applications and systems, including communication servers, payment-switching applications, online

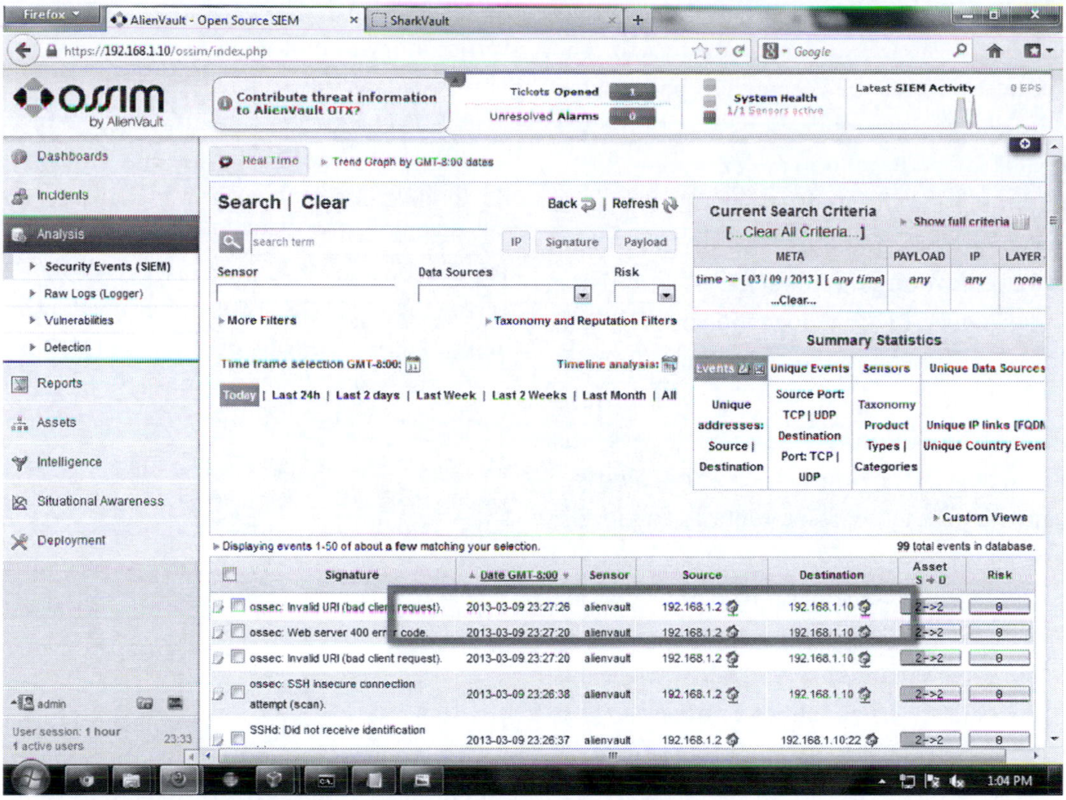

FIGURE 17.2
Origination of events in an SIEM console.

card-management applications, fraud-management applications, and so on. In such cases, the card-management application is the target and/or the origination point for several events and entries. From a security standpoint, it is essential to identify which system, component, and resource was affected by an origin entity/system to give rise to a change of state.

17.2.3 Application Logging Best Practices

In several sections of this chapter, I have mentioned that applications are usually not well-designed to log useful information, especially from the point of view of security. I stress this subject because applications are the most utilized resources in the organization, and if they do not provide useful information through audit trails, then identification of security breaches, flaws, and exceptions becomes very difficult and may be delayed with deadly consequences.

The best practices for logging have been discussed in previous sections of this chapter, but I would like to pay special attention here to the best practices that are required for applications logging in a PCI environment, be they customized applications or commercially available applications.

Good logging practices usually begin with good error and exception handling practices. Attackers look to force error conditions, expecting unhandled exceptions to present themselves with the response from the application. Detailed errors and exceptions provide a gateway to a security breach. The application must be designed to handle specific and generic application exceptions. The goal is to handle all possible exceptions without hindering the application's functionality.

I highly recommend the use of popular application log libraries or APIs like log4j, logger, log4net, log4php, and OWASP ESAPI. These popular APIs and libraries provide an integrated framework where logs can easily be generated, with specific log statements being written in the code to capture all the necessary details, log levels, and so on.

Applications must never be designed to log sensitive data like passwords and card numbers. These details can be used by malicious insiders or external entities in the event that the log server or the logs are compromised.

17.3 THE IMPORTANCE OF TIME AND ITS CONSISTENCY

17.3.1 Time Sync across IT Components

Reconstructing events is a key aspect of log management for the organization. Time is the most important parameter to achieve this goal of event reconstruction. One can best reconstruct events with the understanding of time. This requires two important things: One is to capture time in all events that are logged by multiple systems in the environment. The other is to ensure that time across multiple systems is consistent to provide a chronological analysis of related events (audit trails) possible for analysis. In my opinion, the latter is as important as

the former. This also reminds me of a very strange story in incident management.

I was consulting a client who had suffered a data breach. An external attacker had broken into my client's FTP servers and possibly gained access to some internal servers. We began with some log analysis. The attacker had been able to access the FTP server through the Internet firewall and then ran a remote code execution exploit on the unpatched FTP server. Subsequently, the attacker leveraged this initial access to gain further access to the underlying operating system. The attacker also seemed to have scanned the ports of the internal network from the compromised FTP server. There was one major problem: The time entries on the firewall and the access logs on the FTP server just did not match. We later discovered that the firewall was managed by the client's Australia team; hence, the firewall was configured with Sydney standard time, as opposed to Indian standard time. This discrepancy ensured that our analysis was extremely labored and inaccurate.

This brings me to the primary point of this PCI requirement. Time should be maintained consistently across the PCI environment to ensure that event logs are recorded at the correct time. This is a security measure that extends the functionality of logging by ensuring that log events can be fully reconstructed by correctly recording the time in a consistent manner across the environment.

17.3.2 Network Time Protocol for Time Synchronization

The most popular way to synchronize time across multiple devices is to use the Network Time Protocol (NTP). The NTP is one of the oldest Internet protocols.

The protocol uses UDP for transport on port 123. It can maintain an accuracy up to tens of milliseconds on a WAN (over the Internet) and to the tune of a single millisecond in the case of a LAN (local area network). Lists of NTP servers are maintained by multiple companies and institutions. For instance, my computer is currently synchronized with time.asia.apple.com, an NTP server that is maintained by Apple Corporation, presumably in Asia.

Most large organizations implement their internal "time server," which is nothing more than an NTP server. Subsequently, all devices in the environment are configured to obtain their clock synchronization from the time server that has been placed in the organization. This ensures that time across the organization and its infrastructure is synchronized. The time server itself must be configured to receive time from a public source like time.nist.gov or another source.

I have also come across implementations where the Internet firewall or a single network device serves as a time server. The single device receives time from a public time server, and all system clocks in the organization are synchronized with the single device that is also serving as an internal time server. This might work for smaller companies, but it is ill suited for larger companies with distributed networks. In such cases, it is highly recommended to have a dedicated time server to serve the needs of the company at large. NTP is delivered in UTC time.

Requirement 10.4 of the PCI-DSS mandates that system clocks across the PCI environment must be synchronized with a time server that receives its time from an outside time server.

Apart from configuring the time, it must also be ensured that individuals cannot change the time on critical systems and servers. In several cases, with Windows systems, employees have changed the system time to prolong an application license or to perform a backdated activity. Configuration-access restrictions must be placed on users to prevent them from tampering with the integrity of the time that is being fed using the synchronization with the time server. It goes without saying that the time server that is maintained by the organization must also be protected on the same lines as any other system component to ensure that time settings do not change.

17.4 SECURING AUDIT TRAILS AND LOGS

17.4.1 Business Need to Know: Logs and Audit Trails

Requirement 10.5.1 extends the access-control requirement for business-need-to-know for log and audit-trail data. Logs and audit trails contain highly useful and possibly sensitive information about a system or infrastructure. If this information is in the hands of the wrong individuals, the organization might be subject to a variety of highly focused attack possibilities. Such attacks tend to have a deeper impact on the organization than attempts by an attacker who has to enumerate and perform reconnaissance for a system from scratch. Unfortunately, log data is never given the same protection that servers and workstations are typically given. When my team and I perform internal penetration testing for companies, I often find that log servers are mostly left vulnerable and unprotected. The perception is that the log server does not contain sensitive information or business-critical data. These log servers can often be easily compromised due to poor passwords, lack of system hardening, or delay/lack in patching the system with critical security updates/patches. People often overlook the fact that log servers or system logs contain valuable data about the system's events, actions, errors, and exceptions. A determined and skilled attacker would find immense value in obtaining such data.

A greater danger with logs relates to the integrity of the system logs. I was performing a security assessment at a large manufacturing company. This company had deployed a human-resource-management application to manage its large workforce. The application was obviously a mission-critical application for the organization. The payroll of the organization was also driven through the same application. Due to a shortage of skilled administrators for the application, the organization had temporarily appointed the database administrator to act as the administrator for this application as well. The database administrator began to abuse privileges. The administrator set up fake employee master data and tracked them to some bank accounts that belonged to him and some people he knew. The administrator also deleted the audit-trail data from the application log files. The fraud almost went undetected until an assessment of the human-resources files and the data in the HR-management application did not seem to match. A reconciliation process of user accounts that the organization performed on a quarterly basis led to the identification of this misfeasance.

Malicious individuals or employees who would like to erase their tracks would be very interested in tampering with log information. Experienced attackers ensure that they clear all their footprints after successfully compromising a system. They attempt to gain access to the logs of the system and tamper with the time stamps on the logs, deleting logs or modifying them to convey completely different information. In fact, the popular exploit engine, Metasploit, has modules called "timestomp" and "event_manager" that can be used to change or delete the time-stamp information on a system's event logs. Moreover, the event_manager module can remove events from the target system.

17.4.2 Securing Log Information

Some ways of protecting logs and event information include:

- Strong access control
- System hardening
- Centralized log server
- File-integrity monitoring

17.4.2.1 Strong Access Control

Access-control mechanisms are a popular and relatively easy way to protect the confidentiality and integrity of log information. Let us assume that all Microsoft Windows users in an organization had administrative access to their systems, such that the users might be able to gain access to the event-management module of the operating system and delete log data, and so on. Access rights and permissions have to be configured to preclude regular users from being able to hide their tracks by disabling or deleting log entries and event entries. Unix users can use commands like *chattr* to set access restrictions on the log files and ensure that users cannot tamper with log data.

Effective segregation of duties plays a major role in protection of log entries. For instance, an application administrator could also be the database administrator. This is a recipe for disaster in the event that the administrator decided to turn against the organization. He might also be targeted in social-engineering attacks, and so on, to gain access to multiple abstractions of the system (application and database) to compromise the data and possibly gain deeper access to the organization's infrastructure and data.

17.4.2.2 System Hardening

System hardening is an existing requirement under Requirement 2 of the PCI-DSS. However, system hardening is also very useful to protect the log information stored, processed, and transmitted by the system. Hardening includes the following activities:

- Restricting unnecessary services on the system
- Protecting the system with comprehensive authentication and authorization
- Maintaining stringent security controls over the privileged functions of the system

For instance, if an attacker is able to compromise an administrator account on a Windows domain or gain root access on a Unix box, it is usually "game over." This applies equally to applications, databases, and network devices, where protection of log information is equally critical.

17.4.2.3 Centralized Log Server

Requirement 10.5.3 of the PCI-DSS requires that the logs and audit trails of system components in the PCI environment should be contained in a centralized log server. Log-management applications and SIEM applications connect to all identified systems over the syslog UDP, pull syslog data, and provide real-time analysis of log information from all systems. These tools provide many useful features, including the ability to set alerts on the triggering of severe log entries or events detected by the application in the organization's infrastructure. A SIEM or a log-management application may not always be necessary. For smaller companies undertaking PCI compliance, these applications are often cost inefficient. I have seen creative companies developing/downloading scripts that pull log information from all system components into a centralized log server. Once pulled, there is a parser script that acts on the pulled log data, and then alerts or review reports are delivered to the relevant administrator for information and/or action as necessary. While this is not the most optimal strategy, especially because the scripts are not in real time and are configured to pull logs at specific intervals such as end of day, there is still the possibility that an attacker can tamper with or delete log entries within this time period. Figure 17.3 is a screenshot of a popular open-source SIEM, OSSIM.

17.4.2.4 File-Integrity Monitoring

File-integrity monitoring is a powerful protection practice to protect against the breach of integrity of the logs generated by the system

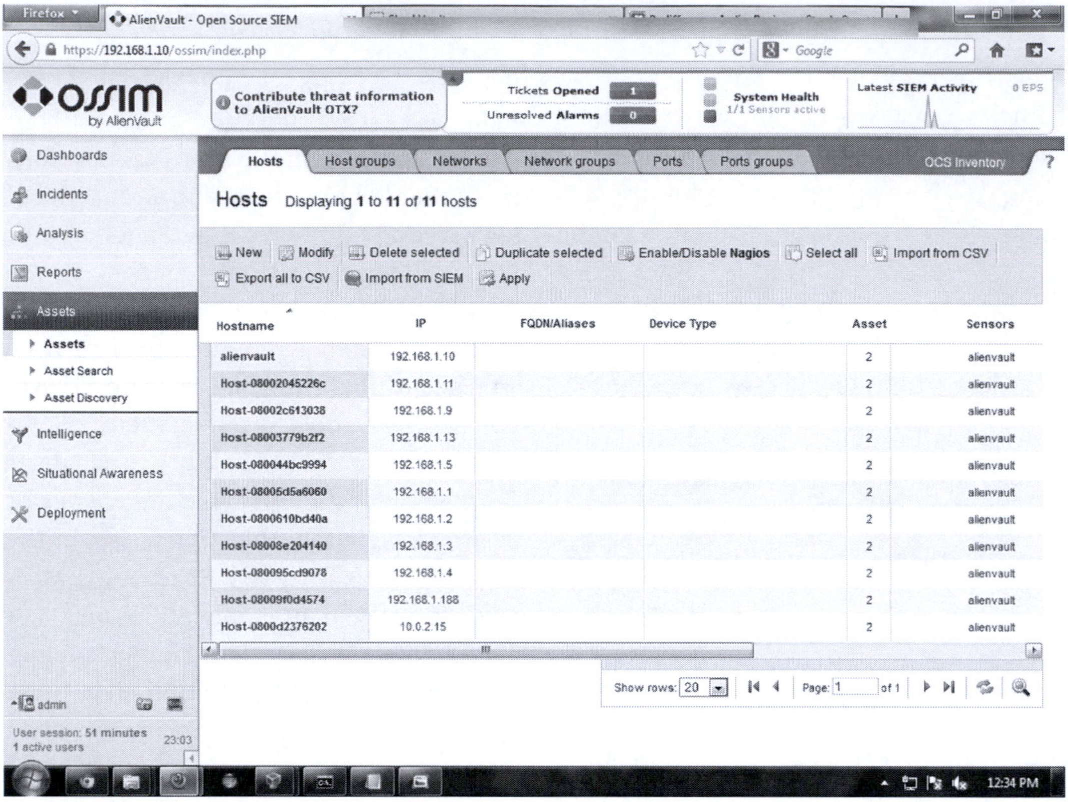

FIGURE 17.3
OSSIM SIEM screenshot.

components in the PCI environment. The practice of file-integrity monitoring essentially means that, in the event of modification or deletion of generated log files, where the integrity of the logs undergoes a change, this should raise an alert to the organization such that it treats the event as an incident and investigates possible misfeasance or attack by an internal or external entity.

Some log-management applications and SIEM applications provide this functionality. They will not raise alerts to administrators when events/logs and audit trails are captured and generated by the system, but when these events/logs/audit trails are changed or deleted, the system raises an alert to the administrators, who would

investigate the issue to identify the root cause of the change.

It must be noted that alerts raised upon generation of new log entries is useless. This would result in a great deal of noise, as new log entries are constantly being generated by multiple system components, and if the file-integrity monitoring solution or practice does not differentiate between genuine events and noise, then administrators might miss actual security incidents and potential breach conditions.

Some popular file-integrity monitoring solutions are:

- TripWire
- Afick
- GFI file-integrity monitor

17.5 LOG MONITORING, REVIEW, AND RETENTION

17.5.1 Requirement 10.6: Log Review and Monitoring

Logs and audit trails are very useful as a detective control in combination with preventive and corrective controls. However, for a log-management practice to be considered comprehensive, logs must be reviewed and monitored. All too often, I come across organizations logging copious quantities of data from multiple system components. But they don't have the discipline, practice, or established tools and processes to review and monitor these logs on a regular basis. Assessors must note that when someone gives you a response like, "We are logging all events in the specific devices" or "We are maintaining all logs in the systems themselves," chances are that they do not have a log-monitoring or review process.

Log-management applications and SIEM applications usually provide for real-time log reviews and log analysis. If the administrators or the security personnel configure alert rules effectively, the tool handles all the complexity of the review process and provides the administrator only with specific data that needs to be addressed.

Requirement 10.6 of the PCI-DSS mandates that the logs from all the system components must be reviewed at least on a daily basis. This requirement effectively rules out manual log analysis. Even if you have a single person reviewing logs from all systems on a daily basis, chances are that that person would be close to exhaustion by the end of a single workday and wouldn't be able to cope with the pressures of the job.

Log-management and SIEM tools must be configured to pull logs from all system components in the PCI environment, including authentication servers, intrusion detection systems, prevention systems, and other system components in the environment. Alerts may be configured for certain events that are captured by the log-management or SIEM applications. Said implementation can be used to optimally handle the rigors of Requirement 10.6.

As discussed previously, some companies use scripts to pull and parse log data to provide easy-to-read formats that can be reviewed by administrators on a daily basis (see Figure 17.4).

17.5.2 Requirement 10.7: Log Retention

Audit-trail and log history can be very useful, especially when investigating incidents and potential security breaches that occurred during previous periods. More than once, it has been seen that attackers have compromised an organization's IT infrastructure, and the organization discovers the breach only after several months. When the health-insurance information from the University of Berkeley was reportedly breached in 2009, it was found that the breach was being perpetrated constantly from October 2008. The breach was only discovered in May 2009.

PCI-DSS Requirement 10.7 states that log information and audit-trail data for the last 3 months must be available for immediate analysis. However, the log information/audit trails for the last year must be maintained by the organization. This requires the following essential facets to be implemented by the organization:

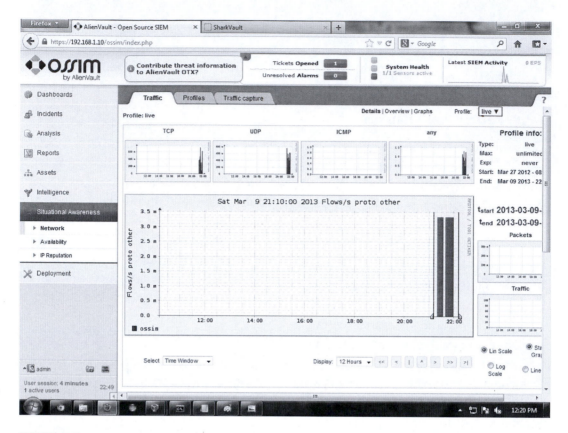

FIGURE 17.4
Events recorded in an SIEM for review.

Log retention on centralized server: Logs from all system components must be retained on the centralized log server for at least 3 months to ensure that the requirement of "available for immediate analysis" is met.

Backup of log information: Consistent practice—I would highly recommend that the log information captured by the centralized log server be backed up with a consistent practice. The backup media must be retained for at least a year, with the similar quality of physical and logical controls over the backup media provided to all other critical data backups of the organization.

The organization must also document the practice of maintaining log information for immediate analysis for a minimum of three months and the backup of the log information for at least a year. I have usually seen this being documented in the organization's log-management procedure or the company's integrated information security policy/procedure. The procedure to perform the analysis and backup should also be detailed in the relevant procedure to ensure consistency and accuracy.

17.6 SUMMARY

This chapter deals with Requirement 10 of the PCI-DSS, which is focused on logging, log management, and audit trails for the PCI environment. We began with an understanding of the need for audit trails and logs. We identified the difference between logs and audit trails: Logs capture the sequence of events as they occur on a system. Audit trails are a sequence of security-specific events that are captured in chronology to provide information about some activity or operation on the system. Requirement 10.1 of the PCI-DSS requires that all user actions should be tied to a user, especially administrative actions. This requires system logs to be enabled and functional.

Requirement 10.2 mandates that the system logs be enabled and functional to capture events such as all individual access to cardholder data, any administrative action, access to audit trails, invalid access attempts, and so on. The focus of Requirement 10.2 is to provide specific security events and logs that might be significant from a PCI environment standpoint. Logs must also capture adequate details for the reconstruction or deconstruction of an event effectively. Details like time stamp, originating user or system, target user, system or process, success or failure indication, and so on, must be logged to provide an effective trail of events. This information must be available under Requirement 10.3 of the standard. It is extremely important to have a consistent time across the environment. If time is inconsistent, log entries would be inconsistent, and tracing events or generating audit trails or correlating events would be impossible. The environment needs to have a single

source of system that may be driven via the NTP Protocol.

Requirement 10.4 mandates that a single component inside the organization must be the time server, which should receive time updates from an industry-recognized source. This server must provide time updates to the rest of the environment to ensure that all system components have the same time and, hence, that their logs will have the same time.

Requirement 10.5 states that audit trails and log events must be secure. Attackers often look to clear their tracks by manipulating or tampering with logs. The PCI-DSS requires the organization to secure logs and audit trails. The requirement specifies the use of file-integrity monitoring mechanisms to protect sensitive log files.

Requirement 10.6 states that logs from all devices in the PCI environment must be reviewed on a daily basis. While this may be a manual process, it is almost impossible to achieve manually. It is always better to use tools or a combination of scripts and correlation to achieve this requirement. I have suggested the use of a security information and event management (SIEM) application like OSSIM. Organizations also use their own scripts for pulling logs from various devices and presenting them in a readable format for daily review.

Requirement 10.7 requires that audit-trail and log information must be retained for immediate analysis for at least three months and retained for at least a year otherwise. This is to ensure that any breach investigation for a period of up to one year can be performed in the event of a security breach involving cardholder data.

18

Requirement 11: Security Testing for the PCI Environment

One of the primary methods to measure the effectiveness of security controls in an environment is to perform security testing against the infrastructure components within that environment. An organization undergoing or maintaining PCI compliance must perform specific security testing against the various infrastructure components in the PCI environment. We begin the chapter with some techniques to be used to meet the PCI requirement of detecting rogue wireless access points.

We will discuss the security testing requirements for the PCI-DSS. I will describe some good practices to perform vulnerability assessments against the organization's PCI environment. We will also understand the PCI requirement for having external-facing testing performed by approved scanning vendors (ASVs). The PCI-DSS also requires organizations to perform internal and external penetration testing for all of its infrastructure components on an annual basis. I will describe the fundamental differences between a vulnerability assessment and a penetration test. We will learn some of the aspects of penetration testing that should be avoided, especially for a mission-critical environment that handles payment-card data. We will also delve into the requirement of file-integrity monitoring for critical systems and configuration files of various system components in the PCI environment as well as some techniques and methods of achieving the standard.

18.1 WIRELESS ACCESS POINT: TESTING

18.1.1 Testing for Rogue/Unauthorized Wireless Access Points

Throughout this book, we have explored several requirements relating to wireless security and security practices for wireless networks. Requirement 11.1 is a wireless security requirement that states that an organization must test for the presence of unauthorized or rogue wireless networks in their environment. Wireless networks are an extremely convenient mode of network access for users in an organization's environment. Wireless networks allow users to move their laptops and mobile devices all around the organization's environment and not be tied down to their desks with physical cables, restricting their movements. Some organizations, like merchant organizations, embrace wireless networks because they provide a great deal of convenience to their shoppers with wireless point-of-sale (POS) devices and billing systems, which increase the speed and efficiency of the shopping experience for the customer. However, other organizations, like service providers, banks, and so on, do not have wireless networks or have wireless networks with limited access for guests and visitors, and so on.

Sometimes, it so happens that users take wireless networks into their own hands. I was recently involved with helping a large third-party processing company achieve PCI compliance for its scoped environment. We were performing a wireless scan in the environment, and we found a single wireless access point that the network administrator confirmed was one that he had *not* authorized or set up in any way. Based on the strength of the signal and the IP address, we identified that an employee in the sales department had installed a wireless access point at his desk to provide wireless access to his entire team for their laptops and smartphones. He contested that they needed wireless network access to be flexible as they moved from one meeting to another throughout the floor. This was even more dangerous because they had secured the wireless access point with a simple WEP

key of five characters. Wireless technology has become even more accessible today, with smartphones serving as tethering devices for wireless access.

The PCI standards require the organization to test for the presence of unauthorized or rogue wireless networks within the organization. This may be achieved with the following techniques:

- Wireless network scanning
- Physical inspection
- Network access control
- Wireless IDS/IPS (intrusion detection system/intrusion prevention system) deployment

18.1.1.1 Wireless Network Scanning

The organization can perform wireless network scanning using specific wireless scanning tools to identify wireless networks in its environment. This can be achieved with wireless network scanning tools like NetStumbler and Kismet. Most of these tools are freely available, and some are even open source. The organization can perform wireless network scans throughout its environment to identify unauthorized and rogue access points that might have been deployed without approvals or by malicious insiders or external attackers. These scanning tools provide a great deal of information about the wireless networks that are available within the broadcast area. Based on the strength of the signal and the reception, the organization will be able to identity whether these networks belong to the organization or otherwise. NetStumbler also offers an application called the MiniStumbler, which can run on mobile devices like the pocket PC. It supports GPS functions that can create a map of the wireless networks identified

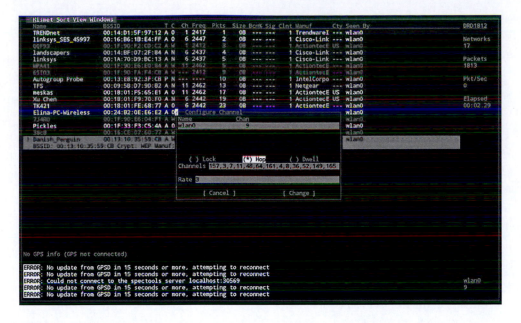

FIGURE 18.1
Screenshot of the popular wireless scanning tool Kismet.

within the broadcast area. Tenable's Nessus, which is a very popular vulnerability scanner, also provides the functionality to scan wireless networks in the broadcast area. The vulnerability scanner provides multiple levels of checks and analyses to identify the operating system (OS) and trace it back to the organization's IT infrastructure. Figure 18.1 is a screenshot of the popular wireless scanning tool Kismet.

18.1.1.2 Physical Inspection

Physical inspection is not the most optimized or efficient way of identifying rogue wireless network access points. Rogue access points are usually connected by wire to a switch or network access point, from where the wireless access point derives its address on the network. Physical inspection involves identifying all physical connectivity to the connected switches to identify any unauthorized access point being plugged into the switch to behave like an uplink

port.* In a large and distributed environment, this can become a very tedious and cumbersome practice that is highly labor intensive. In my opinion, physical inspection must go beyond this, especially in an environment that has DHCP (dynamic host configuration protocol) and no network access control or managed switching. In such cases, users can hook up a wireless access point at their desk and create wireless networks that can be used. In such environments, the physical inspection takes on an additional layer. However, this is even more cumbersome and tedious, and it can take a great deal of time in large environments.

18.1.1.3 Network Access Control

Network access control (NAC) is a concept in enterprise security, where network access is provided to clients in the network only based on a predefined set of rules and

---

* In computer networking, an uplink is a connection from a device or smaller local network to a larger network.

policy parameters. For instance, if a user is attempting to use his/her smartphone to connect to the network and the NAC has been configured to not allow the use of smartphones, then the user will not be able to register and connect to the network. NAC systems perform preadmission and postadmission checks, where preadmission checks are those that are performed prior to allowing a system to gain access to the network. NAC systems can also be either out-of-band systems or inline systems. Out-of-band systems are those where software agents are deployed on the client systems that are to access the network, and the inline system is a single appliance or server concept that acts as a firewall or access control server to enforce policy based on the configured NAC policy.

A NAC primarily performs a preventive function, where unauthorized devices are not even allowed on the network if the configuration and policies are written appropriately by the administrator. However, in the event that one wants to view the devices in an environment, the NAC provides the administrator with the capability of viewing the types of devices that are currently accessing the network (mobile device, Windows 7, etc.). The NAC also provides information on how the device is being accessed, whether over a wired network or over a wireless network.

This is the specific feature that is useful for Requirement 11, where the organization may be able to identify unauthorized wireless networks and access points by viewing the NAC logs and dashboards. The NAC can be used in lieu of a wireless network scanning practice to identify and subsequently prevent access to the network from rogue wireless access points.

18.1.1.4 *Wireless IDS/IPS Deployment*

Wireless IDS/IPS, popularly known as WIPS, is a device that is used to scan the wireless radio spectrum for the presence of rogue wireless access points and misconfigured wireless access points. The wireless IDS can perform more functions by identifying clients that are communicating without encryption with a wireless network. The WIPS relies on sensors that constantly scan the spectrum for wireless networks and then identify and scan the networks for security vulnerabilities. The data from the sensors is collated in a centralized management console, where the administrators can perform policy enforcement actions on the wireless networks. The WIPS also provides alerting capabilities, much like a wired network IDS/IPS. Apart from identifying rogue wireless access points, unencrypted traffic, and misconfigured access points (APs), the WIPS can also identify users and triangulate users based on their locations in the network in the event that the user is circumventing the organization's security policy over a wireless network. WIPS is also used to prevent against denial-of-service and MAC (media access control) address-spoofing attacks.

18.2 INTERNAL AND EXTERNAL NETWORK VULNERABILITY SCANNING

18.2.1 Vulnerability Scanning: Concept Note

Vulnerability scanning, popularly known as vulnerability assessment (VA), is a fundamental concept in security testing. VAs are very popular among organizations that would like to identify vulnerabilities in their IT infrastructure and remediate them based on priority. The vulnerability assessment also forms the basis for a penetration test (PT), which I describe in Section 18.3 of this chapter.

The VA is self-explanatory. It is a technical assessment (set of tests) that is aimed at identifying the specific security vulnerabilities in the IT infrastructure. VAs can be performed either manually, with tools, or by using a hybrid methodology consisting of both. The objective of a VA is to identify specific vulnerabilities to the myriad IT assets in the organization, including network devices, servers, workstations, and applications as well as related infrastructure components like databases, middleware, and so on. There are several tools that are used to perform end-to-end vulnerability assessments.

18.2.1.1 Vulnerability Categorization

Vulnerabilities creep into the infrastructure due to the following four reasons:

18.2.1.1.1 Vulnerabilities in Design

Design vulnerabilities are the toughest vulnerabilities to fix. These vulnerabilities are those in which the security vulnerability arises due to a fundamental design flaw in the system. For instance, when a user entered invalid access credentials multiple times on a Windows 95 system, the system would offer to create a new username and password for the user, making it trivial for an attacker to really "attack" the system. I have also seen several older card-management applications being designed to accept only a four-character password. Breaking a four-character password is trivial. These are

design flaws that introduce a vulnerability into the system. These are usually the most difficult to remediate, as it would require revisiting the entire design and solving the problem, which might even require reconstruction of the entire system.

18.2.1.1.2 Vulnerabilities in Implementation/Development

Vulnerabilities in implementation or development refer to specific vulnerabilities that creep into the system during the development of the system (implementation of the design of the system). These vulnerabilities are tough to fix, but are not as difficult as design vulnerabilities. For instance, if the developers use regular SQL (Structured Query Language) statements instead of prepared statements to query the database, the application might be vulnerable to SQL injection. This is the flaw introduced in the development of the application.

18.2.1.1.3 Vulnerabilities in Deployment

Deployment vulnerabilities are those that manifest themselves in the application during the deployment of the application in an environment. These relate to the configuration of the application and/or its infrastructure components and their security parameters. For instance, let's say an implementer is deploying ERP (enterprise resource planning) software for the organization. The implementer does not change the default passwords of the application, does not configure the password complexity and policy parameters for the application, and does not enable the logging parameters for the application. The application is left vulnerable in multiple dimensions. However, the application is not vulnerable by design or in development. These vulnerabilities are easy to fix, as they involve tweaking configurations for systems to render the system more secure.

18.2.1.1.4 Vulnerabilities in Maintenance

Vulnerabilities in maintenance are those that creep into a system due to nonsecure maintenance and security issues with the running configuration of a system. The key issue with this type of vulnerability is with patching and patch-management practices. Systems usually have bugs and security vulnerabilities. Vendors such as OS vendors, network device vendors, and application vendors develop security updates/patches for these systems. However, if administrators do not test and deploy these patches in time, it could result in attackers being able to successfully compromise the system. For instance, at the time of this writing, there have been several vulnerabilities discovered in the Java Virtual Machine that runs on most clients and servers all over the world. There are also several flaws that have been found with the Web-programming platform Ruby on Rails. If administrators do not constantly watch for these updates and security patches and deploy them expeditiously, then attackers may be able to use the vulnerability to compromise the system.

18.2.1.2 Vulnerability Scanning: Methodology

A critical facet of a vulnerability scan or vulnerability assessment is the methodology. A good methodology is essential to ensure consistency, depth, and repeatability of results. Following a methodology ensures that the vulnerability scan is comprehensive and detailed. I personally recommend the Penetration Testing Execution Standard as a guideline to perform detailed vulnerability

assessments (VAs) and penetration testing (PT).

The following subsections describe a methodology that is generally accepted as an industry-standard methodology for vulnerability assessments

- Reconnaissance and mapping
- Vulnerability discovery
- Analysis and reporting

Figure 18.2 is a visual representation of a VA and PT methodology.

18.2.1.2.1 Reconnaissance and Mapping

Reconnaissance is the first step in a vulnerability assessment and/or penetration test. It is also the most important process of the test. In this phase, the testing team performs active and passive reconnaissance of the target system. During the mapping phase, we identify all the publicly available services running in the target system, or in the case of a Web-application penetration test, we discover all of the pages, files, and directories present in the Web-application environment. Our reconnaissance techniques include performing DNS (domain name system)-based discovery, port scanning, services discovery, and identification of target system and target environment. We also utilize search-engine information disclosure techniques like Google hacking and the use of social networks to gather specific information as would be simulated by an attacker of the system. Some of the techniques utilized in this phase of a vulnerability assessment include:

- Port scanning
- Network packet crafting
- WHOIS and Lookup queries
- DNS enumeration and DNS dumping

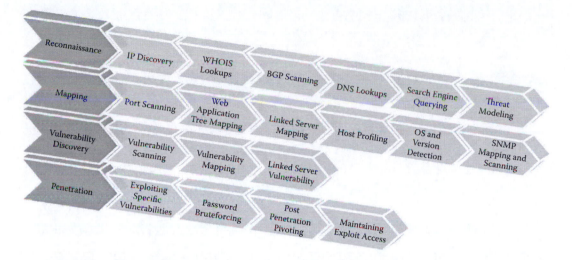

FIGURE 18.2
Steps in a vulnerability assessment and a penetration test.

- Service enumeration
- Web-page spidering
- Web-application directory brute forcing
- Google hacking and specialized search-engine queries, among others

Figure 18.3 is a screenshot of an Nmap port scan.

18.2.1.2.2 Vulnerability Discovery

The discovery phase is a critical phase of the penetration test. In this phase, the testing team identifies all possible vulnerabilities in the target system. We utilize automated and manual discovery processes to identify the most deep-seated vulnerabilities in the

target system. Vulnerabilities could stem from any of the four categories of vulnerabilities highlighted in Section 18.2.1.1. For Web-application vulnerability scanning, it is ideal if business logic security testing is also performed. This type of test identifies business logic flaws that are not identified by any tools or automated vulnerability scanning tools.

Multiple tools may be utilized to find vulnerabilities, including popular vulnerability scanners like Nessus, Nexpose, Qualys, and so on. I utilize multiple commercial and open-source vulnerability-assessment tools, including Nessus, Nexpose, OpenVas, and so on. Each of these tools differ in terms

```
Starting Nmap 6.25 ( http://nmap.org ) at 2013-03-17 15:43 IST
Nmap scan report for 192.168.1.1
Host is up (0.012s latency).
Not shown: 996 closed ports
PORT      STATE SERVICE    VERSION
21/tcp    open  ftp        D-Link DLS-2750U ftp firmward update
23/tcp    open  telnet     Broadcom BCM96338 ADSL router telnetd
80/tcp    open  http       micro_httpd
5431/tcp  open  park-agent?
Device type: general purpose
Running: Linux 2.6.X
OS CPE: cpe:/o:linux:linux_kernel:2.6
OS details: Linux 2.6.15 - 2.6.26
Service Info: Devices: WAP, broadband router; CPE: cpe:/h:dlink:dls-2750u,
  cpe:/h:broadcom:bcm96338
```

FIGURE 18.3
Screenshot of Nmap port scan.

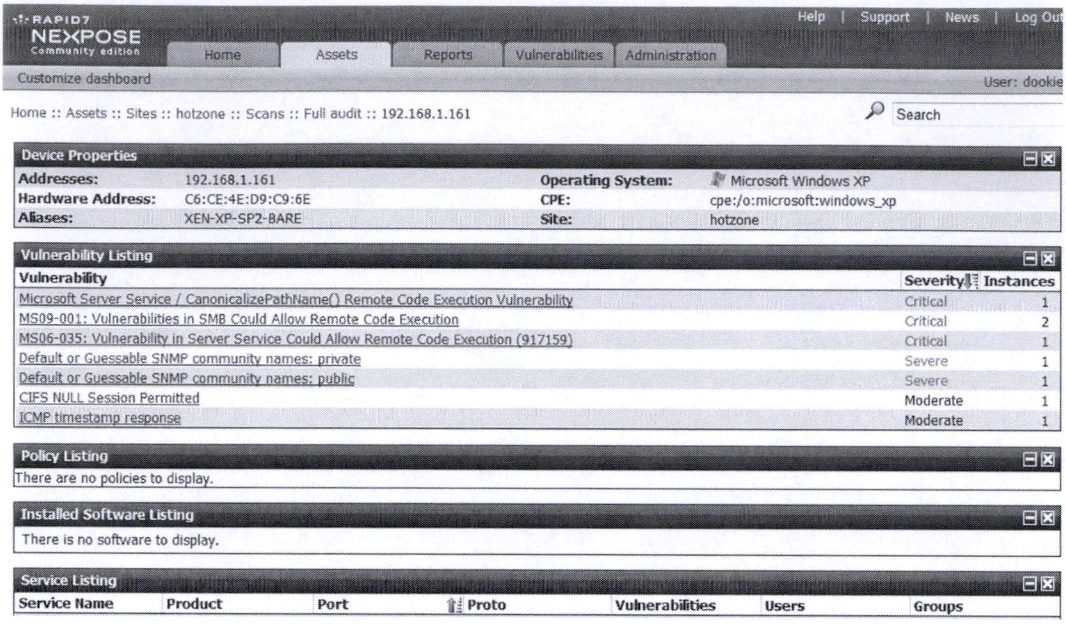

FIGURE 18.4
Screenshot of Nexpose vulnerability scanner from Rapid7.

of features, depth of testing, focus of testing, and so on. Some tools are suited ideally for performing vulnerability assessments against Web applications. Others are suited to perform vulnerability scans against network devices, operating systems, and so on. Figure 18.4 is a screenshot of the Nexpose vulnerability-scanning application from Rapid7.

Modern vulnerability scanners have a great deal of intelligence built in. Testers can run fine-grained scans and specific tests to identify a small or a large set of issues on a target system. Vulnerability scanners like the Nexpose from Rapid7 integrate with the extremely popular exploit engine Metasploit to provide advanced vulnerability scanning and comprehensive penetration testing features.

Vulnerability scanners like Nexpose also provide additional functionality, where the vulnerability scanner can integrate with IPS, GRC (governance, risk, and compliance) tools, log-monitoring tools, and so on, to provide a more comprehensive view of security within the enterprise. Nessus and Nexpose also allow users to set scanning policies based on the type of scan. Most vendors offer out-of-the-box PCI-specific scans, which makes things much easier for vulnerability scanners.

18.2.1.2.3 Analysis and Reporting

The final phase of the vulnerability assessment and/or penetration test is the analysis and reporting. In this phase, the testing team will develop the vulnerability assessment report after analyzing and interpreting the results of the test. Based on the understanding of the target system, the risk ranking of high, medium, and low will be populated with the findings of the test, and subsequently the report is delivered to the client.

Vulnerability scanners usually provide detailed reports that are quite comprehensive. However, I always prefer to add my own explanations to the existing reports, as they are more suited to the situation and the target system.

Most vulnerability scanners, such as Nexpose, come with custom reporting, remediation plans, and so on. Many vulnerability scanning tools also provide XML-based reports that can be consolidated into an integrated report with multiple tools and parsers.

18.2.2 Internal and External Network Vulnerability Scanning

18.2.2.1 Internal and External Vulnerability Scanning

The PCI-DSS Requirement 11.2 states that organizations must perform internal and external network-vulnerability scans on a quarterly basis or after a significant change in the network.

An external vulnerability scan is one where the public-facing devices in the PCI environment are scanned for vulnerabilities from an external network. Public-facing devices like DNS servers, Web servers, firewalls, routers, and so on, are accessible over the Internet (over external networks). Hence, they are subject to different risks than internal devices. In the event that they are accessible to external entities, they may be compromised by external attackers who may be able to pivot their access to the inside network. Internal vulnerability scans must be performed inside the LAN (local area network, i.e., the internal network zone). Insiders often have elevated access to devices and data within the LAN. This can be dangerous if the resources on the internal network are not protected against attacks performed by malicious insiders or

by malware that is targeted at the resources within the internal network zone. For instance, malicious insiders may be able to compromise workstations and servers within the internal network due to a delay in patching a critical security vulnerability. The internal network is subject to different risks, which are sometimes more elevated and dangerous than external risks.

18.2.2.2 Network Vulnerability Scanning

Network-vulnerability scans refer to the identification of vulnerabilities in the organization's network. Network-vulnerability scans focus on the following activities:

- Identifying open ports and services
- Enumerating services and version information
- Identifying vulnerabilities in these services
- Reporting

A network-vulnerability scan is not meant to go into great depth on application-specific vulnerabilities. While most vulnerability scanners can identify some targeted vulnerabilities in applications like open CGI (common gateway interface) scripts, cross-site scripting, and so on, they will not be able to identify deeper application-specific issues like SQL injection, command injection, XPath (XML Path Language) injection, and so on.

True to our methodology, we need to identify open ports and services in the environment. For instance, if we are scanning a Web server, it is likely that port 80 (HTTP) and port 443 (HTTPS) will be open, and some other ports may be open as well. Once we identify the ports that are open and accessible, we must identify the services running

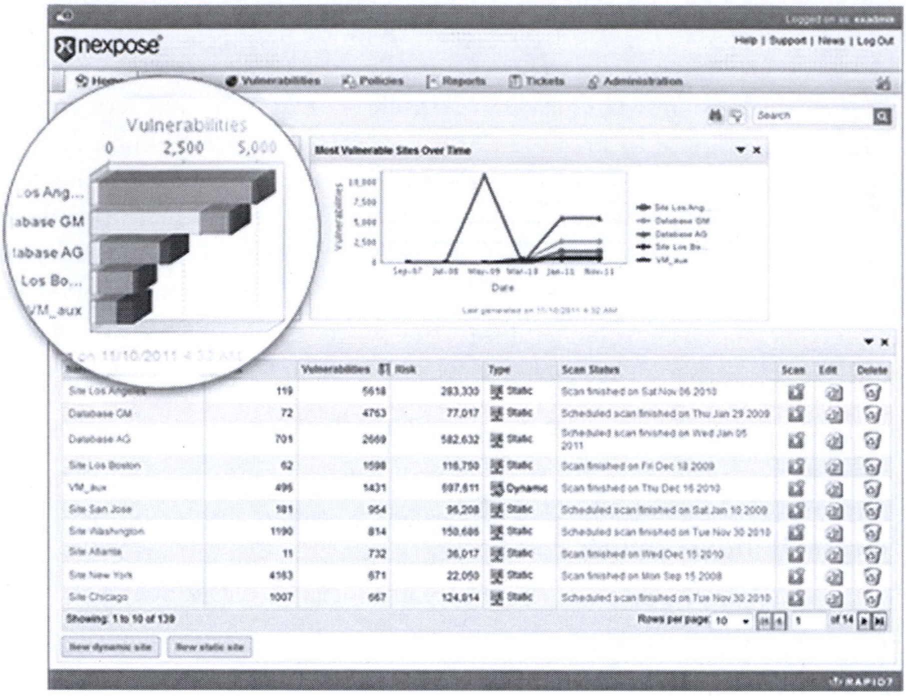

FIGURE 18.5
Screenshot of Nexpose network-level vulnerability scan against a target.

on these ports. For instance, the HTTP server might be an IIS (Internet information server) or Apache. Our scanning techniques must account for services that are running off each port. Once we identify the services, we must identify versions and information about these services and identify their specific vulnerabilities. For instance, if a Web server is running Apache 2.0.64, it might be vulnerable to a denial-of-service attack (e.g., CVE-2011-3192) that can be triggered by manipulating the range header. This vulnerability information is automatically identified by the vulnerability scanning tool. For instance, Nessus or Nexpose would automatically be able to test for the said vulnerability and provide information about the result of the test. Additionally, public databases of vulnerabilities can also be found at sites like http://www.cvedetails.com, http://www.osvdb.com, and http://

www.secunia.com. Figure 18.5 is a screenshot of a network-level vulnerability scan against a target in Nexpose.

Another key consideration in a network-vulnerability scan is the number of ports or services that are tested. Most vulnerability scanners test 1,024 common ports for both TCP (Transmission Control Protocol) and UDP (User Datagram Protocol). However, it may sometimes happen that some ports beyond this range are missed in the vulnerability scan. For a PCI scan, it is suggested that all 65,535 ports be enumerated on both TCP and UDP. However, for large scans, especially on the internal network, this can take a really long time, as the vulnerability scanner must enumerate all 65,535 ports on both the TCP and UDP. For organizations that have extremely large networks to scan for vulnerabilities, I would recommend that the vulnerability assessment team perform a firewall review and identify the ports/ services that are allowed (and blocked). Additionally, perform only port scans on all 65,535 ports (not service enumeration and vulnerability discovery) and subsequently enumerate services only on the open ports. In most cases, when individuals look to run single-instance vulnerability scanning (port scan, service detection, and vulnerability identification) simultaneously on all 65,535 ports for both TCP and UDP, this takes an unduly long time and results in deadlines being missed.

The PCI standards require that the reports obtained by the organization after the vulnerability scanning should be "clean" reports, i.e., if the reports represent severe, critical, or high-severity vulnerabilities, the organization has failed a particular iteration of the vulnerability assessment and must remediate immediately, and justifications for the same have to be produced.

In some cases, organizations run vendor software from IBM, Oracle, and so on. Occasionally, these applications tend to have some incompatibility with the OS or other components in the system. For instance, the application may not work on the OS due to a new security update on the OS. The new OS or database patch might render the application unusable. These are critical apps, and if they become unusable, the organization might not survive. In such cases, the vendor might release the patch only much later or after some months. Until then, it is not possible for the organization to apply the OS patch. In such cases, the organization must be able to produce information from the vendor about the new application patch or update. The QSA (qualified security assessor) must also take a call on the organization's justification. If the QSA believes that the organization's

security posture is generally poor and the unpatched systems are largely due to negligence, then it would do well for the QSA to fail the organization. However, in the event of a genuine business and technology constraint, such scenarios can be dealt with more effectively on a case-by-case basis. In any case, an organization with a non-"clean" report must remediate and rescan to achieve a clean report. Figure 18.6 illustrates remediation actions provided by the Nexpose vulnerability scanner.

18.2.3 Scanning by PCI-Approved Scanning Vendor (ASV)

The PCI-SSC has appointed approved scanning vendors (ASVs). These entities perform vulnerability scans on the external and public-facing servers and devices in the PCI environment. An organization must have all of their in-scope external-facing devices and components scanned by ASVs on a quarterly basis. If the ASV issues a clean report (devoid of critical, high, and severe vulnerabilities), the organization may opt to accept the other findings of the report. However, in the event that the ASV issues a qualified report with high, critical, or severe vulnerabilities, the organization must remediate and rescan until a clean report is achieved.

ASVs are made to go through a rigorous testing process by the PCI-SSC. I will not go into the details of testing coverage, and so on, as it is beyond the scope of this book. However, they are to utilize industry standard metrics like CVSS (Common Vulnerability Scoring System) for measuring the severity of the vulnerabilities identified. A base score of CVSS 4.0 and above is considered a high-severity vulnerability and results in the report not being clean.

1. Default SSH password: root password "password"

Remediation Steps

Fix Default SSH password: root password "password"
Use the "passwd" command to set a more secure login password. A good password should consist of a mix of
lower- and upper-case characters, numbers, and punctuation and should be at least 8 characters long. You may
also want to disable root login via SSH, which you can do in OpenSSH by adding the following to sshd.conf:
PermitRootLogin: no

Assets

Name	IP Address	Site
Microsoft windows XP SP2_eCom	10.2.0.123	Acme_internal_prod
nolo.com.mx	10.2.0.223	Acme_external_prod
web scan_vuln scan	10.12.0.129	MCBQ_internal_service
MCBQ_eCom_pulse	10.12.10.123	Acme_external_service
nolo.com.mx2	10.6.0.145	Acme_internal_prod

FIGURE 18.6
Remediation actions provided by the Nexpose vulnerability scanner.

18.3 INTERNAL AND EXTERNAL PENETRATION TESTING

18.3.1 Fundamental Differences: Vulnerability Assessment and Penetration Testing

I find a great deal of confusion and divide over the concepts of *vulnerability assessment* and *penetration testing*. As a QSA, I would encounter more than one situation where a vulnerability-assessment report would be shown to me as a penetration-testing report. There is a significant difference between a vulnerability assessment and a penetration test. In a vulnerability assessment, the objective is to identify and report multiple vulnerabilities in system components. A penetration test is an extension of a vulnerability assessment. The tester identifies the vulnerability and attempts to exploit the given vulnerability. If the tester is successful with the exploit, he/she attempts to pivot access to the exploited system to other systems and data in the environment. For instance, in a recent penetration test, we were able to gain access to a database using SQL injection. Subsequently, we used this attack to get the root credentials on the database. Using the root credentials on the database, we were able to gain access to the operating system hosting the database server. Pivoting from that access, we ran port scans against other systems on the same network and compromised some of them as well.

In this case, we identified the vulnerability (injection flaws in the SQL of the application) and used the flaw to gain deeper access to the organization, typically the way it would be performed by an attacker. Most penetration tests are bound by some "rules of engagement" that specify the restrictions that the organization places on the penetration tester.

PCI Requirement 11.3 states that internal and external penetration testing has to be performed for all devices in the PCI environment at least annually.

18.3.1.1 Why Perform a Penetration Test?

A penetration test is a very important security test against applications or an environment. I personally prescribe penetration testing heavily, as it provides

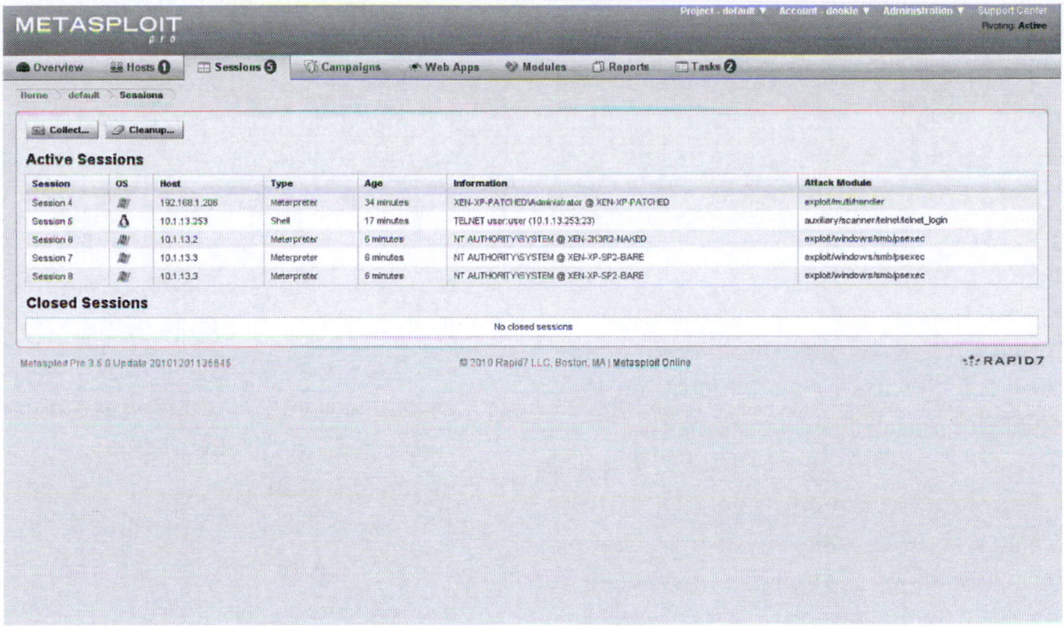

FIGURE 18.7
Example of sessions with a compromised system tested with Metasploit.

myriad benefits for the organization. Some of these are described in the following subsections.

18.3.1.1.1 Proof of Concept

A penetration test is the ultimate proof of concept of any vulnerability. If a tester is able to identify a particular vulnerability and exploit it successfully in a penetration test, it is resounding proof that the vulnerability is exploitable and that its impact and probability metrics are clear and palpable. It's not always that vulnerabilities are exploitable. Some exploits that are tested do not work on the target system either because of a compensating control or the lack of some condition required for the exploit to function. Sometimes, exploits are not available for certain vulnerabilities. Vulnerabilities that cause denial of service are generally not used because they cause downtime of critical business systems. However, if a tester is able to compromise the system using

a penetration test with specific exploits, the results are unambiguous and immutable. Figure 18.7 is an example of sessions with a compromised system tested using Metasploit software.

18.3.1.1.2 Pivot Access to Other Systems

A successful penetration test is one where the tester is not only able to compromise a vulnerable target, but also is able to use that access to gain a deeper access to the data or the other systems in the organization. This *cannot* be achieved with a vulnerability assessment. Often, in a good penetration test, the tester exploits a given system and looks to gain access to more data and systems on the target network (within scope). The organization may be able to unearth more vulnerabilities due to the penetration test, thus providing greater value than just a vulnerability assessment, where visibility is limited.

18.3.1.1.3 Management Buy-In

One of the most interesting by-products of a penetration test is that it manages to get the attention of senior management. Often, I have presented the results of a penetration test to the board or the CXOs of a company, and more than once, I have gotten them to the edge of their seats. A penetration test has the impression of an actual attack. Given the severity of the "breach" condition in a penetration test, management usually looks at this very seriously.

It is not uncommon to hear IT managers and security folks in an organization complain about the fact that management does not really understand or appreciate security, and hence they have difficulty allocating sufficient budgets for it. A good penetration test shakes them out of their possible apathy and helps them recognize and actually see a palpable threat that is clear and present.

18.3.1.1.4 Contractual Requirements, Compliance, and Regulation

Just like the PCI-DSS requires penetration testing, other compliance requirements also mention vulnerability assessment and penetration testing as a security testing practice that can be used by an organization. Often, customer contractual requirements would require that an organization perform a full penetration test of some of its IT components.

18.3.2 Network-Layer Penetration Tests

The PCI-DSS specifies the type of penetration tests that are to be carried out both internally and externally. The penetration test must include both network-layer and application-layer penetration tests. Network-layer penetration tests are those where the testing team/tester must enumerate vulnerabilities at the network and operating-system layer of the IT components. Based on the vulnerabilities, the team must look to perform specific exploits in an attempt to penetrate said devices. Network-layer penetration tests are conducted against all systems, internal or external, in the PCI environment. This includes a similar scope as the vulnerability assessment, as described in the previous sections of this chapter. The tester must enumerate all possible services on the target system, enumerate version information, identify vulnerabilities, and use specific custom or available exploits to compromise the target system and pivot access from there onwards.

18.3.3 Application-Layer Penetration Testing

Application-layer penetration testing is carried out to identify vulnerabilities and use exploits against application components in the PCI environment. This refers to all of the vulnerabilities in Requirement 6.5 of the PCI-DSS, which include injection flaws, cross-site scripting, and so on.

Application-layer penetration testing requires a different set of practices, tools, and training to perform. Often, a team that performs network-layer penetration testing cannot competently perform application-layer penetration testing. Figure 18.8 is an example of an SQL injection exploit against a target Web application.

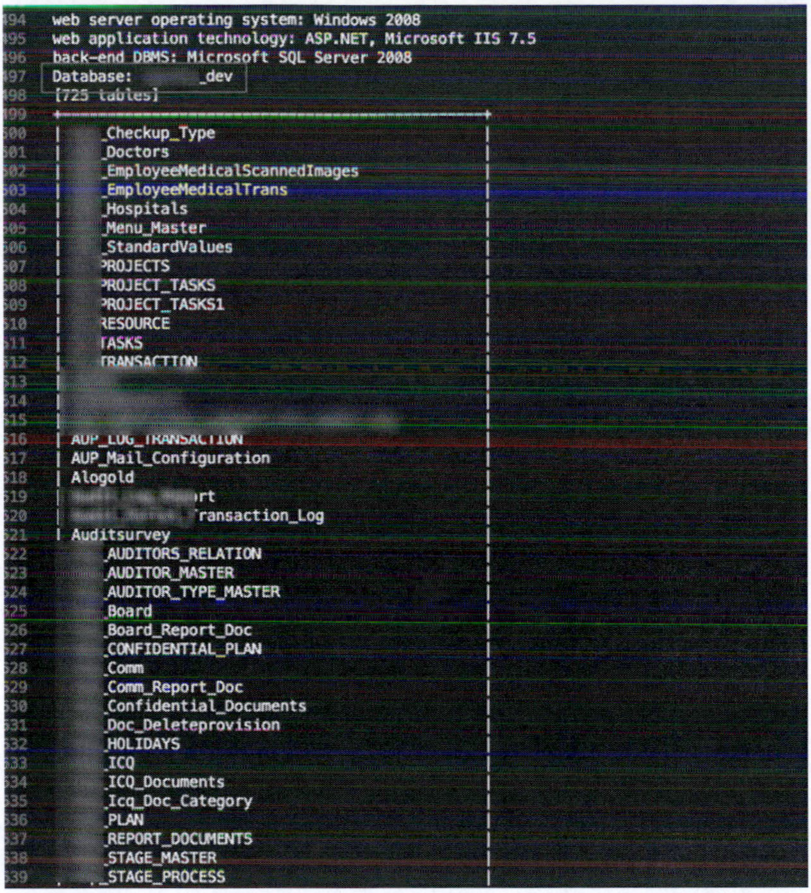

FIGURE 18.8
Example of an SQL injection exploit against a target Web application.

18.4 DEPLOYMENT OF INTRUSION DETECTION/ PREVENTION DEVICES OR APPLICATIONS

18.4.1 Intrusion Detection/ Prevention Systems: An Overview

Intrusion detection systems/prevention systems are network security appliances or applications that are used to monitor network traffic for malicious content to and from the network. An intrusion detection system (IDS), by definition, detects any malicious activity and alerts specific personnel in the organization to take corrective action against multiple attacks. Intrusion prevention systems (IPS), by definition, are those that identify malicious traffic over the network and prevent the traffic from transmitting by silently dropping the packets containing the attack traffic or by raising an alert to specific personnel about the attack.

A network IDS/IPS works on one of three modes of activity, as described in the following subsections.

18.4.1.1 *Signature Based*

A signature-based IDS/IPS contains signatures of attack vectors and traffic types for multiple attacks against systems in a network. In the event that the IDS/IPS detects a given attack vector based on a predefined signature, it flags the traffic as attack traffic. Signatures are based on exploits and vulnerabilities. Exploit-based signatures aim to detect exploit code or traffic containing exploit code to the target system. Vulnerability-based signatures aim to detect the vulnerability in a particular program as well as the exploitability of the vulnerability and the conditions required to exploit the given vulnerability in the attack traffic to the target system. While signature-based IDS/IPS is effective, it is limited to known attacks. In the event of a zero-day attack[*] with no signatures available, these devices might be rendered powerless against the attack. Additionally, there are multiple ways to bypass IDS/IPS using encoding and padding of attack vectors.

18.4.1.2 *Statistical-Based Anomaly Detection*

Statistical-based anomaly detection is a practice where the IDS/IPS is placed on a "study mode" on the network, where network traffic over time is profiled by the IDS/IPS device. Based on the profiled activity, the IDS/IPS is able to gain an understanding of normal or "benign" traffic on the network. In the event of an anomaly in the traffic patterns, the IDS/IPS will block/raise alerts on said traffic. For instance, if a large number of requests are being made from the organization's

FTP server to its Microsoft SQL server on port 1521, it is likely that the FTP server may be compromised, and as this behavior is an anomaly to the normal patterns on the network, the traffic is dropped or alerts are raised to the administrator.

18.4.1.3 *Stateful Protocol Analysis Detection*

Stateful Protocol Analysis Detection is a powerful mode of intrusion detection/prevention. IDS/IPS sensors are loaded with analysis of all possible TCP and UDP network payloads that consist of several protocols like HTTP, DNS, FTP, and so on. The right implementation of these protocols based on the RFCs (requests for comments) and known implementations is provided in the IDS/IPS sensors. If there are anomalous values or payloads in the protocols, then the IDS/IPS can detect the same and block/raise alerts based on the implementation. For instance, if HTTP request headers contain SQL-specific characters, indicating an SQL injection attack, the IPS would be able to detect and drop the packet, thereby protecting the target application. It is not enough if the IDS/IPS can do anomaly detection on network traffic on a single request-response basis. Attack traffic across multiple requests and responses without context would tend to be ignored or missed. Therefore, the stateful protocol inspection features for an IDS/IPS that performs stateful protocol analysis detection is required.

18.4.2 PCI Requirement: Intrusion Detection/Prevention System

PCI Requirement 11.4 states that Intrusion Prevention Systems/Detection Systems should be placed at the perimeter of the

---

[*] A zero-day attack is one that exploits a previously unknown vulnerability.

cardholder data environment and at critical points inside the cardholder data environment. This places a great deal of impetus on the network segmentation scope forming the perimeter of the cardholder data environment (PCI environment). For instance, if there is external connectivity to the PCI environment, then the IDS/IPS must be placed at the perimeter either before or after the Internet firewall or perimeter firewall. Additionally, the IDS/IPS must be placed at the areas that have cardholder data stored or processed. Cardholder data is usually stored in servers in the organization's server farm or data center, in which case the IDS/IPS must be placed in front of the servers to protect against potential attacks that could compromise said servers.

IDS/IPS may also ideally be placed at points where cardholder data is captured and transmitted internally. For instance, a merchant organization might have wireless POS billing systems all across the environment. The POS devices would utilize a wireless network to transmit all billing information to the internal system. The organization must place a firewall and IDS/IPS on the network connecting the wireless network to the internal network or the server subnet as

1. Cardholder data is captured largely over the wireless network.
2. Cardholder data is transmitted over the wireless network into the internal network zone.
3. Cardholder data is transmitted over a wireless network, which is an elevated security risk (that attackers can compromise) compared with wired networks.

The assessor needs to go by the risk of cardholder data exposure and the organization's risk-management practices (covered in Chapter 19) to identify the need for IDS/IPS at various points in the organization.

Placing an IDS/IPS is not nearly enough. The organization must ensure that IDS/IPS configurations are performed effectively and securely. The device must be able to prevent an intrusion or alert specific personnel in the event of an anomaly or possible data breach. The device must be configured to raise alerts on specific conditions that indicate an anomaly or a potential data breach. The assessor must ensure that the configuration of the IDS/IPS is carefully looked into and examined for this requirement.

A strong IDS/IPS is only as capable as its rule base, engines, and baselines. This is especially true for signature-based IDS/IPS systems, where attack signatures provide the IDS/IPS with the capability to detect and prevent an attack against the organization. However, if these signatures, engines, and baselines are not up to date, the device becomes nothing more than an appliance at the gateway passing packets. Most modern automated IDS/IPS devices perform an auto-update from the device vendor's signature databases. The device vendors update their signatures, baselines, and so on, very frequently, and if the IDS/IPS is configured to obtain its updates from the device vendor's servers, then the management aspect of this becomes minimal. However, in some cases, such as when the organization has deployed a manual or open-source IDS/IPS product, the signature and baseline updates have to be performed manually or with scripts that automate a manual process. This is similar to patch management, but requires more focus and speed in terms of updating critical devices like IDS/IPS devices.

18.5 FILE-INTEGRITY MONITORING: CRITICAL SYSTEM FILES AND CONFIGURATIONS

18.5.1 Attacks: Key System Files

When an attacker looks to compromise an organization's data, he/she usually attempts to gain access to the applications and operating system(s) of the target systems to pivot into other systems within the organization. The exploits usually modify (at least temporarily) certain files, processes, or executables in the applications, networks, and operating system. For instance, the popular exploit engine Metasploit provides the Meterpreter, which injects code into a process on a compromised system that will allow the attacker to run commands on the operating system, disable the antivirus (with sufficient privileges), capture keystrokes, enumerate network interfaces, perform port scans, and so on.

Holding true to the concept of defense-in-depth, if there is no control to detect such attacks against the operating system, then the organization might be the target of a more serious, prolonged, and deadly attack.

18.5.2 File-Integrity Monitoring: Critical System Files, Processes, and Content Files

File-integrity-monitoring tools are designed to constantly monitor a set of files for changes. In the event that any of these files are changed, the file-integrity-monitoring application triggers an alert to an administrator who might investigate the event further, based on the severity of the change and nature of the change. Host-based intrusion-prevention systems (HIPS) today usually have file-integrity-monitoring solutions built into the tool that alert an administrator when changes occur to critical files, configuration files, and content files on a target system.

File-integrity-monitoring systems must be deployed for critical systems like operating systems, network devices, applications, and databases in the PCI environment. For instance, if there has been a change in the registry of a Windows server, the file-integrity monitor (FIM) must be able to capture the change and alert the administrator. If there is a change in the rules of the Internet-facing firewall, the file-integrity monitor must be able to alert the administrator. Some of these changes might be required and justified. The organization must be able to define a baseline security configuration for monitoring the integrity of the systems. Based on this baseline, the FIM should provide information and alerts for various systems in the PCI environment. The PCI-DSS requires at least a weekly analysis of integrity monitoring based on the results provided by the file-integrity-monitoring application.

18.6 SUMMARY

Requirement 11 of the PCI-DSS deals with wireless network scanning, security testing, intrusion prevention, and file-integrity monitoring. In this chapter, we began with a detailed understanding of effective security testing for a PCI environment. We initially focused our attention on detection of rogue wireless networks (the focus of Requirement 11.1). PCI environments must be tested for rogue wireless networks in the environment. Wireless networks that are not authorized or required might cause data breaches, as attackers can connect into the network and gain access to the corporate network, and so on. We identified multiple ways of achieving this requirement with wireless scanning tools, physical verification, wireless IDS/IPS, and so on.

As part of Requirement 11.2, we had a deep look at vulnerability scanning. Beginning with the types of vulnerabilities, we then focused our attention on performing internal and external vulnerability scans for a PCI environment. We learned that vulnerability scans are most effective with a consistent and repeatable methodology. We dwelled on some of the finer points of multiple vulnerability-scanning tools like Nexpose and Nessus, including their features and reporting capabilities. Requirement 11.2.2 states that external-facing devices in a PCI environment must be subjected to vulnerability scans by approved scanning vendors (ASVs) every quarter. ASVs are scanning service providers accredited by the PCI-SSC that can perform this scan for PCI-compliant companies.

Requirement 11.3 specifies that internal and external penetration testing be performed annually. We learned that penetration testing provides very interesting and deep viewpoints, especially when a penetration attempt can be used as a pivot to the rest of the environment. We also identified multiple ways to perform penetration tests for large environments.

We then turned our focus toward Requirement 11.4, which states that organizations must deploy intrusion detection and/or prevention systems (IDS/IPS) in the PCI environment at the perimeter. We learned that there are different types of IDS/IPS devices that work on signatures, statistical anomaly detection, and so on. We also learned that IDS/IPS must be configured to alert personnel in the event of a suspected or actual attack.

The discussion of Requirement 11.5 delved into the all-important aspect of file-integrity monitoring for critical system files and configurations. File-integrity-monitoring tools like Tripwire, Afick, and so on, constantly monitor critical system files like the registry and directories for changes. In the event that changes are detected in these files, alerts are raised and sent to administrators, who can then inspect to see whether or not the change is legitimate. This ensures that attackers who affect the integrity of the end system are not left undetected by the system.

19

Requirement 12: Information Security Policies and Practices for PCI Compliance

The foundations of an enduring security practice rest with the organization's policies, procedures, and risk-management framework. Most of what we have discussed in the rest of the book is largely operational and technical security. However, there needs to be a binding frame that ensures that good security practices are consistent, repeatable, and measurable. This chapter focuses on Requirement 12 of the PCI-DSS. This requirement details the need for a binding security policy and operational security procedures. I will also explore an oft-forgotten but extremely important aspect of PCI compliance—risk assessment. We will understand how organizations should truly understand and enhance their security beyond the standard with a strong understanding and implementation of security risk. In this chapter, I will also delve into the important aspects of vendors and managing security of data shared with vendors and vendor compliance, all of which are essential for a company undergoing or maintaining PCI compliance. Finally, we will explore incident management in detail and its importance for any organization that handles cardholder data.

19.1 INFORMATION SECURITY POLICY: PCI REQUIREMENTS

19.1.1 Security Policy Definition

I cannot overstate the need for an information security policy. It is an essential requirement for any organization that wants to have a strong information security practice. An information security policy is a management directive on security for the organization. The information security policy outlines the overall need for security for the organization as well as the security requirements for the organization in different operational areas of security. The security policy is also meant to be a reference to the organization's security posture for their employees, partners, and customers. Requirement 12.1.1 of the PCI-DSS requires that the information security policy address all of the areas covered by the PCI-DSS. For instance, the security policy must link to operational procedures on physical security, network security, and other focus areas of the PCI-DSS requirements. An organization can ensure consistency and repeatability of its security practices by documenting its practices in security policies and procedures.

19.1.2 Risk Assessment: PCI Compliance

19.1.2.1 A Question of Adequacy

Until recently, the subject of risk assessment was mostly pushed to the background in a PCI compliance scenario. The standard was considered to be the guiding document, and every organizational implementation specifically focused on meeting the baseline specified by the standard. I find this to be a misguided stance, and most companies that adopt it find themselves in a position of risk. Several PCI-certified organizations have suffered security breaches in recent times.

The industry was largely divided over the PCI standards. A strong perception was that PCI was largely ineffective in addressing the deeper aspects of security that need to be applied to prevent security breaches against organizations that store, process, and transmit cardholder data. An interesting question emerged from this discussion: "Is compliance equal to security?" There were arguments on both sides of this

question. However, the more dominant side expressed that security was not equal to compliance. I agree with this stance.

An organization can only apply optimal security controls and practices with a sound understanding of *risk*. Risk can be defined simply as the potential impact of a threat capable of identifying and exploiting a given vulnerability. The organization needs to identify multiple risks against its critical information assets. With a sound understanding and ranking of risks and prioritization of risks, the organization must define an optimal risk-treatment plan and security controls to treat specific risks over time.

In all likelihood, the risks and security controls might be of a higher quality than the baselines of the PCI-DSS. This brings me back to my conviction that compliance does not equal security.

I see compliance as a structure and baseline for security controls for the organization. The organization cannot and must not entirely derive its security controls based on a compliance standard. Compliance standards like the PCI only focus on a subset of the organization's overall security risks. The organization must be able to identify, assess, and manage risks for its other critical information assets, apart from just cardholder data.

19.1.2.2 Risk Assessment: Process and Overview

Requirement 12.1.2 states that the organization must undergo an annual process of risk assessment, the purpose of which is to identify key risks, threats, vulnerabilities, and impacts to the organization's critical information assets in a structured and comprehensive manner. If done effectively, a risk assessment provides the organization with a detailed understanding of the impacts of potential risks, threats, and vulnerabilities. This provides the organization with adequate input to devise a risk-treatment strategy, define security controls, and implement these controls in a planned manner. Recall that we also detailed a risk-assessment methodology for an application in Chapter 13. We will now provide an overview of the risk-assessment process for an organization.

Before we commence with the risk-assessment overview for the organization, we must understand that there are multiple methodologies and techniques that are available to perform risk assessments. Some of the popular methodologies include the OCTAVE methodology from Carnegie Mellon University and CERT USA. The others include Standard ISO 27005 from the International Organization for Standardization and NIST SP 800-30 from the National Institute of Standards and Technology. Some organizations have their own risk assessment and management methodologies and frameworks. Organizations are not precluded by standards from using their own risk-assessment methodologies. However, their methodologies must have certain facets and dimensions that are required of a risk-assessment process. Another important consideration for the success of a risk-assessment process is that it must be driven by a team that performs the risk assessment using the same methodology across the organization.

Risk assessment consists of the following activities and processes:

- Identifying context
- Identifying critical information assets
- Profiling threats and vulnerabilities
- Evaluating and profiling risk
- Developing risk treatment plan

19.1.2.2.1 Identifying Context

An enterprise risk assessment should always be tied to the business activities of the organization. In a large organization, there may be multiple business units, departments, and so on. The risk-assessment team must first identify the business units, departments, and activities that are to be covered by the risk-assessment activity. Merchant organizations might have retail operations, finance, marketing, customer relations, human resources, and other departments. Banks might have a larger set of business units, departments, and activities. Third-party processors (TPPs) might have other operations, including card embossing, marketing, compliance, finance, etc.

19.1.2.2.2 Identifying Critical Information Assets

This is the most important activity in the risk assessment. Critical information assets are those sets of information or data that are critical for the organization. These are data sets that are essential for the organization's survival. Information assets are those that provide value to the organization and cause damage to the organization upon breach. Information assets may include data sets such as customer details (personal details), cardholder data, financial information, employee data, and so on. Broad data sets counting as information assets must be identified. Subsequently, specific data elements constituting the data sets must be identified and recorded as part of the risk assessment.

Additionally, along with the data sets, the various processes, people, containers, and technologies involved in the storage, processing, and transmission of the information assets must be identified. For instance, cardholder data might be captured as part of an e-commerce application, as part of a MOTO (mail order/telephone order) transaction, or as part of in-store POS (point of sale) billing. These activities and their touch points with cardholder data must be identified.

19.1.2.2.3 Profiling Threats and Vulnerabilities

Once we identify the information assets, it is important to understand how these assets can be compromised or breached. Compromise or breach of the assets must be captured in terms of confidentiality, integrity, or availability (CIA). I usually begin this process with an understanding of the various threats to the assets. The threats could range from physical threats like accidental disclosure of paper documents containing cardholder data by internal employees to more technology-oriented threats like injection attacks against the e-commerce application or card-management application. I particularly like to combine the OCTAVE methodology of threat profiling and Microsoft's STRIDE methodology for deeper threat modeling to arrive at a comprehensive list of threats. Once threats are identified, it is essential that vulnerabilities also be identified. Vulnerabilities may exist in the organization due to flaws in technology, implementation, processes, and so on. Vulnerabilities that exist across all these dimensions must be identified. This provides the risk-assessment team with a detailed view of the vulnerabilities that the organization has versus the threats that the organization can possibly be subjected to. Detailing vulnerabilities also provides an input into the organization's existing security controls.

An important consideration during threat analysis and vulnerability identification is to provide ranking/metrics to these threats and vulnerabilities based on impact and probability. For instance, an external threat agent being able to compromise the internal card-management system using Web services, or the API (application programming interface) might be a high-impact threat but with a low probability, which would have an impact on how the threat is ultimately ranked in the risk assessment.

19.1.2.2.4 Risk Evaluation

Once we have detailed information about the impacts and probabilities of threats and vulnerabilities, we must evaluate the risks to the critical information assets. Risks must be ranked based on the analysis of threats and vulnerabilities. Risk evaluation is a combination of asset value along with threat impact and probability as well as vulnerability impact and probability. The risk may be evaluated on a qualitative or a quantitative ranking system. Qualitative ranking systems usually rely on judgment and situational vagaries. They are usually captured as high, medium, or low or some similar scoring system. Quantitative evaluation systems rely on historical data, financial evaluation of assets, and so on. These are usually expressed in terms of monetary values.

19.1.2.2.5 Risk Treatment Plan

A risk treatment plan is the first step toward designing an effective security practice. The organization must define, design, and implement optimal security controls for its risks. There are four ways to handle risk, popularly called the four Ts of handling risk. They are:

Risk treatment/reduction: Risks cannot be mitigated completely. Applying security controls for specific risks reduces a risk to an acceptable level. There is always an element of residual risk after risk treatment and reduction, and if this risk is at an acceptable level, then the organization must elect to capture the residual risk and accept the same.

Risk transfer/sharing: Often, organizations elect to insure themselves against data breaches. In the event of a data breach, they are insured for a sum to help them tide over the data breach. This is typically known as transferring of risk, as the organization transfers its risk to another entity. Organizations also commonly share their data with service providers. In such cases, the organization might contractually bind the service provider with some responsibility over the protection of data. In such cases, the risk is shared between the principal and service provider.

Risk termination/avoidance: Risk termination is to terminate or avoid the subject that causes the risk. When the organization finds that a specific activity or data set causes some risk and they can do without that activity or data set, they can terminate that activity or data set to ensure that the risk is completely eliminated. For instance, when I was performing PCI consulting for a merchant, they were storing physical copies of customer cardholder details (scanned cards) in their stores for verification. They realized that they actually didn't need it. It was a major source of risk, as it had to be protected in all of their stores, which was a complex task. They decided that they should eliminate the storage of physical cardholder data

copies in their stores. They incinerated all of their existing physical copies and stopped the process, thereby *terminating* the risk of data breach of physical cardholder data assets.

Risk toleration/acceptance: Sometimes, the cost of treating and reducing a risk, transferring it, or avoiding it is much higher than the cost of accepting it. Sometimes, it might also happen that the organization is constrained against treating a risk in the near future. In such cases, organizations might elect to tolerate or accept the risk.

19.1.3 Annual Review: Policy and Risk-Management Framework

Risks are never stationary. Therefore, the organization's security practices and framework also cannot be unchanging. The PCI Requirement 12.1.3 states that the organizations must review the risk-assessment and security policy annually for any changes. Organizations might add, remove, or modify some of their business activities. A leading issuing processor that I have been working with has decided to add acquiring processing and white-label ATM management to their portfolio. This changes their risk posture considerably over this year, as they will have different business activities and additional critical information assets. Their risk assessment will have to take these changes into account. As the risk profiles change, the security policy would also change. The security policy also needs to be reviewed for changes annually to ensure that it reflects the organization's current security practice that has been evaluated against a structured risk-assessment methodology.

The assessor should consider reading risk assessments and security policies over multiple years to identify changes in the organization's risk profiles and security posture. The assessor must also verify that risk assessments are performed annually or upon major changes to an environment.

19.2 OPERATIONAL SECURITY PROCEDURES

19.2.1 Security Focus Areas

The PCI encompasses enterprise security across multiple dimensions, ranging from physical security to application security to network security. The organization might have scores of tasks that have to be performed by its employees/systems to ensure that their security practice is working and effective. Large organizations especially face this challenge, as they must achieve strong security over a distributed and complex environment. In such cases, documentation becomes essential to provide the organization's employees with knowledge of operational security practices that the organization must perform regularly and periodically. In all 12 requirements of the PCI-DSS, there have been documentation requirements that organizations must have in place apart from the implementation of the security controls. These are operational security procedures that detail the processes and operating steps for specific security implementations. For instance, an antivirus could be documented in an antivirus procedure that specifically describes the working of the organization's antivirus solution and its deployment across the organization. The procedure must also state the maintenance

and exception procedures to be handled in case of the antivirus deployment, and so on. Similarly, other aspects like patch management and network security must have operational security procedures that describe the organization's baseline in meeting security requirements.

19.2.2 Acceptable Usage Policies and Procedures

The organization must define acceptable usage policies on certain user-centric technology elements. For instance, the organization's e-mail system is a very important resource. If an employee used this medium to spread spam within the environment, then it would use the organization's valuable resources and inconvenience other users on the same e-mail system. Similarly, organizations have bandwidth restrictions on the Internet. If employees visit YouTube or other video sites through the day, it could choke the bandwidth and make the resource unavailable for other users in the network.

To regulate and define the usage policies and procedures for such technologies, the organization must define, disseminate, and implement acceptable usage policies. PCI Requirement 12.3 states that the organization must define, disseminate, and implement acceptable usage policies and procedures for such technologies as remote access, e-mail, Internet usage, removable electronic media, laptops, mobile devices, tablets, and so on.

The organization must document its acceptable usage policy/procedure. The document must consist of the following requirements:

19.2.2.1 List of Acceptable Technologies, Applications, and Devices

The organization must provide a list of approved technologies, applications, and devices. For instance, let's assume that the organization only wants to provide Microsoft Windows Remote Desktop Protocol (RDP) for remote access to user systems; in this case, the organization must mention only RDP as a viable remote-desktop technology, as opposed to VNC (virtual network computing), X11, and others.

19.2.2.2 Explicit Approval for Technology Usage

The acceptable-usage policy must enforce a condition where only users with a requirement to use these technologies are allowed to use them. For instance, in a BPO (business process outsourcing) operation that I was assessing recently, most of the call center agents didn't have access to e-mail. This was because company e-mail was not required for them. Only team leaders, who are required to report to management and to the client, were configured with e-mail on their laptops. Once a person is promoted to the team leader position, the project manager sends an e-mail to the IT department commissioning a new laptop for the team leader and e-mail access to the user as well. Often, companies achieve this with a role-based definition. Different roles in the organization have access to different technologies and abstractions.

19.2.2.3 Inventory and Labeling

The organization must maintain an inventory of devices and personnel information linked to those devices as an inventory. The list must be updated when there are changes. For instance, user David has been given a company laptop and a Blackberry. If David must change the laptop after a year and a new laptop is commissioned and provided to him, the inventory must reflect the same.

Devices and assets must also be labeled to indicate organizational ownership. The devices must be labeled with the name of the device, the owner, and contact information along with purpose.

19.2.2.4 Authentication for the Use of Technology

PCI-DSS Requirement 12.3.2 requires that all technologies used by the users of the organization must require the user to authenticate to the device or application. For instance, on desktops, laptops, and servers, the users must be required to authenticate to the device before gaining access to the system. When users access the organization over a remote connection, they must be required to authenticate. In the event that users utilize mobile phones and tablets, the organization must maintain enterprise configuration software like the Blackberry enterprise server and the iPhone configuration utility, where rules over device authentication, encryption, and so on, are specified.

19.2.2.5 Acceptable Usage

The acceptable usage for technology is a list of dos and don'ts for the use of technology in the organization. For instance, the organization might state that users must not download software and applications that are not approved by the IT Department, as downloading software from unknown publishers or developers might result in a malware outbreak. The organization might state that official e-mails must not be used for personal purposes. Acceptable usage defines the way technology—provided by the organization or utilized in the organization or approved to connect to the organization—must be used.

19.2.2.5.1 Approved Network Locations

Network locations are a major consideration, especially for a large company with several devices, applications, and so on. For instance, if an employee is accessing a corporate Web application from an Internet café, there is an obvious threat that the Internet café might have compromised machines where keyloggers and other malware would be installed. In such cases, the employee's username and password are almost sure to be compromised. Similarly, if the user is accessing the organization's network over a public WiFi connection, then it's possible that the user's credentials would be stolen by attackers sniffing network packets. The organization must disseminate information about approved network locations and disapproved network locations to provide clarity to the users on where they can use their devices to access the organization's resources.

19.2.2.5.2 Automatic Disconnect: Remote Access

Users connecting over remote-access technologies also have to be subjected to session idle timeouts and disconnects. Often, when service providers connect into the organization's network and their remote network session doesn't time out, it can result in a possible data breach if not closed. All remote-access technologies provide for session timeout capabilities. Citrix can be

configured to time out in the ICA (independent computing architecture) configuration or in the Windows Terminal Services Configuration. Microsoft RDP can be configured to time out in the Terminal Services Configuration. VNC servers can be configured to time out in the VNC server configuration. SSH can be configured to time out using the ClientAliveInterval setting in the sshd_config file. VPNs (virtual private networks) can be configured to time out after a session idle time using the VPN-session-timeout on Cisco devices. Similar techniques exist on other devices as well.

19.2.2.5.3 Activation of Remote Access: Only When Required

Vendors and third parties who access the organization's network remotely must be allowed to do so only when required, i.e., access to their remote-access credentials must only be activated when required and disabled when not required. This is a requirement because if a vendor has persistent access to the organization's network, potential data breaches might occur, especially if the vendor's environment is affected with malware or if a malicious/negligent employee at the vendor's location maintains persistent access to the organization's network that handles cardholder data.

19.2.2.5.4 Disable Copy and File Transfer: Remote Connections

One of the dangers of allowing users to access the PCI environment remotely is that cardholder data might get copied outside the organization's PCI environment. The organizations must define controls to prevent cardholder data from being copied-pasted or otherwise transferred over a remote connection. This can be achieved on major remote access technologies. On

Remote Desktop, group policies on drive redirection and copy-paste disabling can be defined. For Citrix, the ICA configuration can prevent copy-paste with disabling the clipboard mapping functionality. The usage of rssh (restricted secure shell) can prevent file transfers over SSH (secure shell).

19.3 SECURITY ROLES AND RESPONSIBILITIES

19.3.1 Documentation: Roles and Responsibilities

Requirement 12.4 of the PCI-DSS states that the organization must document security roles and responsibilities as part of its information security policy. Defining security roles and responsibilities is very important for the organization. This ensures that there are multilevel checks and authorization for any decision or change impacting security. Let's assume that the human-resources manager also controls the active directory and human-resources-management application. In this scenario, with a malicious manager, the manager can create dummy employee records in the human-resource files, create active directory credentials for them, and enroll them in the company human-resource-management system (HRMS) application, thereby creating all of the records for the legitimate but nonexistent employee. The manager might be routing all of the dummy employee paychecks to multiple individuals and making a great deal of money from the fraud, thereby causing financial losses to the company.

It is also important to segregate duties in information security management, as specific roles provide individuals with specific areas of focus and expertise. The team or individual managing the firewall cannot possibly perform application security code review. Security is a highly focused industry and is getting more specialized by the day. It is important to have specific roles and individuals with specific skills fulfilling these roles.

The information security policy must state that security roles and responsibilities have been divided among multiple user roles within the organization.

19.3.1.1 The Chief Information Security Officer

The importance of the role of a chief information security officer (CISO) cannot be overstated. The CISO is usually the apex security authority in any organization. The CISO handles the overall security responsibility for matters involving data security and enterprise security. PCI-DSS Requirement 12.5 states that security responsibility should be formally assigned to a CISO or other member of the management staff who is knowledgeable on matters of security. Sometimes, companies merge the role of the CTO/CIO (chief technology officer/chief information officer) and the CISO. While this is not precluded by the standard, I highly advise against this kind of structure. The CTO/CIO naturally has IT as a responsibility, and IT acquires primary focus, often at the cost of security. This automatically ensures that the organization's security posture does not improve and possibly remains in a bad state. Additionally, the CTO as a CISO is a tremendous conflict of interest, as the CISO should be an entity ensuring that the ills of nonsecure IT development, deployment, and maintenance are corrected through a structured process.

19.3.1.2 Distribution of Policies and Procedures and Monitoring of Security Alerts

Apart from the formal assignment and designation of security responsibilities to the CISO, PCI-DSS Requirements 12.5.1 and 12.5.2 focus on the distribution of security policies, procedures, and alerts. There must be clear responsibility assigned to documentation, management, and dissemination of security policies and procedures. This is important, because employees, partners, and customers of the organization must be aware and be following security policies and procedures when in contact with the organization. This is the only way that the organization can ensure that its security framework is strong and in effect. Security documentation is usually under the purview of the CISO or the management representative for information security. These documents must be maintained in version control and must be selectively disseminated to the right people. For instance, the information security policy and access-control policy/procedures might be given to all employees, but the antivirus policy/procedure and the network security policy/procedure may only be disseminated to the network-management team or the network security management, as the case may be.

Another important consideration for security roles and responsibilities is that of security alerts. It is natural that a PCI-compliant organization must have multiple monitoring systems for logs, file integrity monitoring, antivirus, patch management, and so on. Security alerts are likely to be raised by the systems during the occurrence of a security event or incident. In such cases, there must be specific responsibilities

that are defined for people to monitor these systems and to distribute the results of the monitoring, either as reports or security alerts to the right people to ensure that the right action is taken. For instance, if an attacker is attempting to trigger a denial-of-service (DOS) attack against the Apache Web servers in the organization, there must be an individual/designated team to monitor such attacks, and they must alert the responsible team, such as an application-management team, the business owners and the CISO, and so on, to ensure that swift action is taken to control and correct the effect of the attack attempt or possible security breach. This ties in heavily with incident management and incident response, which we will cover during the later sections of this chapter.

19.3.1.3 User Management: Roles and Responsibilities

User management is a very important security aspect. It controls the perimeter access to any system (as user authentication is usually the perimeter control to any system). Users and their profiles must be created, updated, and deleted based only on a structured, documented, and consistent process as opposed to an ad hoc and haphazard process. One of the essential elements of this is to ensure that specific individuals in the company are authorized to manage user accounts and user profiles based on a documented process.

In several large companies that I have seen, they have dedicated user-management teams for regular employees. Recently, I was consulting with a bank where the human resources personnel would send a list of user accounts to be created on the company's directory server.

The user's basic details would be included in the ticket or communication raised by the human resources personnel. This communication would also be transmitted to the physical security officer in charge of physical access. In addition to the human resources communication, the manager in charge of the specific individual(s) would also communicate the user-creation action to the user-management team and the physical access control team. The team in charge of user management would create the user account on the directory on a specific business unit to which the user would be attached. This would automatically create the user's e-mail account and provide access to internal company applications as well. When the user changed his/her profile (like moving to another team or getting promoted), the user's role would be updated through the same communication to the user management through human resources and the supervising business manager. When the user separates from the organization, the user must obtain clearance from his or her supervisor, human resources, and the security department, immediately after which the user's account is disabled and deleted after 90 days. As you may gather, there is a controlled process for user account management that is required when organizations are dealing with data as sensitive as cardholder data.

Requirements 12.5.4 and 12.5.5 state that the responsibilities for user management must be clearly defined and followed. Apart from user management, access to data must be monitored and controlled as well as through formal responsibility assignment.

19.4 PEOPLE SECURITY PRACTICES

19.4.1 Security Awareness Training and Monitoring

"You are only as strong as your weakest link." This is a popular statement that most people (especially in security) have heard. When people mention this statement in the information security industry, it usually has to do with the problem of "people security." One can have the best security infrastructure, security monitoring, and controls for availability. However, if people, either due to negligence or lack of awareness, commit to actions that cause data breaches, there is really *nothing* that even the most security-paranoid organization can do about it.

Organizations must impart security education to their employees. Employees must systematically be taught the tenets of security as well as the organization's policy on security and security practices that will help them stay protected not only at work, but in their daily lives as well.

Requirement 12.6 states that organizations must train their employees (in the PCI environment) on information security and cardholder data security upon hire and on an annual basis.

Security awareness is a powerful practice that, in my experience, is seldom taken seriously. Organizations usually roll out a simple training program that consists of some basic security practices like passwords and physical access that is not really up to the mark or with the times. Today's threats include social engineering with techniques like spear-phishing, browser-based attacks, and so on, that users are really not equipped to handle. The organization must constantly look to provide up-to-date security awareness training to its employees to protect against the human factor in a data breach.

The PCI requirements also state that security awareness needs to be performed upon hiring the employee and annually thereafter. Some of the best companies that I have worked with in this regard have security-awareness training during the employee's induction training. Subsequently, the organization circulates multiple e-mails, online training programs, presentations, videos, and quizzes throughout the year to ensure that employees are always kept vigilant about security. They are forced to see it as a continuous process and not as a single event that happens annually.

Some companies that I work with have also performed specific social-engineering tests by setting up phishing e-mails and simulating scams or online frauds to demonstrate the devastating nature of a successful phishing attempt. We also train the employees on how they can spot illegitimate e-mails and communication.

PCI requires that employees attend security awareness trainings on an annual basis after hire. As part of Requirement 12.6.2, employees must also attest that they have read and understood the company security policies and procedures. For this, I would recommend that companies roll out quizzes for security awareness that actually test awareness and obtain written or online confirmation (through an accept button) that they have read and understood the organization's security policies and procedures. This is meant as a measure to attest and prove that the organization's employees are trained periodically on information security and cardholder data security.

The security awareness training programs to be rolled out by a PCI-compliant organization must focus on the information-security practices and cardholder-data security practices that are to be followed by the employees. Especially for third-party processors, for banks, and for merchants who deal with cardholder data on an almost daily basis, inclusion of cardholder data becomes essential to prevent cardholder data breaches.

19.4.2 Employee Background Verification

PCI-DSS Requirement 12.7 states that organizations must perform employee background verification prior to hiring a new employee into the organization. This is meant as a preventive measure to ensure that undesirables and people with a known criminal or otherwise tainted record are not allowed into the critical PCI environment. Checks such as reference checks, criminal checks, employment history, and so on, must be conducted to ensure that organizations do not hire the wrong people into an environment that deals with cardholder data.

In many countries, especially in the Middle East, the police or the ministry of defense automatically perform background checks. This is useful, as their checks are very detailed and more encompassing than regular background checks. Some countries prohibit certain checks from being conducted against its citizens. In such cases, the PCI would be overruled by the law of the land. Many countries like India have professional agencies and government agencies that perform background checks on corporate employees. These checks range from criminal checks to employment checks to educational qualification checks to prove that the candidate is legitimately qualified.

The PCI also states that for some personnel like store billing clerks, and so on, or individuals who handle a single card at a time for transaction facilitation do not have to be checked for antecedents, as this would be cumbersome for the company to achieve, and the risk would also be limited.

19.5 VENDOR MANAGEMENT AND PCI COMPLIANCE

19.5.1 Vendors: Data Sharing and Risk Management

Companies handling cardholder data often have multiple service providers that render services to the organization in multiple ways. These include back-office data-processing providers, backup providers, physical data storage service providers, managed service providers, cloud service providers, Web-hosting service providers, business process outsourcing companies, software development companies, and so on.

Sometimes companies have to share their cardholder data with their service providers due to their business process requirements. Several merchant organizations outsource their customer service to business process outsourcing (BPO) companies in India, the Philippines, and elsewhere. These BPO call-center agents perform collections, payment management, accounts receivable, order management for the clients over the telephone, e-mail, and so on. In such cases, cardholder data by default is shared with these companies. There are some ways to reduce scope in terms of cardholder data sharing with service providers, such as the use of IVR (interactive voice response), and so on, but it is not always possible.

Requirement 12.8 of the PCI-DSS deals exclusively with cardholder data security aspects when said data is shared with service providers and third parties. The following are requirements of Requirement 12.8 with reference to service providers:

- A list of service providers must be maintained by the organization. Usually organizations maintain lists of service providers where the organization shares data. In the event that the data shared with service providers constitutes cardholder data, then the PCI-DSS requirements apply to these service providers.

- The organization must maintain agreements with service providers to acknowledge that the service provider is responsible for the security of the cardholder data that is shared with them. In certain cases, where the organization's key business processes involve cardholder data, the organization must contractually enforce PCI-DSS compliance and certification on the service provider. Several organizations contractually impose PCI-DSS on their service providers to ensure that their certification process is intact.

- The organization must have an established due-diligence or audit process to evaluate the service provider for security over the sensitive data that is shared with them. Some of the mature organizations I have worked with conduct a risk assessment of the vendors they are engaging with, perform an assessment against the key points of risk, and submit evaluation reports to establish the basis on which the organization engages with the vendor.

- The organization must take steps to monitor the vendor's PCI-DSS compliance on an annual basis. In some cases, where QSAs (qualified security assessors) have performed an audit and certified the vendor organization, the vendor organization must be able to submit the PCI certification on an annual basis from the QSA. In other cases, the vendor must have submitted a self-assessment questionnaire (SAQ) and attestation of compliance (AOC) as evidence of PCI-DSS certification and compliance.

19.6 INCIDENT MANAGEMENT AND INCIDENT RESPONSE

19.6.1 Incident-Response Plans and Procedures

Incident management is a critical requirement for any organization handling sensitive information, especially cardholder data. Incidents have to be handled professionally, efficiently, swiftly, and with a focus on improvement in the future. Security incidents are those activities that result in a potential loss of or adverse effect on confidentiality, integrity, and availability of critical data within the organization. An incident could range from an employee misusing company resources to a potential breach where an external attacker has possibly compromised the organization's database servers. The organization must document the incident-management practices as part of a policy/procedure. Good incident response is highly dependent on performing all of the following activities effectively:

Preparation: Preparation for an incident response begins with a plan, a trained team, specific contact and legal information, and relevant scenarios.

Identification: The incident, in order to be contained and eradicated, must be identified by an incident-response team that must be trained in the processes of identification. This phase involves identifying the root cause of the incident and connected events.

Containment: The first priority in an incident-response situation is to contain the incident at hand. The incident-response team takes containment steps to ensure that the problem or security incident does not get worse. Containment is mostly from a short-term perspective where the problem is temporarily fixed to provide the incident-response team with time to launch an eradication measure.

Eradication: Eradication involves corrective actions that remove the root cause of the security incident. For instance, if malware has infected the environment, an eradication (or corrective) action would be the act of removing malware from all systems.

Recovery: Once an incident has occurred, the recovery phase must focus on returning the organization to normalcy in a safe manner while minimizing losses and damage to the organization. Actions like restoration of off-site backups are examples of recovery actions. Recovery must also include monitoring to ensure that similar security incidents do not arise.

Lessons learned: Security incidents have something to teach the organization. The incident-response team must document their entire process extensively.

After the incident has been concluded, the team must convene and document the entire incident in an incident register. Subsequently, the team must identify the lessons learned and improvements that the organization must now deploy to ensure that the possibility of such incidents in the future is minimized.

19.6.1.1 Elements of Incident-Response Plan

Incident management is a continuous process that is another security framework within the organization. The organization must design an incident-management process based on its data security and commensurate with its risk. One of the key elements for successful incident management is the preparation. Preparation involves developing a practical incident-response plan that takes the following aspects into consideration.

One of the key aspects of a well-prepared incident-management procedure is to have defined roles, responsibilities, communications, and contact strategies. In the event that the organization suffers from an incident, there must be a clearly defined set of roles and responsibilities for the management of the incident. First, there must be a contact list with the names and numbers of people to be contacted on the reporting of an incident. In the event that a breach is confirmed, there must be a communication protocol with the payment brands and affected customers. Notification to law enforcement and regulatory agencies must also be planned.

Incident management is usually driven by a security incident-response team (SIRT) within the organization. This team must be trained on incident management, including visualizing and handling multiple incident scenarios that the organization could face, based on its business and risk profiles.

Another aspect of preparation for incidents is to have some incident scenarios documented by the organizations. The process of handling the incidents must be clearly documented. In the event that an incident of a certain nature plays out, the SIRT is equipped to handle it, as they already have the details of how to handle such incidents. Organizations must also use incident scenarios and learning from past incidents to ensure that they are equipped to handle future incidents with more efficiency and effectiveness.

An important input for an incident-response process is the organization's business-continuity and disaster-recovery procedures. If the security incident elevates to a disaster scenario, then these plans can be invoked. For instance, if the organization suffers from a DOS attack, it might be able to invoke a disaster recovery plan where servers at a different location are activated and DNS (domain name server) entry points toward the new servers.

Loss of data due to an incident is a very real and dangerous scenario. The organization must incorporate data backup procedures for critical data during an incident to ensure that loss of data is minimized. Off-site backups must be maintained to ensure that loss of data to a primary processing facility does not cripple the organization from a data availability standpoint.

The incident-response plan must incorporate the appropriate legal requirements for reporting data breaches. For instance, the California State Breach Security Act (SB-1386) requires a company to disclose a breach to the affected parties.

The incident-response plan must cover the key systems and applications that are essential for the operations of the PCI environment. In the event of a security incident or a business disaster, the organization must be able to continue with operations in the shortest time possible.

The incident-response plan must be tested annually, based on simulations or scenarios with the SIRT.

19.6.1.2 Incident-Response Success Factors

PCI-DSS Requirement 12.9 mentions certain aspects of incident response that, in my opinion, are critical success factors for an incident-response effort, apart from being part of the PCI requirements. They are as follows:

- Certain people in the organization must be designated to handle incidents and be available 24/7 in the light of an incident. This should ideally be a designated security incident-response team (SIRT). I would recommend that this should be a cross-functional team with people from multiple disciplines. It is essential that some IT and security representation be present in this team.
- The SIRT has to be trained in incident response. Large organizations have mature incident-management training programs as part of their security framework. However, there are several courses by reputed institutes like SANS (SysAdmin, Audit, Networking, and Security) that provide incident-response training. Training ensures that the SIRT will be more equipped and better prepared to handle the rig-

ors presented by a challenging security incident.

- We have already discussed the need to include security monitoring systems as a critical input. Monitoring systems provide invaluable details on security incidents within an organization. Incident response must derive as input, alerts, and logs from monitoring systems like intrusion prevention systems (IPSs), file-integrity monitoring systems, Web application firewalls, antivirus systems, patch-management systems, firewalls, host-based intrusion prevention systems, application logs, and so on.

19.7 SUMMARY

Requirement 12 of the PCI-DSS focuses greatly on risk management, security documentation, people-security practices, and incident management. The requirement begins with the need for an organization to maintain an information security policy. An information security policy is a master document that is the management directive for the security framework in the organization and the PCI environment. The information security policy must (a) account for all the PCI-DSS requirements and (b) be derived based on a strong risk-assessment process. Risk assessment is an important process for PCI compliance, as it is a reminder that security is beyond compliance. A structured risk-assessment process provides detailed insights into the organization's critical information assets, threats, vulnerabilities, and possible controls to handle these risks. We learned some techniques and practices using various structured risk assessments that can be performed effectively in the PCI environment.

Requirement 12.2 states the need to maintain operating security procedures to ensure consistency and process in handling operational security practices like patch management, antivirus management, and so on. Requirement 12.3 delves deeply into the need for acceptable usage policies/procedures. Organizations must define the specific technologies and practices that must be adopted when technology is being utilized by the company. The requirement states that acceptable usage procedures must be defined for the use of technologies like remote access technologies, authentication, network locations and devices, mobile devices like laptops and smartphones, and so on. The rule of thumb is that acceptable usage policies/procedures must be defined for any technology, device, or practice that has implications on cardholder data security.

Requirement 12.5 states that roles and responsibilities must be defined clearly for the information security functions of the organization. Clearly defined roles and responsibilities ensure that there is clarity, specificity, and accountability for the organization's stakeholders. A very important role for information security is that of the chief information security officer (CISO). The CISO is critical in establishing, maintaining, and enhancing the information security framework within the organization. This person must be clearly responsible and accountable for security-critical items like incident response, security alerts, implementation of security measures across the PCI environment, and so on.

Requirement 12.6 deals with the human element of information security. Security controls are often powerless if users are unaware of security controls and measures to protect themselves against social-engineering attacks and other such attacks that cannot be prevented by technical security controls.

Requirement 12.7 states that employees in the PCI environment must be screened for their background history. Reference checks, background checks, criminal background checks, and so on, may be conducted to validate that the employee is not an undesirable individual.

Requirement 12.8 is the service provider requirement of the PCI-DSS. Organizations that share cardholder data with service providers must maintain a list of said providers. The PCI compliance of these service providers must be tracked by the organization regularly. Other measures for securing data with service providers include agreements, due diligence, audits, and so on.

The final requirement under Requirement 12 (12.9) is that of incident management and incident response. The organization must be trained to handle incidents, especially those that involve cardholder data. Incident response must handle confidentiality, integrity, and availability considerations during the incident-management process.

20

Beyond PCI Compliance

An organization begins a journey when it achieves PCI compliance. It is usually a starting point for a continuing path to information security and assurance. It is very important for the organization to understand the potential challenges and effectively address them after they achieve successful PCI compliance. In this chapter, we briefly discuss the challenges and success factors that the organization must be aware of to maintain compliance and achieve optimum information security for the enterprise.

20.1 MAINTAINING PCI COMPLIANCE: THE CHALLENGE

20.1.1 The Challenge: The Dilemma Produced by Success

When the organization achieves PCI compliance, it has achieved success in meeting a highly rigorous and competent security standard. However, this is no indication of success in the future. Information security is not an event, but a process. In this process, there are several challenges that the organization must meet in order to remain secure and compliant. In fact, all too often, I see companies that are PCI certified and compliant be breached by simple attacks that could have been easily prevented if they had maintained their security program and rigor throughout. Also, it is important to remember that security is *not* compliance. Compliance is a by-product of a strong information security program. If a security program of an organization doesn't evolve and improve over time, it is likely to have an adverse impact at some point in the future of the organization. Some of the challenges I see are as follows:

- The information problem
- The technology challenge
- A shift in management attitudes

20.1.1.1 The Information Problem

One of the main challenges in remaining secure and compliant is the information problem. Organizations are very coordinated and orchestrated when they are looking to achieve compliance and certification for the first time. However, after the initial certification and the highs that it provides, they tend to wane on their security program. This is not helped by the fact that assessors and internal auditors also tend to go easy on companies in subsequent assessments and audits. This is primarily caused due to lack of accountability and information. Organizations that have strong security programs have these two traits. They have accountability from a group or an individual for security and compliance. They empower this group/person to make decisions and ensure that the security framework and compliance are met. However, this group or person is accountable for the security program or compliance program. Failing that, there are consequences. This group/person is also responsible for getting the right information, at the right time, from the right people to track the state of security and compliance in the organization. However, I have seen that, more often than not, accountability and information are both sorely lacking for an organization that has achieved information security maturity and PCI compliance and is maintaining the same over time.

The information challenge stems from the fact that information updates that are supposed to be present from different stakeholders are not available or are not available in time. Hence, things get delayed, and security is pushed to the backseat. However, information delivered in time and effectively usually has a way of pushing even the most dormant people into action.

Organizations must look at deploying information-correlation tools like GRC (governance, risk, and compliance) applications, project-management tools, and so on, to maintain tight control over the security and compliance state of the organization on a continuing basis.

20.1.1.2 The Technology Challenge

Technology evolves constantly. Organizations are continually grappling with changes in technology. For instance, cloud computing has become a technology paradigm that most companies seem to want to adopt. However, the migration to such technologies is not well evaluated or researched; hence, organizations somehow forget the security impetus that should be there for their technology initiatives. This creates a scenario that might have serious security implications for an organization. With the extremely dynamic nature of technology change, there are always new vulnerabilities and security flaws being unearthed. For instance, several vulnerabilities have been found on the Web-programming Ruby platform that have rendered several Web applications vulnerable by default, just because of a platform vulnerability.

Organizations that have secured their infrastructure and their technology components cannot afford to take things lightly on a continuing basis. They must stay vigilant to ensure that their security framework takes technology risk into perspective.

20.1.1.3 Management Attitude

I am always receiving complaints about management. Some of them have merit, and some do not. More than 25% of the complainants tell me that management wants to forget about security once it achieves compliance. They report that there is a great deal of support from management until PCI certification is achieved. However, once the certification is achieved, management automatically believes that the processes are self-sustaining and largely static, with few changes and evolution cycles. This is untrue. Change is constant. The organization's risk might change, technology paradigms might change, the scale and sphere of operations might change, and so on. This requires security frameworks to be constantly reevaluated and improved.

Management must view security and compliance as business enablers and ensure that these enabling functions receive their due by way of resources and allocations to ensure that their business and their critical data are not at risk.

20.2 SUCCESS FACTORS FOR CONTINUING PCI COMPLIANCE

20.2.1 A Change of Attitude

Security is a process, not an event. Organizations must ingrain this philosophy into all their employees. People should view security and compliance as a continuous process that requires consistent maintenance over time, every day, day after day.

20.2.2 Deep Understanding of Risk and Its Application

Most organizations ignore risks to their own peril. It is absolutely essential to evaluate risk regularly (at least annually). PCI mandates a risk assessment on an annual basis. An annual risk assessment, if done correctly, provides an opportunity to identify and analyze threats that have thus far not been evaluated. Additionally, it provides an opportunity to review existing controls and the effectiveness of these controls. It provides the invaluable opportunity to improve the existing security framework to include a better quality of preventive, detective, and corrective controls.

20.2.3 The CISO

The chief information security officer (CISO) plays a critical role in the organization's security framework. The CISO must be empowered to manage the organization's security framework and practices. Needless to say, the CISO must be one who is well versed in information security practices, technology paradigms, and the organization's business and culture. The CISO must tread a thin line between security and enterprise objectives, ensuring at all times that the organization's security program does not hinder its business objectives and growth prospects.

Also, I have noticed in several organizations that the CISO invariably reports to the CIO or the CTO of a company. This usually engenders a conflict of interest, as these officers are usually in positions of implementation. In such cases, security usually gets lower priority than it requires. The CISO should ideally report to the audit committee or the board. The CISO must also be included in key business and strategy meetings to examine the impact of information security on the organization's initiatives.

20.3 SUMMARY

In this chapter, we briefly explored the factors that could influence the continuing compliance of an organization after it initially achieves PCI compliance. We discussed some of the challenges in maintaining PCI compliance. A significant challenge is the information challenge, where the organization must create accountability and provide information to key stakeholders to effectively manage the organization's security initiatives. We also explored the role of technology change, vulnerabilities, and so on, in the organization's compliance and security challenges. We learned that management attitudes must address improvement and evolution of the security framework within the organization. Management must not view security as a cost center, but as a business enabler that adds value to the business; hence, it must be improved and evolved as a subsystem within the organization.

Finally, we explored the critical success factors for continuing PCI compliance. Significant factors include a sound understanding and assessment of risk and recognizing the importance of the chief information security officer (CISO) in an organization.

Addendum

WHAT'S NEW IN PCI-DSS V 3.0?

At the time of writing this book, the PCI-SSC (Security Standards Council) released the PCI-DSS v 3.0 and the latest standard is currently in effect across the world of PCI Compliance. Given the update, I have developed a separate section dedicated to exploring some of the changes between PCI v 2.0 which you have read throughout this book and PCI v 3.0 that is the latest release. Please note that most of the changes are not major digressions from the original standard. They are what I would call in the family of "enhancements" or "clarifications".

A1 – Current Network Diagram with Cardholder Data Flows

PCI v 3.0 has brought about a slight change in Requirement 1.1.3 of the previous PCI-DSS v 2.0 standard. In the current avatar of the PCI v 3.0, Requirement 1.1.3 is relating to network diagrams of the PCI Scoped Environment. The new requirement mandates that the organization must maintain the current network diagram of the PCI Scoped Environment that highlights the cardholder data flow across the network. This means that the inbound and outbound flow of cardholder data into and out of the PCI Scoped Environment must be highlighted in the Network Diagram. This has already been explained with the same intent and an illustration in Chapter 8 of this book.

A2 – Inventory of System Components in the PCI Scoped Environment

Sometimes, organizations do not maintain a list of 'assets' or system components that are being utilized for a specific environment. Some companies maintain 'asset lists' where all their workstations, servers, software components, network components are maintained in software or as part of several Excel worksheets. However, there is usually no specific list maintained for the PCI Scoped Environment. In PCI-DSS v 3.0, Requirement 2.4 deals with this area of focus. The Requirement mandates that the organization must maintain an inventory of all system components deployed in the PCI Scoped Environment or Cardholder Data Environment. This inventory must consist of all system components, i.e. workstations, servers, software components, laptops, mobile devices, network devices, other hardware devices and so on. I will call this inventory as an 'asset list'.

I would suggest the following:

- Maintain a list of assets (system components) that are being utilized in the PCI Scoped Environment.
- This list of assets must ideally be linked to your Risk Assessment, where each asset has a unique risk ranking, scores on confidentiality, integrity and availability, etc.
- This asset list must be updated as and when there are changes to said assets or the constituents in the PCI Scoped Environment. An example of an asset list is given in Table A1-1.

This requirement has been created to ensure that all system components that are part of the PCI Scoped environment are captured in the inventory and secured with intent and rigour commensurate with standard and the organization's risk metrics. This ensures that components are not missed out (thereby rendered potentially non-secure).

A3 – Malware Protection for Uncommon System Components

There are several system components that are not prone to common virus or malware attacks. This could be for multiple reasons. One of the reasons may be simply due to the lack of scale of said operating systems or software components, which may be unfeasible for malware authors to create malware compromising these systems. The other reason could be that these systems or software could be inherently robust to malware attacks, thereby negating most attack possibilities through malware. However, the world of malware is never stagnant. If anything, it is constantly at work. New exploits are discovered and published every day. Security researchers and Blackhats are constantly in pursuit of the latest vulnerabilities in systems that may be compromised through malware. For instance, for a long time, SAP systems were not targeted. However over the last few years, there have been several vulnerabilities identified and released for these systems, hence changing the entire security threat landscape for these systems. PCI-DSS has introduced Requirement 5.1.2 for systems that are not commonly affected by malware. The requirement mandates that organizations, while may be unable to find Anti-Virus or Anti-Malware products for certain systems, they must be prepared and ready to act in the event of a malware outbreak on these systems.

The best way to achieve this is for the security team to receive information from various anti-virus vendor companies, security research organizations and vulnerability database feeds like OSVDB and vFeed. When an organization subscribes to these information messages, they are constantly updated on the latest security threats to their assets. For instance, if there is a new malware on BSD, these services would receive and disseminate information related to these vulnerabilities. The organization can take adequate steps to add or deploy compensating controls to curtail attack possibilities to the system.

A4 – Enhanced List of Secure Coding Guidelines

Previously, a great deal of focus in the PCI world was given to (Open Web Application Security Project) OWASP Security Coding Guidelines. This created a (wrong) perception that OWASP was the only authoritative

TABLE A1-1

Example of an Asset List/Inventory of System Components

S. No.	Serial No.	Asset Code	Asset Name	IP Address	Confidentiality	Integrity	Availability	Final Value	Risk Ranking	Impact	Probability
1	062PA	SVR001	Oracle Database	10.96.2.1	3	3	3	3	High	High	Medium
2	10AAD	SVR002	File Server	10.96.2.2	3	3	3	3	High	High	Medium
3	99K2F	SVR003	R & D Server	10.96.2.3	3	3	3	3	High	High	Medium
4	9954DF1	SVR004	Antivirus Server	10.96.2.4	3	3	3	3	High	High	Medium
5	SGH8HT4K8E	SVR005	Email Server	10.96.2.5	3	3	3	3	High	High	Medium

source of secure coding guidelines. It also additionally created another wrong perception that secure coding guidelines were only to be used for Web Applications. However, it is well known that the PCI world has several applications that are used in the PCI Scoped Environment of a typical organization. These include web applications and non-web applications like desktop applications, scheduler applications, internal reporting applications and so on. It is essential that these applications also be developed with secure coding guidelines. For instance, if there is an application that has been authored in the C Programming Language, OWASP Coding Guidelines would not serve as the right reference point. There are specific guidelines like the CERT Guidelines for developing secure applications in the C Programming Language. Also, there would be language specific recommendations on secure coding in several resources like SANS, CERT, NIST, etc. Requirement 6.5 of the PCI-DSS v 3.0 mandates that developers are to be trained in and required to use secure coding guidelines from multiple best practices including OWASP, CERT, NIST, SANS and so on.

A5 – Clarifications for Multiple Authentication Factors

Requirement 8.6 of the PCI-DSS v 3.0 has required the same level of controls for authentication factors like smart cards, tokens and biometric authentication, as has been applied for passwords. Similar to passwords, these factors of authentication should not allow sharing between multiple users. The authentication factor must be tied to an individual user. Additionally, the requirement stipulates that only the intended user must gain access to the system.

A6 – Protection of Physical POS Devices

The PCI-DSS v 3.0 has added a specific requirement at Requirement 9.9 for the physical protection of physical payment card capture devices. This requirement is a very valid requirement in the light of the recent merchant cardholder data breaches that have occurred against merchants like Target, Neiman Marcus and so on. Attackers hae also begun tampering with physical POS devices by tampering with the device or by compromising the device at the processor layer. Some merchants have had malware compromise their POS devices. Physical inspection of a Point of Sale (POS) device is seldom done, due to the assumed assurance that these devices are safe. This is a common problem with ATMs where attackers may be able to insert or overlay skimming equipment in the card slot and skim card information from the bank's customers. They can use this information to clone cards and sell card information on the black market.

The requirement stipulates the following controls that organizations must follow to stay protected against physical POS device manipulation or tampering:

- Maintaining a list of devices.
- Periodic inspection of devices – Physical inspections, UV light inspections, XRay Inspections and so on. Serial number verifications and so on.

Additional controls include training for employees to watch for suspicious activity around POS terminals. Reporting of suspicious behavior and Incident Response relating to incidents involving tampering/manipulation of POS devices.

Training must also be specifically given to security teams to facilitate the inspection of POS terminals and devices to identify signs of tampering/manipulation.

A7 – Penetration Testing for Segmentation and Scope Reduction

Penetration Testing has been a key requirement under PCI-DSS. However, there has been a slight addition to the requirement in PCI-DSS v 3.0, Requirement 11.3. The requirement stipulates that there must be an established methodology for Penetration Testing. The second aspect of the change in the requirement is with respect to the Penetration testing for effectiveness of scoping and segmentation.

I have often experienced that the quality of a Penetration Test by several companies and individuals claiming to be Penetration testers, has much to be desired. Often, I have seen Penetration Testing being reduced to a mere 'hygiene' exercise where the company being tested is only interested in getting a clean report and the company testing them is only too keen to comply to such demands. Results, in such cases would obviously be of a poor quality. I think this is a welcome move by the PCI-SSC by insisting that Penetration Testing be performed with a specific methodology as a reference point. For instance, methodologies like the NIST SP800-115, Penetration Testing Execution Standard (PTES), Open Source Security Testing Methodology Manual (OSSTMM) are examples of some quality Penetration Testing methodologies out there. I personally love the PTES as it is written and created by a group of serious Penetration Testers who have been 'in the trenches' and have provided great inputs to other Penetration Testers regarding a quality Penetration Test.

The other change with Requirement 11.3 is with respect to Penetration Testing for effective segmentation and scoping. Often, companies undergoing PCI-DSS compliance specifically segment networks and systems out of scope of compliance. In such cases, the network that has been segmented out must be inaccessible from the PCI Scoped Environment. Often however, this requirement gets diluted. The organization fails to segment networks through effective Access control lists, or firewall rules or OS firewall restrictions. As a result, systems that are supposed be segmented and outside the scope of the PCI Environment are also accessible to systems in the PCI Scoped Environment. This is potentially dangerous as traffic from outside the PCI Scope (the segmented network) can contact and potentially compromise systems on the PCI Scoped Environment as well.

Penetration Testers must perform specific tests to identify if the segmentation between the PCI Scoped Environment and the out-of-scope environment is effective. This can even commence from something as simple as a port-scan of a target system outside the PCI Scope Environment, from within the environment. Additionally, as part of a Penetration Test, the tester must attempt to compromise systems within the PCI Scoped Environment from outside the segmented network to identify possible breach scenarios. This requires the Penetration Tester to not only perform Penetration Testing activities, but also focus on the network architecture, study the details of network segmentation and gain a perspective of the PCI Scoped Environment before performing the Penetration Test against the target environment.

A8 – Vendor PCI Compliance

One of the key areas of focus under Requirement 12 was with regard to Vendors of PCI Compliant organizations undergoing PCI Compliance as well. Until PCI v 2.0, Organizations were required to track and monitor the status of compliance of their vendors for PCI Compliance at least annually. This requirement has been strengthened in PCI-DSS v 3.0 to necessitate vendors to get compliant with PCI Requirements. Requirements 12.8 and 12.9 focus on this area of Vendor PCI Compliance.

The organization must maintain a list of vendors, with whom cardholder data is shared. Organizations must also stipulate the requirements (of PCI-DSS) would be covered by specific vendors. For instance, if a Retail Organization has outsourced their Customer Service Division to a Business Process Outsourcing (BPO) company, then they (the BPO) would be in scope for certain PCI Requirements of the Retail organization. The Retail organization must maintain a list of vendors and map these vendors to the PCI Requirements that they would fall under. The customer organization must track and monitor the Service Provider's PCI Compliance status. Additionally, the Service provider must acknowledge responsibility for maintain PCI Compliance over areas where cardholder data security of their customer is in question.

Index